BACK TO THE GARDEN

BACK
TO THE
GARDEN

Nature and the Mediterranean World
from Prehistory to the Present

JAMES H. S. McGREGOR

Yale
UNIVERSITY PRESS
New Haven and London

Published with assistance from the foundation established in memory of Calvin Chapin of the Class of 1788, Yale College.

Yale University Press books may be purchased in quantity for educational, business, or promotional use. For information, please e-mail sales.press@yale.edu (U.S. office) or sales@yaleup.co.uk (U.K. office).

Designed by Sonia Shannon.
Set in Janson type by Integrated Publishing Solutions.
Printed in the United States of America.

Library of Congress Cataloging-in-Publication Data

McGregor, James H. (James Harvey), 1946–
Back to the garden : nature and the Mediterranean world from prehistory to the present / James H. S. McGregor.
pages cm
Includes bibliographical references and index.
ISBN 978-0-300-19746-4 (hardback)
1. Human ecology—Mediterranean Region—History. 2. Agriculture—Mediterranean Region—History. 3. Mediterranean Region—History. I. Title.
GF13.3.M47M34 2015
304.2'091822—dc23   2014022703

A catalogue record for this book is available from the British Library.

This paper meets the requirements of ANSI/NISO Z39.48–1992 (Permanence of Paper).

10 9 8 7 6 5 4 3 2 1

For Sallie, Ned, Raphael, Anna, and Leila

The world is not with us enough.

—DENISE LEVERTOV

Contents

Acknowledgments

This is a wide-ranging book that engages scholarship in a host of academic fields. My own specialty is literary interpretation and cultural history. Within that broad area I have worked most often in the fields of material culture and the classical heritage. I have visited the Mediterranean repeatedly, lived for extended periods in Italy, and worked on two archaeological digs in the region. Under the direction of Eric and Carol Meyers of Duke University, I participated in excavations at Meiron in northern Israel. More informally and for a shorter period, I was able to work for Joseph C. Carter of the University of Texas on his excavations at Metaponto in southern Italy. I have published a series of books on world cities that includes volumes on Rome and Athens.

As I wrote and revised this book, I received help and encouragement from a number of people. I am especially grateful to Bill McKibben, Gary Snyder, Robert Torrance, and John R. McNeill, who read and responded to portions of the manuscript. Charles Platter, a specialist in Greek literature and philosophy, made corrections and suggestions in his area of expertise. My colleague at the University of Georgia Ari Lieberman corrected my Hebrew and helped me navigate the history of Judaism. Brock Baker refined my approach to Christian ecological thinking. I also received guidance from Carol Meyers, Joe Carter, and the philosopher of aesthetics Ellen Dissanayake. Alexi Worth read an early draft; his strong reaction dramatically reshaped the book. Harry Haskell, formerly classics editor for

Yale University Press, read and reread an unruly early draft and helped give it character and definition. Bill Nelson's excellent maps have sharpened and grounded its argument. Successive classes in the literature and nature course that I taught for many years have been test audiences for successive versions. Wendy Strothman has been a constant champion of the project and an encouraging voice throughout. Steve Wasserman, Erica Hanson, Mary Pasti, and others at Yale University Press have combined unwavering support for the book and sure expertise through every phase of its publication.

The book that has finally taken shape is very different from the one I first imagined. Over the years, it has become more urgent, more argumentative, and more personal. There is a lot in it that my grandfathers, Noah Sylvanus Twigg and James McAlpine McGregor, both passionate and skilled gardeners, would recognize and appreciate. It has been supported and enriched in uncountable ways by my beloved family, to whom it is dedicated.

BACK TO THE GARDEN

Introduction
How Did We Get Here?

On a recent trip to Venice, my wife and I experienced high water. Since we were there in late summer, when the water is usually low, we were surprised and unprepared. So were the Venetians. The next day's newspaper headlined a "nightmare storm that paralyzed half the province." Seasonal high water—*acqua alta*—usually begins in November. Pushed by onshore winds, an amplified tide rolls through the narrow channels that link the Venetian lagoon to the Adriatic. When the tide turns, the wind holds some water against the shore, so with each succeeding high tide, the lagoon gets fuller. The flooding we were experiencing was caused by a heavy rainstorm. A combination of the two events—torrential rain and wind-driven high water—hit Venice in 1966.[1] The one-two punch nearly drowned the city. A return of that fatal combination is what Venetians dread.

Everyone knows that flooding on this devastating scale is a recent threat.[2] And everyone knows that Venice is sinking. Rising seas, the city's own weight, and a falling water table drive it deeper into the mud every year.[3] Storm sewers in any other city would have carried the rainwater away, but in Venice there is no "away." The city has sewers, but they drain into the lagoon. When the tide is in, water rises above the sewer outlets, so rain pools in the streets and piazzas until the next tide. The water runs off only if the lagoon level falls enough.

Venice is the most Mediterranean of cities, not because it is typical—it is certainly not that—but because it is directly linked to the sea and affected daily, even hourly, by the dynamics of sea winds and waves. Because of this unbreakable link, Venice is the canary in the mine for the entire Mediterranean basin. The city's health gives warning of things to come, and at this moment the bird is gasping for breath. Understanding how Venice came to be poised on the brink of disaster points the way to an evaluation of the whole region. Though not as imperiled as Venice, it is certainly under stress. On behalf of the Mediterranean as a whole, Venice poses this urgent question: When and how did our environment become so endangered?

A capsule history of Venice breaks down into two unequal parts.[4] From its founding sometime in the late Roman imperial era to the end of the eighteenth century, it was an independent city-state. Since then it has been a mere city under the rule of outside forces. Napoléon captured Venice in 1797 and stripped it of its assets before he deeded it to Austria. In 1870 the Austrians gave way to the Italians. None of these conquerors had much of an understanding of the city they took over. Their lack of comprehension should come as no surprise. Imagine a powerful, rich, and influential civilization that in 1800 had no use for horses and little use for the wheel. It had few machines more powerful than clocks and relied on human muscle for mobility. A metropolis without roads, it was surrounded not by fields and pastures but by expanses of water. What was any sensible person to think? The sensible Austrian and Italian planners who took control devoted their efforts to making Venice more like the mainland cities they knew.

The environmental crisis in modern Venice is the result of repeated attempts to fix something that was not broken originally but became damaged, perhaps irreparably, by ill-considered mending. The local artisans and managers who had guided the city's development and maintained its ecology for generations were replaced by outsiders who did not understand how Venice worked. The result of their misguided repairs splashes underfoot in the city today. Looking at the outline of Venice on a map, many people see the image of

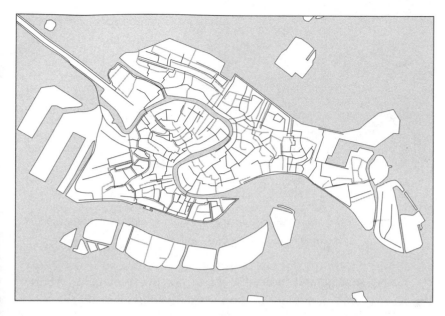

Modern Venice is a fish on a leash.

a fish. Like a fish, the city swims in the waters of the lagoon. But in a most unfishlike way, Venice nearly drowns in those waters on an annual basis. It is a fish on a leash, bound to the land by an umbilical causeway that force-feeds it an unending diet of visitors.

Historical Venice could not have been described as a fish, because before 1800 Venice was not limited to that fishy outline on the map. The city stretched across the lagoon with its multiple islands, mud banks, and sandbars. This curious metropolis was linked by waterways that reached from the barrier islands deep into the marshy mainland coast. The Venetian Empire, comprised primarily of Mediterranean islands, extended the pattern. The urban center was bound to its lagoon—the Laguna Veneta—not just by navigable channels, as it still is today, but in a hundred other ways. Food from island and inland gardens came to the city in boats across the lagoon waters, which themselves provided the fish that formed a major part of the Venetian diet. The traditional relationship between the city and the lagoon was much like the one that existed between terrestrial cities and the fields and farms that surrounded them, except that Venetians farmed the waters as well as that little earth they possessed.

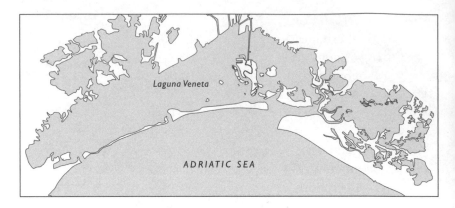

*Historical Venice comprised both land and water, as did its colonial empire,
which extended far beyond the Laguna Veneta.*

Today sewage and industrial waste poison the lagoon. Most of
the islands are abandoned to smugglers, looters, and illegal fisher-
men. The outlines of ancient aquaculture remain, but the fish are few
and poisoned by chemical effluents. Over time the very perception
of the lagoon has changed. What was once understood as a region
under cultivation—an agricultural landscape, though an anomalous
one—is now classified as wild. Modern Venice is a world heritage
urban site set in the middle of a fouled ecological preserve. These
irreconcilable identities cancel the historical interdependence of
the city and its lagoon and hamstring efforts to reverse the damage
to both.[5]

It may be too late for Venice, just as it may be too late for the
Mediterranean region as a whole. There is a good chance that humans
have already abused not just one city or region but the earth itself to
a point beyond its ability to recover health. Continuing failure is all
too apparent as nations struggle to articulate their responsibility to
the planet and act for its benefit. A whirlwind of controversy and
doubt surrounds global warming. Is it real? Is it our fault? Can we
fix it? What will happen if we do nothing? As we struggle for clarity,
we are all but blinded by myths and misconceptions that disguise
our own biological nature and downplay our absolute dependency on
the limited resources of our planet. There is a conspiracy of sorts—
ad men, pundits, and politicians blow smoke and flash mirrors—but
deliberate mystification is just a small part of the problem. A more

significant part, and one more difficult to discern, is played by our intellectual inheritance from the nineteenth century. Much of what we think of as axiomatic in the debate about environmentalism today is a version of one or another nineteenth-century theory. More often than not, we have forgotten the theorists and the background of their thought; we remember their conclusions, though, and take them for truths.

The contemporary environmental crisis is the endgame in a prolonged and culture-wide historical chess match. In a real sense, the global crisis is both an echo and an outgrowth of the Mediterranean disaster.

The Mediterranean can be narrowly defined as a great inland sea and its coast. As a climate zone, it roughly corresponds with the range of the domestic olive tree. Historically and culturally, however, the Mediterranean stretches well beyond these boundaries. When we speak of Europe or European culture, even when we speak of the West or the Western cultural heritage, these vague concepts are largely underwritten by events and movements that flourished first in the Mediterranean. For millennia, Mediterranean societies attracted admiration and envy and served evolving cultures as a model or a foil. Mediterranean nations were the first colonial powers in the world, and the Westernization and modernization of Africa, Asia, and the Americas all began under the influence of Spain and Portugal. Colonialism and its evils matured under the dominance of northern European nations, but in spreading the influence and culture of the West for good or ill, Mediterranean powers cast the mold. The Mediterranean region magnified itself over the long span of its history both physically and in terms of its influence, and we can trace that movement well beyond the Mediterranean Sea.

While Venice has been sinking underwater during the past two hundred years, Mediterranean societies and their scattered offspring worldwide have been experiencing an extended bout of what sociologists call anomie—life without rules—in relation to the earth and ecology. Anomie often follows severe social disruptions, like the Napoleonic Wars that plunged eighteenth-century Venice into crisis. The causes of modern confusion run deeper than any single cataclysm, but today we find ourselves in an equally bad situation. Caught in a desperate state of affairs, people find it exceptionally difficult to articulate problems and to solve them. Without an accepted set of principles or standards that decision makers can appeal to, right and wrong are up for grabs. "The best lack all conviction, while the worst/Are full of passionate intensity," as William Butler Yeats puts it. To make matters worse, in turbulent times the stakes are abnormally high. The wrong decision is easy to make, and the consequences of error are certain to be more dire than they would be in a period of stability.

Before we rush to judgment and ask ourselves yet again, What is to be done?, it might be worth pausing and asking the questions that the fate of Venice prompts. Have things always been this way? Is the present precarious state of affairs the historical norm? Have Mediterranean societies ever responded coherently to the fundamental questions of living on earth? Bear in mind that the roll call of the societies at issue includes many to which we owe some spiritual or intellectual debts and others toward which many of us feel substantial degrees of kinship. Mesopotamia (the Fertile Crescent), Israel, ancient Greece and Rome, the nations of Europe and the Muslim world—could all these societies have come into existence and flourished for so long continually plagued, as we are plagued, by indecision and confusion about issues that are basic to survival on this planet? Did they make their life and death choices with nothing more to guide them than we have? Did they, like us, willfully plunder the land for short-term gain while they compromised the comfort and security of their neighbors, their children, and themselves? Or did they live differently and in harmony with that portion of the earth that they recognized as the source of their well-being?

Looking back, many environmentalists have concluded that the present emergency is just the crisis stage of a malaise that afflicted Mediterranean societies from the start. If we listen to the polemics of some of the more radical among them, we might be convinced that the problem began when human societies turned from a hunter-gatherer lifestyle and took up new technologies of cultivation and domestication. The rallying cry of these activists is "Back to the Paleolithic"—back to following game animals and living directly from what the earth offers unpersuaded and uncoerced. Few of us would survive under such rigorous conditions, and most of those who study the Mediterranean past do not advocate such a radical turnaround.

They might logically do so, however, because many of those who critique our deep environmental history base their polemics on more or less the same turning point: the Neolithic invention of agriculture. Nutritionists argue that the human species is adapted genetically to the Paleolithic diet and that we have had insufficient evolutionary time to readjust to the increased starch and decreased activity that communities embraced when cultivated grains replaced a diet based on foraging and hunting. They trace the roots of modern obesity and heart disease back to the Neolithic. One popular writer on ecological history, Jared Diamond, has been among the most vocal critics of the Neolithic. He has portrayed Mesopotamian agriculture as a prolonged disaster directed by self-interested elites who managed their resources for the benefit of themselves and their families while others' needs went unmet. Other environmentalists have joined Diamond in his effort to portray Mesopotamian agriculture not as a triumph of social organization and land management but as the start of a prolonged slide into the infertility that haunts the Fertile Crescent today.[6]

The historian Lynn White argued many years ago that "the roots of our current environmental crisis" lay in the book of Genesis.[7] In the story of the creation, God commanded the first human to "be fruitful and multiply and fill the earth, and subdue it; and have dominion over . . . every living thing" (Gen. 1:29). God's fiat would seem to justify any amount of human manipulation or exploitation of nature, and White argued that the Christian community had carried out this divine instruction to the letter. For White, Mesopotamian societies were not the culprit; the blame lay in the Holy Land.

The ecologist Aldo Leopold had his own idea about the roots of the crisis. He did not see environmental degradation springing from official mismanagement or obedience to a divine commandment but arising as the consequence of a long-standing moral vacuum. In one of his most influential essays, Leopold argued for the existence of an evolutionary or progressive trend in the ethical thinking of Mediterranean societies.[8] His argument was based on the gradual expansion of rights that can be seen as a deep background theme in Western culture. Rights of full participation in the community were once the privilege of the noble few. Over time these rights extended to all free males, then to those who had once been held in bondage, to women, and in lesser degree to children. At present some activists are arguing for the extension of rights to unborn fetuses; others press for animal emancipation. Leopold believed that this historical expansion of rights would encompass the biological world someday and that we would come to understand ourselves as citizens of the ecosystem and not solely of the human community.

Many other theories of similar character trace the current environmental crisis into the past and posit different starting points for disaster. The response that all these theories provoke is this: If the crisis is so deeply rooted, why did its effects take so long to be felt? While some equivocate, suggesting that Mediterranean ecology was compromised almost from the start of the agricultural revolution, the best data do not support that position. Things have been starkly, demonstrably bad in the past two hundred years, and they were far better before that. Indeed, compared to the present state of the region, even the most extreme view of past environmental damage must acknowledge it as benign.

The more common answer accepts as a given the contrast between the ecologically healthy past and the demonstrably abused present. Its response to the question of Why now? typically assumes a gradual worsening to the crisis stage or points to technology. Proponents of the technological argument agree that although ancient societies may have been inept, misdirected, or lacking in ethical attitudes, the consequences of their ignorance were muted because the societies were technologically limited. In this view, nothing really bad happened before the nineteenth century, when the crescendoing use of mechanical and chemical energy gave societies the means to carry out their designs on the earth.

I offer a different picture of the origins of our crisis. I argue that the present state of affairs both regionally and worldwide is much like the situation of Venice. Today's crisis is not an extension but a contravention of the norms of the historical past: our era came to birth when a once-powerful consensus on the constructive management of the earth, a consensus that had developed along with agriculture, was eroded to extinction. The slow process of erasing this constructive worldview—which I have called First Nature—was substantially complete by the late eighteenth century, and when the last vestiges of the consensus were eradicated, there was nothing to take its place. There were no rules, customs, or standards of conduct to limit exploitation. So technology did its damnedest. With proper cultural guidance, technology might have been a powerful force for human and planetary well-being, as it promises to be in a more enlightened future.

I explore this historical development from the forging of First Nature through its perseverance to the current age of crisis. Finally, I propose remedies to the modern environmental disaster that are based on a creative reworking of the principles that sustained the Mediterranean region for so long. The First Nature vision can be revived and renewed to make it an effective tool for recovering world ecological health.

PART I

Forging First Nature

CHAPTER ONE

The Paleolithic Landscape

The Paleolithic age has attracted the attention of ecological theorists in recent decades. Some of their interest can be explained by nostalgia for a time that appears unequivocal, clear, and simple as we look backward from our troubled present. But there is much more to be learned from even a short look. The ecological sophistication of both Neanderthals and the anatomically modern humans that gradually supplanted them is striking. Even more striking is early humans' artwork. In sculpture and especially in cave painting, people chronicled and celebrated the biological world that sustained them. Not only were they capable of deriving a living from a precarious environment, they were able to represent the natural world they experienced and describe how their human community fit into it. Of all the lessons to be learned from the epochs that preceded our own, an appreciation of earlier people's ability to assess and express their place in nature is perhaps the most valuable of all.

In 1856 quarrymen in the limestone hills east of Düsseldorf, Germany, discovered part of the skull, the thick ribs, and some heavy long bones of what they thought was a bear. The skeleton soon came to the attention of local scientists who recognized it as human; they identified the remains as those of a deformed soldier from the era of the Napoleonic Wars. A leading anatomist, Rudolph Virchow, saw in the bones the thickenings and distortions symptomatic of rickets and osteoporosis. In 1863, four years after Darwin published his *Origin of Species*, anatomist William King declared that the skeleton was not that of a diseased modern human at all but evidence of a new species, to which he gave the biological name *Homo neanderthalensis*.[1] From the start, the newly named hominid species, Neanderthal Man, created terrible problems. Darwin had refused to speculate on human evolution in *Origin of Species*, but his account of the historical development, progressive differentiation, and frequent extinction of life forms made the existence and subsequent disappearance of hominid species a clear possibility. Fearing a hostile reaction to his work because of these implications, Darwin had delayed publishing *Origin of Species* for more than a decade.[2] As Darwin had feared, readers immediately realized that his theory opened the door to human evolution, and the great Oxford debate of 1860 between Darwin's self-appointed advocate, Thomas Henry Huxley—who became known as Darwin's Bulldog—and the lord bishop of Oxford, Samuel Wilberforce, focused on this issue.[3]

The discovery of *Homo neanderthalensis* raised the question of the species' origin and fate and its links to anatomically modern humans. In the nineteenth century, the answer to that question was unequivocal. Scientists and laypeople alike tended to identify evolution with the idea of progress, a link that Darwin himself found unpersuasive. By the logic of progress, hominids of the past must necessarily have been less competitive and less competent than those who replaced them. In our era, when the idea of progress has lessened its grip, the genetic profile of the Neanderthals has been repeatedly probed to assess potential links. Applying newly discovered techniques of DNA analysis to genetic material unexpectedly preserved in bones from the original site, scientists in 1997 concluded that Neanderthals and modern humans last shared a common ancestor five hundred thousand to seven hundred thousand years ago. That dating and the general conclusion of this pioneering study have been reinforced by ambitious surveys that promise to describe the entire Neanderthal genome. But the case is by no means settled; research and speculation continue to keep Neanderthal genetics a hot topic.[4]

About half a million years ago Neanderthals migrated to Europe either through southwest Asia, where they also have a long history, or, less likely, but still a tantalizing possibility, across the Straits of Gibraltar, which would have been periodically narrowed by glacially induced drops in sea level.[5] For the entire course of their history as Europeans, Neanderthals were shaped by advancing and receding ice. During the past five hundred thousand years, ice ages have ebbed and flowed in cycles of about one hundred thousand years. As each cold period reached its maximum in extent and intensity, the polar ice cap surged deep into the European continent. Not only the Neanderthals but every living organism was forced south into frigid but ice-free lands along the Mediterranean coast. Species found refuge from the ice in the Iberian Peninsula, in Italy, and in the Balkans. At the end of each glaciation, as the ice barrier receded, the distant offspring of those who had fled to the south generations before re-colonized a continent wiped almost clean of life.

Cold climate survival put selective pressure on the Neanderthals, favoring individuals whose short stature and compact frames made them better able to retain body heat. Presumably, too, though this is less often discussed, coping with repeated and dramatic changes in habitat put a premium on individuals with inventiveness and dexterity.[6] Successfully harvesting animals, turning their hides into clothing, and crafting useful tools are skills that the Neanderthals developed and maintained with little variation over unimaginable stretches of time. They also buried their dead and in some cases buried objects along with the bodies; a few corpses were colored with red ochre, a natural dye.[7] Pollen residue in a Neanderthal burial in Iraq suggested to some archaeologists that the dead might sometimes have been strewn with flowers. A second Iraqi burial revealed that Neanderthals cared for their sick and wounded. There is also some evidence that they built fires inside caves in primitive hearths.[8]

Every prehistoric culture is represented archaeologically by its repertoire of tools and tool-making techniques. The French archaeologist Nicholas Mahudel first proposed differentiating early societies in this way in the early eighteenth century; a hundred years later, in the 1820s, Christian Jurgensen Thomsen classified exhibits at what became the Danish National Museum using similar techniques. Every ancient culture could in theory be represented in many other ways as well, but the durability of stone ensures it a disproportionate place in the archaeological record. Only in rare instances are organic materials like hides, wood, and plant fiber preserved. Pollen, which is remarkably enduring, has only recently been recovered and studied. Typical Neanderthal sites are rich in animal and human bones, in stone tools, and in the litter of stone fragments struck off in the tool-making process.

There is great controversy among experts about the kind and level of intellectual and social life that sustained this toolmaking. We might imagine a flint knapper planning to make a certain tool. He shuffles around the bone-littered cave floor looking for the perfect nodule of flint but fails to find it. Suddenly he remembers an outcropping with just the right quality of flint laced through it. He packs a lunch, grabs a spear, and heads out on a hundred-mile round trip. This sequence of actions, which could be taken for granted in modern humans, requires imagination, planning, organization of behavior, and spatial memory that many archaeologists are hesitant to ascribe to hominids like the Neanderthal. Trade might also account for the long-distance transport of high-quality stone, but trade also seems unlikely among a group that is generally believed to have been incapable of language or intricate social organization and interaction.

Whatever their social and intellectual abilities might have been, in their choice of home sites the Neanderthals showed a high level of insight and intelligence. Preserved sites show a preference for river valleys, and shelters with a commanding view of the surrounding countryside. These locations gave Neanderthals access to water and the prey that water attracts. They also chose sites where supplies of flint or chert were abundant. The archaeological evidence suggests that they preferred south-facing caves sheltered from the north wind and heated by the sun. Many of the caves that they occupied over thousands of years passed into the hands of the anatomically modern humans who followed.

From their choice of shelters, their tools, and from the evidence of their hunting and scavenging, it is possible to draw a picture of the Neanderthal in the landscape. In the typical museum installation, we see hairy creatures none too clean, draped with skins and looking slightly unfocused. In a tableau at the Smithsonian National Museum of Natural History they are grouped in a cave looking at the burial of one of their fellows in the floor beneath them. If we imagine the same beings standing outside this crude domestic setting and looking over the landscape that they hunted and foraged in, the picture changes dramatically. If a species' success is measured by survival and adaptability, then the Neanderthals were a great success. They endured in an unstable landscape that recurrently became too harsh to sustain any form of life. Furthermore, they survived for hundreds of thousands of years without disfiguring or destroying their environment. From a technological point of view they were primitive; from an ecological point of view they were exemplary. The environmental activist Dave Foreman made this point in a striking way: "Unlike our own bull-in-the-china-shop kind, there is no evidence that Neanderthals ever got out of balance, ever upset their environment, ever forgot their place in nature, ever caused the extinction of other species." Perhaps, he speculates, "Neanderthal genes were picked up thirty millennia ago by the Cro-Magnon gene pool . . . thereupon to drift along beneath the surface, bubbling up now and then in a Lao Tsu, a Saint Francis . . . a Thoreau, a Muir . . . a Rachel Carson."[9]

Our species, *Homo sapiens*, began arriving in southwest Asia about seventy thousand years ago. By about forty thousand years ago modern humans were in Europe. After tens of thousands of years of technological inertia, Neanderthals suddenly began to work antlers and bones, materials that they had always discarded unshaped in the past. Among the objects they crafted from the newly adopted material were needles, which suggest a revolution in the way their clothes were made. They began to collect seashells, too, perhaps to wear in necklaces or bracelets.

The anatomically modern humans who moved into the old Neanderthal territories in Spain and southern France were given the name Cro-Magnons by Edouard Lartet and his son Louis.[10] Details of the living patterns of these people emerged from excavation after excavation. When they first entered the region, they produced a characteristic set of material remains. This initial culture shared many characteristics with Neanderthal tools.[11]

Did the newcomers learn their technologies from the Neanderthals, or is the reverse true? If there had been more dynamism in the Neanderthal tradition, it would seem more likely that the new arrivals learned from the old hands. With some flint-working techniques this must have been the case. But since the Neanderthals had never before shown any interest in bone tools and little, if any, in personal adornment (aside perhaps from red ochre), the influence seems to have come from the opposite direction as well. Since Cro-Magnon people often moved into Neanderthal caves, they must have gained insight from their predecessors into proven ways to use local resources. The sum of the evidence suggests that each group learned from the other. Sharing requires a period of coexistence, and the archaeological record suggests that this period of coexistence was in some areas extremely long. The odds are that anatomically modern humans and Neanderthals overlapped in parts of their home territories for up to ten thousand years. That is five times the interval that separates us today from the reign of the Roman emperor Augustus. Whatever ultimately brought the Neanderthals to extinction, it does not appear to have been contact with modern humans.[12]

Even during the earliest incursions into Europe, Cro-Magnons seem most dissimilar from their new Neanderthal neighbors in their cultivation and preservation of what is useless. Beads and marine shells, brought in over long distances in some cases, are among the most characteristic finds in Cro-Magnon sites. A fragment of bone with deeply etched images of two female deer, discovered in the mid-1830s, is one of the earliest such finds that still survives. As this object and the many similar, though undatable, finds that joined it over the next forty years or so were to demonstrate, the Cro-Magnon people, unlike the Neanderthals, not only collected trinkets but created images of the world around them. Cro-Magnons embellished utilitarian objects like spear throwers with sculptures of animals. They created small animal images and statues with no link to any tool. Cave painting, their most ambitious and exciting art, was not happened on till the last quarter of the nineteenth century.

More than any of their other arts, cave painting gives us insight into the way that anatomically modern humans understood the world around them. From their widespread paintings of herd animals and predators, we gain a sense of their close observation and evident reverence for the creatures that sustained them. The first prehistoric cave paintings were recognized in 1879.[13] Additional caves were discovered throughout southern France and northeastern Spain.

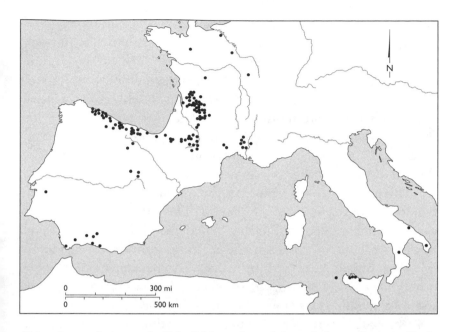

Painted caves dating to the Paleolithic are located throughout northeastern Spain and southern France.

Over the years, many other painted caves have been found in a broad arc that extends from the Iberian Peninsula almost to the Urals. Nearly half of those caves are in France. The Abbé Henri Breuil, the great synthesizer of cave art, identified six caves as having special importance.[14]

Recent discoveries have added to this master list. The Chauvet Cave, near Pont d'Arc on the Ardèche River, was first visited in 1995. It became the subject of a feature film in 2011. Unlike many other caves discovered by amateurs, the Chauvet Cave was immediately recognized as a site of extraordinary importance, and from the moment of discovery every effort was made to protect it. Walls richly decorated with paintings of a kind not found elsewhere are the most compelling feature of the site, but the cave offers other extraordinary things. Some of the working materials of the artists are still in place. A cave bear's skull set on a rock and two bear femurs thrust into the mud remain where they were put millennia ago. Probably the most evocative feature of the cave is the many footprints preserved on its floors. The path traced by an adolescent who visited the site can be followed across the hardened clay. To make sure that he or she could find the way back out of the cave, the child made soot marks with a torch on the ceiling. The carbon in these smudges has been dated to twenty-six thousand years ago. A wolf on a similar path may have come through at roughly the same time. The wolf's prints are unusual. Its middle toes are shortened like those of a domestic dog. If the child and the wolf passed through together, that would be evidence for domestication of the dog twelve thousand years earlier than is generally accepted.[15]

The paintings in the Chauvet Cave have been dated to thirty-two thousand years before the present. This makes them the oldest cave paintings found in Europe. When the child passed through twenty-six thousand years ago, the paintings were already an incredible six thousand years old. In many ways they are unique, but in others they resemble work that other cave painters created ten–twenty thousand years later. The cultural tradition of the Neanderthals stretched over a period of hundreds of thousands of years. The time scale of the Cro-Magnon way of life was accelerated by a factor of ten. Still, the endurance of cultural practices and the pace of change are glacial by contemporary standards.

Painters in the Chauvet Cave used red ochre pigment or charcoal to create their images. The clay has traces of branches and twigs they dragged inside. They made fires in hollows where cave bears had curled up or among stones stacked against the walls of cave chambers. The fires warmed and illuminated the work area and provided drawing materials at the same time. Whether in ochre or charcoal, the drawings all appear to date from the same time. The wild animals that these early artists painted include species that remained staples of cave art for millennia, as well as images of creatures that were seldom depicted again.

Among the most typical images at Chauvet are wild horses, reindeer, red deer, bison, and mammoths. The atypical images include two strange stylized representations that look like abstract versions of a butterfly and a beetle. There are sixty-five representations of rhinoceroses, three times the total found in all other caves combined. There are even more images of cave lions. The ibex, rare elsewhere, is also well represented at Chauvet, along with a spotted cat and other indeterminate animals. The outlines of human hands created by spraying red ochre are common; otherwise, the human image is virtually absent, as in most painted caves.

Whether common or rare, the animals depicted share several characteristics. The drawings or etchings are generally free and fluid. In most cases the animals are defined by the particular curves of their spines and the graphically simplified details of their heads and mouths. Legs are less often represented. The impression a viewer gains is that all these animals were observed and remembered by people who looked at them from a slight elevation as the animals stood or crouched in vegetation that obscured their lower bodies. The animals are sometimes depicted alone, but more often in groups or pairs. They are usually drawn about half life-size on cave walls at about head height.[16]

Among the most evocative features of the cave are the massing of figures in groups and the artists' imaginative response to the cave contours. Irregularities in the wall surface must have suggested to the painter the beginnings of some images. A mastodon in one of the chambers is drawn on a stalagmite with a humpback contour and columnar forms like legs or a trunk. In many cases, the animals seem to emerge from cracks or curves in the walls.

The most unusual and puzzling image is painted on a rock pendant. The centerpiece of the image is the pubic triangle of a woman, an abstraction found etched or drawn elsewhere in the cave. The inner curve of thighs appears to be traced below it. A human figure emerges from one of these thighs topped by a human torso. The armless torso ends in a bull's head shaded in black and drawn in profile. The bull's bright white eye seems to stare straight toward the viewer. Beyond this composite figure is a cave lion walking away but looking back. The apparently human trunk and legs with a bull's head attached is unique not only as a representation of the human figure but also as an assemblage of body parts that do not cohere in nature. The singularity of this minotaur-like creature has led investigators to call it a shaman.

The drawings in Chauvet Cave pose the questions that cave art has raised from the start—namely, Who was it for? What purposes did it serve? Explanations range from the literal to the symbolic. For literalists, the cave paintings of animals represented targets. The primitive hunter threw spears at the representations in preparation for the real hunt. Some painted animals bear marks like those that a spear might make, but the overwhelming majority do not. A more common explanation is symbolic. The paintings, especially those in the deepest and most inaccessible areas of caves, represented shrines associated with hunting. Here the magic of the hunt was prepared through some unknown ritual action. Related to this hypothesis is a second one with broader implications: identifying the decorated caves as the retreat of hunter groups, societies of men who performed secret rituals associated not just with hunting but with the cohesion of the band and the ritual mustering in of adolescent recruits. The shaman figure and the pubic triangle certainly lend support to the idea that ritual played a part in the use of the caves. The links between a hunting cult, a shaman figure, and a symbol of fecundity are also attested in widespread sites.[17]

Two common assumptions run through all these theories. Analysts have always seen the caves as the analogues of shrines or temples, and all their theories suggest that the sites were visited repeatedly and used systematically. Most assume that the sites were reserved for hunters, who they assume were adult men. Neither of these conjectures is supported by the little secondary evidence that survives. Indeed, the few places where footprints and traces of visitors have been preserved suggest a different scenario. Typically, as at Chauvet, the paintings were created within a short period of time, then abandoned and ignored. Subsequent visits to the cave were few and far between, probably the result of accident rather than design. Perhaps most surprising of all, the footprints preserved in cave floors are disproportionately those of children and adolescents.

Perhaps it is not using the art but creating the art that was most significant to the cave painters. For us, it may be more valuable to ask why the paintings were made rather than how they were used. Art in some form is nearly universal among known human populations of the past and the present. Art concerns itself with such matters of biological significance as reproduction, death, and health. Arts like dance and music play a role in organizing and coordinating group activities. Children make and enjoy art.[18]

Based on these fundamental characteristics, a philosopher of aesthetics, Ellen Dissanayake, has proposed a theory about the origins of art that takes into account its long history and near universality but focuses on an artist's ability to create works that are "meaningful, valuable or compelling." Artists, she writes, "simplify or formalize, repeat (sometimes with variation), exaggerate, and elaborate in both space and time for the purpose of attracting attention and provoking and manipulating emotional response."[19]

The context in which Dissanayake sees these patterns on display in their most widespread and influential form is in the special language of words and gestures that parents use when they talk to babies. In her view, "talking to babies, who have innate linguistic capacity, but no acquired language, calls on all the techniques that artists use to make their art meaningful and arresting. Baby talk is simplified and repetitious; it features exaggerated stresses and uncommon rhythms; it is accompanied by exaggerated facial gestures."[20]

The instinct to create art is as characteristic of our species as toolmaking, language use, or symbolic behavior. "This universal ability or proclivity is to recognize that some things are 'special' and even more *to make things special*—that is to treat them as different from the everyday."[21]

Throughout this book the view of art that Dissanayake pioneered is taken for granted. Art, whether in the form of sculpture, painting, epic, or hymn, is assumed to call attention through formal techniques to the things that matter. For many of us today, bewildered or alienated by the art of our own era, this is not an easy assumption to make. For whatever reason, modern artists appear to have withdrawn from the world as most of us experience it into a private realm with little observable connection to those things that matter most. The crisis that art is experiencing today should not blind us to the ability of art historically to represent fundamental truths.

Following Dissanayake's lead, we can see that cave art represents a simplified and abstract world in which everything has been reduced to the animals that sustain human life and those that threaten it. Survival depends on complete and concentrated attention on these two groups, and because of the care in depicting their eyes, the animals themselves seem to be paying attention, to be watching the artist and the viewer. In cave art, vigilance characterizes both hunter and prey.

The anthropologist Richard K. Nelson describes a culture in which vigilance plays a dominant role in his study of the Koyukon Inuit of northern Canada. These indigenous people live in villages, but they have subsisted historically, and still to a large degree survive, on the animals they hunt. "The intimacy of their relation to nature is far beyond our experience," he notes, which must have been equally true of Cro-Magnon people. The lives of the Koyukon are characterized by physical dependence on the environment and an "intense emotional interplay with a world that cannot be directly altered to serve the needs of humanity."[22] For the Koyukon the world in which they live is aware and alert. Animals watch the movements of the hunter in the landscape. Disrespect, the violation of prohibitions, any impropriety on the part of the hunter, is immediately known and punished. Because the animals are vigilant, the hunter must be doubly vigilant to succeed in the hunt and to avoid fatal missteps.

It is not hard to imagine that the world of the cave painters was similar to the world of the Inuit hunter. The early humans, like today's, lived off the land and depended for their survival on the resources that it offered. Without imagining particular prohibitions or ethical norms, it is still possible to imagine the Cro-Magnon painter capturing a world in which survival required heightened awareness. Indeed, the cave paintings themselves are products of exactly this kind of awareness. The ability to draw animals with such grace, fluidity, and expressiveness requires more than manual dexterity and artistic technique. It also calls on resources of memory that have been built over a period of time during which animals of all kinds have been carefully observed. The hunter and the painter, like the animals portrayed, are all watchers.

Certain traits of the cave painters' worldview are only noticeable through comparison with other representations. In succeeding chapters, it will become clear that most shared visions of what the world is like have focused on things that humans have made. From the Neolithic onward, human societies commonly represented their worlds through lenses of their own creation. The Cro-Magnon almost never represented themselves, and they never represented objects they themselves made. They did not show any of the ways that they may have reshaped the landscape. Indeed, they did not represent land forms at all, just those animals in the landscape that mattered to them. In this way their art called attention to the specifics on which their survival hinged. Their pictured world was a reduction to its bare essentials of the ecosystem that sustained them.

CHAPTER TWO

Neolithic Revolutions

From the arrival of the Neanderthals in Europe through their replacement by anatomically modern humans and for millennia afterward, the food supply of any human community was limited to what the ecosystem offered. Paleolithic foragers could eat only what was there to be hunted, and cave art reflected their understanding of this fundamental fact. Not just the pattern of individual lives but the size and character of early settlements depended on foraging. Prehistorians reason that only small, mobile bands could sustain themselves by living directly off the land. Groups that were too large would be driven by hunger either to fragment or to starve. Sedentary groups of any size would soon exhaust the resources within reach and would have to move on or starve. Everything changed when farming developed. So dramatic was the change this invention brought about that it is often described as a Neolithic Revolution.

In recent decades new research into agricultural history has overturned the paradigm that many of us learned in school. We were taught that large-scale farming began in the Fertile Crescent when Mesopotamian chieftains consolidated their hold over multiple towns and created bureaucracies that coordinated the complex work of irrigating grain fields. Social hierarchies of specialists and multitudes of laborers, homogeneous crops of cereal grains—these were the origins of agriculture and civilization.[1] This theory had its roots in nineteenth-century concerns and combined elements that preoccupied a broad spectrum of people. Focused as it was on Mesopotamia, the theory located the origins of agriculture and the origins of large-scale political organization in the same place, tying together accounts of the rise of domestication of crops and animals and the rise of the nation-state. The narrative of state formation, which was a major political preoccupation of post-Napoleonic Europe, was further linked with the origins of the coercive power of the community—that is to say, with the origins of war. For theorists imbued with the thought of that era, three distinct theoretical concerns were inextricably blended together. The history of cultivation and domestication, the rise of the nation-state, and the story of warfare are distinct, but nineteenth-century historiography joined them in a way that contemporary theorists must struggle to undo.

What prehistorians now believe is quite different. The agricultural revolution came about in fits and starts; it was by no means the creation of a single culture. Its great effect was achieved by the combination of scattered discoveries into a readily adaptable package of seeds, herds, and techniques of cultivation. This new history undermines the chronology that the earlier picture enshrined and breaks the links that nineteenth-century theory forged between domestication, state formation, and organized violence. Not every scholar has kept up with these developments. Some of the most influential writers on the Neolithic agricultural revolution, among them its harshest critiques from both an ecological and an economic perspective, remain unaware of the new picture of the past that has emerged from the accumulated evidence of the past decades.[2]

While archaeologists and others were drawing this new picture of the agricultural revolution, researchers in other fields began to revise long-accepted views of the nutritional soundness of cultivated crops. What for generations had seemed to be a positive, progressive emergence from the dark uncertainties of the Paleolithic period was turned on its head. A utopian view of the Paleolithic is now far more common, along with a nagging sense that a lot of today's problems can be traced to the Neolithic Revolution: the beginning of farming. I take issue with this view. This chapter chronicles both new thinking about the origins of agriculture and research centered on the nutritional controversy. In subsequent chapters, devoted more to culture than to the pragmatic conduct of agriculture, I chart the development of the First Nature view.

Three Cities: Jericho, Abu Hureyra, and Çatalhöyük

Jericho was the first archaeological site to indicate that the history of cultivation was more drawn out and more elusive than anyone had imagined. When excavators reached the earliest levels at the site, what they found contradicted everything they believed. Pottery had always been seen as a necessary part of the agricultural revolution. Theorists believed that it was required to store grain and oil and to carry water to houses and fields. Yet there was no pottery in the earliest levels at Jericho. The people of Jericho were sedentary and lived in houses surrounded by a high wall, but much of their diet came from hunting and foraging. Hunting gazelles and gathering wild plants went side by side with farming to produce a mixed economy halfway between that of a Paleolithic hunter-gatherer and a Neolithic farmer. The third feature of Jericho that confounded theory was the importance of trade to a society with no obvious social hierarchy. Theorists believed that long-distance trade, like urbanization, depended on large-scale agriculture and powerful rulers. Jericho showed trade in an entirely different light.

The ruins of ancient Jericho lie in a desert that is part of a geological feature known as a rift valley. It is an area where the large plates that underlie the continents are drifting apart. The Jordan Valley is part of an interconnected system that reaches into Africa. It runs north from the Red Sea, through the Dead Sea and the Sea of Galilee, to Syria and eastern Turkey. Easy passage through the Jordan Valley supported regional trade that was crucial to the city's development. The long mountain chain that separates the Mediterranean coast from the rift creates a rain shadow that all but deprives the valley of moisture. Farming that depended directly on rainwater was impossible there. Still, the valley was not without water. The rain that fell in the mountains fed streams that flowed west toward the Mediterranean and others that flowed east down dry slopes into the fringes of the valley.[3]

Once rainwater reached the valley floor near Jericho, it flowed underground, where it nourished a desert spring called Ain es Sultan that provided water for the city year round. The spring, which continues to flow today, also offered a feature that was easy for archaeologists to overlook—namely, damp ground. Without irrigation or rainfall in the valley itself, the farmers of Jericho were able to cultivate grain in this very special and very limited environment. Once archaeologists recognized that cultivation at Jericho had depended on this unexpected resource, they began looking for similar environments.

One of the most common landscape features in deserts is a fan-shaped deposit of soil at the mouth of a seasonal mountain stream. After the brief annual rains, these streams suddenly fill, and over a few days or weeks they transport not just water but enormous amounts of soil from slopes to the valley flatlands. Over time, these seasonal river courses, which are called wadis in Arabic, create fan-shaped deposits of mountain soil at their outlets. For a period of weeks or months after the water ceases to flow, the deep and rich soil that makes up these fans stays moist. Cultivated like the damp ground near the Jericho spring, they could be extremely productive.

Floods saturate the soil in spring, just at the moment that new growth can begin. The same inundations make yearly deposits of nutrient-rich soil while they sweep the fan clear of weeds and brush. Once the floods are finished, seeds can be broadcast on the wet soil or set into shallow pits or trenches traced with a stick. Soil moisture causes the seeds to sprout and continues to nourish the growing plants. Because these fields are continually reinvigorated by mineral-rich transported soils, they supported annual cultivation for hundreds or even thousands of years.[4] On these sites, farming was sustainable, and its environmental impact was low.

The noted prehistorian Andrew Sherratt argues that the first agriculture in West Asia sprang up on sites of this kind. He calls this kind of agriculture "floodwater farming." At Jericho and elsewhere, grain cultivation did not replace hunter-gatherer activities; cultivated grain supplemented the traditional diet. The grains that these special and unusual sites produced were, Sherratt maintains, a rare and therefore precious commodity. Since relatively few areas were suited to their production, for many hundreds of years grain was a luxury commodity rather than a staple and had a high barter value.

An alluvial fan is under cultivation today. (Photograph from NASA.)

It would have been traded for goods that the inhabitants of Jericho needed but did not produce locally. Among these goods was obsidian, a glasslike, durable volcanic rock that can be fractured to create exceedingly sharp-edged tools. Grain harvesting required sickles of some sort, and obsidian made keen blades. The early inhabitants of Jericho also traded for seashells from the Mediterranean. These more exotic shells supplemented the shells that could be gathered from the Dead Sea nearby. The inhabitants of Jericho offered grain in exchange for these goods, but also bitumen, a soft, sticky form of petroleum that welled from the earth near the site. Bitumen had a variety of uses. It served as a caulk and waterproof coating, and it was widely used as an adhesive to bind stone tool heads to wooden handles.

A lot of ecological diversity is packed into the Jordan Valley and its surrounding steppe and mountain habitats—a relatively small territory. The development of agriculture within this unique environment drew on this diversity. Transplanting grain from its native environment to the desert spring was the most obvious example of the benefits of connection. The movement of resources—grain and the knowledge of how to cultivate it, obsidian, bitumen—from one part of the region to another were also important. The exploitation of diversity and regional cooperation through trade were the keys to the process.[5]

Excavations at Abu Hureyra in Syria also revealed a Jericho-like mixture of hunter-gatherer lifestyles and emerging agriculture. The digging there was carried out in the early 1970s, and in 1974 the site was flooded when a dam was built on the Euphrates River. Prehistorians have continued to analyze the data obtained in these digs for forty years. The first occupation level at the site dates to 9500 BCE. At that early period, the only form of food production that can be documented in the archaeological record is hunting. Five hundred years later, there is evidence of plant gathering, and by 6400 BCE the local diet had expanded to include hunted gazelle, foraged plants, and some cultivated cereals. One thousand years later, the residents were growing peas and beans along with cereals.[6]

The food supply at the equally precocious Anatolian city Çatalhöyük was similar to one part of the diet that sustained Jericho. In the earliest phases of city life the meat of wild aurochs was the mainstay (the auroch is the wild ancestor of the ox). Excavations in the 1960s also uncovered evidence of widespread and diverse trade.[7] The quantity and quality of the imported goods that the city could afford poses the question of what they had to offer in exchange. Noting that the skulls and bones of aurochs preserved in the site became smaller over time, Sherratt and others have suggested that Çatalhöyük may have been the first place were wild aurochs were domesticated. Over generations, these wild cattle went through a series of genetic changes, becoming less robust and less aggressive. These useful beasts were what the city had to offer in exchange for imported goods. When domestication of cattle became a widespread practice, the city lost its commercial edge and simply vanished.

Located in the highlands of what is now Turkey, the abandoned city of Çatalhöyük was buried in two enormous mounds that cover an area of more than thirty acres.[8] James Mellaart, the first excavator, identified ten layers of mud-brick cities piled one on top of the other and indeterminate layers beneath separating level X from virgin soil. Level X, the earliest distinguishable layer, has been dated to 6400 BCE. The highest level at the site dates to 5700 BCE. After that, the site was abandoned for five thousand years, then reoccupied in the late classical period.[9]

As Çatalhöyük emerged from the ground during the first excavations, it soon became clear that nothing like it had ever been seen before. (The sites that anticipate the architecture and culture of Çatalhöyük were excavated later.) The complex had been conceived as a single architectural entity and laid out in an asymmetrical grid. The houses had no doorways, and there were no streets. Entry to each house was through a hatch in the roof. The city was higher in the middle and lowest at the outer edge. The walls of the outermost houses formed the city boundary.

The degree of coordination among the individual housing units was high. Builders used wooden forms to create mud bricks from which every house was built. The forms were of uniform dimensions, so bricks throughout the city were of the same size. Houses could be bigger or smaller, but all were designed in the same way. From the roof hatch a ladder angled down to rest against the southern interior wall, where the hearth and the oven were placed. There were platforms of different sizes—probably for sleeping and resting—set into the floor against the north wall. In many houses, bodies have been discovered, buried beneath the floors. Males were buried under the easternmost platform and females under a platform to its west. The westernmost platform in a house could cover the remains of either men or women. These segregated burials suggest that the platforms were perhaps rigorously assigned to either men or women.[10]

Plaster-covered interior walls and successive layers of replastering suggest that the houses lasted on average about a hundred years before becoming unstable. Vertical buttresses, often painted red, braced some walls. Wooden beams, typically salvaged from aban-

Excavations at Jericho, Çatalhöyük, and Abu Hureyra uncovered signs of early farming and animal domestication.

doned houses, supported roofs. Since traffic within the town passed across the rooftops, there was no space between adjacent houses. Intermittent openings seem to have served as dumps for waste and debris.

While some houses were bigger than others, their essentially random placement within the city suggests to the excavators that their scale reflected family size rather than family status. No palace complex was discovered, and no quarter of the city appears to have been devoted to people of a superior social rank. The excavators also failed to find evidence of occupational specialties.[11]

Like the cave painters of the Paleolithic, the men and women who lived in Çatalhöyük used wall art to represent the world as they understood it. Scattered among the houses were buildings identified by the excavators as shrines. Structured like houses, the shrines were distinguished by their decoration. One of the most elaborate shrines was uncovered at level VII.9.[12] The main room of the shrine seems designed to support multiple and complex cult activities. Its main decorations are sculpted aurochs' heads. There are subdivisions of the walls, depressions and platforms on the floor, and multiple low entrances to secondary rooms. The east wall of the room, for example, is subdivided by two buttresses into three sections. Each of the buttresses supports a large idealized bull's head crafted from clay plaster. A shelf runs the full length of the wall, and it supports a third, smaller horned bull's head between two larger ones. There is a shallow depression in the floor slightly off center in front of these bull masks. A small secondary depression is next to it. A tiny opening in the wall under the shelf leads to a small adjoining room. A low doorway—typical of the sort that leads to household storage rooms—opens in the near corner of the south wall.

The opposite wall of the shrine is subdivided again into three sections. Three superimposed bull masks with widespread wavy horns decorate one of the buttresses. A single bull's head with two sets of horns juts from the second buttress, and a third bull's head is centered in the open space between them. There are no openings or floor depressions here. Two conventional low doors in the north wall open into a shallow second room.

In another shrine from the same level (VII.35) the repertoire of decoration is slightly different. Bulls' heads are combined with idealized pairs of breasts arranged both horizontally and vertically on the wall. The nipples have been replaced by vultures' beaks.[13] One of the most highly decorated bull shrines was uncovered at the somewhat later level VI. There, multiple altars with sweeping bulls' horns face the corners of a room where one of the buttresses is extended by a benchlike projection flanked by seven sets of bulls' horns.[14]

The activities that took place in the shrines can only be imagined. Sherratt emphasized in his late work the continuity between the first phase of agriculture, domestic architecture, and a forager's worldview.[15] At Çatalhöyük settlers continued to depend on animals for their livelihood and passed fairly seamlessly from foraging to animal domestication. They continued to understand and symbolize their world through animal images. Their cults linked symbols of

power, death, and fertility—animal images and images of women—
in architectural settings. The vitality of the city and the power of
animals were interdependent in their minds.

What became of all these communities? Abu Hureyra, Jericho,
and Çatalhöyük were abandoned many millennia ago. It seems clear
that resource depletion, a factor repeatedly invoked in modern critiques of ancient agricultural civilizations, was not the problem for
any of them. The causes were not ecological but economic and technological. Jericho thrived on floodwater farming as long as domesticated grains were luxury trade goods. Low annual production made
the city noncompetitive when new methods of farming made grain
a commodity. Çatalhöyük grew rich on the obsidian trade, which
failed when materials like fired clay and metal replaced stone. Its other
source of wealth, a monopoly on the production of domestic cattle,
was short-lived. These sites were abandoned because their success depended on products that lost their market and on farming and herding that were limited in scope. There is no evidence that they depleted
the soils or the herds on which their livelihood depended.

For Sherratt, the eminent reviser of the early history of agriculture, the important factor is not domestication in and of itself.
Grains transformed from a forager's resource into a farmer's staple
were important but did not cause the Neolithic Revolution.[16] That
revolution rested on the combination of single domesticates into a
larger pattern of cultivation. This combination depended on the
geographical diversity of the Jordan Valley, where a variety of cultures exploiting different ecosystems traded goods and technologies.
The resulting synergy produced and combined technological and
cultural advances that together made the Neolithic Revolution.[17]

What the Founders Grew

The Mediterranean founder crops, or "primary domesticates," are
few in number. They include two or three varieties of wheat along
with barley, lentils, peas, chickpeas, and bitter vetch. Rye was cultivated at sites on the fringes of the Fertile Crescent, but it was not a
large element in the regional diet. All these crops were descendants
of wild grasses that foragers, like those living in the earliest period at
Jericho and Abu Hureyra, had gathered for hundreds of years. Edged

tools for cutting the stalks of wild grains and grinders for transforming their seed into meal existed long before the grasses became domesticated. Both technologically and temporally, the transition from a forager's lifestyle to that of a cultivator was slow and incremental.

As foragers morphed into farmers, the wild plants they cultivated changed as well. Wild plants that are adapted to their environment have genetic profiles that match the climate and soil they depend on. When farmers cultivate these wild grasses in a new environment, they replace those natural conditions with artificial ones. The change in environment does not stop the genetic process, but it introduces new conditions that redirect it. Many traits that existed before remain essential to a crop's success, but some features that helped the plant survive in the wild are not favored by cultivation, so over time these diminish or disappear altogether. Alterations of this kind are what make cultivated grains different from their wild progenitors and what make domestication traceable in the archaeological record.

In the wild, ripe seeds that fall from a grass germinate at different rates depending on the thickness of their husks. Some sprout during the next season when conditions are right, but others lie in the soil for years before germinating. This variability in the pace of germination allows wild grasses to hedge their bets. The next growing season might be a good one, or it might not. Thin-husked seeds that sprout then may not mature, but thicker-husked, slower-germinating seeds that can wait out one or more summers may survive to sprout later on. In a farmer's field, however, seeds that do not sprout in the year they are planted rarely get the chance to produce offspring. The rhythm of sowing and harvesting favors quick-sprouting thin-husked grasses.

Thinner-husked, faster-germinating seeds are richer in starch, whereas thicker-husked seeds have more proteins and fatty acids. By favoring faster-germinating seeds, farmers produce domesticated grains that are starchier and lower in oils and proteins. Seed for seed, they are less nutritious than their wild forms. Domestication makes up for this drop in the nutritional value of a single seed by vastly increasing the available supply of grain, but the subtle switch from protein-based to starch-based nutrition poses metabolic problems for some humans.

Harvesting also shapes the crop. Wild plants must drop their seeds so that they can sprout, but with cultivated grasses, only those seeds that remain on the stalk at harvest time are gathered and reseeded. Grains that mature slowly are infertile when harvested early and do not sprout if sown as seed. Simply by sowing and harvesting, Neolithic farmers over many generations changed wild grasses into crops that were different from their wild forms.[18]

The thousands of modern varieties and hybrids of the Fertile Crescent founder crops feed much of the world today. Foods like wheat, olives, and wine are our strongest and most intimate link to the deep past of the Mediterranean. But as difficult as it might be to imagine, the world's entire diet today remains rooted in a limited number of Neolithic events that occurred in different parts of the globe.[19] The full range of founder crops from all the Neolithic centers feed every person on earth. The biggest component of the contemporary world diet that owes its origins to the Mediterranean region is wheat. Although there are now many varieties of wheat, descendants of the earliest cultivars are still widely grown. *Triticum dicoccum*, or emmer wheat, is the domesticated descendant of a wild grass called *Triticum dicoccoides*. According to the food authority Alan Davidson, in the modern world it is grown primarily to feed animals, "although good bread and other baked items could be made from it," as they undoubtedly were for many thousands of years.[20] *Triticum monococcum*, or einkorn wheat, which many believe is the oldest variety of wheat in cultivation, still grows in poor soils in many parts of the Mediterranean littoral. Modern wheats would not flourish in this environment, but einkorn wheat is one of the most grasslike in its ability to tolerate drought and low levels of soil nutrients.

Today the most widely grown wheat is *Triticum aestivum*, spring or winter wheat. This variety is called a hard wheat not because its kernels are particularly tough but because its seeds contain a lot of the protein that forms gluten. Gluten binds the ingredients of bread together in an elastic mass that stretches around the bubbles of carbon dioxide exhaled by yeast in the loaf. Durum wheat, as its name suggests, actually does have hard kernels (*durum* is Latin for "hard"). Ground durum wheat produces semolina, the basis of couscous, the North African staple, and the preferred flour for making pasta.

Barley may have been collected and cultivated before wheat. Stores of wild barley gathered ten thousand years ago were uncovered by excavators in Syria. Barley became the main crop of the Fertile Crescent partly because of its tolerance for salty soils, and its cultivation spread both east and west. It grew in Spain seven thousand years ago, in India five thousand years ago, and in China four thousand years ago. Barley contains little gluten and is difficult to bake into yeasty loaves. It was boiled and eaten like oatmeal or baked into flatbreads. Some beer was made with barley. Today most barley is grown as animal feed, but it is still used in soups in the West. In Tibet, where the cold climate favors this hardy grain, roasted and ground barley is a primary food.

Most of the commodity foods of the modern world—foods that are mass-produced and unspecialized—are cereals or tubers. Legumes like peas and beans, which played a major role in early cultivation, are now only secondary food crops. Both farmers and dieticians know how unfortunate this is. Unlike cereals, which deplete the soil, legumes collect nitrogen—a vital soil nutrient—in nodules on their roots and restore it to the soil as they decompose. Legumes are nutritious in themselves, but their proteins also complement those in grains. Wheat contains all the major amino acids—the building blocks of protein—that humans need except lysine. Legumes are rich in lysine, so a diet that combines grains and legumes is nutritionally complete. Vegetarians recognize this fact, as do the millions worldwide whose diet rests on rice and beans or a similar combination. The founder legumes are the common or garden pea, the lentil, and the chickpea, along with another member of the pea family that people seldom eat today, bitter vetch.

Even though cereal farming was important in the Mediterranean basin, agriculture there came to be focused on a different suite of crops and crop technologies.[21] The intensive and widespread cultivation of olives, grapes, and figs has been fundamental to Mediterranean agriculture since its first development in the late Neolithic. The widespread creation of terraced hillsides for the cultivation of these three crops has had a profound effect on the regional landscape.

The range of the olive tree virtually defines the limits of the Mediterranean region. Three categories of olive-related trees exist around the Mediterranean today, and their proliferation and variety made the job of finding the origin of the olive difficult. The oleaster is the indigenous species from which the cultivated olive was developed. Some modern oleasters, however, are actually the offspring of domestic olives—a kind of genetic return to the wild. During each ice age, the oleasters of the Mediterranean, like every other plant and animal species that survived, were forced into isolated refuges. Repeated glaciations and retreats led to the creation of distinct regional varieties of the plant. Given these complexities, it is no surprise that the genetic history of the olive tree is vexed. It appears to be the case that cultivated olives are closer genetically to the oleasters of the eastern Mediterranean than to those of the western part of the region. This suggests that the cultivated olive originated in the east and spread through the Mediterranean basin in much the same way as cereal crops,

The genus *Ficus*, to which the domestic fig belongs, thrives in tropical or semitropical climates worldwide. The historical domestic fig comes from a wild variety of West Asian origin called the caprifig. The botanical name of one domestic variety, *Ficus carica*, reflects the Greek belief that Caria in West Asia was the home of the fig. It is more likely that the city on the western coast of modern Turkey was only a way station on the pathway of the domestic fruit, not its point of origin.

Like the fig, the grape exists in many varieties worldwide. The particular variety that flourished in the Mediterranean, *Vitis vinifera*, the wine grape, is indigenous to areas east of modern Turkey and south of the Black Sea. Both genetic and archaeological evidence confirm the long-held view that grape cultivation began in this area and spread both around the Mediterranean toward Spain and eastward toward China. Recently the picture has been complicated by genetic studies suggesting that crosses with wild grapes may have occurred along the way that produced a measurable genetic difference between the grape varieties of the eastern and the western Mediterranean.[22]

Scientists continue to argue over the exact routes that led to the near universal adoption of agriculture in West Asia, Europe, and North Africa. One of the few places in the Mediterranean basin where the transition from foraging to farming can be studied systematically is Franchthi Cave in southern Greece. A decade of excavations begun there in 1967 revealed an incredibly long history of repeated occupation. The first datable use of the cave occurred more than twenty thousand years ago. From then on, hunter-gatherers visited the cave from time to time. The bones of the animals they killed and ate show a gradual change in their quarry as the climate cooled, then warmed. Twenty thousand years ago, they ate more wild horses than anything else. By the end of the Paleolithic, some ten thousand years ago, red deer were their most important prey. They also foraged for wild plant foods. By about 11,000 BCE, they had discovered wild stands of pistachios and almonds and ate nuts along with wild vetch and lentils.[23]

Deer and small animals remained a major part of their diet in the post-glacial period. Fish from the Mediterranean played an increasing part, and the size of some of the fish they were catching suggests that they had boats that could take them into deep water. Pieces of obsidian from the island of Melos, which could only have come by sea, reinforce this notion. Wild oats and barley became a common part of the local diet, and stones to grind them became a common implement.

The Neolithic layers at the cave are sharply divided from the older remains beneath them. In the Neolithic layers the skeletons of domestic sheep and goats show up. Domesticated wheat, barley, and lentil abound, and a variety of new stone tools make their appearance. After a relatively short delay, pottery is present. When these tools and fruits of cultivation make their debut, evidence of the traditional diet vanishes. There are no more seeds from the wild varieties of oats, barley, lentils, and peas that had been staples of the foragers' diet.

Franchthi Cave is at a crossroads on a major cultural highway. From this exceptionally well-documented and thoroughly published site, it is possible to get a sense of the revolution that passed through in Neolithic times. There is no question that the transition from foraging to cultivation was relatively swift. Nor is there any doubt that the particular grains, pottery, and domestic animals that suddenly show up in the Franchthi subsoil are just like the ones found to the east. The Neolithic Revolution was undoubtedly an easy sell at Franchthi. Unfortunately it is still hard to tell exactly how the change came about. In the continuity between wild and domesticated grains, some researchers see evidence that the inhabitants of the region turned from gathering to cultivating local grasses.[24] For other specialists, the sudden appearance of the full Neolithic package strongly suggests, if not colonization, at least an undeniable influence from the east. Did traders in boats bring the knowledge of farming from the east coast of the Mediterranean to this spot? Or did the same boats bring colonists from the east equipped with all the multiple parts of the Neolithic package? DNA research, which has not been published for Franchthi, might resolve some of these questions.

The Neolithic Revolution Comes Together

Floodwater farming of the sort that sustained Jericho and Abu Hureyra is rarely possible. Alluvial fans and similar wet spots were and are few and far between in the arid Levant. Domestication of the kind that the residents of Çatalhöyük practiced was not adaptable to all climates either. Natural grasslands provided seasonal food for domestic cattle just as they did for wild cattle, but pasturing cows in other types of terrain was difficult. During the second phase of the agricultural revolution, what Andrew Sherratt called the "Secondary Products Revolution," these problems were solved by the exploitation of new energy resources and the opening of new ecosystems to farming.

Both developments grew out of and depended on the millennial history of the first agricultural revolution, and both relied on the combination of tools and practices that characterized this epoch. The first-phase "Neolithic package" had bundled cereal cultivation and limited domestication with village architecture and the use of pottery, although not every site made use of every part of the suite of crops and technologies. The second phase added two elements that overcame the limits of floodwater farming and turned agriculture into an ever more widely exploitable resource. The plow and cart pulled by draft animals were one. The other was water management techniques, which made farming flexible and adaptable over a range of ecosystems. As agriculture developed, differences of climate and differences of ecology created a technological divide between cultivators who used groundwater resources—rivers, streams, springs, and lakes—and cultivators who depended on rainfall.

While tradition had long pointed to cereal cultivation as the basis of the Neolithic Revolution, Sherratt argued that cereal cultivation became widespread not because of any improvement in grain stock but because of a magnification of the power available to cultivators. Digging sticks were sufficient for seeding the relatively small areas that floodwater farmers exploited. The much larger areas that irrigation opened up for cultivation required a more powerful tool. The ard, sometimes called the scratch-plow, filled the bill. The ard—formed from a crooked branch with a stubby spur to cut into the earth—created a shallow channel where seeds could be sowed.

Humans can pull or drive shallow plows, but animals do a much better job. They are heavier and more muscular, and their skeletons are better framed for pulling. Getting an animal to perform this or any task, however, was a formidable challenge. At first herders must have maintained an uneasy distance between themselves and the dangerous and excitable cattle that they managed to impound. Herding then played the role of modern canning or refrigeration: it kept the meat fresh until it could be used. As the tradition of herding continued, animals became smaller and more docile. Herders became more adept. Eventually it was possible to work more closely with the animals. The ox-powered plow can be heavier and dig deeper than any plow that humans can pull. It can be used to till large fields in the short period of time that seasonal conditions impose. And with an oxcart, the harvest is gathered and transported efficiently.

Pulling and carrying are not the only things that make domestic animals useful. Goats and sheep produce wool that can be spun into cloth. In the modern world of synthetic fibers, this may seem inconsequential, but in the ancient world, the exploitation of wool expanded the range of garments people could wear and dramatically increased the range of ecosystems that could produce useful products for home consumption and for trade. Before sheep and goats were domesticated, linen was the only cloth manufactured in the Mediterranean. Linen is a lightweight, generally loose-textured cloth that makes clothes suited to warm climates, but it has real disadvantages. Linen is produced from flax, a cultivated plant that competes with food crops for field space and labor resources. Wool is easier to spin into thread than linen and produces heavier yarn and cloth with greater insulating qualities. New raw wool, rich in lanolin, sheds water. Unlike many other fibers, wool remains a good insulator even when it is soaking wet. Because wool makes warm clothing, it extends the range of habitable climates. And because the animals that produce wool, goats and sheep, can live happily in climates that have short growing seasons, raising them increases the range of habitats that can be productive without impinging on scarce arable land, as flax does.

The life of the shepherd is very different from that of the farmer. Farmers live in a village and tend nearby fields. When the fields are idle or fallow, they attend to other tasks that probably do not take them far from home. Shepherds, like traditional foragers, are mobile. The sheep and goats move from one pasture to another and may range over long distances.[25] In many Mediterranean economies, flocks have for millennia migrated from low-altitude winter pastures to mountain meadows, where the animals fatten on grass available only during the short summer. This seasonal pattern, called transhumance, provided one of the background rhythms to Mediterranean life from the third century BCE to the twentieth century CE. Though now almost extinct, vestiges of this pattern can still be seen in central Italy, southern France, North Africa, and the Levant. Nomadic herders range even more widely. Exploiting the seasonal availability of forage in harsh climates, nomads travel to widely scattered sites. Unlike the pattern of transhumance, which is repeated every year, the nomad may trace a lifelong pathway with limited repeats.

The activities of shepherds, nomads, and farmers combined to produce a regional economy, and the three groups lived in a symbiotic relationship that was maintained through trade. Their relationship duplicated the geographical relationship among climate zones and cultures that characterized the Jordan Valley and its surroundings. The relationship was easily adaptable to any mix of flatland for grain cultivation and highlands for pasturing. From its point of origin in a particular regional geography, it became a concept, a widely applied system of land use. As such, it was exported regionwide as part of the Neolithic Revolution.

Sherratt emphasizes milk as a significant secondary product of domestication. Though it might seem obvious that the earliest herders would have seized on milk as a nutritious and easily available food, this notion is unrealistic. Cows only produce milk when they have a calf to nourish. Where forage is poor, they can produce only enough milk to feed their offspring. The herder who forced the issue might obtain a little milk at the expense of a valuable calf. Even when there is excess milk, the job of collecting it may not be easy. The cow's ability to express milk involves an involuntary response— the "let-down reflex"—that makes the milk available in the teat. Early images of milking show penned cows with calves nearby. Seeing a calf triggers the let-down reflex and makes the milk flow. Over generations, as cattle were selected for the abundance and richness of their milk, as well as its availability, milking became routine. Modern dairy cows produce enormous quantities of milk daily, and anyone who learns the knack can milk a cow.

Milk, then, was originally a seasonal product that was only available from calving time in the spring to sometime in autumn, when the calves were weaned and the cows' milk dried up. Preserving milk for year-round consumption was desirable, and over time a number of techniques were discovered to make this possible. These techniques varied widely from region to region. The rich variety of preserved milk products that exist today is a survival of such techniques. In the Mediterranean region, where thousands of cheese varieties are still made, the raw materials include sheep, goat, buffalo, and cow's milk. The cheeses made from this variable stock range in texture from rock hard to runny. Cheese may come in wheels that weigh hundreds of pounds or in disks or wedges weighing a few ounces. Climate has a strong effect on the composition and preservation of cheese. Mediterranean cheeses tend to be made of sheep or goat's milk rather than cow's milk because of the kind and extent of pasture. Cheeses that are soft and quick to form predominate. The region also produces other preserved milk products. Yogurt and kefir are probably the best known and most widely used.

Like meat, milk is rich in proteins; it also contains large amounts of calcium and the vitamin D that metabolizes calcium in the body. Processing milk to make cheese or yogurt preserves most of the protein and calcium along with a percentage of the vitamin D. The material difference between processed and unprocessed milk is a surprising one. Milk is produced by mammals to nourish their young. After the young are weaned, their small intestines produce decreased amounts of the enzyme lactase, which breaks down the lactose in milk into easily metabolized sugars. By adulthood, many humans, like other mature mammals, have stopped producing this enzyme altogether. Without lactase they become "lactose intolerant." Processing milk does away with a large percentage of the lactose, so cheese is more digestible for many than raw milk. In yogurt and kefir, bacterial cultures predigest the lactose.

Scientists have recently discovered the genes responsible for switching off lactase production in adults. This genetic switch that triggers lactose intolerance is widespread, especially in Asia and Africa. The lowest levels of lactose intolerance are found in northern Europe, where milk and milk products have formed an important part of the diet for millennia. Attempts to link the gene for lactase production with the advance of the Secondary Products Revolution have not, however, been successful.

Using the milk of domestic animals increased the food supply and made storing food possible. It also increased the efficiency of herding. Butchering a cow for meat yields a bonanza of calories for human use, so slaughtering a cow is like winning a lottery. Milking a cow over a number of years turns the lottery into an annuity. Milking not only harvests more calories for human use but recovers a larger percentage of the energy the cow herself has harvested from the ecosystem. Efficiency of this kind is relatively unimportant when cattle can get all their nourishment from uncultivated pastures. In some Mediterranean climates, however, winter forage is not available, and animals eat grain that has been cultivated and harvested. In that situation, it is extremely important that the farmer make the most efficient possible use of all the potential animal products. When cattle compete with humans for cultivated grain, the total calories produced may well shrink. Grain-feeding rather than pasturing cattle that are destined only to be slaughtered, an increasingly common modern practice, is incredibly wasteful for just this reason.

Other animals entered the domesticated community in different times and places. Dogs, which make animal herding and protection easier, began their partnership with humans at least fourteen thousand years ago, much longer ago if the snub-toed footprints at Chauvet Cave belonged to a domesticated dog. Cooperation between humans and dogs probably began when wolves followed human hunters or foraged for scraps on the edge of campsites. Dogs do not have to compete with humans for food; they are willing scavengers of discard and waste.

Cats, which have never been fully domesticated, probably began their association with humans when stores of wild or domesticated grain attracted rodents to villages. Cats entered village life in the Levant where agriculture began, and the domesticated cat, which has a single genetic origin, followed the same path as the expanding frontier of Neolithic agriculture.

Current research suggests that the ancestors of today's chickens originally came from Southeast Asia. They were domesticated in China eight thousand years ago and reached the Mediterranean through central Russia sometime in the Neolithic. They were and remain an important source of food throughout the Mediterranean region. In the modern world, the great majority of chickens eat grain like every other domesticated animal. But just like dogs, chickens are content to scavenge for scraps of discarded food and scratch for grubs and worms like other birds. They do not have to compete with humans for food.[26]

The wild boars from which modern pigs descend were, like chickens, native to Southeast Asia. From there they spread across the Asian continent and into Europe. Recent DNA research on domestic pigs reveals a degree of genetic variability that suggests that pigs were domesticated in several different places.[27] Though pigs are intelligent and as capable of learning as a dog, they are not herd or pack animals, so it must have been difficult to learn the techniques of driving them. Since no valuable secondary products are produced by pigs, they might have been an impractical animal to domesticate. In the Middle Ages, pigs and dogs foraged together in city streets. This may have been true in the Neolithic as well, but their more important source of food throughout premodern history came from an ecosystem that no other domestic species could safely exploit. Wild pigs were native to forests, and domestic pigs found food in an environment where sheep and cattle would starve. Acorns and other nuts, along with grubs, roots, edible fungi, small animals, and carrion nourished pigs. While humans occasionally ate acorns, they were never a major source of nutrition, so by and large, pigs extended the range of exploitable ecosystems rather than competing with humans for food, as they do today. Today pigs consume enormous amounts of cultivated grains and other manufactured foods, of which they return only a small percentage as usable calories. Like grain-fed chickens and cattle, pigs create an ecological deficit.

Neolithic people continued to forage and hunt, and they grew other crops that supplemented their diet and gave it variety. Considered as a whole, the human diet of the Mediterranean littoral was rich, varied, and nutritious. It reflected the interaction of multiple cultures—herding and farming—and relied on the cooperative use of products from multiple ecosystems. It is admirable as an intricate and carefully managed means of food production. It is equally admirable because agriculture as an industry today, its abuses notwithstanding, remains based on the suite of crops and techniques that were introduced in a few Neolithic events. In our day, when food literacy is becoming increasingly important, it is essential to remember that our appreciation and understanding of what nourishes us cannot be limited to the farm-to-table connection. We need to be aware, too, of how the crops we enjoy arrived on the farmer's doorstep in the first place. Neolithic domestications brought them there.

Was the Neolithic a Nutritional Mistake?

Theorists and researchers long shared the belief that the Neolithic Revolution led to population increase and longer life. They took it for granted that agriculture and domestication had erased many of the dangers and uncertainties of a hunter-gatherer lifestyle. Conflicts with large prey and competition with other predators, the continual handling of weapons, and the high risk of an unsuccessful hunt suggest that life before agriculture was a difficult one. The English philosopher Thomas Hobbes described this era in history as one in which humankind lived in a state of constant apprehension. "In such condition there is no place for industry, because the fruit thereof is uncertain: and consequently no culture of the earth; no navigation, nor use of the commodities that may be imported by sea; no commodious building; no instruments of moving and removing such things as require much force; no knowledge of the face of the earth; no account of time; no arts; no letters; no society; and which is worst of all, continual fear, and danger of violent death; and the life of man, solitary, poor, nasty, brutish, and short."[28]

For many reasons, scholars in the late twentieth century began to find Hobbes's view unacceptable. The impression grew that the Paleolithic was something of a utopia and the Neolithic its antithesis and destroyer.[29] Nutritionists point out that the kinds of food that the Neolithic Revolutions made available were considerably different from the foods that humans and their hominid ancestors had eaten before cultivation. Cultivated grains and meat from domestic animals were higher in fats and sugars than foraged food. This trend toward fats and sugars has been dramatically accelerated in the contemporary diet, which contains large amounts of processed foods, but some effects would have been felt in the early Neolithic. Sugars in foods increase blood glucose levels and stimulate insulin overproduction, which may lead to insulin resistance. Diseases related to this syndrome include obesity, coronary heart disease, type 2 diabetes, hypertension, and other "diseases of civilization."[30] Changes in the Neolithic diet created vitamin and mineral deficiencies associated with eating a small variety of foods and caused an increase in food acidity. The balance between two essential electrolytes in the body, potassium and sodium, also changed as humans switched from foraging to cultivation. Introduced in the Neolithic and exacerbated by modern food production, these changes have created the characteristic patterns of modern mortality. What we die of, like what we live on, was shaped by the Neolithic Revolution.

In the archaeological literature it has become commonplace to see the Neolithic as generally characterized by "an overall degradation of the quality of human health."[31] Though this conclusion is based on research that has become increasingly precise and definitive in the past few decades, the amount and kind of change in human health has been overstated. In 1958 members of the Greek Speleological Society explored Alepotrypa Cave in the southern Peloponnesus. Excavations began there in 1970 and continue to the present. The cave and the areas around it were occupied between seven thousand and fifty-two hundred years ago, until an earthquake sealed it off and preserved its archaeological remains. Artifacts and animal bones collected there point to a Neolithic lifestyle. Skeletal remains from a minimum of 160 persons have been found in the cave and meticulously studied.

The detailed picture of Neolithic health that the site paints is less

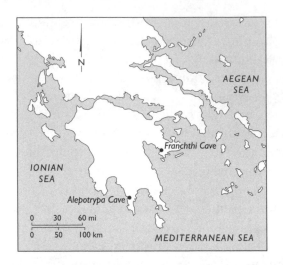

Franchthi Cave and Alepotrypa Cave provide glimpses of culture, diet, and health during the Neolithic.

dire than predicted, given the gloomy views of many in the archaeological community. It probably comes as no surprise that Neolithic life spans were, on average, shockingly brief by modern standards. The expectation of life at birth was under eighteen years. This dramatic figure, however, is misleading. If an average baby can hope to live only eighteen years, it is because a great many babies in such communities die in infancy or childhood. In fact, this population shows an "unusually high prevalence of child mortality." By age ten, though, the picture looks quite different. For the child who survives, the horizon has expanded. The researcher concludes that "after the critical age of ten years, individuals can be expected to live to a mature age." Still, the oldest individual in the sample died at age fifty, and the average age at death was twenty-nine.[32]

As contemporary television programs show, skeletons can offer testimony about a life lived. Like worked stones, however, their range of expression is limited. What the skeletal remains from Alepotrypa represent are lives marked by the effects of Neolithic agriculture. Anemia was widespread and afflicted almost 60 percent of the population. In most cases, the anemia was mild; only a small fraction suffered severely. Iron deficiency is the most common cause of anemia, although rickets and scurvy leave similar marks on bones.

Since cereal crops are low in iron, the deficiency is common in agricultural communities. There was some evidence for occasional halts in the growth of bones. Severe malnutrition can cause breaks in the pattern of bone growth. One failed crop can produce this effect.

Though the population was generally young, arthritis was common. Other skeletal evidence suggests prolonged stress. Those bones belonged to people who traveled long distances on foot, carried heavy loads, worked hard often on their knees, and used their hands. Despite these hardships, there was little evidence of injury. The only indication of trauma came from the skulls of nine individuals. Each had small head fractures that were well healed by the time of their deaths. To the researcher, these injuries suggested "interpersonal aggression and conflict but not lethal encounters. . . . Blunt objects such as stones might have been used to inflict this kind of trauma."[33]

Teeth show the effects of Neolithic life most strongly. We might expect a diet rich in cereals to have little effect on hard tooth enamel, but oddly enough, the opposite is true. Grains may be soft, but the mortars and pestles that ground them were typically made of stone. As the grain was ground, the stone wore away, and the fine grit that eroded from it ended up in food. The teeth of the Alepotrypa farmers have shallow dish-shaped wear patterns on all their chewing surfaces. Otherwise, tooth health was remarkably good; there were few cavities and little evidence of infection.

The evidence from Alepotrypa confirms the general impression among archaeologists that human health and vigor decreased in the Neolithic period. The strongest impression that the data give, however, is that things could have been a great deal worse. Infant mortality must have been high, but there is little evidence of severe, prolonged anemia or chronic malnutrition among adults. Physical labor imposed its stresses, but crippling illness and severe trauma were not at all common. The researcher concludes that the evidence points to "a slight overall decline of health status with the transition to agriculture."[34]

These conclusions take for granted that populations before the Neolithic would have been healthier, but skeletons of Paleolithic populations in the Old World remain scarce. Without that kind of background data, it really is impossible to say whether the Alepotrypa Cave data indicate a general decline in health, as most researchers assume, little change, or actual improvement. One set of research data, which has not received wide attention, does offer comparative information. Two Hungarian demographers looked at skeletal data for Paleolithic and Neolithic populations in a similar geographical setting. Their data suggested that life expectancy at the beginning of the Neolithic rose by about four years.[35]

The best general assessment of the impact of the Neolithic on human health is a measured one. Two factors need to be weighed. One is the enormous increase in the human population that the Neolithic created. The other is what appears to be a dip, though a slight one, in human health and an increase in endemic disease. The "diseases of civilization" have their remote origins in the Neolithic diet, but their prevalence today reflects the dramatic upswing in fats and sugars that characterize the modern industrialized diet and the simultaneous stripping away of such traditional causes of death as infection. A judicious observer might reject Hobbes's gloomy assessment but would have to concede that without the Neolithic foods on our tables today, there would be many fewer humans populating the world, and those few would be living a life that was far from utopian.

CHAPTER THREE

The Spread of Farming Culture

F irst developed in the Levant during the tenth millennium BCE, farming spread into Anatolia by the eighth millennium BCE, then crossed the Aegean Sea to the Greek mainland in the middle of the seventh. From there the movement took two separate paths more or less simultaneously. Pioneers from Greece heading north brought the technology and culture of farming to the Danube Valley. A separate group made its way across the Adriatic to southern Italy, Sicily, and the Iberian Peninsula. Italy was settled by the mid-seventh millennium BCE. Sardinia and Corsica followed soon after and served as jumping-off points for the spread of farming to southern France and Spain, where agriculture was established by the mid-sixth millennium BCE. Europe north of the Alps was colonized by farmers from the Danube Valley.[1]

Along with the founder crops and domestic animals, farming brought a radically new form of communal life to each successive region it affected. Architecture and pottery offer the most enduring evidence of this dramatic change, but there are many intangible aspects of culture associated with the advance of farming, including the organization of society, the relative status of men and women, language, mythology, and the conduct of worship. The new world picture that farming created as it transformed communities gave shape to social institutions. Without question, Mediterranean culture in

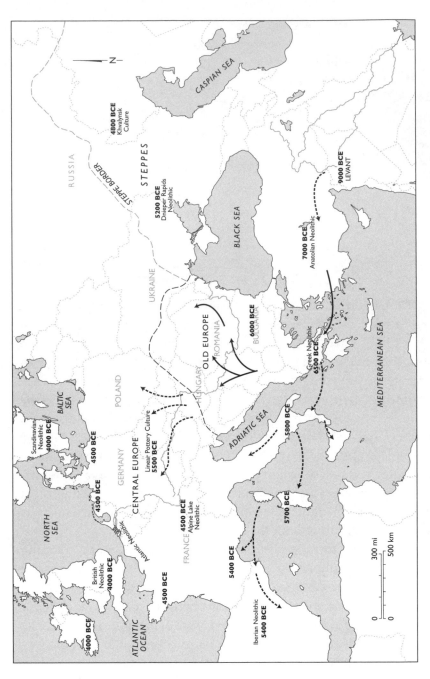

Farming culture spread from the Levant to Greece and from there to the rest of Europe.

its formative period was agri-culture. And like the foods on our dinner tables that date from the Neolithic, many of the languages spoken today are arguably part of this agricultural legacy.

The origins of language and mythology, along with their connection to social structure, have been hotly debated since the nineteenth century. In 1869 the historian Johann Jakob Bachofen argued in a highly influential book that Western societies had first been governed by women and only gradually evolved what, from his and his era's point of view, was the more advanced social system of patriarchy. Karl Marx's collaborator, Friedrich Engels, picked up the idea, and an English novelist turned mythographer, Robert Graves, incorporated this notion in his compilation *The White Goddess*.[2] In that book Graves argued that the patriarchal Olympian gods supplanted the primal goddess of the woman-centered Greek religion. Synthesizing emerging archaeological evidence with discoveries in comparative mythology, folklore, and linguistics, the prehistorian Marija Gimbutas refined the notion in a series of influential books in the mid-twentieth century. Her belief that early societies were matriarchal and worshipped a female deity—the Goddess—has captured the imagination of many outside the academic world. Essentially, she argued that "past societies in Europe and the Near East, especially prior to the so-called invasion of Indo-Europeans circa five thousand years ago, ... were Goddess-worshipping, female-centered, in harmony with their environments, and more balanced in male-female relationships, in which the status of women was high and respected."[3]

The goddess hypothesis describes the domination of nature as a masculine ideal; adherents assert that in the period of matriarchy, relations between human and ecological communities were harmonious. A contemporary school of thought that merges environmental thinking with feminist literary and social criticism makes a similar point. Called ecofeminism, it "focuses on the connections between the domination of women and the domination of nature."[4]

Home ground for the matriarchal view of early societies is a group of farming communities that began to spread through the Danube Valley seven thousand years ago. Archaeologists became aware of these communities only during the twentieth century, and for much of that time, study of them was fragmented among competitive neighbors. After the fall of the Soviet Union, cross-cultural and international studies of these sites increased. The result of this still-active investigation has been the recognition of a culture of "Old Europe." This culture flourished in much of the Danube basin from the western coast of the Black Sea eastward into the rich soils of Hungary. The culture was precocious and long lasting. It rested on a Neolithic package that originated in the Levant and reached the region through Greece. Between 5000 and 3500 BCE, the civilization of the Danube Valley was one of the largest and most technically proficient in the world.

The cultures of Old Europe refined the techniques of floodwater farming. Rather than cultivating small plots of stream-deposited soils, these communities cultivated the rich soil of the Danube Valley, which had many of the same qualities. The earth was moist, deep, and easy to cultivate. Fertility was renewed by intermittent flooding that added nutrients to replace those lost to crops. Unlike the desert, where the total area that could be intensely cultivated was quite small, the Danube floodplain covered hundreds of square miles.

Large expanses of rich soil encouraged housing clusters, and the villages of Old Europe could be quite large, certainly bigger than any housing concentrations that had existed before this time. Only the cities of Mesopotamia, which did not come into being until the fourth millennium BCE, would have rivaled them. Old European towns also existed for long stretches of time. As houses decayed, they were replaced by new structures built on the rubble of the old. So, like many Levantine sites, the villages of Old Europe became tell-like prominences in the flat alluvial landscape.

Excavations at these sites have revealed a communal pattern that is similar in many ways to life in Çatalhöyük. Houses were relatively uniform, though the towns had streets, and the houses had doors. Interiors in a typical village were roughly the same size. Though plenty of pottery and skilled metalwork have been found in burials throughout the region, the villages had no potters' or metalworkers' quarters, nor any evidence of social hierarchy. There were no obvious headmen's houses and certainly no palaces. There is no evidence of a priestly caste, and there are no distinct shrines or temples. Religion appears to have been a matter of household practice. The undifferentiated architecture of the Old European villages, like that at Çatalhöyük, suggests an egalitarian social structure, which

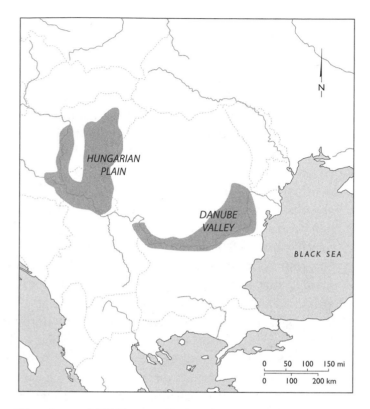

*The cultures of Old Europe, which included the Danube Valley and
the Hungarian Plain, featured floodwater farming, communal
dwelling, and a matriarchal society.*

would be consistent with the goddess hypothesis. Whether or not
these societies supported matriarchies or a culture of a goddess, their
non-confrontational ecological attitudes embraced not just foraging
but the cultivation of the soil and the domestication of animals.

The art of Old Europe has captured the attention and imagination of generations of researchers. Architectural elaboration is the
norm at Çatalhöyük, but the most common art objects found in
Danube sites are small, portable figurines. A few of these represent
men. A larger number represent a range of wild and domestic animals. By far the greatest number of representations are of women.
Though often found in isolation, female figurines are sometimes
found in groups. One of the most striking finds of this kind was a

clay jar containing twenty-one figures and thirteen small chairs. The figures were shaped and fired in the early years of Danube settlement.[5] There are fifteen larger figures and six smaller ones. The chairs are on the same scale as the larger figures, who are usually exhibited seated in them. The physiognomy of each figure is about the same, but there are differences in shape, size, and painted or incised decoration. Each figure rests on enormous buttocks and thighs. Each has a small cylindrical torso with stubs for arms topped by an extended neck. Faces are indicated by pinched noses and incised eyes and mouth. The top of the head is typically flattened.[6]

One obvious characteristic of the figurines is their obesity. Whether that represents an ideal of beauty or even of fecundity, the figurines clearly show the effects of plentiful nourishment. In that way they may represent the community's acknowledgment and celebration of agricultural success. The goddesses are fat because the soil and herds are productive and food is abundant.

Female figurines reveal much but not everything about the structure of Danube societies.[7] Female dominance in one sphere did not carry over into another, and contemporary specialists believe that these communities were not strictly matriarchal: "Men seem to have controlled external relations involving trade and negotiations with neighboring chiefs, while the rituals represented by female figurines seem to have emphasized the dominant role of women inside the house, and perhaps were connected with ancestor cults centered on their mothers and aunts."[8] The norm was not matriarchy, then, but a sharing of power, with dominance of one gender in the external sphere and the other in the domestic sphere.

The goddess hypothesis may not be fully confirmed by archaeological evidence, but it remains a compelling ideal for many. The theory not only describes the characteristics of the putative age of matriarchy but also offers a conjecture about the forces that brought the era to an end. In Gimbutas's view, matriarchal societies in Europe were overwhelmed in a series of invasions that began in the late fifth millennium BCE. Old Europe offers some confirmation of this theory. Archaeology shows that an astonishing number of settlements in the lower Danube Valley were burned and abandoned around that time. At a site in north-central Bulgaria, burned houses and human skeletons suggest a massacre. No new village sites from that era have come to light, but new kinds of graves are characteristic. These graves contain technologically inferior goods. Horse sacrifices mark some of these graves as well, and the consensus appears to be that a nomadic people erupted into the Danube Valley. One possibility is that, as Gimbutas suggested, Old Europe collapsed under pressure from the eruption into the lower Danube Valley of people who were mobile herders, possibly mounted on horseback, from the steppe grasslands of what is now Ukraine. A migration from the steppes does seem to have happened at about the same time as the collapse, but contemporary archaeologists are uncertain whether it caused the collapse or came about when a collapse brought on by some still-unknown factor had made Old Europe vulnerable.[9]

The eruption of mounted nomads from their homelands in the steppes has played a major role in shaping the thinking of a number of theorists. Not only have such invasions been invoked to explain the destruction of matriarchal society, they have also been linked to the history of the region's languages. The broad family of what are called Indo-European languages includes existing and vanished tongues native to a swath of geography extending from Iceland in the North Atlantic to Bangladesh in South Asia.[10] Within this range, there are areas where non-Indo-European languages prevail.[11] In general, however, the languages of Europe, eastern Europe and the Balkans, Russia, Iraq, Iran, Afghanistan, Pakistan, northern India, Bangladesh, and Sri Lanka are all members of a single extended family. This family of modern languages is linked genealogically to others that are no longer spoken, including Ancient Greek, Ancient Persian, Latin, and Ancient Sanskrit. Many researchers believe that the commonalities among languages across this vast region could only have come about through mass migration of a distinct people.[12]

The task of giving this hypothetical people a name and a cultural identity was taken up by Gimbutas. What she identified as the Kurgan Culture was, in her mind, "a patriarchal, semi-nomadic, Indo-European-speaking group of stockbreeders who originated in the vicinity of the lower Volga and migrated westward across much of Europe." Till the end of her life, Gimbutas continued to argue that the Kurgan Culture was the bearer of language and also of "patriarchy, patrilineality, (social) ranking, animal domestication (including that of the horse), pastoralism, mobility, and armament."[13]

How widespread such an invasion might have been remains unclear. The archaeological record shows changes in culture that might
correspond to an invasion. It is equally possible, however, that these
cultural changes came about through the adoption by indigenous
peoples of new ways of life. With this thought in mind, prehistorians
began to ask themselves what movement in the Neolithic period had
such a broad disruptive effect that it could produce massive shifts in
language, culture, and mythology.

There are two possible answers to this question. One is the mass
movement of peoples, the horse-powered invasions that Gimbutas
argued for. The second is a social revolution of such magnitude that
it led to the abandonment of an older way of life and the adoption of
a new culture that included new language and new mythology. This
would imply a revolution so widespread and so powerful that it
made the rituals, symbols, myths, and sacrifices that reflected and
supported an earlier way of life utterly meaningless. Society would
have been rebuilt around an entirely different set of social and environmental conditions.

The spread of farming technology occurred at about the right
time to explain the new social institutions, and it was certainly revolutionary. Could it be that the expansion of farming technology or
developments within its system of values spread new myths, cultures,
and languages? If so, the most likely group to introduce language and
culture would not be nomadic invaders whose actions disrupted an
agricultural way of life but the agricultural pioneers themselves. The
most persuasive contemporary thinking about language spread recognizes this fact. The argument here is that migrants introduced
Neolithic culture, technology, and *language* to new areas in a leap-
frog movement across the Mediterranean and beyond.

Genetics and Linguistics

In the mid-1960s a pioneering biological researcher named Luca
Cavalli-Sforza began studying what is now called population genetics. Like Gimbutas, he was looking for evidence of migrations that
could have spread a new culture and language across the Mediterranean world. Rather than turn to archaeology, Cavalli-Sforza in-
vestigated the human genetic record. So-called genetic research on

human populations had been going on for a hundred years by this time, but that work had focused on visible variations like skin and hair color, eye and skull shape. Since many of these characteristics were associated with race, much of this investigation amounted to little more than a justification for nationalist and racist agendas.[14]

Cavalli-Sforza and his associates focused on a hidden phenomenon that had no racial or racist implications. Genetics determine the human blood groups or types, which, like skin color, serve as markers of heredity. From the beginning of mass conscriptions in World War II, industrial societies took blood samples and recorded blood types for individual troops. Soldiers from around the world participated in these levies, so enormous amounts of data were collected. These data, furthermore, include a sampling from nearly the entire world.

What Cavalli-Sforza first looked for in his data was any pattern in the distribution of different blood types that might suggest a movement of Mediterranean population from east to west. He found exactly that in a blood type that predominated in the Levant. This discovery suggested a population movement that seemed to correspond with the pathways by which farming technology had spread. The fledgling science of genetics had stepped in to settle a question that had stumped older and better-established disciplines.

In the last decades of the twentieth century, researchers developed and perfected two new forms of DNA analysis that gave good results from a relatively simple examination of genetic material. The first of these methods to come into widespread use focused on mitochondrial DNA. Mitochondria, the energy producers in cells, are alien bodies suspended in human hosts. They are the descendants of bacteria that invaded the primate body multiple generations ago and established a symbiotic relationship with its cells. Mitochondria have DNA, but it is isolated from the human genome. It is passed intact from generation to generation without taking part in the sharing of genes that marks sexual reproduction. The mitochondrial DNA of each human being is identical to that of his or her mother.

In theory, then, the mitochondrial DNA of each living human should be identical and indistinguishable from that of the first woman. In time, however, DNA mutates. Over the multiple generations that separate us all from a common mother, our mitochondrial

DNA—like our genomic DNA—has changed character. We are no longer all alike; we no longer fully resemble an Eve. Variations in human mitochondrial DNA create broad groupings that biologists have used to answer a number of questions about human origins and human affiliations.

At first, the mitochondrial DNA evidence appeared to confirm Cavalli-Sforza's conclusions. The Mediterranean dispersal pattern from east to west that his research on blood types had demonstrated also showed up in surveys of mitochondrial DNA. In a short time, however, this apparent confirmation became a challenge to Cavalli-Sforza's theory. Blood-type distributions lack a degree of resolution that mitochondrial DNA provides. Tracing the mutation history of the genes not only shows affiliations within a population but creates a timeline that was missing in blood-type research. Biologists assume that mutations of the kind that make a permanent impact occur quite infrequently. They estimate that on average such a change happens every ten thousand years or so. By counting the number of mutations that distinguish two populations and multiplying by this rough-and-ready figure a researcher reaches a conclusion about when two populations were last in contact.

Although the mitochondrial DNA evidence showed that the westward migration that Cavalli-Sforza argued for was correct in its geographical dimension, it also showed that his time scale was off. The number of mutations that distinguished the eastern and western ends of the population that shared an eastern Mediterranean blood type suggested that most of the migration Cavalli-Sforza attributed to the spread of early farming actually occurred many thousands of years before. Cavalli-Sforza's blood types had traced Cro-Magnon era migration, not the movement of early farmers.

Though the bulk of mitochondrial DNA evidence pointed to a westward migration during the Paleolithic, not all of it did. Geneticists identified one marker that dated to the Neolithic. It, too, showed a progression from east to west, but the migration that it represented was small compared with the earlier one. The marker is most common in the Levant, so its origins are assured. It is found along the Mediterranean coast all the way to Spain, then northward along the Atlantic and into Britain. About 20 percent of the European population share this marker.

Farming might conceivably be spread by such a small population, and those who have looked to Cavalli-Sforza for support of their ideas about early farming have welcomed his data. Language spread, however, is not so easy to account for. The simplest model for language spread is population replacement, and the Neolithic marker in European mitochondrial DNA is much too scarce to suggest anything of the kind. The archaeological evidence, too, suggests that adoption rather than displacement is the most likely way for farming to have spread. If we accept that the immigrant population is smaller than the indigenous population, can we still link the spread of agriculture with the spread of language?

Numbers are crucial to the argument. If we imagine that every forager in the preagricultural Mediterranean spoke a single language, then a wave of new people that was smaller than the indigenous population might have been able to impose an elite language like Latin or French on the people they encountered, but it is far more likely that the incomers' descendants would have ended up speaking the indigenous language. The Paleolithic foragers of the region probably did not speak a single language to begin with, however. In analogous situations in historic times, linguistic fragmentation has been the norm among hunter-gatherer groups. A rough count of indigenous languages of the pre-Colombian Americas, where foraging was widespread (though by no means universal), yields more than 1,300 names of languages, and these are just the names that have been recorded. Without doubt, the number understates, perhaps by a high percentage, the total number of different languages that Amerindians spoke before 1492.

Where linguistic fragmentation exists, the numbers game of language replacement changes. An incoming group that is linguistically and culturally unified can be small in comparison to the total indigenous population of a region in terms of genetics but overwhelming in comparison with any single language group within the region. Over time the incomers will be absorbed genetically. Yet as their distinctive genetic marker becomes increasingly rare in the population, their language could predominate. Population dynamics are the key to language change and the dominance of an incoming language over multiple indigenous languages.

Researchers, particularly the archaeologist Colin Renfrew, have adopted a "modified wave of advance" model to describe the simultaneous spread of farming and language.[15] Cavalli-Sforza's original wave-of-advance model had two phases. In the first phase a colony of farmers entered a territory where foragers had lived for millennia. The foragers and the farmers interacted rather than competed, since they used different resources in their shared ecosystem. Eventually they intermarried, and some percentage of foragers and their descendants took up farming. Boosted by the nutritional bonanza that farming created, the agricultural population grew much more quickly than the forager population. Foragers disappeared (or became herders) as farming expanded. Eventually the farming community reached the tipping point where the labor supply exceeded the cultivable land. Then the second phase of the wave of advance began. A portion of the farming colony migrated to new territory. The genetic signature they bore was already an unequal mix of imported and indigenous DNA. In their new colony, they repeated the process of interaction, intermarriage, and assimilation. As the population expanded, the process continued until the wave of advance reached the end of arable land. With each surge in the wave of advance, the DNA that characterized the original colonists was diluted still further. Through this mechanism a small migrant population could create a large cultural change while leaving a relatively small genetic trace.[16]

The wave-of-advance model is probably not the last word on the origins of Mediterranean languages. Still, the links between language and farming are persuasive. The effects of the Neolithic Revolution evidently spread westward from the Levant. It is not too much to imagine that language and social life spread along with the cultivation of the land. Mediterranean culture in its most fundamental sense is agri-culture.

Towns and Temples

Early researchers imagined towns and cities as a late phase in the history of cereal cultivation. The excavations at Jericho, Çatalhöyük, and a host of other sites in the Levant long ago overturned that assumption. Urban architecture arose from the lifeways of sedentary foragers like those at Çatalhöyük right at the start of the Neolithic

Revolution. As that revolution extended its hold on community after community in its outward spread from the Levant, it eventually reached the territory of well-established and highly successful forager populations on the Atlantic and western Mediterranean coasts. These communities were among the last to adopt cereal cultivation and animal domestication. They were late, too, in adopting the most visible component of the Neolithic package: domestic architecture.[17]

For many of these late converts to agriculture the concept of the village was more important and more useful than the dwellings that made it up. They adopted the village as a symbol rather than as a place to live. In the process they transformed functional structures into idealized ones. Stonehenge is the most widely known monument of this kind, but it is only one among a multitude of structures scattered in a wide arc from Scandinavia and the British Isles along the Atlantic coast and south into the Mediterranean islands. These monuments represent a common response to the spread of domestication, but they take many forms. Stonehenge is a ring of monoliths, and there are similar, though smaller, rings in many other places. In some regions there are single standing stones or towers; in others, houselike structures called dolmens. The anthropologist Ian Hodder characterizes these monuments as a response to the agricultural package that communities new to farming adapted to their own particular needs. Hodder believes that megaliths "referred symbolically to earlier and contemporary houses in central Europe and, to a lesser extent, in Western Europe."[18]

Viewed in a certain way, what the builders of these monuments did was not so different from the actions of the well-known cargo cults of New Guinea, who built simulated airstrips in isolated jungles, believing that the structures themselves were sufficient to call down planes loaded with rich goods. Neolithic imitators were not so naive, and the structures they created in imitation of houses or housing clusters served their societies in essential ways. In many coastal areas it was impossible for people to live close together and still exploit the resources that they depended on. Still, for agriculture to be successful, community coordination was important. In societies of this kind, unity came through acting in common rather than living in common. Buildings that could be created only by a coordinated community effort encouraged cohesion. Once built, these same structures could be used to host rituals that continued to promote and celebrate cooperation.[19]

In the Mediterranean region the most striking megalithic monuments are found on the remote, tiny island cluster of Malta. These islands were settled by Sicilian colonists sometime in the sixth millennium BCE. Steep limestone hills sustained scattered farms, but the main source of nutrition for the islanders seems to have been their herds of sheep and goats, pigs, and a few cattle.[20]

Excavators and explorers began to take note of these monuments in the early eighteenth century. By the mid-twentieth century most had been fully excavated and their descriptions published. Before the use of carbon dating, it was assumed that the "temples" of Malta were built at a relatively late date. Many experts thought that the example of the Egyptian pyramids might have inspired the temples, or that Egyptian artisans might have built them. Others turned to the architecture of the Greek islands or West Asia as possible sources. Carbon dating has shown that the earliest of the temple complexes on Malta itself and its largest adjacent island, Gozo, antedate the pyramids and the fortifications of the Minoans of Crete. It is now generally accepted that the temples on Malta are the most ancient architectural monuments not only in the Mediterranean but in the world.[21]

The temple of Ggantija in Xaghra, on the island of Gozo, dates from sometime between 3600 and 3200 BCE, after the fall of the Danube cultures but before the first great urban areas were created along the Euphrates and the Nile. The Hagar Qim temples near the village of Qrendi stand on a hilltop overlooking the Mediterranean and a nearby rocky island; they date from the same period. Just downhill from their commanding site is the more sheltered temple of Mnajdra. The most complete and most intricate temple site in Malta is at Tarxien on the outskirts of the rapidly expanding Maltese capital, Valetta. Though the active use of the Maltese temples lasted a millennium or more, the form of the complexes from Ggantija through Tarxien remained remarkably constant. Giant stones, some rough, others shaped, create solid perimeter walls. Each temple has a single entry that leads into a long central passage. This corridor widens in two or more spots to accommodate an intersecting pair of round-ended rooms. Most temples have two pairs of these lobed

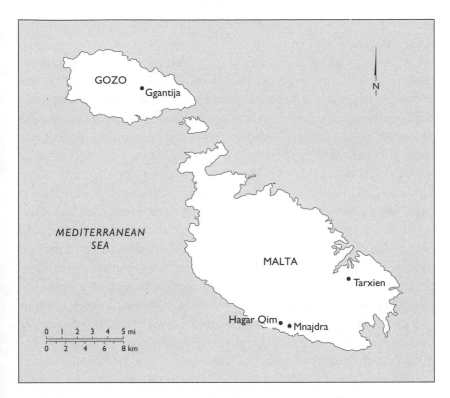

Temple sites on Malta and Gozo have the oldest architectural monuments in the world.

rooms. Some have a small apse at the end of the central path. The evident focal point of the temples is the niche at its far end, but this may not have been the case originally. Set at the endpoint of the temple's central axis and in some of the apses, the niches are structured in much the same way as the doorways that lead to them. In Maltese art, the shorthand representation of the temple is this doorway niche.[22]

Carved panels in shallow relief decorated the temples; some of the wall slabs are incised with images as well. Tarxien is rich in blocks with shallow engravings of curling tendrils, generally organized into geometric patterns; in some cases, the tendrils curl into full spirals. Other blocks show long lines of animals in profile. Goats with sweeping or curled horns alternate with pigs in one long procession. A much-damaged block shows a sow and piglets alongside a bull. There are fire bowls and fire pits and the marks of fire on interior walls. There are large urns or bowls.

Figurines and statues are among the most revealing objects turned up by the excavators. Almost all of these are representations of human beings. In many cases, the images have enlarged buttocks, thighs, and calves, though this is not universal. There are many images of women and of others that are sexually ambiguous. Among cult objects, phalli alone or in clusters are most common. The most striking single object is the base of a larger-than-life-size statue of a standing figure, usually interpreted as female, who wears a skirt with a pleated hem. She stands on small feet from which enormous calves balloon.

The emphasis on fertility and the combination of animal and human figures are similar in the art of the Danube cultures, although a direct relationship is not likely. Because the temples mimic domestic architecture and because figures of women play so large a part in their ornamentation and in the objects associated with them, Hodder argues for a close link between the temples and the Maltese society that produced them. In his view, the temples were architectural expressions of the special status of women in this agricultural society.

Hodder suggests Maltese agriculture in its earliest phases could expand only as long as the labor supply increased. After a while, there were enough laborers to farm all the available land. At this tipping point, the social foundation began to change. Once there were plenty of field hands and shepherds, human reproduction was no longer the primary social engine, and the entire apparatus of rituals, architecture, and cult objects devoted to it lost their importance. Symbolic power passed from the house and the mystical body of the woman and refocused on landholding and inheritance. Symbols of masculine power and status took center stage.[23]

For Gimbutas, such a change would have been evidence of a sweeping substitution of aggressive patriarchy for nurturing matriarchy. Hodder's theory is more conservative and, to my mind, more convincing. He argues that the symbolic role of women within the real or idealized household ceased to be the primary societal concern in Malta. Land replaced labor as the thing that mattered most. As this transition occurred, the gods and the rituals of fertility lost their magic and their believers; new cults took their place.

Though particular to Malta, Hodder's theory might apply more broadly to the shift from undifferentiated female-centered societies to male-dominated ones. Rather than rely on invasion and the substitution of one community by another, his theory rests on an internal agricultural dynamic. The shift from foraging to agriculture multiplied the nutritional resources available to a community and increased its population. The wave of advance theory recognizes this fact by positing that when farmer communities outgrew their resources, some percentage of their members moved on to new territories. When migration reached the continental limits, however, migration was no longer an option. There was no place to go. At this point communities began to experience the pressures of limited resources. Labor became abundant and lost value. Land became scarce, and those forces, both real and symbolic, that controlled land gained prestige and influence. The old lifeways and mythologies that extolled female reproduction as the engine of abundance ceased to be plausible. A new system of beliefs replaced them.

Malta represents one of the best examples of the fundamental changes in community life that the Neolithic Revolution created. The dynamics of agricultural change were responsible both for the development of the temples of Malta and for their abandonment. Power remained the same, though its realm and its expression changed radically. What drove social transformation again and again on Malta and throughout the Mediterranean world was the regime of cultivation and domestication.

From a modern perspective, we might describe the cultural change that led to the abandonment of the temples as an environmental crisis. The anomie that the Maltese must have experienced during this period of conflict and confusion would probably be familiar to us. What prevented the Maltese from experiencing the full disaster that modern societies are going through now was the essential stability of their agricultural routine. Their crisis of belief was profound, but it was not grounded, as the modern one is, in the degradation of the physical link between their community and the biological world. Their crisis was spiritual, emotional, and intellectual. Though modern theorists are prone to treat the contemporary ecological situation as essentially a crisis of understanding, they are mistaken. Agriculture is not an idea; it is a practice. Repairing the modern ecological crisis requires not just an intellectual adapta tion to changed conditions, like the one that the Maltese achieved, but a pragmatic readjustment of our partnership with the earth that nourishes us. We must think differently, yes, but we must act differently as well. Ideas will guide the change, but they are insufficient in themselves.

CHAPTER FOUR

Uruk and Egypt,
the Great Powers

D evelopments in farming and herding led to the creation of large and complex communities in Old Europe. As this culture was disappearing, both Mesopotamia, under a series of different ruling elites, and Egypt, with its more sedate rhythm of dynastic change, were expanding. In Egypt the Nile and in Mesopotamia the Euphrates nurtured enormous stretches of potential cropland. In Anatolia—home of the third great regional power, the Hittite Empire—there was no single great river or river system, so agriculture depended on rainfall. All three civilizations developed sophisticated and intricate systems to nourish the founder crops. All used oxen for plowing and hauling and donkeys (later horses) to speed communication within their territories. All developed systems of writing that widened the reach of central authority and ensured coordinated action throughout each realm. These mature states were not, as it was once universally believed, the originators of agriculture, but they were great consolidators of the discoveries of multiple cultures scattered throughout the region. As we saw earlier, the nineteenth-century linking of state formation, agricultural expansion, and warfare—a complex that remains intact in many contemporary critiques of Neolithic agriculture—was based on the mistaken belief that these societies were the inventors of agriculture.

Uruk and Mesopotamia

Mesopotamia lies entirely outside the geographical and climatological limits of the Mediterranean region. Culturally, however, the land crossed by the Tigris and Euphrates rivers long experienced the influence of, and exerted power over, the communities of the Levant and the Mediterranean basin. The city of Uruk was the first great power in Mesopotamia. Now some twelve miles distant from the meandering course of the Euphrates River, the city originally stood on its banks. Mentioned repeatedly in the Bible under the name Erech, Uruk is in Sumer, the southernmost part of Mesopotamia; its location was pinpointed in the mid-nineteenth century.

While northern Mesopotamia is a region of high plains that rise in a series of steps from the Tigris River valley to the Zagros Mountains, southern Mesopotamia, the site of Uruk, is low-lying and flat. The shifting intersection of the Tigris and the Euphrates dominates a floodplain and a delta that are crisscrossed by active and abandoned river channels, isolated lagoons, and extensive marshes. This territory was once a rich habitat for deer, wild boar, birds, and fish. The lotus, which has edible roots, and the date palm grew wild. The areas beyond the marshlands were desert. With sound water management, both the marshy soil, too wet for cultivation, and a portion of the arid desert were transformed into high-yield farmland.[1]

New excavations and explorations have updated the Uruk story. Once it was believed to be unique and foundational—it was the only large city anywhere around—but it is now clear that there were other cities like it upriver. Hamoukar, near Syria's border with Iraq, has been the scene of excavations during the past decade. Preliminary reports from the still-ongoing explorations indicate that a walled city stood on the site sometime in the first half of the fourth millennium BCE, earlier than the founding date for Uruk in the mid-fourth millennium. Hamoukar had complex architecture that indicated social differentiation, ovens for communal bread-baking, and a symbol system for identifying ownership of goods. Trade in obsidian from a source nearby appears to have been the city's mainstay. About fifty miles east of Hamoukar, a city buried beneath Tell Brak had monumental buildings that also predated Uruk. Massive walls protected a city there that covered an area of at least one hundred acres. Excavators found ceramic-, stone-, and metal-working areas.

Satellite towns ringed the urban center at Tell Brak. Aerial photographs supplemented by exploration on the ground have revealed more than a hundred towns within a five-mile radius. Between these outliers and the center were large uninhabited spaces that may have been fields or pastures. The regional population might have reached twenty thousand.[2] With big cities the traditional regional focus of archaeologists, village cultures have often been forgotten. The common account suggests that with the creation of large cities, one form of the organization of community life gave way to another. But villages continued to grow and thrive while cities developed. Villages aligned themselves with major centers and were no doubt subject to more supervision than they had once experienced, but they did not disappear. Cities, on the other hand, proved to be more volatile. The history of Mesopotamia is marked by repeated conquests of one city by another. In a country without natural protections that could act as a bar against invasion, walled cities were the only viable form of defense. Armies could take refuge behind city walls and shoot down on an attacker from their heights. Destroying the enemy meant capturing and destroying its city strongholds. Villages were mostly undefended and were easier to rebuild if overwhelmed. While cities rose and fell, villages rebuilt and persevered.

Even though modern research has shown that Uruk was neither the only city nor the dominant urban center, it still repays attention. The characteristics that distinguish it and its sister cities from earlier organizations of social life are momentous. Monumentality and a differentiated society that reflected status as well as occupational specialization, an effective leadership hierarchy, large populations densely settled in a complexly organized space, widespread trade, and some kind of symbiosis between center and periphery are their defining traits. The characteristics of Uruk in particular as they have been reconstructed through a century of digging and research are ones that became an integral part of the repertoire of political organization in the ancient world.

The demotion of Uruk and Mesopotamian cultures generally

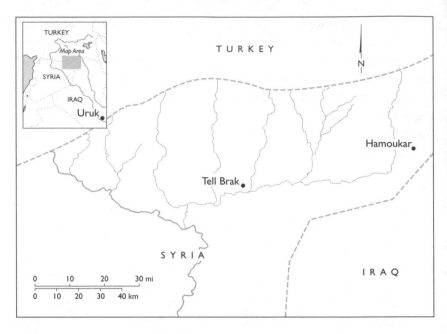

Urban centers like Uruk, Tell Brak, and Hamoukar flourished in Mesopotamia in harmony with the environment, notwithstanding modern charges of causing environmental degradation.

from their position as the founding sites of the agricultural revolution has important intellectual consequences. For historians and theorists rooted in the nineteenth-century political and social world, the primacy of Mesopotamian cultures in the agricultural historical narrative made sense. Their own world was one in which great powers were struggling to manage their resource bases, to govern territories and colonies and assure their monopoly over coercive violence within their territories, and to hone warfare for political use beyond their boundaries. Mesopotamia seemed to them to be a founder society which had—at the very beginning of the agricultural revolution as they imagined it—succeeded in addressing, if not necessarily harmonizing, all three of these concerns.

As we now conceptualize the agricultural revolution, on the basis of the pioneering work of Sherratt and others, Mesopotamia is no longer the point of origin for cultivation and domestication. Grain cultivation, the mainstay of Mesopotamian agriculture, is no longer the key element of the domestication complex, and the proto-nation-state is no longer the necessary moderator of domestication. The history of agriculture, the history of the rise of the political community, and the history of warfare did not cohere inextricably and inevitably as they were once thought to have done.

Irrigated agriculture made possible Uruk and the cities like it that dotted the banks of the Euphrates River. Upriver from Uruk, small rectangular fields bordered a complex of irrigation channels cut into the river's levees. These fields were flooded in midwinter and the water allowed to soak into the ground. Once their surfaces were dry, the fields were plowed and sown with barley or wheat. The water captured and held by the soil was sufficient to nourish the crop before the summer drought. Downriver from Uruk the field system was different. The fields there were enormous rectangles, up to a hundred acres apiece. At one of its narrow ends, each field abutted an irrigation canal. Fields of similar dimensions were grouped side by side along secondary canals to ensure that every bit of land that could be irrigated was linked to a waterway.

Teams of oxen plowed the long fields in furrows perpendicular to the water source. When the canals were breached and water flowed into the fields, the furrows served as channels for the water to irrigate the entire field. Once the water drained away and left the fields dry enough to work, teams of oxen pulled seed drills through them and deposited seeds in holes at the base of each furrow. This careful deposition of the seed increased productivity, and the fields of Uruk grew enormous quantities of grain.

Compared to plowing and sowing, which could be mechanized, harvesting was labor intensive. Bent low over the furrows, workers grabbed grain stalks by the handful and cut them with sickles. The number of sickles required quickly outpaced the supply of flint or obsidian blades. Ceramic sickles were a substitute, which Uruk potters mass-produced. Clay with a high silicon content produced blades that were sharp when first fired but useless once their edges grew dull. But the blades were so easy to produce that their short life was no problem. Once cut and bundled in sheaves, the harvest was hauled from the fields in ox-pulled carts. Threshing took place on hard-packed earthen floors. Teams of oxen pulled heavy sledges with parallel rows of flint blades on their lower surface to separate grain from straw and chaff.

Surviving records show measurements of field size—both length and width and, with increasing accuracy over the centuries, area. Routinely the scribes recorded information about expenditures for seeding and plowing, crop yields, and ownership of the harvest. Using standardized measures, the scribes estimated outlays of grain for feeding oxen and seeding the fields. During the periods of planting and harvest, overseers issued graded rations of barley to field hands according to a standardized system. Uruk potters created sturdy jugs of a fixed volume to distribute these rations.

Writing

To collect, analyze, and store the wealth of data that made the irrigated field system work, the city administration relied on symbols inscribed on clay tablets. As recordkeeping evolved, they produced the well-known cuneiform tablets that scribes throughout the region used. Tens of thousands of such tablets have survived. The earliest documentary tablets now known were uncovered in Uruk. Though their absolute date is hard to fix, they appear to belong to the time between 3200 and 3000 BCE. While later cuneiform tablets were archived, these early examples were preserved entirely by accident. Around 2000 BCE, major buildings in central Uruk were expanded. To prepare the ground for this ambitious project, dirt and rubble collected from many locations around the city were transported to the site. Among the debris were large numbers of discarded and broken clay tablets. As luck would have it, many of these tablets found their way into the fill dirt beneath the new structures, where they were recovered four thousand years later.[3]

The earliest surviving texts from Mesopotamia do not preserve sacred hymns or laws, philosophical speculations or astronomical data, but the ephemeral "paperwork" of day-to-day agricultural management. This administrative recording system is a distant ancestor of later writing systems. The earliest recordkeeping materials of the Uruk civilization were clay tokens in a variety of shapes that represented commodities. To create an inventory for a shipment of sheep, for example, an appropriate number of sheep tokens were placed in a bag to be handed over at delivery. Since it was all too easy for an unscrupulous trader to remove tokens from a bag and change the official record of a transaction, more foolproof methods soon became common. Typically a number of clay symbols were placed inside a ball of wet clay. Once it hardened, the symbols inside could not be removed without destroying the ball and giving the game away. Next, representations of the contents came to appear on the outside of the clay ball so that shipments could be tallied and verified en route without breaking it. Some products were identified with clay tags attached by strings and marked with a symbol. As shipments were assembled, scribes copied these symbols onto tablets along with notations of quantity. Often the contents listed on the front of a tablet were totaled up on the back of the same tablet.

The shift from inscribing symbols that represented objects to writing symbols that represented words was a crucial step in the development of writing. Many accounting systems like the earliest ones used in Uruk have turned up in various parts of the world. Frequently their discoverers have identified them as the "earliest use of writing" or the "independent invention of a writing system." But specialists accept that the invention of writing means the invention of a graphic representation of language and not just the picturing or symbolizing of objects. In Uruk the transition from symbols representing things to symbols representing words is easy to document. When the sign for a particular object began to function as the representation of the sound of the object's name, writing took on the characteristics of a rebus, as today pictures of a pool cue, a bent knee, an eye, and an income tax form might represent "cu-ne-i-form."

Cuneiform scripts were eventually used to represent all the languages of ancient West Asia. (The Egyptians developed a system with an independently derived set of graphic signs.) The regional predominance of cuneiform is remarkable. It is also a tribute to the usefulness of a ready-made set of phonetic representations. Sumerian, the first written language, is what linguists describe as an "isolate." It has no affiliation with any other known language. Akkadian, the second language to adopt the Sumerian system of representing syllables graphically, is a Semitic language. It had no etymological links with the freestanding Sumerian language, and what is worse, not much overlap with the phonetics of Sumerian. A lot of sounds and sound combinations native to Akkadian were not present in Sumerian. Still, the Akkadian scribes adopted the Sumerian writing system, evidently convinced that its advantages outweighed its inconveniences. Through the course of the third and second millennia BCE, languages using cuneiform writing continued to grow, though there were many simplifications and adaptations. It was only the adoption of the Phoenician alphabetic system that displaced cuneiform. Even then, the system held on. Cuneiform inscriptions from the first century CE have been found.

By all measures Uruk was huge. By the end of the fourth millennium BCE it covered almost one square mile and may have been home to fifty thousand people. At the center of the city were two temple complexes. The temple of the goddess Inana defined the area called Eanna; the second major temple complex, in the area called Kullab, served the god Enlil. Though on a much-expanded scale, these two structures echoed the smaller temples that anchored village life.

This enormous community was under the control of an interlocked elite of political, religious, and military leaders who took an active, official role in many aspects of daily life. Crafts like potting that were loosely organized at smaller centers were industrialized in the city. Small-town potters built their vessels by hand for the most part, but in the city potters turned clay on wheels. With the potter's wheel they could work at a much faster rate, and they were also able to standardize production to suit official needs. Other workers may have been organized in guilds or overseen in other ways. The state maintained close control over a portion of the agricultural labor pool.

City leaders encouraged and protected trade in important commodities, both those that sustained the life of the urban population, such as grain, cheese and dairy products, and produce, and those that marked off the privileged elite, such as gold, silver, and precious stones. Trade in metal that served agriculture, crafts, and the military was also closely supervised by the state.[4]

Egypt

Egypt may be geographically on the Mediterranean, but through much of its history, the sea played little part in the life of the kingdom. The Mediterranean marked the limit of productive land in the north, just as the desert marked the limit of cultivation to east and west. Only as a continuation of Nile shipping did the sea eventually gain importance for the Egyptians, though it had long served their neighbors. The richest part of Egypt was the Nile Delta. There the river branched out and created a broad triangle of exceptionally rich agricultural land. Currently 50 percent of the population of Egypt lives in the Delta. Memphis, the long-term capital of the ancient kingdom, stood on the southern edge of the Delta.[5]

Our image of ancient Egypt is a product of more than two hundred years of archaeological investigation and almost five hundred years of scholarly speculation. Archaeologists, artists, and surveyors accompanied Napoléon's troops as they invaded Egypt in the last decade of the eighteenth century. They collected artifacts and painstakingly made drawings of surviving monuments. This quixotic campaign, which Napoléon himself abandoned when his political fortunes were suddenly on the rise at home, created both Egyptology and the early nineteenth-century fashion for objects in the Egyptian style. From the start, the ruins of Egypt struck both popular and scholarly imagination with almost equal weight. Egypt has kept its large following; other archaeological enthusiasms have come and gone.

The Egyptians' cult of power, their extraordinary attention to the well-being of the dead, their abundant use of durable stone for building, and the country's desert climate combined willy-nilly to preserve overwhelming amounts of archaeological material. Egyptian belief in life after death led people of the highest social rank to have their remains preserved. Since they imagined eternity as similar to the life they had enjoyed on earth, they filled their tombs as if they were packing for an extended trip. Not everything would fit in even the most elaborate tombs, and because the lifestyle of distinguished people depended on the labor of innumerable servants and slaves, there was also a staffing problem. Human sacrifice may have been practiced in the earliest periods of the kingdom's history, but it was not long before a simpler and more economical solution was arrived at. Images replaced actual objects. Scenes painted on the walls of tombs and models filled with little figurines doing all the things necessary to sustain the life of the rich and powerful came to be substituted.

Egypt's dry climate discouraged the growth of molds and fungus that feed on organic materials. Tomb robbers, on the other hand, stole much of what had been preserved, but since they were more interested in valuables than in archaeological remains, they left a lot of interesting things untouched. Supplementing the artifactual record is an extraordinary wealth of written information. Inscriptions on stone in the hieroglyphic writing of the Egyptians survive in thousands of locations. Decoding the writing was one of the great breakthroughs of nineteenth-century archaeology.

Once decoded, however, these texts offered a surprisingly narrow window on the country's long history. Whereas cuneiform texts are rich in economic detail, the Egyptian writing system was so complex that it could be mastered by only a relatively small number of people. Hieroglyphic writings are richest in religious texts and royal declarations. Inscriptions tell the official versions of dynastic history, chronicle events in the religious cycle, and memorialize those among the dead who had power and influence.

The life of the nation is only obliquely represented in the art of tombs and in texts and inscriptions. The personalities and concerns even of powerful and distinguished individuals are concealed behind a facade of official actions and attitudes. While it has often been the role of archaeology to bypass the official story that texts present and to chronicle the lives of people who were not considered worth writing about, that has not typically been the case in Egypt. Most Egyptologists have concerned themselves with much the same world that writing presents. Monumental and official culture are well represented in archaeological publications, the cult of the dead is abundantly documented, but the remains of small communities and the patterns of daily life beyond the royal household and the estates of wealthy men and women are not. The relationship between archaeological Egypt and the living nation of the past is distinctly skewed.

The most dramatic proof of that skewing is visible in any voyage along the Nile. Built of stone, the country of the dead—land of

The Nile floodplain and delta are ideal for farming and problematic for archaeological preservation. (Photograph from NASA.)

monumentality and pharaonic absolutism—still stretches along the Nile at a safe distance from the annual flooding. The agricultural engine that propelled the nation lay in the floodplain itself and in the Nile Delta. Indeed, from the third millennium BCE the Delta was the Egyptian heartland. Here was the breadbasket of the country and its most densely settled part. Thousands of villages built not of stone but of mud brick housed those who fed the kingdom and guaranteed its survival. The Delta and the floodplain, however, are poor environments for archaeological preservation. Muddy soils replenished annually and humid air replace stone and the dry desert climate. The river water that swept over the land destroyed structures while it reinvigorated the soil. What the Nile did not sweep away, the plows of hundreds of generations of farmers broke down or dug up.

In the remains of the era before the pharaohs became monument builders—the Predynastic Period—and the periods of Greek and Roman occupation, archaeologists have uncovered the agrarian substrate of Egyptian life. Several distinctive Neolithic cultures have come to light. One of the earliest is called Badarian; it may have been in existence as early as 5000 BCE, about the time Old Europe started to flourish, but the confirmed dates are later. The culture appears to have been at its height between 4400 and 4000 BCE.

Known Badarian sites stretch along the Nile well south of the Delta, and traditionally archaeologists had looked to the south for the culture's origins. The Egyptians themselves believed that their civilization began when African migrants moved upriver. Although the people of Egypt, like all other people on earth, originated in Central Africa, looking for the roots of the Badarian culture in the south proved to be misguided, since Badarian artifacts and forms of subsistence were both firmly linked to the Levantine Neolithic. Domestic architecture and pottery were part of the Neolithic package. So were the wheat, barley, and lentils that the Badarians cultivated. Circular foundations at Badarian sites, once identified as the ruins of houses, proved on further investigation to have floors covered with a thick layer of sheep or goat dung: they were stalls or stables, which adds another imported element to Badarian culture. To reach the Badarians, farming and herding technologies must have traveled from the Levant, along with animals and seeds, by passing through the eastern desert and then going downriver. The Badarians adapted these practices to their environment. What they could grow and when they could grow it depended on the flood cycle of the Nile, which was entirely different from the seasonal cycle of the Levant. There is no evidence of hunting as a way to supplement the diet as there is in West Asia. Fish, however, played a large part in the Badarian diet.[6]

The great Egyptologist Flinders Petrie first identified the next historical Egyptian culture after the Badarian at a site far south on the Nile where thousands of modest graves were uncovered. The burials were so simple that a generation of archaeologists trained to expect monumentality had found them positively un-Egyptian. It was generally believed that these were the graves of unsophisticated invaders who had somehow established themselves in the kingdom of the pharaohs. A French archaeologist was the first to suggest that the graves might represent something else. He identified them as the remains of a Predynastic culture. This was a novel idea at the turn of the twentieth century, when the earlier Badarian culture was still unknown. It had been a foregone conclusion throughout the nineteenth century that Egypt had come into being through the power and political skill of the pharaohs. The suggestion that any sort of culture might preexist these rulers was met with skepticism.

Cultivating the Nile floodplain, raising domestic animals, and fishing remained the major forms of subsistence at this far southern site. There were new crops to supplement the wheat, barley, and lentils traditionally grown, including Levantine founder crops like peas and vetch. Jujube, a tree that produces a fruit something like a date, and an ancestral form of the watermelon increased the variety of foods available. Pigs and cattle joined the herds of goats and sheep. Wild gazelles brought down by hunters supplemented fish as a source of protein.

The suburb of Maadi near Cairo gave its name to the first culture uncovered in the Delta. While cemeteries had been the representative sites of the Badarian and far southern cultures, excavations at Maadi centered on villages. The material remains of Maadian culture paint a fairly clear picture. The Delta region, also called Lower Egypt, was a crossroads where influences from the Levant and Upper (southern) Egypt blended. The extensive dig turned up houses that mixed Levantine and Egyptian styles. Pottery was cross-cultural. Footed jars from the Levant mixed with flat-bottomed pots made from local clays. The Levantine jars had come filled with oil, wine, or resins. Donkeys, descendants of the wild asses that had long inhabited the region, were the main beasts of burden. The Delta diet was similar to the diet farther south. Wheat and barley were its mainstays. Lentils and peas supplemented the grains and rounded out the protein supply. Pigs, oxen, goats, and sheep were abundant. Dogs were also common and may have been a food source as well as village scavengers and shepherds' aids.

The last centuries of the fourth millennium BCE were the final Predynastic years in Egyptian history. Increased efficiency in cultivating the Nile floodplain produced enormous amounts of grain. The archaeological evidence, primarily from burials in Upper Egypt, shows that elites were gaining power and wealth. The wealthiest were laid to rest with huge quantities of grave goods around them. As the Upper Egyptian culture matured into its third phase, the regional culture of the Delta disappeared. Archaeologists have long argued that the absence of a Maadi legacy meant that the powers of Upper Egypt had invaded and conquered the Delta. The official records of Egyptian dynasties stretch far into the past, but they do not reach 3000 BCE when the Upper and Lower regions were unified. Archaeology has extended the roster of kings, adding two rulers of special importance, King Scorpion and King Narmer, to the list and pushing back the traditional beginning of the Dynastic Period.

Though sharing crops and linked by trade, Egypt and Mesopotamia had distinct cultural and agricultural traditions. Irrigation in Mesopotamia depended on breaching the banks of the Euphrates and allowing river water to flow into the fields. The annual Nile flooding could be exploited without engineering. The pattern of water management that developed in Egypt was an extension of a natural process. The Nile floodplain had low ridges running parallel to the river that had been created by the river itself as its volume increased or decreased and its course meandered over the millennia. As the waters fell after each annual flood, pools collected behind these natural embankments. Farmers learned to increase the volume of water captured in this way and to use it for irrigation. The process required no central oversight or coordination to make it work. Water capture and irrigation were the job of each village rather than a centralized task, and Egypt remained a country of relatively independent small farming villages into the modern era. The state was highly centralized politically but only loosely organized in other ways. The nineteenth-century belief in the necessity of centralized power to call agriculture into being and supervise its conduct are contradicted by the Egyptian case.

The annual deposit of a thin layer of silt and the natural scouring away of potentially harmful mineral salts made the soils of the Nile Valley and its delta a continually rich agricultural environment. Nineteenth-century Europeans may have been generally contemptuous of agriculture in the Ottoman Empire, but they marveled at the productivity of Egypt. Napoléon reportedly called the country the "breadbasket of the Mediterranean." It remains highly productive and agriculturally diverse today.[7]

Political theorists held that the pharaohs called Egypt into being. Pragmatic theoreticians argued that the practical necessity of coordinating labor for huge projects like building the Sphinx or the pyramids was the real propulsion toward social cohesion. More poetic thinkers thought of Egypt as the "gift of the Nile." The reality of Egypt's past, however, was not successfully summed up by any of these abstractions. Wealthy, royal Egypt was created by powerful kings who consolidated their hold over the countryside and secured for themselves and others of noble rank or priestly occupation a major share of the abundant preexistent agricultural wealth of the country. This is the Egypt that has long dominated the archaeological record. The annual flooding of the Nile was nothing but an inconvenience to people living near the river until the techniques of farming were imported from the Levant. Then the annual mud bath became a blessing for those with the skills to exploit it. Egypt, like Mesopotamia, was a great power because it was a hugely productive agricultural region. Both great powers were creations not of their rulers or of the waters that fed their fields. They were gifts of the plow.

The reputation of the agricultural powers in the ancient world has suffered at the hands of modern critics. Egypt, which retained its fertility into the present, has been less subject to attack, but Mesopotamia, at present reduced to a barren condition, has been the object of consistent reproach. Since the nineteenth century, Mesopotamian

regions like those around Uruk have been charged with environmental neglect and degradation. The motives for both the nineteenth-
century critique and the modern one are complicated. In "Ozymandias" the English romantic poet Shelley describes the fallen statue of
an ancient despot and the inscription on its base. "My name is Ozymandias, King of Kings;/Look on my Works, ye Mighty, and despair!" Surrounding the statue is nothing but desert where the "lone
and level sands stretch far away." Shelley's poem had nothing to do
with ancient environmental neglect. Ozymandias did not create the
desert that surrounded his image. The king's inscription is a symbol
of self-delusion and pride. It was meant as a warning to modern
rulers who thought their fame would last forever, not as an indictment of kings long dead.

When nineteenth-century excavators explored the ruins of the
civilizations of Mesopotamia, they transformed this poetic cliché.
Early archaeologists were not immune to the charge that they
were interlopers in the country of a foreign power—the Ottoman
Empire—and infidel trespassers in the territories of Islam. As a way
of justifying their incursions, they exaggerated the differences between the grandeur of the past and the squalor of the present. This
theme, which is common to archaeological and colonial reporting,
aimed to break any ancestral link between the communities of the
past and those currently occupying the region. It was a tactic, not
an offhand observation, and it allowed Europeans to claim that they
were the true stewards and rightful heirs of the cultures they were
unearthing.[8]

During the nineteenth century, the devastation of Mesopotamia
was attributed to the Arabs, because that accusation suited the ideological needs of the time. In our day, the indictments have been re-
located further back in the past. In a recent book, the environmental
activists Paul and Anne Ehrlich made the case for resource depletion as the reason for the decline of ancient Mesopotamia, a region
which they epitomize in Nineveh, a successor city to Uruk and
Babylon. Their critique opens with the contrast between the region
in its political and agricultural heyday and its barren surroundings
when modern excavators first reached it in the 1840s. (The authors were apparently unaware of the mixed motives of nineteenth-
century observers of the Arab world and took their reports as faithful

accounts.) While they recognize that warfare and invasion played a role in weakening the region, they point to environmental degradation brought on by official neglect as the source of Nineveh's decline.

Archaeologists have discovered that the Assyrians and their successors were slowly weakened up through the fifth and sixth centuries AD, by a decline in their natural resource base. One underlying cause of the gradual deterioration of the entire region was deforestation in the hills and mountains, the source of the area's water supply. Another was environmentally unsustainable irrigation. Indeed, cuneiform tablets from more than 4,000 years ago, before the time of the Assyrian Empire, tell us that irrigation was already causing salts to build up in the soil, and the Mesopotamians lacked the artificial drainage technology that could counter the process. Growers switched from wheat to more salt-tolerant barley, and the area in which any crops could be cultivated was steadily reduced. Those processes weakened the cities and made them more vulnerable to capture. They fell victim to a series of invaders, culminating in the Middle Ages with the Mongols.[9]

On its face, this is a damning critique of environmental degradation traceable to the "overweening pride, arrogance, and presumption" of ruling elites who were "focused on maintaining their social position, fighting their frequent wars of conquest and defense ... but paying little attention to the gradual environmental decay that was undermining the foundations of their civilization."[10]

A close reading of the Ehrlichs' text, however, shows little, if any, connection between the policies and attitude of Nineveh's rulers and regional resource failure. The Ehrlichs' implicit reliance on the nineteenth-century link of state formation and agricultural productivity has betrayed them. Taking note of the dates in their description makes it clear that changes in regional productivity had little to do with Nineveh at all. Even by their reckoning, environmental degradation began a thousand years after the fall of the city in 612 BCE. What finally brought an end to the environmental viability of

the region, as they see it, was the Mongol invasions of the thirteenth
and fourteenth centuries CE. Clearly, some degree of agricultural
productivity in the region survived the fall of Nineveh by nearly two
thousand years.

But even that time frame is too short. Though commonly portrayed as devastating, the Mongol invasions of the Arab world did
not put an end to regional agriculture; much irrigated land returned
to cultivation after the invaders were expelled. What finally put an
end to widespread agriculture in Iraq was not environmental failure
at all but the oil wealth that started flowing into the country in the
twentieth century. The oil bonanza made farm labor unattractive in
Iraq, as it did in many parts of the oil-rich Arab world. Iraq became
a net importer of agricultural products because it could afford to do
so, not because it had to. The region's environmental decline in the
present day has been accelerated by the damming of the Euphrates
River in Syria and Turkey.

Cuneiform records show that salinization only became a problem when population pressures reduced the possibility of letting
fields lie fallow. Even in these circumstances, administrators made
efforts to counteract salinization by increased sowing of barley, as
the Ehrlichs note, and by cultivating *shok* and *agul*, inedible plants
that served no other purpose than to lower salt concentrations in
fields. Far from being an example of neglect, Mesopotamia reflects,
in the response to salinization, a constructive adaptation to changed
circumstances.

The true history of the regional environment contrasts dramatically with the story told by harsh critics. While individual cities like
Nineveh lost their dominant positions, as others had done before
them, farm villages continued to produce, and the overall health of
the region and its ecology remained on the plus side. Statistics over
a long time span—5000 BCE to the present—show a regional population of roughly half a million in the Uruk period, a dip in population in the Assyrian period immediately afterward, then steep growth
from the era of Alexander the Great into the Middle Ages. The regional population before the Mongol invasion is estimated at about
1.5 million people.[11]

In an op-ed piece published in several American newspapers,
Jared Diamond describes Mesopotamia's "ecological suicide," though

he views the disaster as "inadvertent": "Just as the region's rise wasn't due to any special virtue of its people, its fall wasn't due to any special blindness on their part." Unlike the Ehrlichs, Diamond recognizes that the "ecological failure" was slow paced: "The original flow of power westward from the Fertile Crescent reversed in 330 BCE, when the Macedonian Army of Alexander the Great advanced eastward to conquer the eastern Mediterranean. In the Middle Ages, Mongol invaders from Central Asia destroyed Iraq's irrigation systems. After World War I, England and France dismembered the Ottoman Empire and carved out Iraq and other states as pawns of European colonial interests."[12]

Diamond's chronology is more accurate than the Ehrlichs', but his, too, reflects the nineteenth-century belief that agriculture, state formation, and warfare are indissolubly linked. He takes it for granted that vulnerability to military conquest is a valid measure of the vigor of the resource base of an ancient society.[13] This assumption reflects the continued influence of an outdated narrative about the origins of domestication. The yoking of politics, domestication, and warfare characterized theories of the origins of agriculture that have been undermined by modern prehistorians. Ancient warfare and modern warfare differ dramatically in their dependence on a combatant's resource base. Modern armies supply themselves, but ancient armies lived off the land. An ancient city under siege and the army besieging it shared the same resource base, which was fixed by what either side was able to forage from the areas that it controlled. When critics argue that vulnerability to military attack is a valid measure of ancient resource viability, they are overlooking this fact. They are also overlooking aspects of the historical record.

To demonstrate the weakness of the Mesopotamian agricultural economy, Diamond points to the conquest of the region by Alexander the Great. For him that successful invasion is compelling evidence that the Tigris and Euphrates Valley succumbed to mismanagement. What Diamond fails to point out, however, is that after conquering Mesopotamia in 330 BCE, Alexander went on to conquer Egypt. The "breadbasket of the Mediterranean," which no one contends was committing ecological suicide, fell victim to the same conqueror who overwhelmed Mesopotamia. In this head-to-head test, then, the strength of the agricultural base did not determine which civilization would be conquered. Egypt's healthy agrarian system was no defense against Macedonian aggression.

Alexander's campaigns are not the only test case of the limited power of agricultural viability to predict success or failure in warfare. During the seventh century BCE, successive Assyrian, Babylonian, and Persian armies—all based in Mesopotamia—repeatedly invaded Egypt and occupied its capital. Countries characterized as "resource depleted" recurrently conquered a country that was undoubtedly resource rich. There is no reason to accept the conclusions of modern polemicists who argue that ancient Mesopotamia suffered agricultural collapse. The old-fashioned link between the history of state formation, warfare, and domestication is wrong, and it inevitably leads to misinformed conclusions.

CHAPTER FIVE

The Primacy of Landscape
in West Asia

The charge that ancient leaders failed to give adequate attention to the fields and flocks that sustained their peoples has become a commonplace of ecological writing. But in fact the very character of ancient culture made it impossible for leaders to be deceived about the realities of agrarian life or to neglect them. Ancient culture, whether material, literary, or artistic, was an outgrowth and an expression of farming. All ancient culture was agri-culture. Nothing in language, myth, or literature created an alternative reality where farming could be evaded or overlooked.

In the modern world, we have particular ways of talking about the relationship between humans and the nonhuman ecosystem. Our conversations about this important area of life tend to be both analytical and factual. We aspire to exactness and testable theories; we embrace scientific modeling and methods of proof. In the absence of scientific insight and precision, many would argue that there can be no meaningful conversation about ecological imperatives. Since such thinking was unknown in the ancient world, we assume that communities must have lacked the ability to assess the resources on which their lives depended.

The reality of ancient life was quite different. The language of priests and poets was not analytical, but it was not fanciful or empty either. The same truths that we express today in different language animated it. Hymns to the gods and epics about heroes acknowledged and celebrated the way farming and herding sustained the life of ancient communities. Literature and art reflected the agricultural base. The order and organization of the cultivated landscape served as the model for order throughout the universe. Societies represented their relationship with the world around them in a variety of different ways, but all of them put cultivation and domestication in the center of life, and all of them understood their relationship with nature through the lens of agriculture.

Landscape and World Order in Uruk

The transition from writing as a means of accounting to writing as a means of representing spoken language was slow. Although the earliest written texts from Uruk date to the end of the fourth millennium BCE, the great age of written texts begins about five hundred years later. During the interval, the subtlety and range of writing grew. By the second millennium BCE, a variety of texts existed, many in multiple copies. Once texts were created and preserved, it became increasingly possible to record not just facts and figures about the productivity of fields, the cost of labor, and the transport of commodities but much more. Texts began to give some sense of the feelings that various parts of the landscape inspired in people. Some locales were described with fear or wonder; others evoked deep feelings of reassurance, even erotic power. The way the world was put together and how humans fit into it was not only understood intellectually but felt viscerally, and writing preserved all that.

One of the richest sources for this kind of information about Uruk are the hymns of Inana and Dumuzid. Inana was a love goddess and Dumuzid her mortal lover. In Sumerian mythology, the pair also represented one aspect of kingship. In this hymn that relationship is explicit.

Ninšubur, the good minister of E-ana, clasps him by his right hand and brings him in bliss to Inana's embrace: "May the lord whom you have chosen in your heart, the king, your

beloved husband, enjoy long days in your holy and sweet
embrace! Give him a propitious and famous reign, give him
a royal throne of kingship on its firm foundation."[1]

Once wedded to her royal husband, Inana offered multiple blessings:

May he, like a farmer, make the fields productive; may he
make the sheepfolds multiply, like a trustworthy shepherd.
Under him, may there be flax, may there be barley; in the
rivers may there be carp floods. Under him, may there be
mottled barley in the fields; in the marshes, fish, and may the
birds chatter. Under him, may the old reeds and the young
reeds grow tall in the reed beds. . . . Under him, may the wild
sheep and wild goats multiply in the forests; under him, may
the irrigated orchards produce syrup and wine. Under him,
may lettuce and cress flourish in the garden plots; under
him, may there be long life in the palace.[2]

These endowments were the products of fertility, an appropriate
area of expertise for an ancient love goddess. Under her influence,
the cultivated land and domestic animals produced abundantly.
Through their association with the goddess of love, the crops and
herds were eroticized. They became representations of human desire
and its gratification. This emotional weighting means that people
had deep sentimental attachments to domestic animals and agricultural land and positive feelings about them.

The eroticized fields and pastures were surrounded by a wilderness that the hymns presented in darker terms. Together, what was
cultivated and what was uncultivated constituted a world that was
founded on the pragmatic use of landscape but was also fully reflected in emotional life. This systematized and strongly felt world
picture is what the Greeks would later call a cosmos, using a word
that combines ideals of order and beauty. At the center of this cosmos was "Uruk of the wide plazas," home of the royal palace and the
chief temples of the gods. Surrounding the city were irrigated fields
where many people worked at jobs that were difficult and—in the
short seasons of intensive activity, especially harvest time—unremitting. Labor in the fields must have brought pain and hardship to

many, but the croplands were also the city's mainstay. Sumerian mythology acknowledged what the fields produced, not the effort required to produce it.

The city and its croplands together formed a cultural comfort zone, a place where people felt safe and well taken care of among reassuring scenes and activities. Beyond the croplands and overlapping with them seasonally were the pastures where the herds of sheep and cattle were kept. In late summer and winter, when the herds fed on the stubble and the unharvested grain in the fields, they were a daily sight for anyone leaving or entering the city. During the summer animals left the lowlands and were guided to distant high pastures. The herds went far beyond the places where most people traveled, but their actual physical remoteness did not change their image. Domestic animals, like the croplands, were the focus of strong feeling. They were represented in poetry by their warm wool and especially their milk and butter. The last two were the most heavily eroticized of all the agricultural products in Sumeria.

Rejoicing in the palace, Inana pleads with the king: "Make the milk yellow for me, my bridegroom, make the milk yellow for me, and I will drink the milk with you, my bridegroom! Wild bull Dumuzid, make the milk yellow for me, and I will drink the milk with you, my bridegroom! . . . fill my holy churns."[3]

Beyond the croplands and the pastures lay territory that felt entirely different. For the Sumerians, it had no innate characteristics. It was a residual space, left over after all the cultivated spaces had been subtracted from the ideal world map. It was not so much a place in its own right as an emptiness. This empty space, which we would call wilderness, was not, in their estimation, wild by nature; it was wild because it was unmarked by human cultivation. So it was not familiar or nourishing, and it was empty of erotic potential. It was a place for wariness and fear. Only the courageous could go into it, and even they could not be assured of safety or success.

Although the Sumerians' conception of wilderness is related to ours, the place that wild space held in the Mesopotamian imagination was markedly different. What modern cultures share with this ancient one is an association of the wild with supernatural forces. For the men and women of Uruk, wilderness was a place where the fearful power of divinity was close to the surface of things. At any moment, it might erupt and overwhelm a human hapless enough or daring enough to enter it. Wilderness was a place of awe-inspiring power. When wilderness entered the modern consciousness, near the end of the eighteenth century, it had a similar character. What early writers emphasized were the qualities in nature that they described by the word "sublime." Though this quality inhered in all of nature, it was most evident in places like the Swiss Alps, where nature had created massive and overpowering landscapes that dwarfed and endangered humans while it inspired them with terror.[4]

During the eighteenth and nineteenth centuries, these wild places gradually became synonymous with nature itself. Even today, environmentalists at all levels of professional competence and ideological commitment have accepted this identification. But wilderness is only one ecosystem type in a range of types. We may see it as the one in which natural process is best exemplified, but genetic laws and environmental constraints govern in all ecosystems equally, whether humans take part in them or not. In ancient Mesopotamia, as in the ancient Mediterranean in general, the ecosystem that all communities viewed as representing nature was the landscape transformed by farming and herding. Wilderness was as peripheral to their environmental consciousness as farming is to ours.

Domestic metaphors fit Inana when she was ready for love, but when she was angry, metaphors of the wild drove them out: she is a "leopard of the hills, ... raging"; she is a "great bull trusting in its strength; no one dare turn against her"; "she casts her venom."[5] In her terrifying mood, the pliant seductress was replaced by a leopard, a raging bull, a poisonous snake. The transformation froze any erotic impulse. If this were the end of the story, it would suggest that wilderness was the realm outside the cultivated areas, a place where people were understandably afraid to go. The wrath of Inana, which was expressed by wilderness, was not confined to this distant and abstract realm, however.

> Her wrath is ... a devastating flood which no one can withstand. A great watercourse ... Inana rips to pieces the spacious cattle-pens. The fields of the city which Inana has

looked at in anger ... The furrows of the field ... grass.
Setting on fire, in the high plain ... speeding ... fighting ...
conflict.[6]

This fragmentary text highlights many of the forces that threatened the city, including floods that destroyed the levees along the
river, overflowed the fields, wrecked the irrigation canals, broke down
the cattle pens, and beat down the crops in the fields. The remnant
crops rotted away. In another manifestation of her anger, the goddess could be like wildfire that swept through the high pastures where
the sheep and cattle grazed in summer, scattering the herds and destroying the grass they depended on.

Angered and unappeased, the goddess revealed that wilderness
was not an isolated geographical zone but a condition. In a safe,
productive world, wilderness remained at the fringes of civilization,
but that was not its permanent resting place. Wilderness was displaced and distanced by the work of city building and cultivation. It
could be driven to the edge of communal space by an enormous and
continuing effort. But it could always flow back into the places that
had been cleared and reassert its dominance, as an angry Inana asserted her power and control.

Overall, the goddess combined the power of the wilderness and
the seductiveness of the fertile fields. When she married the king,
she brought both aspects of the landscape—the nutritive and the
forbidding—to their marriage bed. When the marriage was con-
summated, the king lived in harmony with the natural world that
sustained life and with the powers within the natural world that both
animated it and threatened to destroy it. What might happen if the
king ignored or chose to reject his divine bride? In the Sumerian
epic *Gilgamesh*, Inana offered herself to the king of Uruk for whom
the poem is named. Rather than accept this union as ritual and custom demanded, Gilgamesh mocked the goddess. He reminded her
of the fate of all the lovers that she had taken in the past, whom she
drained of vitality, then abandoned. Gilgamesh was making a com-
monsense decision. But given his role as king, his choice was wrong.
However perilous, his partnership with the goddess was vital to the
well-being of his community.

To avenge the humiliation and rejection she suffered, Inana demanded that the gods unleash a monster called the Bull of Heaven and send it to devastate Uruk. Gilgamesh and his companion, Enkidu, fought the monster and overcame it, but Inana was not defeated. Now she demanded from the gods the death of a hero. The gods resisted at first, but when Inana threatened to open the underworld and unleash the dead, they agreed to the death of Enkidu. Saddened and frightened by the death of his companion, Gilgamesh searched for immortality, but it eluded him. In the end, the poem celebrates the pleasures of the earth and the joys and satisfactions of a life attuned to the community and its sustaining landscape.

Mythology in Ugarit

Almost as soon as excavation began at the Ras Shamra tell, on the northern coast of modern Syria where the ancient port city of Ugarit had stood, multitudes of cuneiform documents were discovered. Though a few were written in Akkadian, the bulk were written in an alphabetic script that had not been seen before. The language represented by the script was not an outlier like Sumerian but a northern Semitic language with links to Hebrew and Aramaic. As the tablets were transcribed and deciphered, documents recording the daily life of the vanished coastal city came to light along with mythological texts of great interest.

Narratives from Ugarit included references to divinities like Baal, which were well known to biblical scholars, along with others whose historic links to biblical divinities no one had anticipated. Both El and Yahweh, alternative names of God in the Hebrew Bible, were found among the gods of Ugarit. Since the first explorations in 1929, publications of these texts have sparked enormous curiosity among biblical scholars. Thanks to consuming interest in what might be called the prehistory of monotheism, Ugaritic texts, which would have excited little interest in themselves, have found a wide audience.

Ugarit flourished in the second millennium BCE. Though centuries of time and crucial differences in culture and environment separated Uruk and Ugarit, there were important links between the two societies in their agricultural practices, and both shared a view of the world that I have characterized as First Nature. That original Neolithic worldview pictured the universe as a partnership between the human and biological communities that was exemplified and symbolized by their meeting place, the landscape shaped for cultivation. In the fields outside the city, the organization of the town and the creative power of the natural world merged with each other and came together in a constructive union. This First Nature ideal, so foreign to our own, was nonetheless a foundation for environmental thought and action during all but the last two centuries of Mediterranean history.

Both Uruk and Ugarit were urban cultures sustained by cereal crops and the milk, cheese, and meat produced by sheep and cattle. Both cultures enriched their own resources through long-distance trade, and both levied armies for offense and for their own defense. The palace and the temple were primary institutions in both. Uruk was built of mud brick and Ugarit primarily of stone, but the structure of each city and of the elites that ruled them were similar.

A First Nature landscape-based view of the world was common to both, but Ugarit represented wilderness in a different way. In large part, this difference reflected the varying environments that sustained agriculture in each region. Inland Mesopotamia depended for its livelihood on the management of irrigation. Coastal Ugarit depended on a rainy season that nourished farming but could also threaten the fields with lightning, torrential rains, or destructive winds. Baal, a mountain-dwelling god who presided over both the nourishing rain and the destructive storm, was the ascendant deity in one of the most influential myth cycles from Ugarit.

Sumerian texts are rich in metaphor; by comparison, the literature of Ugarit is spare. Erotic scenes show the difference particularly well. In Sumeria they may be intermittently graphic, but they are, for the most part, concerned with seduction rather than copulation and feature flowery and indirect language. In Ugaritic the scenes are all business.[7] The lack of symbolism means that many fewer passages in the mythology of Ugarit give a sense of how people felt about the world around them. In one hymn to Baal, though, these feelings emerge.

Baal sits like the base of a mountain

. . . .

A tree-of-lightning [in his] ri[ght hand].

His head is magnificent,
His brow is dew-drenched.
His feet are eloquent in [his] wrath.
[His] horn is [exal]ted,
His head is in the snows in heaven,
[With] the god there is abounding water.
His mouth is like two clouds,
[His lips] like wine from jars.[8]

Dew, snows, clouds, and water are all important parts of the description, and it is clear that the god is well represented by the mountain: he is both a rainmaker and an entity that looms majestically over the landscape below. In the mythology of Ugarit the rain on which the life of civilization depends comes from the heart of the wild. Wilderness is inaccessible, majestic, frightening, and mysterious. Its power over the cultivated is absolute. Passages in the Baal Cycle let us see more about the link between the god and the mountain. Speaking to the warrior goddess, Anat, Baal urges her to "bury war in the earth, set strife in the dust."

[For I have a word] that I would say to you,
A message [that I will repeat to you]:
[a word of] tree
And a whisper of [stone],
[a word unkno]wn to me[n]
[and which the multitudes of the ea]rth [do not] understand
The si[ghing of the heavens to the ear]th
Of the deep t[o the stars].
[I understand the lightning]
Which [the heavens] do not know:
[come and I shall] re[veal it]
[in the midst of] my [div]ine mountain Saphon.[9]

The wilderness that frightened the Sumerians was an empty place. The wilderness that Baal gave access to was eloquent in its own right, and Baal spoke its language. Baal understood what trees say, and the whispers of stone, the sighing of the heavens and the sea to the earth and stars, even the language of the lightning, which heaven itself could not interpret. Wilderness as the Baal hymn presents it is full of information, but that information can be accessed only through him. Like the mountain in storm, the inner truth of nature is wrapped in cloud.

The terrifying face of wilderness can best be seen in descriptions of Mot, the god of death, who at a crucial point in the cycle sends a threatening message to Baal.

> My appetite is the appetite of the lion in the wasteland
> As the desire of the shark is in the sea;
> As wild bulls yearn for pools . . .
> Since [Mot] scorched the olive,
> The produce of the earth,
> And the fruit of the trees.
> Valiant Baal was afraid of him.[10]

Eventually Mot conquered Baal, but not before the storm god had fathered a son to be his successor. The son soon proved unable to step in for his father, so the goddess Anat went in search of the dead god. To bring him back to life, she must destroy Mot.

> She seized divine Mot,
> With a knife she split him;
> With fire she burnt him;
> With millstones she ground him;
> [with a sieve she sifted him;]
> On the steppe [she abandoned him;
> In the sea] she sowed him.[11]

Anat put Mot through some sort of agricultural process, but scholars disagree about what it was. It was something like grinding flour or making beer, but neither of those familiar procedures has anything to do with sowing the steppe or the sea. It is clear, though, that Mot was treated like the grain that Baal's rain nourished. It is also clear that his death restored the agricultural world to health.

In the wake of Mot's destruction, Baal came back to life and returned to his throne. He impregnated Anat, who gave birth:

a bull is born to Baal
And a wild ox to the Charioteer of the Clouds.
Valiant Baal rejoiced.[12]

The poem ends on that upbeat note. The biblical scholar Mark S. Smith has noted that the "struggles of Baal mirror the struggles of humanity against the vicissitudes of a dangerous world, but his victories re-invigorate not only the world of the divine pantheon but also human society." The Baal hymn "interrelates humanity, nature and divinity and thereby yields an integrated political vision of chaos, life and death."[13]

This is certainly true, but it is only a partial truth attuned to nineteenth- and twentieth-century concepts of wilderness and contemporary associations between wisdom and divinity. While biblical scholars might appreciate the character of Baal in abstract and anthropocentric terms, the men and women of Ugarit saw all the god's activities in terms of the cultivated landscape, on which their survival depended and over which Baal ruled like a tyrant king. His epic struggle with Mot was fought to banish infertility and starvation.

Mythology in Hatti

In Hatti, the Hittite kingdom of central Anatolia, a story similar to the Baal story was told at about the same time. Telipinu, like Baal, was a protector of agriculture and the son of a storm god. The story begins with Telipinu's fierce reaction to an ill-defined threat:

Telipinu [. . . screamed]: "Let there be no intimidating language." [Then he drew [the right shoe] on his left foot, and the left [shoe on his right foot.]

Mist seized the windows. Smoke [seized] the house. In the fireplace the logs were stifled. [At the altars] the gods were stifled. In the sheep pen the sheep were stifled. In the cattle barn the cattle were stifled. The mother sheep rejected her lamb. The cow rejected her calf.

Telipinu too went away and removed grain, animal fecundity, luxuriance, growth and abundance from the steppe, from the meadow. . . .

The mountains and the trees dried up, so that the shoots did not come [forth]. The pastures and the springs dried up, so that famine broke out in the land. Humans and gods were dying of hunger. The Great Sun God made a feast and invited the Thousand Gods. They ate but couldn't get enough. They drank but couldn't quench their thirst.

The storm god sent an eagle to search for his son, Telipinu, but the eagle failed to find him. He then turned to the matriarchal goddess, Hannahanna, for advice. She sent out a bee that succeeded in find-

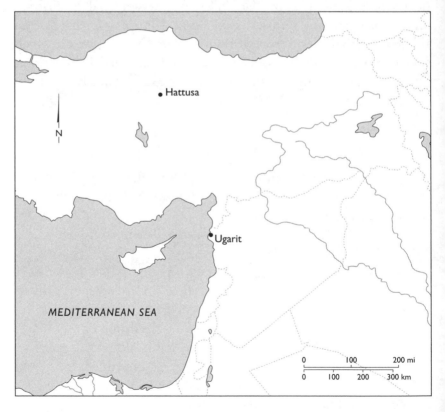

Ugarit and Hattusa both had a landscape view of the world but differed in the view of wilderness.

ing Telipinu. Once Telipinu was found, the goddess Kamrusepa assuaged his wrath. Telipinu returned home and reversed the damage that he caused. The tale ends with the assurance that society will once again enjoy "plenty, abundance and safety."[14]

Because crop success in Ugarit depended on annual rainfall, city dwellers worshipped Baal, a mountain god whose cooperation was needed so that the crops would thrive. The people of central Anatotolia depended on rainfall too, so the storm god was an important figure there, but they had a more northern climate to contend with. Seasonal extremes of heat and cold set limits to the agricultural year; rain alone could not make the crops grow. The season of infertility was represented by the annual anger of the storm god's son and the divine searching and propitiation that each year encouraged his return.

Agriculture, which is the largest and most active technological sphere in each of these societies, is at the center of each myth system. What the crops need and what the farmers fear are the essential underpinnings of plot, theme, and feeling in each. The orderly universe that the texts project is a landscape-centered one, with each human community firmly set in its cultivated space. At its focal point is the city, comfortably surrounded by croplands and pastures. Beyond is wilderness, which continually threatens the city in Sumerian myth or both threatens and nourishes it in Ugaritic or Hittite myth.

The gods that the myths describe were, like the people who created and narrated them, fully Neolithic. They lived in houses, they organized themselves in families and extended societies, they dueled with words or with weapons, they were nourished by sacrifices that depended on the bounty of field and flock. This ideal connection between myth and landscape was sometimes reinforced by a linking of myth and geography. Uruk was a real city. The heroic adventures that began and ended there stretched outside the world of human experience to engage gods and monsters. This narrative pattern gave the city a place in the world of the gods and in the idealized cosmos. It turned the city into a stage upon which the great dramas of Sumerian mythology were played out.

The myth system of Ugarit was also anchored in locations of varying specificity. Yamm, the sea god, lived in the Mediterranean. Mot lived somewhere underground. The palace of Baal was the most precisely fixed. He lived on what the text identifies as Mount Sapan. Over a mile high, Sapan—called Jebel el Aqra in modern Arabic—is twenty-five miles north of the city and a few miles in from the coast. With more than fifty inches of annual rainfall it is one of the wettest spots in the region.[15]

As conquerors, the Hittites came across gods associated with the landscape again and again. They often captured gods by transferring their statues to a new temple in Hattusa, their capital. If the new temple was satisfactory and the god willing to make the move, the relocation would transfer the deity's protection from the conquered people to their conquerors. Often these transported gods retained their original geographic names, even if their allegiances had shifted to their new home. The Hittites recognized and sustained numerous storm gods, for example, from a number of different conquered towns and cities. The ability to uproot geographically based gods was a useful skill. It made conquest simpler and more beneficial. Not only was new territory acquired with each successful expedition, but new divine sponsors were acquired as well. More importantly, divorcing real-world geography from spirituality created new ways of conceiving of space.

Mediterranean cosmology rested in large part on human needs and on the adaptation of landscape to fill those needs, but this was not entirely a matter of cultures imposing their will on a passive landscape. The character and particular features of the regional landscape underwrote the mythological association. The city-cropland-pasture-wilderness cosmology cannot be universal. It would not be the world picture of steppe dwellers in Central Asia or forest people in northern Europe or Central Africa. Since these peoples could see only one set of landscape features, their cosmologies did not have the same components.

As Sherratt pointed out, the early Neolithic first developed in a part of the world where steppe and mountain ecosystems were close together and linked by a third, low-lying ecozone that aided communication between them. He argued that the diversity of distinct ecological zones lying close to each other enabled the creation of agriculture, which, in its earliest form, involved the transposition of species native to one ecosystem to another one nearby. Ecosystems with different properties lying next to each other continued to characterize landscape use while they formed the basis of imaginative cosmologies throughout the Mediterranean world.

Biblical Cosmology

The cosmology of the Bible had roots in the legends of Mesopotamia, Ugarit, Canaan, and other Levantine communities. And like their neighbors, the creators of the Bible reflected the dominance of agriculture in Neolithic life and thought. That link has not always been acknowledged, but it is evident from the earliest chapter in the book, called Bereshit in the Torah and Genesis in the Christian Bible.

The revelation of God's interaction with the Israelite community begins in an account of the world he made.[16] As Genesis unfolds, an initial silent act of creation brings an empty and formless earth into being. From that point onward, God makes recognizable things. His task is broken down into six subunits that are labeled as days. A seventh day of rest concludes the sequence. For literalists, these days are twenty four-hour intervals; for others they represent the billions of years that the geological record now chronicles. These differences of interpretation divert attention from the symbolic importance of the days of the week in the Genesis account. The seven-day week is such a familiar feature of our own calendar that it is hard to realize how unusual it was or to appreciate just what it meant. The recurring week is intangible but every bit as consequential as the physical limits of a house, a sacred precinct, or a field. Abraham, the patriarch and idealized founder of the Israelite community, was portrayed as a nomadic shepherd for whom geographical boundaries were an alien constraint, not a reassuring ordering of the world he and his extensive family inhabited. Antagonistic to spatial organization, or unable to adopt it, he and his community may have expressed the Neolithic urge for system and order in another way. Like the megalith builders who re-created a cluster of village houses in a symbolic structure, these nomads transformed the spatial order that underlay Neolithic cosmology into an organization of time. That order was so fundamental to their way of thinking about themselves that they grafted it onto the foundational act of their God. Genesis presents the seven-day week as a blueprint in the divine mind that is manifested when the world is built.[17]

In the work-week, the difference between Tuesday and Thursday may be minimal. In the week of creation, however, the events obey an inner dynamic, from God's fashioning of the inanimate earth and sky through the creation of sea and land animals and, on the penultimate day, human beings. Humans were made in God's image, they were marked off from the rest of creation because "God blessed them" (Gen. 1:28). He also endowed them with rights and powers suited to their climactic position in the crescendo of creation. "Let them have dominion over the fish of the sea, and over the fowl of the air, and over the cattle, over all the earth, and over every creeping thing that creepeth upon the earth" (1:26). This entitlement is repeated and amplified a few verses later when God speaks to the newly created humans and charges them to "Be fruitful and multiply and fill the earth, and subdue it; and have dominion over . . . every living thing (1:28). What limits or defines the dominion that God grants to humans is a matter of fierce debate at the moment. Historically, however, human dominance has been interpreted quite literally. As beings at the pinnacle of the creation hierarchy, men and women are distinct from the rest and gifted with authority over all other creatures.

This interpretation is not unique to the English translation of the Bible. The Hebrew verbs that are translated into English as "subdue" and "have dominion over" are strong ones. "Subdue" is a translation of the verb *kavash*, which means "to overpower and subordinate, to 'place one's foot on the captive's neck.'" The second verb is equally harsh: *radah* means "to rule legitimately like a queen over her people or a master over his slaves," but it also means "to dominate and control someone." Both verbs suggest that the relationship between Adam and the rest of creation is politically or socially based and reflects the dominance of one human being over another.

The historian Lynn White published a ground-breaking article more than forty years ago titled "The Historical Roots of Our Ecological Crisis." In it he identifies the biblical fiat as the source of the unrestrained exploitation of the environment that characterizes the modern world. "Man named all the animals, thus establishing his dominance over them. God planned all of this explicitly for man's benefit and rule: no item in the physical creation had any purpose save to serve man's purposes. And, although man's body is made of clay, he is not simply part of nature: he is made in God's image."[18]

Like White, Paleolithic foragers would have had a difficult time with this view of the human role on earth. A forager's way of life did not set them above or separate them from nature. They had no supervisory role to play and no authority over the rest of the creatures and the land that sustained all life. Not until Neolithic times could people imagine themselves as having any sort of dominion over the earth and the creatures that inhabit it.

White's critique is important, and I will return to it in Chapter 9. In relation to the Torah and to ancient Israel, however, it is overstated. Genesis offers not one but two accounts of the creation of Adam. In Genesis 2:7 the creation of man is reiterated in words with different connotations. "And the Lord God formed man of the dust of the ground." Here the standard English translation does not reflect the Hebrew perfectly. The phrase that is translated into English as "dust of the ground" is 'afar min ha'adamah. The name Adam is a pun on this 'adamah, and that linguistic echo reflects the source of his creation. 'Afar min ha'adamah does not primarily mean dry and fugitive dust but, more literally, "soil from the earth." Adam was made from fertile earth, the material of cultivation.

God put Adam in the Garden of Eden. Eden was a special place, marked off from the rest of creation. Its traits particularly suited the needs and the character of the being who was its privileged occupant. This mythical place, described as "a garden" (2:8), included "every tree that is pleasant to the sight, and good for food" (2:9). God placed Adam in this paradise (a *paradeisos* is a walled garden) "to till it and keep it" (2:15). Adam labored in the garden as a cultivator (the modern translation) or pruner (the original King James translation). The Hebrew verb here is 'avad, which has a multitude of meanings depending on its context. The root meaning, however, is the exact opposite of the kinds of activity reflected in the verbs of Genesis 1:28. 'Avad is the action not of a dominant figure but of one who is subjugated or controlled—in the social context it means "to serve"; in a religious context it means "to worship." As an agricultural verb it means "to tend the crops and the animals."

Historically, little has been made of the implications of this second passage. In a controversial book published a decade ago, the theologian Theodore Hiebert argues that the Genesis 2 account reflects an ecologically responsible view of the relationship between the Israelite community and the landscape. He asserts that the emphasis on subjugation and dominion can be traced to a nineteenth-century cultural synthesis that was strongly influenced by the political dominance of the West and the power of the industrial revolution.

In Hiebert's view, Genesis 2 gives us a different picture of the link between the ancient Israelites and the land they cultivated. At the same time, it offers a new idea of how that community sustained itself. Rather than being nomadic shepherds, like the modern Bedouins who eke out a living in the most arid environments, Hiebert believes the men and women of the patriarchal era were farmers. They lived in the hill country inland from the Mediterranean coast and tended both herds and crops. If they moved around at all, they seldom traveled far. They valued the earth, they valued the fruits of the earth that they cultivated, and they identified with those fruits that originated from the same *'adamah* as themselves. He believes that they practiced a "religion of the earth." They worshipped their God in urban centers and in local shrines where he had appeared to them. Their conceptual world, like the world of their experience, was not divided between strong opposites. They did not pit their deity against nature or the desert against the cultivated land. They did not despise cities or contrast nature with history. Such uncompromising dualism, which is characteristic of much Torah writing, Hiebert argues, belongs to the late Apocalyptic period of Judaism, when links to the land and the soil had already been severed.[19] If Hiebert is right, the way of life of the founders of Judaism was much like that of their neighbors. It was a version of the First Nature consensus; its upholders were fully conscious of their dependence on the cultivated landscape.

Neither Genesis account of the place of humans in the landscape was based on the idea of wilderness. Wilderness has no place in the Genesis worldview, which is entirely dominated by a cultivator's perspective. In one mood, that cultivator sees himself as the servant of the landscape from which his body was formed and on which his sustenance depends. In a different frame of mind, he imagines himself as the controller and director of that landscape, the unique,

powerful figure capable of imposing his will on the compliant, productive earth. But in neither case does he imagine the world as a
natural space that is beyond human influence and control. However
the patriarchs may have lived, or however they felt about their place
in the landscape, believers today are free to choose either an exploitive
or an ecologically responsible attitude toward the environment. In
the past two centuries, facile reliance on the dominion text has both
reflected and licensed ecological exploitation. In the current climate
of ecological thinking, a return to the First Nature values of the
'adamah seems the right choice.

Cosmology beyond Landscape

The idea that humans are distinct from other beings and have superior abilities and responsibilities is reinforced by the Bible's representation of the deity in whose image humans were created. The
wilderness concept, which has no place in the Genesis account, is
represented in metaphors that describe God. Whatever his designation, El, Elohim, or Yahweh, God was linked with nature in ways
that were meant to separate him from other storm gods of the region. During the years of desert wandering that transformed the
captives of Egypt into the successful invaders of Canaan, God manifested himself several times. In the early chapters of Exodus, God
appeared to Moses from within a bush "that burned with fire, and
the bush was not consumed" (Exod. 3:2). Later in the same book,
God appeared to the entire nation as "a pillar of cloud, to lead them
the way; and by night in a pillar of fire, to give them light" (13:21).
The moment when God delivered the tablets inscribed with the Ten
Commandments was a high point not only of the desert wandering
but of the entire biblical story. At that crucial moment, "Mount Sinai
was altogether enveloped in smoke, because the Lord descended upon
it in fire; and the smoke thereof ascended as the smoke of a furnace,
and the whole mount quaked greatly" (19:18).

The smoke and fire at Sinai looked atmospheric but were not.
The storm god Baal, in contrast, was shrouded in cloud that was
occasionally pierced by lightning. The biblical transformation of the
thunder and lightning of the storm into fire and smoke linked God
with Baal and distinguished the two at the same time.[20] Baal inhab-

ited a particular mountain in the Levant. God chose Mount Sinai as a place to communicate with his people, but it was not his native place. Baal deployed thunder and lightning to manifest his will but also to perform his natural task as weathermaker. God chose a physical form that could be seen and understood by the people. The substitution of smoke and fire for cloud and lightning underscored the difference between Baal, who was part of nature, and God, who could manifest himself in natural forms but who was outside nature and beyond it.

God's transcendence of nature was emphasized again in his dialogue with Job. In that text God manifests himself as a whirlwind (Job 38:1) and is described at length in images of storm that are clearly to be understood as metaphors. God responds to Job's demand for justice and understanding by posing a series of rhetorical questions, starting with "Where wast thou when I laid the foundations of the earth?" (38: 4) and going on for 128 verses. Overwhelmed by this torrent of rhetorical questions, Job admits that he spoke without understanding (42:3). God's non-answer to Job's question establishes him as a being beyond human comprehension and simultaneously outside creation. God escapes human conceptualization, it would appear, to the same degree that he stands outside nature. God's character is enigmatic because it is unnatural. Wilderness metaphors may represent aspects of the divine, but the divine is not natural, nor is the natural divine.

Since about the sixth century BCE, the Jewish cosmological tradition has been preserved in a compact body of texts. Those texts have inspired an enormous and rich corpus of secondary texts called the Talmud whose authors comment on, elucidate, puzzle over, and make assertions about every letter of the Torah. During Babylonian exile the Jewish community lost its connection with the landscape. This caused a turn away from certain practices, like the ritual of the Temple Mount in Jerusalem, that were impossible to transfer from their original sacred site. In response to this divorce from the land, the religion turned inward, and Jews began an intense scrutiny of the relationship between God and his chosen community based on a painstaking examination of the sacred text. The Roman destruction of the Jerusalem Temple in 70 CE forever deprived Judaism of its ritual center. Again the religion was forced to take a decisive turn away from the land and back to the text. Understanding the Torah and the Talmud, rather than knowing God through contact with his actions in the promised land, became the dominant theme of exilic Judaism.

The shift from landscape to text made it possible for Judaism to survive the crises of repeated exile. It also changed the character of the religion in fundamental ways. Exegesis, the science of meticulous reading, became the primary activity by which the community could understand its place in the world. The tools of exegesis are abstract; they are grounded in an authoritative text and a system of logical interconnection among textual elements. Interpretation seldom invites the outside world to intrude, and in time a text-based system evolves in directions that have a strong internal logic but less and less contact with the limits and constraints of the world. Having originally identified themselves and their communal life in terms of cultivation and domestication, the Jews gradually came to conceive of themselves as a community that could only be understood by the logic of the book. This was a significant change of direction that influenced not just that community but the two religions that grew on its foundations. It was one of these communities at a point much later in time that Lynn White had in mind when he wrote his article condemning the influence of Genesis 1:28 on ecological thought.

CHAPTER SIX

Mediterranean Trade and Regional Cooperation

The Neolithic culture that took shape over thousands of years involved an assemblage of domesticated crops and animals, a repertoire of techniques, and acquired practices that united the human community with the natural world in a consensus view I call First Nature. Assembling this package was the work of limited population movements combined with multilevel regional trade in seeds, animals, technologies, and concepts. Sharing through trade was the engine that enabled Neolithic communities to capitalize on discoveries and innovations made in distant parts of the region. Time and again, trade overcame the limits of geography and helped to transform the Mediterranean into a cooperative community. Understanding the way this transformation came about and grasping its particular character are essential both to understanding the region in the past and to realizing its contemporary potential.

During the late second millennium BCE, during the so-called Bronze Age, the Mediterranean came into focus as a group of human communities interlocked by trade partnerships. At first, regional trade rested on geographical diversity as the unique products of one region were exchanged for those of another. Over time, trade came to specialize in agricultural commodities or such secondary animal products as wool and cheese. In its first phase, trade spread the wealth of the region's resources and brought about a regionwide sharing of naturally occurring materials. In its second phase, trade enabled areas with few natural resources to enter a regional economy by trading the secondary products of animal cultivation.

Trade goods traveled in a variety of carriers. Boats were the most technologically advanced and most efficient bulk carriers. Pack and dray animals also came into use, themselves secondary products of domestication. Oxen and oxcarts, donkeys, camels, and finally horses moved goods around the region and beyond. Trade has many detractors both ecological and political, but their arguments are less persuasive in the Mediterranean than in many other parts of the world.

The Uluburun Shipwreck

Some of the most powerful testimonies to the extent and nature of ancient trade have come from the archaeological examination of shipwrecks. One such wreck, a trading vessel that foundered off Uluburun on the southern coast of Turkey sometime around 1300 BCE, provided a detailed snapshot of the range and influence of Mediterranean trade in the heart of the Bronze Age. The wreck helped to pinpoint the breadth of trade and the complex relationship among trade, culture, and politics. Discovered by a sponge diver in 1982, the wreck was excavated by underwater archaeologists during a ten-year campaign that began two years later. The wreck site, which was surveyed, chronicled, and excavated with meticulous care, has yielded a wealth of information about the ship's cargo, personnel, and destination.

The main cargo on board was copper ingots. More than three hundred ingots weighing a total of ten tons were stacked in the ship's hold. A ton of tin ingots, the proper percentage to turn the whole mass of copper into bronze, was also stowed on board. Ingots of cobalt blue glass were stacked near the copper and tin. These heavy cargoes make the ship seem like a bulk carrier, but bronze and glass, despite their abundance in this cargo, were luxury goods almost certainly on their way to a high-ranking ruler in mainland Greece.[1]

The excavators found scattered logs of ebony, a precious wood imported from a region as far south as modern-day Somalia, which

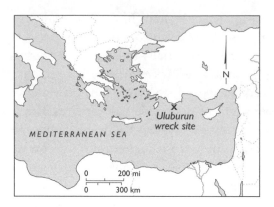

The Uluburun shipwreck gives evidence of fair trade and diverse exchange around the Mediterranean.

regional craftworkers used to make high-quality furniture. Traders brought elephant ivory either from the same region or from North Africa; on board there was one large tusk along with fourteen hippopotamus teeth from Egypt, a substitute for ivory. Like the glass, wood, copper, and tin, the ivory had not been worked, which led the excavators to conclude that artisans attached to the court of the purchaser would be ready and able to make it into luxury items of local design.

The Uluburun ship also carried large amounts of a naturally occurring arsenic derivative called orpiment, which was used as a pigment in paints and cosmetics. Portions of the shells of the murex, a mollusk, used for making a costly incense, were also on board. Resin from a species of pistachio tree was also being shipped. It was used as a preservative in wine and added as a scent to oils. Olives formed a substantial portion of the cargo, as did pomegranates. Spices shipped included coriander, black cumin, and safflower. There were, in addition, some finished goods and a large supply of beads.

The goods gathered in this one cargo combined products from many parts of West Asia and Africa. Goods that had traveled overland from as far away as the Baltic in the north and the Indian Ocean in the east were included, but most of the cargo came from Egypt, Anatolia, Cyprus, and other parts of the Levant. The copper came from mines in Cyprus, but the odds are that the Uluburun ship picked up this cargo along the Levantine coast. Trade in copper often passed through the city of Ugarit. The sandstone anchors of the ship, plus its lamps and cookware, all came from the same general area, which led the excavators to conclude that some city on the Levantine coast was the ship's home port.

A team of high-ranking merchants from the Levant were evidently responsible for the ship and its cargo. Accompanying the merchants aboard the ship were two Mycenean ambassadors and their heavily armed guard. The merchants probably represented some West Asian government in its dealings with the ruler of a large and wealthy Greek city. The Uluburun shipwreck suggests that trade in the late second millennium BCE involved partnerships within a cosmopolitan cultural environment. The bulk goods on board suggest that there was no disparity in technology between the trade partners.

Not all trade was like that represented by the Uluburun wreck. During the Paleolithic, trade with few exceptions rested on regional differences in geology. Low-quality flint was exchanged over short distances. High-quality flint and obsidian were traded over much greater distances. Bitumen, like that found near the site of Jericho, gold, lapis lazuli, amber, and other precious commodities were widely exchanged. Even the first steps in cultivation and domestication created new and fundamentally different trade goods. The grain harvested at Jericho at first supplemented and then for a short while may have eclipsed the bitumen trade that had secured the city's wealth. At Çatalhöyük cattle became a unique trade good that briefly catapulted the city to wealth and regional prominence.

Cultivated grain and domesticated cattle were early proof of the economic power of the Neolithic. The value of domesticates as trade goods, however, was not secure. As the technology of cereal cultivation spread, a low-volume producer like Jericho could no longer compete. Çatalhöyük was bypassed in the same way. Agriculture, rare in the earliest Neolithic, became commonplace as time passed. Both grain and cattle soon lost their status as luxury items and became valuable only in volume.

As long as livestock was simply meat on the hoof, the value of cattle was limited. A localized trade between herders and farmers— an exchange of grain for live animals to be slaughtered within a short period of time was certainly possible and continued into the mod-

ern era. Widespread trade in animal products, however, depended
on preservation. Milk and meat spoil quickly and cannot be carried
long distances. Cheese, on the other hand, can be transported for
days or weeks without spoiling, and it offers many more calories, fat,
and salt than the same weight of unprocessed milk. This extra nutritional value makes it possible to sell cheese at a price that offsets the
labor costs of producing and transporting it.

The most important of all secondary animal products from an
economic standpoint was wool. Sheep and goats could be pastured in
areas that had no other agricultural potential. They grazed in summer in mountain meadows where the growing season was too short
for grain, olives, or grapes. They fed on slopes that were too steep for
cultivation or even for terracing. The supply and demand of wool
had an enormous effect on the structure of regional life. Wool is
durable and compressible, making it easy to ship over long distances
and to store. It can be sold raw or spun into thread or woven into
cloth, so labor in one region can be paid for at a distance when the
finished product is sold. Wool is also a flexible commodity. Depending on how it is processed, it can suit a variety of economic and market
conditions. A shepherd might wear a sheepskin or a heavy woolen
pullover knitted from coarse-spun, unwashed yarn. Wool from the
same flock might find its way to the workshop of a specialist where
it is stripped of oils, dyed, spun, and woven into luxury garments for
the very wealthy. Clothes do not last forever. There is a constant
need to replace them, so wool does not saturate its market. All these
characteristics made it an economic product with revolutionary potential. More than any other good, wool transformed the Neolithic
trade structure from one that was dependent on the vagaries of geography to one in which human industry was primary.[2]

Oil, especially olive oil, is a product with a similar history. Olive
oil and preserved olives can be shipped over great distances without
deterioration. Oil must, however, be stored and shipped in containers. The containers, made of clay, add to the bulk and especially the
weight of the commodity, so the best way to transport olive oil over
a distance is in cargo ships. What is true of olive oil is also true of
wine. Wine is more perishable than oil, but sealed in clay amphorae,
it can with luck be preserved for years. Wine worth exporting is an

elite commodity, and its higher price per unit more than repays the cost of shipping.

Trade and Ecology

The advantages of trade have long been recognized by economists, though in recent years there has been considerable criticism of the unequal partnerships that prevail when powerful nations coerce their weaker neighbors into exchanging goods and services at disadvantageous prices. What the Uluburun shipwreck shows is the absence of this kind of one-sided trade relationship in the Bronze Age. If such a relationship cannot be said to have existed between the powerful and sophisticated states of the Levant and less developed Greece, then the regional pattern was probably one in which fair exchange was the norm.

The economist can point to scattered Mediterranean islands and note that most of them were uninhabitable in the Paleolithic because their stocks of wild animals were too small to sustain hunter-gatherer communities. With the introduction of sheep, goats, olive trees, and cultivated plants other than the olive, the islands became habitable. Economies based on imported technologies and domesticates could and did sustain themselves for thousands of years without depleting the soil, water, and natural vegetation on which their survival depended. If this is an acceptable ideal, then there is benefit in trade.

From the ecological perspective, trade is not typically viewed in such a positive light, because trade favors the movement of species from one habitat to another. An ecologist might single out the same islands analyzed by the economist and note the destruction of their megafauna during the Paleolithic and the damage caused to native plants by domesticates and the weeds that traveled with them. The devastation of island habitats worldwide is a familiar and important cautionary tale. Introducing foreign species into fragile ecosystems can indeed have dire consequences. Though the Mediterranean contains many islands, the region as a whole is not a place where ecosystem development occurred in isolation, and islands are not a good conceptual model for understanding its regional biogeography. The

Mediterranean is the very opposite of an isolated biological community; it is a massive crossroads at the edges of three continents where species have repeatedly migrated and settled.[3]

The Mediterranean basin is a robust and flexible bioregion. It has a long history of accommodating invasive species from the multiple different environments that border it. Species are abundant and various there precisely because so many once-exotic species have found a welcome niche. The route by which domesticates spread from the eastern to the rest of the region replicated one of the pathways that invading species had taken for millions of years. Trade in domesticates was the way that the human community unselfconsciously followed these ancient patterns of regional interaction. Diversity is the regional theme, not homogeneity, and trade is one of the forces that harnesses the wealth of diversity.[4]

Technologies of Trade: Ships

The movement of goods in the Bronze Age depended not only on the production of new commodities but on the ability to transport both luxury goods and bulk commodities. The Uluburun ship was not an isolated piece of technology. Rafts and boats made from bundles of reeds carried goods up and down the rivers that irrigated the fields of Mesopotamia and Egypt. Indeed, boats probably made their way along those rivers even before the fields were cultivated. Boats were certainly in use for many thousands of years before any other large volume carrier, like the oxcart, was invented. Until the middle of the nineteenth century boats remained more cost effective than any land-based transport.

River boats were important, but their use was restricted by regional geography. The open frontier that boats eventually conquered was the Mediterranean Sea itself. But the differences between a boat that could navigate the Nile or Euphrates and one that could safely set out on the Mediterranean were substantial—not that humans waited for technological innovations before they set out to sea. There is surprising new evidence that Neanderthals reached Crete on some kind of watercraft. Mesolithic people sailed to the Aegean island of Melos, gathered obsidian, and brought it back to the mainland, where it was traded overland for hundreds of miles. Boats descended from the ones that carried these early traders allowed people in the late Neolithic to migrate permanently to many of the Aegean islands. The main thrust of settlement occurred during the Bronze Age, when seagoing ships came into wide use.[5]

Ships from many ports sailed the Mediterranean during this era. There is ample evidence of commerce among cities that could only be connected by sea and a wealth of documentary evidence about the goods imported and exported by ship. Descriptions of ships are preserved, along with models of ships and representations that range from room-sized bas-reliefs to graffiti scratched on shards of pottery. There are also surviving bits recovered from shipwrecks and actual preserved boats in Egyptian tombs. Despite this wealth of evidence, however, many details about Bronze Age ships are still controversial, and the archaeology of ancient ships remains one of the most fascinating and challenging disciplines.

Technologies of Trade on Land

Transport on land depended on humans for thousands of years. Then, when domesticated animals entered the picture, a host of new carriers came into use. Aurochs, the first animals to be domesticated, were already doing work for the human community early in the sixth millennium BCE. Almost two millennia later, the ox-pulled cart was developed in Mesopotamia. From there, the oxcart spread both east and west. Ideal for hauling heavy loads over short distances, the oxcart is ill adapted to long-distance travel. A human can easily cover two and a half miles in an hour; an ox a bit less. Oxen require large quantities of food and water, which limits the climates in which they can survive. Carts also have their drawbacks. They work well on flat terrain but less well on slopes. Although they do not require a roadway, in boulder-strewn fields, deserts, and marshes they fail. To be reliable as long-distance transport, ox-drawn carts need the infrastructure of roads and strategically placed reserves of water.

Most long-distance land transport in the Mediterranean region before the Romans built their marvelous network of roads depended on pack animals. The donkey was the first to be domesticated. There may have been multiple domestications, but the wild asses, or onagers, of East Africa and the Levant, of which tiny populations still survive, began to be tamed sometime in the fifth millennium BCE, more than a thousand years after the first attested use of oxen for plowing. Donkeys are compact and short-legged. They are sure-footed, too, so they can be used in terrain where an oxcart would founder or overturn. They eat considerably less than oxen, and since their natural habitat is arid, they require less water. Modern authorities estimate that a pack donkey can carry about one-third of its own weight—seventy to one hundred pounds. Fully loaded, the donkey walks at about the same pace as a human being.[6]

There are two varieties of domestic camel in the world today, the product of two separate domestications. The single-humped dromedary was first domesticated on the Arabian Peninsula at about the same time as the donkey. Bactrian camels were domesticated in the uplands of western Iran at roughly the same time. Through subsequent history the two species have remained the most practical and functional animals in the difficult terrains to which they are native. The Bactrian camel is at home in the cold northerly steppes and deserts that stretch from Iran eastward to China. The dromedary is still widely used in the hot desert countries of West Asia and North Africa. The ability of both species to forage on scrub and to go long distances without drinking is legendary. A single dromedary can carry the load of six or eight donkeys. A Bactrian camel can carry a one-ton load on its back. Both can cover thirty miles a day in terrain that is too arid and unstable to support a donkey.

Horses and Horse Power

In regions where the horse could survive, it became the dominant, multipurpose animal. Domestication began sometime around 4000 BCE in the steppes north of the Black Sea. From there the horse spread rapidly both east and west. As ships increasingly linked communities around the Mediterranean Sea, the horse transformed land transportation. The horse was the ideal animal to bring the kind of swift and decisive change that Gimbutas imagined overtaking the ancient world of matriarchy. Where Gimbutas and earlier archaeologists saw mounted invaders, however, contemporary archaeologists, supported by genetic evidence, see a wave of advance. This view is

attuned to the slow pace of cultural change. What it lacks is the dynamism of invasion theories, a dynamism connected historically with
the horse.

The cave painters of France often represented wild horses, and
the remains of horse bones in cave deposits show how important a
part of the Paleolithic diet horse meat was. At the end of the last ice
age, climate change promoted the growth of forests, and the open
plains where horses had thrived became overgrown. This dramatically reduced the range of the wild horse, which ceased to be an
important source of meat in areas where it had once been primary.
About 4000 BCE horses show up again in the archaeological record.
Wild horses had survived and thrived north of the Fertile Crescent
in the open grassy steppes of the Caucasus. Nomadic peoples there
captured and used them in a variety of ways.[7]

Once the horse had been tamed in the steppes, it soon showed
up elsewhere in Asia and Europe, as the archaeological record shows;
it expanded rapidly into areas where it had not been seen for thousands of years. Unlike most domesticated species, however, which
show a single point of origin and a gradual spread from the Fertile
Crescent both east and west, horses spread in a more complicated
pattern.[8] Evidence for the unusual pattern of repeated domestication of horses comes from genetic studies of modern horses, which
show greater diversity than any other domesticated animal. This genetic diversity has led to the conclusion that the widespread use of
horses "occurred primarily through the transfer of technology for
capturing, taming, and rearing wild caught animals."[9]

Sometime in the early third millennium BCE, the horse reached
Mesopotamia. At first horses were treated like faster oxen and yoked
to carts and plows. Not all carts carried grain. Rulers and warriors
had their own vehicles, a few images of which have survived. Typically their carts were four-wheeled conveyances with a raised front,
side rails, and room for two to stand inside. In a surviving copper
model from about 2500 BCE, two oxen pull the cart. In a battle
scene from a wooden box called the Standard of Ur, a chariot is
pulled by a team of four donkeys. Two of the donkeys are harnessed
to the yoke pulling the cart, and two others are bridled but otherwise free. The outer two free donkeys set a pace which the inner pair,
despite the weight they were pulling, would attempt to match.

Heavy chariots with four solid wooden wheels were neither fast nor maneuverable. It would not be hard for foot soldiers to get out of the way of ox-pulled chariots. Both speed and turning were improved when chariots were mounted on runners rather than wheels. Sleds could turn corners more easily than four-wheeled carts, but friction was an obvious problem in many terrains. Two-wheeled carts were lighter and faster and more stable on turns, but the solid wooden wheels kept speeds down.[10] Oxcarts might travel at two miles an hour; horses pulled light chariots at speeds of up to twenty miles per hour.[11] Sometime in the second millennium BCE, lighter and stronger wheels with an outer rim supported on spokes were invented; they quickly became standard equipment on chariots throughout West Asia. Between 1600 and 1200 BCE the region was embroiled in recurrent wars, and the chariot became a major resource for every regional fighting force. Numbers, though hard to pin down, suggest horses were used for war on a staggering scale. Solomon, who ruled over a minor regional power, claimed to have twelve thousand horses ready for battle.[12] The rulers of the great powers must have commanded many more.

By about 1000 BCE, a new way of using horses began to develop, perhaps first among the steppe peoples who had the longest experience with them. Instead of harnessing horses to carts, people mounted horses and rode on their backs. Bridles developed for handling cart horses could readily be adapted to this style of riding. Saddles, which developed next, improved riders' ability to hold their seat. As skills and agility increased, mounted riders armed themselves with short bows. The Scythians of the Caucasus and the Parthians of West Asia were adept at this style of fighting. Because of their special fighting abilities, they were able to resist attacks by the great powers of eastern Asia and their successors, the Greeks and the Romans. Most experts believe that the stirrup was the only major tool of horse management that was unknown in the ancient world. Its invention is usually dated to the early Middle Ages.

Diversity and Fragmentation

Trade not only spread commodities and techniques across the Mediterranean; it also brought different cultures into prolonged contact, and contact often led to settlement. People of one culture began to live within the boundaries of another culture group. Multiethnicity, which we might also call diversity, was not valued in the nineteenth century, and its presence in the historical record was typically downplayed or overlooked. Indeed, there was considerable prejudice in the nineteenth century against the mixing of peoples; intercultural and especially interracial marriage, for example, were strongly condemned. It is probably safe to say, however, that ethnic unity played a relatively minor part in the majority of world political systems before the nineteenth century. The history of conquest in the Mediterranean region from the Bronze Age onward underscores this thought. Regional communities with governments that change with the tides of conquest are not likely to be ethnically uniform.

The benefits of ethnic uniformity are obvious, and the romantic folk-based ideologies of the nineteenth century enumerated and extolled them. In these systems everyone shares a common culture and a common language; everyone's beliefs and values are substantially the same. It is wise to remember, however, that the rise and spread of these ideologies coincided with the rise of the modern nation-state and that thinking of this kind helped to suppress divisions within societies that had been long-standing. Although diversity has many advocates today, its advantages are less obvious. Diverse systems inevitably pit contrasting beliefs against each other; they invite clashes of culture and misunderstandings that reflect lack of a common experience, a common religion, or a common language.

Despite the potential for conflict that diversity inevitably produces, its benefits can be substantial. Culturally diverse systems tend to be more dynamic than homogeneous ones because a wider range of cultural predispositions means a wider range of potential responses to threats and opportunities. Ethnic and cultural diversity in the social order function in a way that is analogous to the division of labor in the economic order, and in many instances, the two systems interlock. Throughout history, occupational specialization and ethnic difference have often coincided. In many societies herders have been ethnically and culturally different from the populations that lived in towns and grew crops. In other societies it has typically been the case that particular skills or occupations are associated with particular ethnic groups. Some Egyptian temples were frescoed by Minoan artists from Crete. Pharaohs hired Greek soldiers to protect them. The Nile Delta, which connected Egypt to the rest of the Mediterranean, was also home to many foreign colonies. We have imagined diversity to be a contemporary ideal, but it has a long and important, if underappreciated, history. It was a significant feature of the Mediterranean throughout its history.

PART II

Perseverance and Attack

CHAPTER SEVEN

The Greek Link between
Landscape and Cosmology

A s the layers at the Franchthi Cave illustrate so dramatically, the Neolithic Revolution came to what is now Greece early and in full force. The dissected Greek landscape put different soils and microclimates in close proximity, making the peninsula and associated islands ideal places to adopt a broad swath of Levantine crops and herds. Like the anonymous poets of Uruk, Ugarit, the land of the Hatti, and the Bible, Greek men and women reflected the Neolithic consensus in many different ways in works that have come down to us not as anonymous classics but as the crowning achievements of known and celebrated authors. The *Iliad* and Hesiod's *Theogony* and his *Works and Days*, among other texts, are foundations of ancient Greek culture and remained persistent influences in the Mediterranean tradition.

What Greek farmers built and what these poets celebrated would have been understood and accepted anywhere the Neolithic agricultural revolution was central to culture. What distinguished Greek culture in its classical period, however, was the work of philosophers whose pursuit of logic led them to repudiate fundamental features of the First Nature consensus. They were the first great dissenters in the Mediterranean tradition, and their works mark the beginning of the intellectual abandonment of the consensus view as a foundation for social understanding and action. Although their influence in their own era was slight, their ideas were enormously consequential in later eras.

Because the Greek philosophical tradition is still with us, the concepts that characterized it and their historical development remain important today. The Greeks and their view of nature influence us for an additional reason. During the nineteenth century, scholars of the classics synthesized what they believed to be the ancient Greek view of the relationship between the human community and the natural world. They saw this relationship as one of opposition based on two Greek terms: *nomos* and *physis*. *Physis* is the word from which English derives terms like *physics* and *physical*. In the ancient Greek vocabulary, it represented what we would call the natural or the instinctual. *Nomos*, on the other hand, was a general word for the ruling principles of the human community. These were not natural or instinctual but based on custom and principle. What governed the natural world—the realm of *physis*—was a set of immutable physical laws. *Nomos*—the product of memory and deliberation— governed human communities.

These terms are reliable indicators of important differences between the human community and the natural community, but scholars of the nineteenth century, for reasons of their own, treated the communities as distinct and antithetical. Theirs was an anachronistic and mistaken position derived from principles that were developed in their own era and rooted in the rapidly evolving reconception of nature as something distinct from and antagonistic to the values of the human community.

The ancient Greeks conceived of the natural world in many different ways. No single picture was accepted by everyone. More importantly, the *nomos–physis* distinction was not universal among Greek thinkers, and it was certainly not the foundation or the sole standard of their thought. And while the loudest and ultimately the most influential voices among the Greeks were those of the philosophers, it is important to understand that the purpose and scope of ancient philosophy was very different from that of modern academic philosophy, which during the twentieth century shrank to little more than a critique of language.

Greek philosophy began as an offshoot of poetry. It was narrative before it was logical, and narrative remained important throughout its history. Greek philosophy was also closely related to Greek religion—but not the state-sponsored worship of the Olympian pantheon, which was something that philosophers in the Greek world frequently came into conflict with. Greek philosophy was like the Greek cult religions. These were small-scale group-based spiritual movements that promised their practitioners access to secret information and power, especially the power to transcend mortality and live eternally as gods. Plato and Aristotle, who seem to us to be supreme rationalists, were both leaders of philosophical schools that promised benefits of this kind to their initiates. It is important to realize, too, that Greek philosophy, with one exception, was a pursuit of the rich and well-born. It was not available to the masses, and it had little influence on communal thought in its own era. Given its importance today, and the host of misconceptions that surround it, a reexamination of ancient Greek thinking about nature and a look at actual Greek agricultural practices is essential.

Before Philosophy

Like the Sumerian epic of Gilgamesh, the Greek *Iliad* took an oblique approach to the human relationship with the environment. In *Gilgamesh*, the fateful rejection of the goddess-lover forced the king to undergo a series of harsh experiences that led him to accept his human nature and its limitations. The great epic poem that is often seen as the foundation of Greek literature and thought, Homer's *Iliad*, follows a similar path. Although it is, like *Gilgamesh*, a warrior epic, a key passage of the poem steps outside the action to describe a symbolic object: a shield made for the poem's hero, Achilles, by the god of fire and artifice. Its theme is the agrarian landscape. After experiencing violence and death, Gilgamesh is able to embrace the joys that community and landscape offer, but Achilles is not so lucky. His early death is decreed by fate, and he must be content with an image of the orderly universe that his bloodthirstiness has helped to reinvigorate.[1]

In the *Iliad*, violence is universal; both humans and gods experience it. Soon after the poem begins, the human and the divine worlds are caught up in a cosmic epidemic of murderous anger, which over-turns the patterns of normal life and narrows the gap between im-mortal and mortal. As the contagion of violence works through to its conclusion, the divine world and the human world return to their proper spheres. The fierce partisanship that individual gods felt for one side or another yields to fate, which decrees the destruction of Troy. As the surge of wrath ebbs, the shield of Achilles offers its image of an orderly cosmology that both gods and heroes are finally ready to accept and affirm.

The shield is hard to visualize, but it clearly represents a cosmology built on the cultivated landscape, a verbal picture of First Nature. Its images seem to be laid down in concentric rings that ripple out from two cities at the shield's center. Though one of the cities is at peace and the other at war, discord is present in both. In the central marketplace of the peaceful city, a murder trial is under way. The killer confronts representatives of the victim's family and offers compensation for the crime while a circle of judges prepares to decide his fine. Like war-torn Troy, the city is not without discord, but it has ways to limit aggression and to judge between rival claims. Side by side with the murder trial, a wedding is taking place. The marriage ritual governs desire, the force that drove Paris to lure Helen from the home of her husband, Menelaus, in the abduction that began the Trojan War.

The second city at the center of Achilles' shield is, like Troy, under siege. Two armies surround it and debate whether to attack or accept a payoff. Those inside the city prepare an ambush to steal the enemies' food. Learning of the attack, the besiegers rush to head it off, and open battle breaks out. "The armies aimed their bronze-headed spears at one another. With them were Strife and Panic, and Fatality who was dragging three men after her . . . and her robe was stained with men's blood."[2] This second city is threatened by the forces that the first is able to discipline and contain. Their presence side by side on the shield suggests that either fate is possible for any city. The plot of the *Iliad* shows how the cycle of wrath and violence determines the fate of cities like this one and like Troy, and how through the brutal therapy of war, it brings each back to a state of equilibrium.

Just beyond the walls of the conjoined cities, at no apparent distance from the ambush site, is peaceful cropland where teams of men plow a field. As they reach the end of a furrow, servants hand them a cup of wine. In the next field over, reapers are cutting the grain in long straight swaths. At midday they will feast on a roasted sacrificial ox that servants prepare in the shade of an oak. Beyond or beside these fields is a vineyard hung with ripe grapes. A single path leads through the thorn hedge that encloses it. Down this path a steady stream of men and women carry baskets filled with fruit. A boy walks beside them singing and playing the lyre.[3]

Just as the poets of Uruk infused scenes of cultivation with erotic images, Homer made the fields and vineyards places of delight. The plowmen look forward to a cup of wine at the end of each long furrow and the harvesters to their feast. Music makes labor in the vineyards easier.

> [Hephaistos] also made a herd of horned cattle. . . . The cows mooed as they came full speed out of the corrals to feed among the waving reeds that grow by the banks of the river. Four shepherds followed the cows and their nine fleet dogs went with them. Two terrible lions had fastened on a bellowing bull that was with the cows, and bellow as he might they pulled him away, while the dogs and men chased after. The lions tore through the bull's thick hide and were gorging on his blood and entrails, but the herdsmen were afraid and only sicced on their dogs; the dogs hung back and barked, keeping out of danger.[4]

At first, the world of the herdsmen seems comfortable and reassuring. The hungry cows released from their nighttime enclosures head to the pasture with a chorus of moos. The herders look forward to an easy day. But the lions change all that. They drag a bull away and devour him while the shepherds look on in terror. Even their dogs cower. The herds are pastured in a place that borders on wilderness. Security is fleeting. There is no sure protection from disaster.

In the final zone of the shield, which is as far from the city as the cow pastures, life is tranquil and rewarding again. Just as the central image of the shield contrasts a city at peace with one in turmoil, the shield's two outermost bands show scenes of peace and security alternating with scenes of violence and terror on the fringes of wilderness. The shepherds leave their work and sing and dance in an open field. "There was a bard to sing to them and play his lyre, while two acrobats performed for them as the poet struck up with his tune." Beyond the pastures, at the edge of the inhabited world, lies the encircling ocean.

The cosmos that Homer sketched on the shield would have been comprehensible to the poets of Uruk, though almost two thousand years intervened between their compositions. The city surrounded by fields and pastures, then by wilderness, would be entirely familiar. The sense of comfort or danger that characterizes each zone would also resonate. In neither civilization is the city or the wilderness permanently fixed and secure. The shield is not simply a statement about the way things are. It is also a statement about the way things ought to be, and it responds to a deep human need for order and justice. A justly ordered cosmos in which men and women lead lives that are rewarding is fundamental to the Homeric ideal. The shield illustrates a world in which humans and gods are distinct, strife and desire ubiquitous, and death inevitable. The landscape-based cosmos of the shield answers all those threats by celebrating the reassuring and nourishing order of First Nature.

Hesiod on Work and Striving

Homer's focus on violence and desire as the forces most likely to destabilize the agricultural community is echoed by the poet Hesiod, who wrote his *Works and Days* sometime in the late eighth century BCE. Hesiod's concern was the question that had also preoccupied the authors of Genesis, namely, Why is it so difficult for people to thrive in the world that divinity has created? The biblical answer is the disobedience of Adam and the human expulsion from the garden. Hesiod put the blame elsewhere:

> For the gods keep hidden from men the means of life.
> Else you would easily do work enough in a day to supply you
> for a full year.[5]

Zeus, "father of gods and men," brought order to the cosmos. When he organized the world, fire was withheld from men and reserved for the gods. Prometheus, son of an earlier generation of gods displaced by Zeus, violated the divine mandate by stealing fire from heaven and giving it to humankind. This may seem to be an act of kindness—Prometheus is often considered one of humanity's benefactors—but his act narrowed the gap between gods and humans, an essential prop of the world order that Homer had represented. In some versions of the story, Prometheus suffered eternal punishment as a consequence of his act, but in Hesiod's version, punishment fell on human beings. To carry it out, the gods created a seductive and talented woman named Pandora.[6]

Before Pandora was created, "men lived on earth . . . free from ills and hard toil and heavy sickness." When Pandora arrived on earth, she opened a jar prepared for her by the gods that contained sorrow, misfortune, and illness. The world was transformed from a place where a man could feed himself for a year with one day's work to a wasteland choked with weeds and thorns, demanding hard labor and offering little but disappointment. Reproduction and labor were the forces that sustained a similarly adverse world in the Bible. Hesiod, for his part, relied on the power of "strife," which was personified in the Greek cosmos by the bloodthirsty war goddess, Eris. In his view, there were two kinds of strife, one destructive and the other constructive. Harmful strife was represented in Hesiod's poem by the theft of fire and the creation of Pandora. These aggressive acts produced hostile responses and led to discord and disorder. The other kind of strife—competition—"inspired even lazy men to labor." Strife is discordant, but it can lead to striving, which Hesiod saw as the main remedy for the nasty trick that Zeus had played on humans.

Challenging the Visible World Order

Hesiod was interested in representing the cosmos as Homer described it, but he was also intent on identifying the abstractions that threatened order. Desire was one threat, wrath was the other, although both have their positive sides as well. In the early Greek philosophical tradition, which developed a little after Hesiod's time, these two abstract principles—desire and strife—played an extremely important part. For Homer and Hesiod, describing these two forces required telling a story. At first the people we now call philosophers were storytellers who explained their ideas in pithy expressions or in fictional tales. Despite their use of narrative, the philosophers were distinguished from the poets by their reliance on logic and abstraction. It was mainly the ascendancy of logic that slowly transformed the writings of the philosophers from an explanation of the hidden forces at work in the landscape-based cosmology to a full-scale rejection of it.

Empedocles, one of the first great philosopher-storytellers, lived in a Greek colony on the island of Sicily during the first half of the sixth century BCE. He outlined his philosophy in two poems, one of them called *On Nature* and the second, *Purifications*. Only fragments of either poem survive. In a tightly compressed and obscure passage in the first poem, Empedocles describes several things at once.[7] First he lays out what he believed to be the large-scale rhythm of cosmic function, described as a "twofold tale." He links two alternating states of the universe: times of coming together and times of fragmentation. Their back-and-forth rhythm results in an endless dance of opposites. The principles that govern the dance are two abstractions like those that were important to Homer and Hesiod. One of these forces is love, which Hesiod personified as the fatal Pandora and Homer as Helen. Unlike Hesiod, who thought of love as a disturbing force, Empedocles believed that love was constructive, and he emphasized its ability to bring things together and to perpetuate species. Strife, for Empedocles, was the opposite of love, and it played a role that was similar to the role that violence and wrath played in the earlier stories.

When love dominated the cosmos, things "grew to be one alone out of many," but when strife prevailed, the same things "grew apart to be many out of one." The objects that obeyed the pull of strife and love were what Empedocles elsewhere called the "roots." They were four in number. Empedocles named them in another fragment: "fire and water and earth and the immense height of air." Empedocles' roots—more commonly known as elements—were tools for describing the composition of inorganic and organic substances from the sixth century BCE through the late Renaissance.[8]

Empedocles' biographer Diogenes Laertius reported that the philosopher wrote his poems in reaction to another Greek thinker, Parmenides, who argued that the world is unchanging. What people regard as change, Parmenides asserted, is actually a misperception. We think we perceive birth, death, growing, and disintegrating—all the different forms of becoming—but we are wrong. If we look at "becoming" from a logical point of view rather than relying on the evidence of our senses, our illusion is exposed. Being is absolute, Parmenides argued, so nonbeing is impossible—in fact, a contradiction in terms. Parmenides' reasoning was based on his perception that a simple negative statement like "There is no X" implies a fundamental paradox. Paraphrased, the sentence might read, "There is such a thing as an X, and it is not." Restated in this way, the sentence both posits the existence of X and its nonexistence. Because of that internal contradiction, Parmenides argued that all statements about nonbeing must be ruled out as logically unsound.[9]

Parmenides pursued the implications of his discovery still further. If, he reasoned, there is no nonbeing, then there can be no less or more being. The word "being" must function like our word "unique." "Unique" means "one of a kind," so when people assert that something is "more unique" than something else, the error is easy to spot. The qualities of the verb "to be," in Parmenides' view, are similar. If being is absolute like uniqueness, then one thing cannot have more being than another. Nor can one thing have more being at one time and less at another. If being is like uniqueness, then there can be no becoming, since becoming must inhabit a no-man's-land between more and less being.

If being cannot be negated or diminished, then nothing that has being can ever cease to exist, because that would require a loss of being. Consequently, there is no passing away of things, since death or dissolution also negate being. Most improbably, but logically, in Parmenides' philosophy, everything that ever was still exists and will continue to exist eternally and unchanged. Things were always the way they are right now, and they always will be. Yet humans perceive things as coming into being and dissolving. We *perceive* change, which Parmenides' logic told him cannot occur, but rather than question logic, he decided that something must be wrong with our perceptions. However unlikely the result, we must dismiss our sense impressions and accept only those truths that our intellect offers.

This choice of logic over appearance, of hypothetical being over experiential becoming, was made by all the pre-Socratic philosophers;

it was not solely Parmenides' choice. Even though we know that scientific truths are often counterintuitive, the outright rejection of sense perception that came so naturally to these philosophers strikes us as implausible. Their all-too-ready acceptance of intangibles, however, rested on an important part of their education. Unlike most people today, Greek philosophers were overwhelmingly influenced by a rigorous training in geometry, the model intellectual system of their time. As a means of calculating angles and areas, it has pragmatic links to the observable world, but its most remarkable power is the link between its few axioms and its deductive methodology. A geometric proof can be complex and elegant, and although it may be represented in a drawing of intersecting lines and angles, its truth does not rest on an accurate diagram but entirely on internal logical consistency. Firmly convinced of the power of this kind of thought, Greek philosophers were willing to grant conclusions based on logical reasoning greater authority than the sense evidence the conclusions contradicted. In time, this rejection of the material world and the dismissal of common perception proved fatal for the First Nature cosmology that was grounded in the real landscape that people inhabited.

Understanding Empedocles as someone who struggled with Parmenides' recognition of a conflict between being and becoming makes his work more comprehensible. Empedocles' twofold tale is intended to reconcile our perception of becoming with the realm of absolute being that logic imagines. In his philosophy, the four elements—earth, air, fire, water—and the two dispositions, strife and desire, are constant and universal. Their natures do not change, and they are neither created nor destroyed. They do not become, and they do not pass away. They are the embodiments of Parmenides' permanent being.[10] When these unchanging elements interact with each other, they create a world in flux.

Driven by the forces of strife and love, which physicists today refer to by the less anthropocentric terms "repulsion" and "attraction," the elements combine or separate. United by attraction, they form compounds; divided by repulsion, they fragment and return to their elementary state. Empedocles' "twofold tale" describes long periods of oscillation between these two states, which in his view characterized the history of the physical world. Human senses register the dynamics of this history, but only logic can infer its eternal and constant character.

Like Parmenides, Empedocles drew a sharp distinction between sense data and insight. Speaking of the goddess of love, he wrote: "Her must you contemplate with your mind, and not sit with eyes dazed. . . . She is perceived by no mortal man as she circles among them; but you must listen to the undeceitful ordering of my discourse."[11] Empedocles' description recalls scenes in Greek literature where gods and goddesses appear to mortals in disguise. In Empedocles' poem, this description shows that logic, like divine favor, sets a person apart. Guided by this insight, Empedocles explored the relationship between humans and deities in his mysterious second poem, *Purifications*. The doctrine expounded there and its relationship to the cosmos that Empedocles sketched out in *On Nature* are enigmatic.

Speaking in the first person, the poet announced that he had become an immortal god.[12] This is considerably beyond the range of possibilities that the *Iliad* or even the *Odyssey* offered most mortals, and Greeks in general did not believe in immortal life. Special groups of Greeks, however, did believe in immortality and also believed that they could teach others how to achieve it. These groups formed mystery religions or mystery cults that promised immortality in the form of deification to their fully initiated members. Although not everyone belonged to a cult, everyone knew that they existed and where they were centered. They knew members were promised godhood, but the public was not supposed to know how initiations were carried out. In time, the Greek philosophical schools became much the same. Everyone knew some of what they taught. What philosophers passed on in secret to their successful students was similar to what the mystery cults promised: the secrets of a blissful and immortal life.[13]

From what has been pieced together of the rest of *Purifications*, it seems that the immortality Empedocles boasted of at the start of his poem was hard won. The situation he alluded to is unclear, but he apparently went through a prolonged period of expiation before reaching that state.[14] This part of *Purifications* links the cosmology of the first poem with the personal history of the second. As the world passed through alternating cycles of the blending of the elements in harmony and their violent dissolution when strife dominated,

Empedocles experienced them, too. During what seem to be reincarnations, Empedocles linked to each of the elements. "The force of the air pursues him into the sea, the sea spews him out onto the floor of the earth, the earth casts him into the rays of the blazing sun, and the sun into the eddies of the air; one takes him from the other, but all abhor him."[15] As he is reborn generation after generation, he experiences life in these spheres as a foreign soul rejected by each in turn. Strife dominated his life, not comfort or reassurance, just as strife dominated the cosmos. At the end of a cycle, which came just as the philosopher completed his purification, the disposition of the universe changed, and the reign of Joy and Aphrodite, goddess of love, that he invoked in the opening passage began.

The underlying theme of his philosophy might be described, then, as living according to nature, as long as we understand that what he meant by nature was not the visible landscape of First Nature and Achilles' shield but an invisible and insensible universe delivered to the prepared mind by logic. Empedocles rejected the senses as reliable guides to understanding, and his ideal cosmos was vastly different from the world of human experience. The materials from which the world of his imagination were composed, however, were basic things—earth, air, fire, and water. They were the tangible and commonplace materials that sustained plant and animal life. Both the individual and the cosmos were made up of these elements, and they were acted on by the same elemental forces. So while Empedocles repudiated the First Nature cosmological vision common to West Asia, he still recognized the importance of the material building blocks of that landscape.

Plato's New Cosmic Model

Even Empedocles' tenuous link between the landscape that sustained human life and the work of philosophy was obliterated in the philosophies of Plato and Aristotle. In place of the traditional First Nature view, which the pre-Socratics had already compromised, both philosophers proposed an idea of natural order based on the regular motions of the stars and planets. Although there were important differences between the cosmologies that each man articulated, as there were in every other aspect of their philosophies, both separated the earth from the sky, and both associated aspects of human nature with celestial rather than earthly models. The consequences of this shift were muted in the short term but were eventually enormous, amounting to an absolute redefinition of human nature that severed a practical and conceptual link that had existed for millennia between the human community and the agricultural landscape that sustained it.

Plato articulated his views on the order of the planetary system in his dialogue *Timaeus*.[16] In the same dialogue, he described his views on the origin of the universe.[17] That vision was strikingly different from Empedocles', although it included some of the same concepts. The biggest difference was Plato's assertion that the universe was the work of a divine creator: the craftsman (*demiourgos*). Plato's craftsman was good, purposeful, and rational; he created the universe according to a geometrically grounded plan. Before his act of creation, the material of the universe lay around in a state of disorder. Rather than create the universe out of nothing, as the God of the Pentateuch appears to have done, the craftsman built the ordered universe from these eternally preexistent materials.

Like the craftsman who created it, Plato's universe was rational, orderly, and good. It was also alive. Because it had life, Plato believed that it had a soul. This is a troublesome word in the modern vocabulary, but Plato understood and used that term to represent an eternally enduring combination of intellect and emotion. This soulful, living universe with its fully developed intelligence embodied both sides of the Empedoclean worldview, the realm of eternals and the realm of becoming. Pragmatically, the movement of the heavenly bodies marked earthly time, but in an ideal sense their motion symbolized eternity. In Plato's view, as in the view of his society, the stars and planets that represented eternity were themselves immortal and divine. For Plato, the ability of the universe to express order and beauty through the motion of the celestial bodies was the prime demonstration of its intellectual capacity.

All living things, including humans, were made from the same raw materials that the craftsman used to make the planets. Unfortunately, by the time the craftsman turned from shaping stars to shaping our world, he had used up most of the best stuff. The earth and the beings that inhabit it had to be made from inferior raw material that was impermanent and subject to decay. Humans found themselves inside disease-prone bodies and condemned to exile on a changeable planet. Earthbound souls, which retained a bit of divine substance within them, struggled with their bodies in a coarse and troubled world.[18] In *Timaeus*, Plato argued that humans could recover their divine nature and separate themselves from their bodies and the world by studying the divine pattern that is written in the stars. By emulating the rational beauty and order inscribed in the night sky, the individual soul could recapture the divinity that was its true heritage.

What made the *Timaeus* so much more influential than Empedocles' poetry was in large part Plato's rhetoric. Empedocles and the rest of the pre-Socratics had transformed the ideals traditionally invested in a landscape-based cosmos into abstractions. Their cosmologies were intellectual, and intense conflicts flared up over the minutiae of rival systems. Though an even more abstract thinker than the pre-Socratics, Plato understood the power of a visual image to ground theory. When he embodied his ideas in the observable planetary system, he created a symbol that was easy to grasp. It was also a symbol that aimed to eclipse the landscape-based First Nature cosmology by subsuming it within a larger system of order.

In forging a new ideology that contrasted with the *Iliad*'s symbolic shield and with the confusing speculations of the pre-Socratics, Plato spun out an important thread of earlier philosophy. The cosmos in *Timaeus* was not for all comers. It was reserved for those most deeply initiated in the speculations of his school. Those in the know might espouse the idea while the rest of the community remained in ignorance. The privacy of the philosophical life and the secrecy of initiates helped to insulate Plato's cosmology from public view. The norm in West Asia had always been the unity of community and individual cosmology. In Plato's world, as in that of Empedocles, it was possible for the two to be completely divorced from each other. Platonic philosophy was an intellectual exercise for wealthy and entitled young men of Athens. Its practitioners did their best to shield the school from common life and from common people, whom they had no wish to influence or engage.

A passage from Plato's *Critias*, an incomplete dialogue that carried on the conversation begun in *Timaeus*, has attracted the attention of environmental historians. They see this passage as offering authoritative evidence that deforestation and catastrophic soil erosion were widespread in Athenian territory in Plato's day. The passage describes what Plato's speaker imagines Greece to have looked like nine thousand years before his time:

> At that epoch the country was unimpaired, and for its mountains it had high arable hills, and in place of the "moorlands," as they are now called, it contained plains full of rich soil; and it had much forestland in its mountains, of which there are visible signs even to this day; for there are some mountains which now have nothing but food for bees, but they had trees no very long time ago, and the rafters from those felled there to roof the largest buildings are still sound. And besides, there were many lofty trees of cultivated species; and it produced boundless pasturage for flocks. Moreover, it was enriched by the yearly rains from Zeus, which were not lost to it, as now, by flowing from the bare land into the sea; but the soil it had was deep, and therein it received the water, storing it up in the retentive loamy soil, and by drawing off into the hollows from the heights the water that was there absorbed, it provided all the various districts with abundant supplies of springwaters and streams, whereof the shrines which still remain even now, at the spots where the fountains formerly existed, are signs which testify that our present description of the land is true.[19]

All too often this description of environmental degradation has been taken as a factual account inserted into the *Critias* without thematic purpose. Plato's motives, however, should be clear to any reader of the *Timaeus*. What he is describing is the natural deterioration of a planet made of inferior materials and existing in the contingent world of becoming. It is not a factual inset in a philosophical discourse but a just-so story that purports to describe the character of a world that is not immutable like the stars and the other planets but material and subject to long-term change.

Aristotle on Cosmology

Aristotle reaffirmed many of Plato's thoughts about cosmology in his brief introduction to *On the Parts of Animals*. For him, there was no divine craftsman; rather, nature itself functioned in a workman-like way.[20] Aristotle imagined a patterning force within nature—we might see it as similar to the genetic code—and he ascribed to this built-in program a goal or purpose.[21] Aristotle's celestial realm, unlike Plato's, evolved from innate natural principles like those that govern animal growth and development. Still, his heaven exhibited the same high level of clarity and order that separated Plato's sky from the murky material world that humans inhabit.

Aristotle believed that the pattern of universal order was written in the stars far more clearly than on the earth. He also introduced some elements into his cosmology that had lasting detrimental effect on thinking about the earth's place in the cosmos. Aristotle asserted that an object in motion on the earth traced a straight line, whereas objects in motion in space—the stars, moon, and visible planets—moved in circular paths around the earth. This misperception led Aristotle to conclude that physics supported the distinction between earthly and celestial. The celestial objects traced circles, the shapes of perfection. That a ball rolling across an open field on earth did not trace a circular path was a compelling demonstration of the distinction between the two realms. This notion went unchallenged until the era of Galileo and Newton.

Both Plato and Aristotle also redefined the role of the city in human life. In Socrates' understanding, the city was already markedly different from the cities on the shield of Achilles, and Plato followed suit. Rather than recognizing the interdependency of city and countryside, Socrates divorced the two and described urban life as if it were self-sufficient. Aristotle also studied the city. He used the same logical tools that Plato relied on, but he tempered these with a more accurate representation of the realities of daily life.

When several villages are united in a single complete community, large enough to be nearly or quite self-sufficing, the state comes into existence, originating in the bare needs of life, and continuing in existence for the sake of a good life.

And therefore, if the earlier forms of society are natural, so is the state, for it is the end of them, and the nature of a thing is its end. For what each thing is when fully developed, we call its nature, whether we are speaking of a man, a horse, or a family. Besides, the final cause and end of a thing is the best, and to be self-sufficing is the end and the best. Hence it is evident that the state is a creation of nature, and that man is by nature a political animal. And he who by nature and not by mere accident is without a state, is either a bad man or above humanity; he is like the "Tribeless, lawless, heartless one," whom Homer denounces.[22]

In this passage Aristotle tells his own just-so story to explain the rise of what this translator calls the state but which Aristotle called the polis. The polis was a political organization that embraced the city and its surrounding villages. Arguably, it is the name for the complex of settlements, croplands, and pastures represented on the shield of Achilles. Its defining characteristic is a productive interdependency between city and countryside that creates self-sufficiency for the whole though not for either part. Aristotle thought that the polis had evolved out of necessity. It came into being originally to satisfy the "bare needs of life": food, clothing, and shelter. Agriculture, in other words, was the foundation of political organization. Aristotle also identified the family, which he saw as a polis in miniature, as an agricultural work group. "The family is the association established by nature for the supply of men's everyday wants."[23] Once the polis achieved its primary goal of feeding all its members, it entered into a second phase with a higher purpose. Communal life no longer focused on survival but on fostering the good life for its members. Only when society reached a level of organization and complexity that allowed the city to mature, to enter this second phase, could people live up to their full potential. The city made possible the transition from a life preoccupied with material concerns to a life in which intellect and spirit could thrive. Despite the late appearance of the polis in the history of human communities as Aristotle imagined it, it was the organization best suited to maximize human potential.

Aristotle's ideas about the evolution of communal life have been enormously influential. They are, however, wrong in significant ways.

Prehistory has taught us that spiritual and intellectual life go hand in hand with every form of human organization. The idea that they would be secondary concerns, something humans were free to attend to only after the needs of survival had been met, is not borne out by the facts. It is hardly even logical. The work of survival is never assured and never finished, so there can be no period when leisure for thought is guaranteed. It is even more unrealistic to think that intellect and spirit make no contribution to the task of feeding and housing a community. Aristotle described intellect and spirit as aspects of successive phases of human development because he wanted to separate what he regarded as the material work of survival from the intellectual's pursuit of leisure, but the dichotomy was and is false, and its consequences have been cataclysmic.

It is impossible to imagine much of an interest in the material world among philosophers who continually exalt the immaterial and the otherworldly. Plato and Aristotle, given their theories, had no real motive to study the raw materials that sustained life or the labor of beasts and humans that transformed those materials into food, clothing, and shelter. Like landscape, labor and science fell victim to the turn toward idealism. But the labor that agriculture continued to demand and the dichotomy between intellectual and manual labor that the philosophic tradition took for granted prevented the philosophers' ideas from changing Greek life.

The Agricultural Base of Greek City Life

Aristotle's ideal polis, anchored in the productive household, is represented in a Greek text from the same period that is not well known. Xenophon, one of the most prolific followers of Plato, wrote a book called *Oeconomicus*. Sarah B. Pomeroy has given her translation the title *Discourse on the Skill of Estate Management*. Pomeroy's presentation of the dialogue differs from that of earlier readers, including the noted classicist M. I. Finley and the materialist philosopher Karl Marx. These critics and others saw the work of small farmers as marginal to the economy of the polis. Pomeroy argues, however, that it was fundamental to the economy of Greece in the fourth century BCE and beyond. She also emphasizes the role of the family as an economic unit and is alert to the contributions that Xenophon attributes to women. In Pomeroy's view, Xenophon portrayed the estate as a cooperative enterprise in which both the (male) manager and his wife played key roles. Working together, the two created security and wealth.[24]

The estate of Ischomachus, which Xenophon described, was not as small as many farms that were worked by a single family. Still, it was tiny by comparison with large estates managed by overseers and staffed by crowds of slaves. The household of Ischomachus was mixed. It included the family of the owner, but also a close-knit group of slaves who worked under the direct supervision of husband and wife. Together, masters and slaves farmed a collection of fields. The dispersal of the fields caused some difficulties—travel time and the challenge of protecting crops at a distance from home—but it also brought advantages. Fields in different places with different soils and exposures supported a variety of crops.

Most, but not all, of the labor expended on the farm went toward the cultivation of grain, olives, grapes, and figs. Food for the household was stored. The rest of the food produced was sold. The wealth that the household generated was essential not just to the well-being of its members but to the polis as well.[25] The distinctions that an Athenian of good birth might aspire to were all sponsored by the polis, and all required payment. A prominent person confirmed his status by "paying for sacrifices, public banquets and benefactions, entertaining guests, maintaining horses."[26] These expenditures, along with occasional tax levies, contributed to the public resources of the polis. The aim of a marginal farmer might be survival, but a person of ambition like Ischomachus worked to accumulate wealth. Much of this wealth would be tied up in land, household goods, farm stock, and equipment, but the demands of a public life could be met only by a steady supply of cash.

Profit from selling crops was the main revenue stream, but it might be supplemented by selling slaves or domestic animals. Selling any one of these, like selling land itself, might have negative consequences. Although slaves were treated as a commodity by some owners, the *Oeconomicus* recommends incorporating slaves into the extended family of the owners and offering them rewards rather than coercing their labor—that they be given incentives to produce and offered the possibility of manumission. Without their labor and without that of the animals that pulled the plows and transported the harvest, the farm would become less productive and yield a lower income.

Labor in the fields, vineyards, and orchards was supplemented by labor at the loom. Just as Pomeroy draws attention to the partnership between husband and wife that made the household productive, she also points to the economic value of women's work. From the time of Homer to at least Xenophon's time—for several centuries—the clichéd qualities of a good woman remained the same. Besides her appearance and her manner, the trait most often singled out was her ability to weave cloth. In fifth-century BCE Greece, woolen cloth, the most widely traded commodity of the Secondary Products Revolution, was produced almost exclusively by women working in individual households.[27]

What Xenophon depicted, then, was the life of the polis seen from the agrarian countryside. With the point of view reversed, the dependency of the city on the resources of rural farms was thrown into strong relief. The city relied on its fields for grain, wine, and oil. Its most viable commercial products, wool and cloth, come from its pastures and household looms. Levies that supported the cults of the gods and the public displays that enriched social life flowed in the same direction. The interdependence that Aristotle grudgingly acknowledged and Plato refused to recognize remained vital for the welfare of the Greek city. Archaeology on the Greek mainland has been unable to confirm much of what Xenophon described, but excavations in Greek colonies in southern Italy and on the Black Sea coast have shown that small fields and, at least potentially, dispersed and diversified holdings were indeed the norm.[28]

Stoic Cosmology

Plato and Aristotle focused their attention on the wealthy elite, but other philosophies were more widely taught. The Stoic school concerned itself for the most part with ethics, and it was best known for the emotional ideal—stoicism—that its name still connotes. Stoics worked to achieve a state of detachment from the ups and downs of life. They were studiously indifferent to good or bad luck and worked to insulate themselves from the powerful emotions of lust, anger, jealousy, and remorse. This cultivated apathy, for which the group became famous, was rather surprisingly grounded in cosmology. The Stoic watchword was "Live according to nature." Rejecting emotion might seem anything but natural, but what the Stoics meant by this would have been familiar to Parmenides or Empedocles. Like the earlier philosophers, the Stoics viewed the emotions as a barrier to right understanding. Fear and desire prevented the individual from knowing and embracing logically grounded truth.

As close as this might seem to the views of Plato's followers, there was an important difference. The Platonists argued for an ideal realm distinct from the world of everyday experience. The Stoics, on the other hand, believed that the quotidian world was the only one that existed and that ideas not grounded in reality were fantasies. Once confusing emotion was stripped away, the world could be perceived as it really is—which was of paramount importance to them. For the Stoics, as for Aristotle and Plato, planetary cosmology was a foundation of their system. And like the idealists, they accepted a geocentric view of the structure of the universe.

One of the few surviving texts from the early Greek Stoics is a hymn to Zeus attributed to Cleanthes. In the hymn Zeus is labeled "nature's sovereign" and credited with "governing all by law."[29] This Zeus is a far cry from the Zeus of the *Iliad* or Hesiod's *Theogony*. In the *Theogony* he is sneaky and lustful and fitfully presides over a disorderly family of rash but independently powerful deities. The Stoic gods are more compatible with the Platonic conception of the gods: incapable of doing wrong and united in their will to further the good.

Cleanthes asserts Zeus's omnipotence, especially in relation to nature.

This whole [universe] wheeling around the earth, submits,
Obediently following your lead
As, with unconquered hands, you wield the ready
Forked, fiery, ever living thunderbolt
By whose stroke nature's deeds are all accomplished.
By it you guide the common, all-pervading
Plan interfused with light both great and small
. . . .
No deed on earth is done without you, god

.   .   .   .
Save by the wicked in their arrogance.

Zeus controls the universe and guides the "common, all-pervading plan" that controls its functioning. The Stoics did not believe in a creator god like Plato's craftsman who stood apart from his work, but, as the hymn suggests, they saw the creator more in Aristotelian terms—as an animating and directing presence within creation. Zeus's thunderbolt, which probably represents fire, seems to be an expression of his ubiquitous presence. This presence guides the common, all-pervading plan that is also manifested by the greater and lesser lights, the sun and the moon.

In Cleanthes' hymn, humans can learn the organizational scheme of the universe. That seems to be the sense of the puzzling phrases at the beginning of the hymn,

> For rightly mortals may address you,
> Since, born from you, to them alone of creatures
> Crawling the earth, your echo's trace remains.

Zeus creates everything and is in everything, but only humans have the ability to discern the slim "echo's trace" of divinity in the universe. Realizing this fundamental truth, they may choose to either embrace or reject it.

> Thus good and evil you have joined in one,
> So that the one everlasting plan rules all,
> Which wicked men shun, in their misery
> Always craving more goods, and forfeiting
> Nobility of life by foolishly
> Flouting god's common law—both deaf and blind.
> Madly each rushes to his own destruction.

Clearly, in a system as intricate as this one, where ethical choice is primary, the grounds of choice must be secure. That is why Stoics had to see themselves as living according to nature rather than living out some code that was grounded in opinion or social convention. The geocentric world system recognized by all and underwritten by

an all-pervasive god of truth had to remain secure, or their philosophy crashed with it.

Stoic and Epicurean Philosophy in Rome

The Roman poet Lucretius, who died in 50 BCE, wrote his epic
De rerum natura near the end of his life. A brilliant poet, Lucretius
was also a thoroughgoing and articulate Roman exponent of the Epicurean philosophy, typically painted as the diametrical opposite of
Stoicism. Epicureanism attracted brilliant individuals but could not
compete with the widespread appeal of the Stoics, especially because
of their ability to gain political favor.[30] Stoicism was well suited to
the moralistic and authoritarian tone of the Roman Augustan era; a
"don't ask, don't tell" policy made it impossible to acknowledge an
allegiance to Epicureanism.

Lucretius's poem has many themes in common with Cleanthes'
hymn to Zeus, but from the start, important differences surface. The
all-pervading deity of the *De rerum natura* is not Zeus, father of gods
and hurler of the lightning bolt, but Venus, goddess of love. This
suggests a milder divinity, one more in keeping with the appetites an
Epicurean might be thought to indulge, but Venus is also another
name for one of the twin forces that early Greek writers invoked
under the name of eros, or attraction. The ascendancy of Venus underscores the poem's message. Reading the poem will reveal the truth
about the world, and that truth will erase oppression and fear. The
reader is presumed to be suffering from a "terrifying mental darkness," which the light of day cannot dispel. The only remedy is an
understanding of the "ordered ways of nature." The prescription
sounds remarkably like an approach to the Stoic belief in a god-
centered cosmology, but this is not the case. The Epicurean cosmology is earth focused, but its teachings are unusual:

> Fearfulness holds all mortal men in bondage
> When they observe, on earth and in the heavens,
> Events whose cause no reason can explain,
> And think divinities have made them happen.
> Thus when we see no thing can be created
> From nothing, we shall better understand

Our object: both the source of all creation
And how it comes to pass without the gods.[31]

According to Epicureanism, the universe is a system that follows its own laws—a contention familiar to any Stoic. These iron-bound laws are imposed by fate and necessity, and even the gods cannot break them. Again, no Stoic would be surprised or upset by such an assertion. The twist comes when Lucretius deploys this cosmology as a way of undermining the authority of the gods and erasing the awe and terror that their presumed powers inspire. The universe follows its own course, coming into being and dissolving. The gods do not control or manipulate this process, which means that they cannot reward reverence or punish those who displease them. Right understanding of the universe as an autonomous being driven by its own internal forces liberates humans from misconceptions and the fears that false beliefs create.

There is more to the poem and to the Epicurean philosophy than the removal of negative emotion. "No thing returns to nothing; all, when sundered, return to their material elements." Lucretius sounds this note repeatedly, and although it seems to be little more than what modern physicists call a conservation law, the poet develops its implications in surprising ways.

Raindrops die when the atmospheric father
drops them into the lap of Mother Earth,
But shining crops grow upward, and branches
Leaf out; trees bear ripe fruits.
By these humans and animals are fed;
By these joyful cities bloom with children
And young birds sing in leafy groves.
This fattens the flocks and rebuilds their worn-out bodies
In rich pastures, where white milk streams
From swollen udders; from these the playful young
Come on unsteady limbs to play in the new grass,
Nurtured on strong milk.[32]

The passage amplifies the axiom that matter is neither created nor destroyed, but it would be absurd to reduce it to this bald statement. What the passage records is the death of the raindrop, which is not death at all but a mutation. In an act that mimics impregnation, the sky sends the drop into the lap of earth, where the raindrop's extinction becomes an act of creation. Lucretius follows that creative act into a realm that the philosophical cosmologists had long abandoned. Rather than chronicle events in the starry heavens among the planetary spheres, Lucretius returns to the ground that the hymn writers of Uruk had explored more than two millennia before.[33] Under the influence of the rains the earth buds and blossoms. The fields and trees nourish the herds and the human population. Nourishment leads to fecundity. The city rejoices in the birth of children.

Once the grass has sprouted, herds recover the weight lost during the winter. The ewes give birth. Lambs bounce around in the fields and grow fat on the rich milk of their well-nourished mothers. The drop of rain in its final mutation turns into the drop of milk. Lucretius takes the arid assertion that nothing truly perishes and makes it a joyful celebration of the process by which life perpetuates itself through new growth. In the same way, he reintegrates philosophical cosmology with a deeply felt connection to the world of the city and its surrounding agricultural lands. Because he dismisses heavenly gods and the promise of immortality, his cosmos can reconnect with the earth and the agricultural landscape.

Lucretius represents the road not taken in the philosophical dethroning of First Nature. After adopting a landscape-based cosmology wholeheartedly in the great foundational poem of the Greeks, the pre-Socratics undermined it, and Plato and Aristotle replaced it, substituting a cosmology based on the celestial order. Their new view was underwritten and reinforced by the Stoics, who gained increasing intellectual and political power. In the Roman world, under the emperor Augustus, their power was ascendant. The alternative— an earth-based, landscape-anchored view of order and life—was brilliantly represented in the masterpiece of Epicurean literature, but it was a minority view that was strictly censored. Lucretius's celebration of what I call First Nature became a suppressed counterstatement to an official orthodoxy that divided the material and the spiritual and gave authority to ideals that subordinated landscape.

CHAPTER EIGHT

Roman Agriculture
Three Case Studies

Despite a deep commitment to the ideals of First Nature landscape cosmology, Lucretius had no influence on the conduct of Roman agriculture. Fortunately, the Roman world had little need for a philosophical grounding of its institutions. Farming, the foundation of Roman life, was fully supported by a pantheon of agricultural deities and a calendar packed with agricultural commemorations. The Roman world may seem familiar to many readers. It was hierarchically organized and bureaucratic, strong on infrastructure, and, above all, enduring. Given the role that Rome—along with Greece—still plays as a cultural underpinning of the modern West, its closeness to us seems even greater. But if the Roman Empire existed today and could be directly compared with modern states, our reactions would be very different. By all contemporary measures, the Roman Empire, even at its second-century CE height, would rank as a third-world country. The birth rate was high, but infant mortality and a low life expectancy kept population stable. (In the late years of the empire the demographic picture became decidedly negative, and population declined.) Commerce was widespread, but industry employed only a small fraction of the population, and most jobs were in agriculture.

Wealth, much of it derived from trade in natural resources and food, was concentrated in the hands of a few. Though the empire was dotted with populous cities and towns, the majority of the population lived in the countryside. Most importantly, the Roman world was governed not so much by reason as by ritual. Daily life and especially agricultural life were ruled by tradition and a packed calendar of festivals that commemorated every phase of cultivation. This calendar of commemorations, more than anything else, marks Rome as a premodern society with a mature, articulate, and integrated religious belief system that justified and regulated every aspect of life. This belief system is one of the most detailed pragmatic expressions of the First Nature consensus that has come down to us.

Ritual and the Agricultural Life

The state religion of the Roman Empire was an important part of public life at every level, and it was one of the fundamental ways the state provided cultural support for farming. The gods of Rome's Capitoline temples—the triad of Jupiter, Juno, and Minerva—were formally worshipped in special-purpose buildings set next to the marketplace in every imperial town. The religious responsibilities of the state extended far beyond the worship of the major Olympian gods, and officials performed rites on behalf of the entire society on many days during the year.

The official state cult was attuned to the rhythm of cultivation and celebrated its sponsoring gods in festivals from seedtime to harvest. Sometime in late January a sowing festival was held to honor Ceres, goddess of grain, and Tellus, goddess of the earth. This festival, celebrated in Rome and other cities as the *sementina dies*, was duplicated throughout the countryside in festivals called *paganalia*. Games in honor of Cerealia, another grain goddess, who entered the pantheon in the third century BCE, were held in mid-April. On April 25, priests of Quirinus, one of the avatars of the war god Mars, celebrated the Robigalia festival, in which the god Robigo was asked not to infest the young crops with blight or mold.[1] A festival to Venus on May 1 honored the first of the new wine. August, the month of harvest for many crops, was crowded with festivals. The god Ops—abundance—was honored on the first of the month. Vertumnus, god of orchards, was worshipped in midmonth. Ceres was celebrated again in early October.

Individual households, both urban and rural, were considered to be under the protection of gods who were invoked from time to time in a pattern that echoed the official calendar of festivals. Each household honored the several gods devoted to its care. The lar was the protector spirit of the house, the neighborhood, and the fields. This god was honored at shrines in homes and at crossroads and street intersections in towns and cities. Along with the lar, a family shrine contained representations of the animating spirits of the father and mother of the house. The lares shared their shrine with the penates, whose responsibility was the household stores, the provisions that kept everyone nourished throughout the year. Their combined shrine received frequent sacrifices, in some households as often as twice a day. On the first, ninth, and fifteenth day of the month more elaborate honors were required.

Many other gods and goddesses looked after the family and its well-being. Like the penates, many of them were concerned with nourishment. Priapus was the best-known figure of this kind. His image, a little man with an outsized swollen phallus, represented agricultural fertility. The richness of the fields was his responsibility. Faunus was a general fertility god. Flora was the goddess of flowers. Picumnus and Pilumnus presided over both productivity on the land and the birth of children. All received honors on a regular basis. Throughout cities and the countryside, there were local shrines and sacred places. For help with special problems, individuals could pray to Olympian gods. Venus was invoked in matters of love. Hercules, whose labors involved traveling, was invoked by merchants, as was Hermes, the go-between of the gods and the sponsor of liars and thieves. Asclepius, a god borrowed from the Greeks, was the patron of healing, and his shrines were centers for healing as well as the dissemination of medical knowledge.

Cincinnatus and Farming

If the *Oeconomicus* is accurate, the small farmer was the backbone of Greek agriculture. In a heavily mythologized vision of the Roman past, the historian Livy represented Lucius Quinctius Cincinnatus,

a Roman farmer, as the ideal of early Roman rule. Having served as
consul in 460 BCE, Cincinnatus was called on again some three years
later to serve the state in an extraordinary capacity. In a battle with
a neighboring city, a Roman army had been surrounded. The Senate
sent emissaries to Cincinnatus, whom they found plowing a field at
his farm. The delegation informed Cincinnatus that he had been
named dictator for six months with absolute authority over the state
and the army. As dictator, Cincinnatus organized his forces and
opened negotiations with the enemy that resulted in a bloodless victory. Sixteen days after his appointment, with his work completed,
he resigned and returned to his farm.[2]

Cincinnatus was the proprietor of a small family farm like the
one Xenophon described in *Oeconomicus*. Cincinnatus was also a
Roman citizen prominent enough to be a member of the Senate. In
the earliest period of Rome's history, citizens lived both inside and
outside the city limits. They met in the forum on market day to decide issues of law and policy. Market day was the most convenient
time for those living outside the city to attend these meetings. In
time, however, the coordination between market day and assembly
day was deliberately broken. From then on, power was in the hands
of those within the city walls; Romans who lived on the periphery
were disenfranchised.

The Roman republic began as a polis—a cooperative urban-farm
community. The cooperation ended in political divorce, and the city
emerged not just as the seat of government but as the ideal of political organization. The model of all forms of Roman administration
was the city of Rome. Political enfranchisement within every successive Roman polity, whether it was widely or loosely extended, was
termed "citizenship"—literally, "membership in the city." Like many
Greeks, Romans exalted the city and substituted the rationale of its
government for the more inclusive enfranchisement of both city
dweller and exurbanite that the polis had embodied.

On the social side, the divide was equally important. A Roman of
standing was a city dweller, focused on the business, the legal conflicts, and the social life of either the capital or a city that imitated
its characteristics. The manners and perspective of city dwellers,
their *urbanitas*—urbanity—were the hallmark of proper behavior.
Though a founding father like Cincinnatus might be admired for

his simplicity, the manners of real country people were despised. When Romans went into the country, as they often did, it was to enter a space that was defined most clearly by an absence. The countryside provided relief from the pressures, temptations, and risks of the city. The horror of every Roman of importance was real rustication— losing touch with the urban scene and being forced to live life in the boondocks.[3] Once the Roman Republic became the Roman Empire, suburban retreats gained in popularity among wealthy Romans. These second homes were within easy reach of the cities, and from the most desirable of them, the city was actually visible, at the end of a long garden, say, and through a vista framed by trees. When the busy public servants of the imperial period—Livy's readers—returned to their farms, it was not to resume their interrupted plowing but to carry out an entirely metaphorical action. They were participating in a way of life that had been packaged and idealized through literature, architecture, and the manipulation of landscape.

Meanwhile, the agricultural countryside carried on its own productive life. That life was, in many instances, attached directly to properties owned by urban dwellers, but there were also many different structures that sustained agriculture. Some of these structures were grandfathered into the Roman Empire and reflected the adaptive use of landscapes by indigenous peoples.

Area One: The Biferno Valley

The Biferno Valley in southeastern Italy is one of the most intensively studied agricultural regions of the Roman world. The Biferno River begins in the Appenines, the spine of the peninsula, not far from the modern city of Campobasso. It flows northeastward some fifty miles to empty into the Adriatic Sea near Termoli. The Appenines guard the western entrance to the river valley, and ridges on the east separate its drainage basin from the Trigno River to the north and the Fortore to the south. This region offers a variety of environments, from mountain slopes to bottomlands, that have been inhabited and exploited for millennia. During the 1970s the British archaeologist Graeme Barker and a team of collaborators carried out a series of pioneering surveys there. Additional studies in the following decades led to a two-volume publication of their remarkable data in 1995.[4]

In historic times the valley was a stronghold of the Samnites, one of the most powerful and enduring antagonists of the Romans in their battle to subdue the Italian Peninsula. Conflict between the rivals began in the fourth century BCE and continued until the Romans finally prevailed around 80 BCE. Before the Romans arrived, the Samnites had organized the river valley into two separate regions, which reflected important differences in terrain, climate, and culture. Dominated by the mountain flanks, the upper valley was cooler; its terrain was steep and its soils shallow. In the lower valley the climate was milder; the ground was flat, and the alluvial soils were deep and rich. Because of these different conditions and the different opportunities that they offered, the Samnites used each part of their territory in different ways.

Hill forts in the uplands guarded the mountain passes and protected the valley from invasion. Again and again they held the front line in the multicentury warfare between Samnites and Romans. Guarding the border was their primary role, but they also protected upland grazing from raiders. Middle-altitude areas with flatter lands supported small villages. These, too, might be fortified, though less substantially than the upland outposts. Pathways connected these villages with the forts and with upland pastures. At the junctions of these pathways, the Samnites built shrines. Some of the largest and wealthiest were the scenes of costly animal sacrifices. Others were small and undistinguished.

Both small and large farms dotted the countryside. Villagers apparently worked fields within walking distance and returned to their homes at night. More distant land with available water and workable soils was cultivated by farmers who lived year-round in relative isolation. The lower altitudes at which villages and farms flourished made cultivation of grain and other crops, especially grapes, possible. An excavated Samnite farmhouse may be typical of the architecture. The building, made of local limestone, is square, about forty feet on each side. Its main entrance leads to a central courtyard surrounded by rooms that are for the most part also square. Hearths in two of them suggest that they were used for eating and sleeping. Some of the interior rooms appear to have been used for grain storage. Stables and sheds stood against the southeast wall of the structure. There was plenty of timber in the region for building. Tiles manufactured locally covered roofs. While some richer farms may have had more elaborate architecture, the remains of huts scattered through the valley suggest that a portion of the population lived in much more primitive shelters.

With the exception of the hill forts, upland settlement and building types—towns, farms, villas, and shrines—were widespread in the lower valley as well. What distinguished the two zones was the presence of a large and powerful city in the flatlands. This city, called Larinum, controlled the fields in the floodplain of the Biferno. It also sat at the nexus of roads that served the entire region. Larinum had an organized grid of streets, impressive buildings made of dressed stone, a separate temple quarter, and an area were artisans congregated. Its most valuable exports were grain and wool. Larinum was evidently a cosmopolitan center where speakers of the Samnite language, Oscan, mingled with speakers of Latin and Greek.

Grain was cultivated on the valley floor, and the country around Larinum was said to be especially fertile. Grapes and olives grew abundantly, but there is no evidence of trade in these commodities. Even in the lower valley, the Samnites raised a great many animals. Sheep and goats were evidently favored, with pigs running a close second. The Samnites also raised cattle for plowing and kept small numbers of horses. Pork was the most commonly available meat, but pigs were typically slaughtered near important upland shrines and consumed in ritual feasts. Sheep, goats, and cattle were slaughtered more rarely, typically at the end of their working lives. Some hunting still went on along the mountain slopes, and an occasional deer or rabbit was killed. People in the lower valley supplemented their diet with fish, including some deepwater species, as well as shellfish and oysters.

Rome's conquest of Samnium in 80 BCE led to Romanization, but the Samnite base was preserved. The conquerors did not substitute Romans for the indigenous people or Roman practices for traditional ones. Under Roman rule, people in the region did about the same things that they had always done, but they did them more intensively and with a greater level of organization. By integrating the

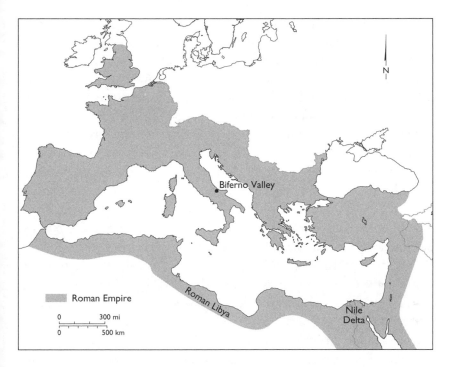

The Roman Empire encompassed the entire Mediterranean Sea at the end of the fourth century.

valley into their own international economy, the Romans brought wealth into the region in amounts that exceeded the investment in infrastructure and administration that the Samnites had made.

With the resolution of conflict between the Romans and the Samnites, the hill forts protecting the border were abandoned as unnecessary. On a few sites, Roman towns supplanted Samnite villages. Saepinum in the upper valley was one of these. Its street grid and many of its houses remained in place but were incorporated into an urban pattern that within a few years looked Roman. The town was walled, and there were gates allowing access to two main roads that crossed at the heart of the town. In a Roman colony planted in open country, these roads would have been oriented due north and south and would have met in the center of town. The builders here worked with old roads that were not geographically oriented, did not meet at right angles, and did not intersect in the center. Still, the

Roman engineers used their intersection as a location for defining structures. They built a forum and a capitolium, a temple dedicated to the three principal gods of the Roman state. Near it was a basilica, where law courts met. These government buildings were surrounded by houses, shops, and workshops and by a building that excavators have identified as a slaughterhouse. On the edge of town there were a theater and public baths. An aqueduct supplied the city with water. It appears that the fields outside the towns were resurveyed in the Roman period. There is sketchy evidence of what is called centuriation, the gridlike laying out of rectilinear fields that Roman surveyors created. Tombs, again typical of Roman towns, lined the roads into Saepinum. Prominent families built their monuments as close to the town as possible and made them as lavish as they could afford.

A Samnite Rip Van Winkle returning home after many years would have found the fields around the town bigger and more regular. He would have been shocked by the tombs and surprised at the height and strength of the town wall. The slaughtering of animals in the city center rather than in a shrine, like the consumption of meat in a nonreligious setting, might have struck him as improper. Despite these innovations, he would probably still have been able to find his home and the street he grew up on, but the old neighborhood would now be embedded in a town that bore all the marks of standardized Roman urbanism. The city would have been the same on the neighborhood scale but dramatically different on a large scale.

In the lower valley the Roman style of agriculture had its greatest impact both in the towns and in the countryside. The modest and rough-built Samnite farmsteads that had served as the base for cultivation throughout the territory were replaced in the lowlands by fewer and larger Roman villas. An excavation at Matrice shows how a Samnite farmstead grew into a larger Roman country house in the early years of occupation and then into an extensive villa in the Roman imperial period. The rough Samnite walls enclosing a small area survived and formed the core of the house throughout its lifetime. Rather than build over that area, owners in the Roman era added on to it. A first set of walls, apparently built in the early years of occupation, simply enlarged the perimeter of the old compound while keeping its shape and proportions. Building in the imperial period took a different direction. The older structures were retained, but additions more than doubled the size of the house. Its stolid square shape was modified to produce a building that was either a long rectangle or one with two end blocks of rooms united by a long corridor.

Excavations at other sites confirm what literary sources describe, that the country homes of wealthy Romans who settled in the region were comfortable and elegantly decorated. Remains of terra-cotta pipes show that some villas had water distribution systems that were analogous to those of towns and cities. Some rooms, especially rooms with baths, which many larger villas included, were heated by furnaces that pumped hot air through spaces beneath their floors. Walls might be covered with fresco paintings or veneered with marble. Colorful mosaics decorated bare floors. These refined and expensive features were confined to the part of the villa reserved for owners and guests; it was called the *pars urbana*. The rest of the farm population lived in much more modest quarters, on the site but at a distance. The best evidence of their presence comes from cemeteries.

The basis of the wealth that produced the villas and justified the employment of vast numbers of laborers and the purchase of numbers of slaves was large-scale agriculture. Through an accident of history we have some literary evidence of that development. Wealthy Romans from the town of Larinum figured in a criminal case that Cicero argued. His speech for the defense, published as the *Pro A. Cluentio*, contains incidental details of the agribusiness that made the Romanized town and its leading inhabitants wealthy. The client is described as owning multiple houses, commercial interests, and livestock in the countryside around Larinum. References elsewhere in the argument suggest that the herds included pigs that were slaughtered for market and sheep that moved from winter grazing in the fields outside the town to summer pastures that were either in the mountains where the Samnites had pastured flocks or in upland fields that lay to the south in Apulia.

Both the elegant villas and the wealthy town were centers of agricultural production that was similar in kind to the cultivation practiced by the Samnites but notably different in scale. Samnite farmers had always raised pigs, but pork production expanded during the Roman period, and evidence from throughout the Roman world shows that pork was the Romans' favorite meat. For them it was a decidedly secular food, and pork production in the empire became a profitable industry. Pigs can be driven to market, and this practice continued well into the imperial period, but pork can also be cured in salt or smoked, which increases its shelf life and its economic potential.

After 100 CE or so, cultivation changed in the Biferno Valley. The inhabitants stopped trying to compete as suppliers of grain, wine, and oil and seem instead to have concentrated on herding. The record of silt deposits at the river's mouth shows that the fields the Romans had opened up in the early years of their occupation were no longer worked annually. They were being allowed to revert to pasture as the business of the region shifted from diverse agricultural production to a monoculture driven by market forces. The money was in pigs and sheep, and the grain fields (and their annual silt deposits) shrank as the pastures grew.

Area Two: Roman Libya

About the same time that Biferno Valley producers were putting their money into pork futures, farmers on the other side of the Mediterranean were investing in a remarkable kind of infrastructure. The Romans had won North Africa from the Carthaginians during a long series of wars that culminated in a decisive victory in the second century BCE. Not until two centuries later, however, did Rome consolidate control over the former enemy and began to integrate Carthaginian territory into its regional economy. Roman garrisons kept the peace, and Roman administrators established boundaries to control the indigenous Berber people. In Libya, as in the Biferno Valley, development was sparked by Roman occupation but carried out by local farmers. What distinguished development in Libya from that in the Biferno Valley was the difference in climate and in the Roman technologies that made agriculture possible there.

Modern Libya, like the rest of North Africa, is arid, except in areas along its Mediterranean coast. Inland annual rainfall averages one to three inches per year. It is generally agreed that farming that relies on rainfall requires a minimum of about eight inches annually. In contemporary North Africa, areas of lower rainfall are classified as pre-desert. No farming takes place there. Yet it was these arid regions that sustained not just subsistence agriculture but marketable crops in the Roman period.[5]

The Romans have always been recognized for their genius in water management. Roman aqueducts running across the landscape on arcades that rise or fall with the terrain are found wherever they built towns and cities. Despite their virtuoso handling of urban water supplies, the Romans are not particularly known for irrigation projects. Most of the areas where they built did not require them. But in Libya, on the threshold of the desert, irrigation offered the only hope for agricultural success.

The structures that began to appear in the first century CE did not look anything like aqueducts, and they did not perform exactly the same work, though there were sizable overlaps. Roman aqueducts began far from the city in a network that gathered surface or spring water and fed it into the arcaded channels that carried the water from its source to its outlet. In the Libyan system, the job of collecting water was all important and the transfer insignificant. Essentially, the Libyan system was an improvement on floodwater farming, the earliest form of Mediterranean agriculture that has been identified. Just as the traditional system had done thousands of years before, the Libyan system relied on wadis—dry ravines—to concentrate seasonal rain. Rainfall on each square foot of ground might be scanty, but the wadi and its feeders collected the water that fell over a wide area. That water was directed to fields that were much smaller than the collection area. This disproportion effectively multiplied the amount of rainfall available for agriculture. Three inches of rain collected from a hundred acres become thirty inches of rain when spread over only ten acres. The collection could not be 100 percent efficient, but the system still multiplied the amount of rainfall available to each square foot of cultivated land from a trickle to an amount that was sufficient to nourish crops.

The heart of the Libyan system was a series of barriers that slowed runoff and captured water. Enormous effort was invested in clearing land of stones, transporting the stones, and using them to build not just one dam at a wadi mouth but a series of dams in every wadi and its tributaries. This was a public work on an enormous scale, every bit as complex and extensive as an aqueduct system, but the character of the work was such that the dams could not be built, supervised, or maintained as a single project. The system of dams in one wadi and its feeders was entirely independent of the system in another. Both worked on the same principles, but their builders needed to understand the particular dynamics of each individual watershed.

Building the dams not only depended on local expertise but demanded extraordinary commitments of local labor. There must have been master wall builders who directed construction, but the job depended on a huge workforce. People were needed to collect stones to be transported to multiple worksites. More people were required to carry and pile up the stones in hundreds of separate sites. Walls properly sited and built to hold water and withstand the force of floods required skilled labor. Like so many of the forms of labor on which the traditional agriculture of the Mediterranean depended, this complex task could not be duplicated by earth-moving machines. Like terracing or cultivating crops under trees by hand, water collection on this scale demanded incessant, skilled manual labor in quantities and of a kind that is unavailable in most areas of today's industrialized world; it is certainly unavailable in contemporary Libya. The captured water was fed into selected fields along the sides of the wadis and especially in the broader and flatter areas where the wadis ended in alluvial fans. By impounding the water during the brief rainy season, conserving it, and selectively releasing it to the fields, crops could be produced in areas that had been only modestly productive before this period and that have declined dramatically in productivity since about 700 CE.

Evidence from archaeological digs shows that during the Roman era Libyan farmers cultivated a broad range of crops in these carefully tended plots. They grew barley, durum wheat, bread wheat, lentils, peas, field peas, and watermelons. They produced oil from olives, safflower, and flaxseed. Their diet was sweetened with a number of fruits, including grapes, figs, almonds, pomegranates, peaches, and dates.

Remains of slaughtered domestic animals include sheep, goats, cattle, pigs, camels, and a few chickens. Large game like antelope and gazelle and smaller animals like rabbit, porcupine, and even jackals supplemented the meat ration. Hunting not only enriched the diet; it also destroyed animals that might otherwise have eaten the grain in the fields or competed with the herds for forage. During part of the year, domestic animals were pastured in the grain fields, where they could graze on the stubble and where their dung increased the fertility of the soil. There is also evidence that Libyan farmers planted a relative of the alfalfa plant, a crop that significantly increases the productivity of arid fields.[6]

What was most astonishing to the archaeologists who surveyed the region was not the widespread evidence of subsistence farming but dramatic evidence that the region had produced a marketable crop. Olive presses were found everywhere in the area, and experts estimate that the annual export of oil to Rome probably totaled a million liters. More oil went to other markets around the Mediterranean.[7] Pollen evidence confirms that the bulk of what the Libyans cultivated in their carefully watered fields was olive trees. Other food crops may have been grown underneath the olive trees in many areas.

The Roman demand for agricultural products was unprecedented, and their organization of the entire Mediterranean basin into a single market economy has never been duplicated. Olive oil from Libya and pork from the Biferno Valley were only a small portion of the many agricultural goods that this market supplied. As the Roman dominance of the Mediterranean disappeared, local agriculture changed. Pioneering historians misperceived the causes of this shift and attributed it to environmental neglect: "The image of the ruined cities of North Africa, from which olive oil and timber were exported in ancient times but which later were buried beneath the desert sand, epitomizes the environmental factor in the decline of civilization."[8]

This much-repeated argument about desertification holds that intensive agriculture leads to overuse of soil and depletion of its nutrients. Wind or water erosion follows, and then the transformation of productive regions into desert or semidesert. This sequence does not fit the Libyan evidence, however. Intensive agriculture there led to soil enrichment, not depletion. Political collapse, not environmental exhaustion, led to the abandonment of the Libyan fields. Roman North Africa did not fail in its job of producing food for the regional market. Just the opposite occurred: an international market failure brought on by invasion and fragmentation within the Roman Empire made export based agriculture unsustainable. Political change, not environmental irresponsibility, led to the abandonment of productive infrastructure in North Africa.

Area Three: Egypt

The destinies of Roman politicians have been described as rising and falling with the amount of bread supplied to the large population of the capital city. Typical arguments suggest that the imperial houses won the goodwill of the Roman poor through lavish public entertainments and an unending supply of free food—the "bread and circuses" (*panem et circenses*) that the satirist Juvenal talked about. It is certain that grain shortages had great political repercussions and that the demand for grain in Rome was necessarily vast. An estimated 150,000 tons of wheat came to the city from Egypt every year, and that was only one source. Sicily also provided a huge amount. It happens that the archaeological evidence for the Egyptian supply is more complete than the evidence for other regions.

In Egypt as elsewhere, the grain that found its way to Rome came from two sources. Taxes imposed by the Roman Empire on those that it controlled were often paid not in money but in produce. It was useful to the state to collect taxes in the form of grain, which it could redistribute. Much of the grain collected in this way went to feed the Roman armies, which were more or less constantly engaged on the various frontiers of the empire. A certain percentage of it fed the slaves in public enterprises. Only a portion of it found its way into the grain ships heading to Rome.[9] The second major source of Egyptian supply was imperial properties. One of the peculiar features of the Roman Empire was the accumulation by successive emperors of large estates in every part of the world. These estates in time became an imperial legacy. Though they belonged to the imperial family, they were typically put to use for the benefit of the population as a whole. In Egypt the imperial family owned enormous estates that provided much of the grain that Roman citizens consumed.

As we saw in Chapter 4, archaeology in Egypt traditionally focused on the tombs and temples that spread along the Nile Valley south of Cairo. In the great age of Egyptology, interest in the era of Roman occupation was minimal. Lack of interest coupled with a bias against exploring the life of ordinary citizens meant that many sites were unexplored. Only in recent decades have survey archaeology and selective digs opened up the literally thousands of sites in the Delta that reflect the centuries of Roman occupation and the agricultural communities and estates that sustained it.[10]

Archaeological discoveries in the Delta suggest that Romanization altered the landscape there in predictable ways. Romans built roads that made communications faster and more secure between cities and towns. Roads also made it easier for authorities and military forces to respond to emergencies and streamlined commerce between inland areas, the agricultural zone, and the port of Alexandria. At the same time that roads were improved, canals linking the multiple branches of the Nile were built, and much of the grain produced in the region was floated in barges to the port. Villages that had been small and disorganized in the pre-Roman period grew larger; their streets now met at right angles, and in larger towns the typical Roman complex of forum and capitolium took center position. Population appears to have increased—by some estimates, to levels that were not matched again until the nineteenth century. The main crop of the region was wheat, and Roman farming and field improvement combined with traditional Egyptian techniques of field irrigation to produce large yields. These crops fed the agricultural communities, the city of Alexandria, and the privileged citizens of Rome. Between the fall of the western Roman Empire and the Muslim capture of Egypt, the same fields provided grain for Constantinople (now Istanbul), the eastern capital of the empire.

Although the Romans added some dikes and canals to the Nile and its tributaries, they made no attempt to alter the annual flooding schedule of the Nile, so the Egyptian agricultural season remained what it had been. Grain was harvested early in the year and stored in dockside warehouses in Alexandria. Some portion of the Roman grain fleet probably overwintered in Egypt. The ships were loaded soon after the harvest but were held in port until the winter weather with its strong winds and unpredictable storms had subsided. Because of the prevailing winds, the route out of Egypt had to be circuitous. Some ships headed straight north along the eastern coast of the Mediterranean toward Cyprus. There they turned west toward the island of Rhodes. From Rhodes the route led south of Crete to Malta. From Malta the fleet turned north toward the Straits of Messina, which separate Sicily and Italy. Once through the straits the ships followed the coast to the port of Ostia. An alternative route lay along the North African coast with a sharp northern turn off Libya. Once in Italy, small ships could sail directly up the Tiber to be unloaded at the commercial docks on both sides of the river below Tiber Island. Larger ships were emptied in Ostia, and their cargoes were transferred to barges that could navigate the river. The luckiest and fastest ships might complete the trip in a month. The trip between Alexandria and Rome—cities that are no more than twelve hundred miles apart—more commonly took two months.[11]

For the first and only time in history, Rome capitalized on the full potential for productivity and exchange within the Mediterranean basin. Goods from every part of that diverse ecozone circulated through the region. Areas that had not flourished before and have been barren since were important parts of an intricate region-wide web of production and exchange. Though the countryside had long given way to the city as the dominant political and social institution, Rome remained an agricultural society. It was characterized by high rural populations and narrowly held wealth that rested primarily on commerce in agricultural commodities. The empire functioned because Roman agriculture was widespread and effective. It sustained the lives of citizens, and it maintained, indeed increased, the productivity of its soils. Had it not been marred by extensive and cruel agricultural slavery, we could cheer its unmatched record of sustained success.

CHAPTER NINE

Medieval Christian
Ecological Understanding

The dissolution of the Roman Empire in the western Mediterranean brought on one of the most complete social changes that the region has ever experienced. Every person, rich or poor, cleric or lay, was affected. The collapse of central power and the central bureaucracy was accompanied by dramatic changes in transport, trade, and economic life. Disintegration of the regional networks that supported large-scale commercial farming eradicated the most characteristic form of Roman agriculture. What survived at every level of daily life were fragments of a broken system.

The consequences of all this disruption might well have been devastating for the environment. Many scholars have assumed that this was the case. Some have argued that a breakdown in law and custom must have left forests without protection and subject to irresponsible grazing and cutting. Others reason that the abandonment of large-field agriculture meant the cultivation of shallower upland soils with a high potential for erosion. These assertions, however, are not been borne out by the facts. Indeed, the pragmatic response to the destruction of the Roman way of doing agribusiness was one of the brightest occurrences in the history of the Middle Ages. The regional agricultural heritage was resilient enough to absorb the loss of commercial farming and herding and to adjust to new market conditions. Peasant farmers carried on the rhythms of the First Nature consensus while they innovated and adapted.

The greatest attack on the consensus came from educated people. In the late Roman period, as traditional elites were marginalized, cults and occult philosophies replaced political life, from which all but a few were excluded. With the conversion of the empire to Christianity in the mid-fourth century CE, the religious underpinnings of First Nature were replaced with a theology that had little place for the agricultural landscape or for nature itself. The adoption of Christianity suppressed the multiple cultural practices and liturgies that had, in a thousand subtle ways, articulated the consensus. Had it not been for the pragmatic survival of the First Nature consensus in the work of generations of farmers and shepherds on the land, it would have perished completely in the western Mediterranean with the fall of Rome.

Medieval Agriculture in the Christian World

The fifth-century collapse of the empire in the West left authority and responsibility there in the hands of the Catholic Church. The pope assumed control of a share of imperial territories. From Rome, he ruled directly over a territory in the middle of the Italian Peninsula with fluid boundaries, a territory that today has shrunk to the limits of Vatican City. The church was a spiritual institution suddenly charged with immense secular responsibility, a task for which it had extremely limited preparation and one in which it had little real interest given its otherworldly perspective. The Roman infrastructure—cities with their public amenities, sewers, and aqueducts, the roads that connected the empire—was left to care for itself. The church had insufficient military power to protect its territory and no navy to protect its trade. The large estates that had sustained Roman agriculture in the imperial period disappeared along with the international trade in grain, oil, and wine. Shipping in the western Mediterranean almost vanished. Though more stable, the eastern Mediterranean also experienced the effects of invasion. A period characterized by large-scale commercial agriculture was followed by a period of social turmoil.[1] The large estates of rich entrepreneurs and high government officials were fragmented. As the interdependency of different regions in the Mediterranean basin collapsed, towns and villages were forced to become self-sufficient, and many simply disappeared.

Along with the collapse of international trade and large-scale farming came a shift in land use. According to some historians, the end of Roman estate farming meant that areas suitable for large-scale cultivation were either abandoned or allowed to revert to pasture. The money crops, to the extent that these existed at all, ceased to be products like wheat, barley, and oats and became instead the products of pasturage. Sheep were the only late antique and medieval agricultural commodity in the western Mediterranean. Most Western agriculture became subsistence farming—in striking contrast to the agriculture of the Roman past and, as we will see, in equally striking contrast to the agriculture of the Islamic countries. Crops were produced for local consumption and no longer for trade.

Fields of the kinds that the Romans had used for their commercial farming of cereal crops were typically in lowlands, where flat terrain and alluvial soils favored the creation and cultivation of big fields. Abandoning these fields meant abandoning lowland agriculture in favor of upland farms. Population decline was one cause of the shift, but lowlands were also more vulnerable to attack from marauders and pirates. When the security of the seas could no longer be guaranteed, raiders were a recurrent menace. But fear of coastal raiders was not the only reason to abandon what had been the richest agricultural lands of the Romans. Even more than the threat of piracy, what kept the lowlands from being brought back under cultivation was malaria.

Malaria is a disease that thrives in warm weather wherever there are pools of stagnant fresh water. The excavations at Metaponto have shown that many Greek colonists in southern Italy suffered from malaria.[2] During the long centuries when Roman farmers cultivated the lowlands, it has been argued, malaria was kept at bay by the steady draining of marshes and wetlands. When intensive work on the land ended, the wetlands reformed and, with them, the habitat of the anopheles mosquito. Over centuries, mosquitoes reclaimed the coastal and riverine areas of the Mediterranean and transformed them from the heartland of grain production to abandoned and dangerous environments valuable as winter pasture for livestock but otherwise unhealthy and uninhabitable. The loss of these resources meant that the most fertile and productive soils in the region were out of bounds. Post-Roman populations were forced to rely instead on uplands where the soils were thinner, less nutrient-rich, and more fragile. Those fields could not produce the same number of food calories that the older fields had produced, and the inevitable consequence was a smaller population.

Mountain soils also favored different kinds of crops. Grain growing was impacted most heavily; olives and other tree crops, grapes, and vegetables were less affected. As one historian explains, "Mountains and hills were also more likely to be covered with woodlands than lowland areas. During the Roman era, these woodlands were protected. Forest legislation under the Roman Republic dates to the fifth century BC. The Republic claimed ownership of forests in land it controlled and relied on a cadre of forest custodians to guard and patrol it. This ancient 'forest service' eventually became responsible for tending and managing the forests, for controlling harvests, and for protecting of watersheds."[3]

With the destruction of the Roman government, control over forests all but disappeared. In the absence of control, forest resources were subject to abuse. Trees might be cut down for building or firewood. Grazing animals like goats, who are especially destructive of young trees and green shoots, might be turned loose in them. What resulted?

> There is a clear indication that the human-induced clearings
> . . . were enhanced by the political crises of the 3rd and 5th
> centuries AD and they became stronger in the Middle Ages
> because of the large-scale expansion of sheep and goat herding, which replaced the previous agricultural economy, and
> because of the absence of any organized agricultural policy
> throughout the Middle Ages. . . .
> In other words, the largest landscape change occurred
> after the Roman Classical Period, and the previous clearings
> had been relatively minor until that time. So, the Roman
> Classical Period vegetation can be considered a close ap-

proximation to what the vegetation might be in present times if it had not been destroyed by human action.[4]

While this analysis is substantially correct in its appreciation of Roman conservation, like most descriptions that depend on deforestation as a primary cause of landscape degradation, it overstates the extent to which widespread forest use meant forest clearance. Even in the absence of government control and supervision, many forces limited the exploitation of woodlands. Big timber is valuable and likely to attract the interest and protection of powerful people whether they are figures of authority or not, so dense forests and sizable woodlands would typically have been off-limits to random exploitation. Jobs like building ships and roofing large structures require big timber. Demand was low, since shipbuilding was pointless when commerce was virtually nonexistent, and large structures are more usually built when population is increasing and cities are growing. Even where demand existed, transport remained a problem. The high cost and difficulty of felling a great tree was negligible compared with the expense and challenge of moving timber overland from the forest where it was harvested to the shipyard or building site where it was to be used.[5]

A factor that is harder for us to appreciate in an age when chainsaws and wood splitters are widely available is the technological limitation on harvesting forest giants. Big trees contain many times the potential heat energy of small trees, but harvesting them and reducing them to wood that is useful for burning is a formidable task. The small hand tools that most villagers possessed were hardly up to the job. Even if a tree were to be successfully felled, the job of cutting it into pieces small enough to feed a cooking fire still remained. A householder was better off gathering and using small pieces of wood. For fires, fallen or hanging branches that had dried out over the course of a year or so were preferable.

Two forest management techniques that Roman writers on farming advocated continued to be widely used after the fall of Rome. They survived not because they were mandated but because they were practical methods of producing renewable supplies of the small-dimension wood that met the needs of farmers. These techniques, known as coppicing and pollarding, are occasionally still practiced

today, and many Mediterranean forests still bear the marks of this
kind of cultivation. The purpose of coppicing is to transform a single-
trunked tree into a producer of multiple fast-growing shoots that
can be periodically harvested. Mature trees are cut to the ground,
then allowed to sprout multiple trunks. A coppiced woodland is typically divided into sections that are harvested on a rotating basis. The
length of the rotation depends on the speed with which the trees
grow and the use to which the branches are to be put. Fast-growing
trees might be harvested every four years; slower-growing trees, like
oak, might require a fifty-year rotation. Instead of big trunks difficult to harvest and slow to regrow, coppiced woods produce multiple small-diameter sticks and poles. Pollarding works on the same
principle as coppicing, but trees that are pollarded are cut back to
a main trunk rather than to the ground.[6] Where wild or domestic
animals graze in forests, the shoots that grow from coppiced trees
at ground level are likely to be eaten. With pollarded trees the productive source of new growth is raised above the level where animals
browse.

Neither deforestation nor upland erosion was widespread after
the fall of Rome. Terracing enriched upland soils rather than depleting them. Freed slaves, Roman tenants, and the families of migrat-
ing tribes appear to have adapted well to changed conditions. They
fell back on the time-tested technologies of the First Nature consensus, cultivating olives, figs, and grapes and herding sheep. Grain,
the largest Roman crop, continued to be raised on small plots or on
terraces shaded by olive trees or vines. The sustainable agriculture
that had characterized the region before the great Roman explosion
once again served the inhabitants.

Christianity and First Nature

While the pragmatic conduct of agriculture kept the First Nature
consensus active on the land, its articulation in the sacred calendar
of the empire and the households of its people came to an abrupt
end. It was not the invasions of the barbarians or the destruction of
Roman infrastructure that muted this cultural conversation. The
force that brought the expression of the consensus to near silence
was the newly institutionalized imperial faith, Christianity.

Roman religion had celebrated the rhythms of daily life and ritualized the agricultural cycle, but the state gods offered no ethical guidance and little comfort to individuals eager for personal or mystical religious experience.[7] This lack of personal religion became more keenly felt as political developments changed the social character of the Roman Empire. Before the imperial period, active public service was the ideal for Romans of status. The best expression of a prominent Roman's character was his record of holding government office. He began his career by seeking election to a minor position, and with connections, luck, and perseverance he would progress up the public hierarchy throughout his life. In the imperial period, public service became both more precarious and more uncommon. Slaves of the imperial household assumed much of the work of government. Individuals were forced to look elsewhere for a sense of personal fulfillment. Many found it in religion; others found it in the philosophical schools.

By a series of imperial acts, Constantine and his successors changed the official religious life of the empire. Constantine chose to lend imperial support to a single religion that he thought could satisfy both the state's need for divine underwriting and an individual's longing for religious assurance. In Rome, Constantine and his successors managed the difficult public relations job of reconciling the newly tolerated faith with the city's religious heritage. The temples of the gods in the city's historic center were kept up, and Christian worship was excluded. The large buildings that the Christian community required were provided at imperial expense and on imperial lands on the city's margins.

Within the empire as a whole, Constantine took a similar approach to reconciling the new religion with the old. Aware that Rome could never be divorced from what was becoming its "pagan" past, Constantine founded a new capital in the East. Byzantium, later named Constantinople (and even later, Istanbul), was built virtually from scratch to express the union between the Christian emperor and his Christian state. Though power sharing between Rome and Byzantium, between East and West, was the ideal, the concentration of imperial power there ended up marginalizing not just Rome but the entire western Mediterranean.

The ecological implications of the official adoption of Christianity were far-reaching. When Christianity became the cosmological grounding of the Roman Empire, it canceled the official cult of state worship and ended the festivals that marked the high points of the agricultural year. This was in keeping with Christianity's refusal to support religious toleration, but it also reflected the lack of interest among Christian theologians in the productive landscape. Jesus had little to say about agriculture, domestic animals, or indeed about nature in general. He referred to people involved with these concerns but only in a metaphorical way. Afloat on the Sea of Galilee, he urged his disciples to become "fishers of men." Sheep and shepherds play a large part in the metaphorical language of the New Testament, too, as they had in the Old. Jesus told the parable of the good shepherd and is himself referred to as both the Good Shepherd and the Lamb of God.

In his actions, as in his language, Jesus continually emphasized his immunity to natural law and natural causation. He walked on water. He turned water into wine. He raised the dead; he cured the blind, the lame, and the paralytic. At the end of his life, though he died, he rose from the grave and reinhabited his own body marked with the telltale wounds of his crucifixion. Jesus's metaphors and his miracles recalled the transcendent Old Testament God, for whom nature was a vehicle of self-expression accommodated to human understanding, rather than a sphere of being in which he occupied a fixed place. Jesus' main concern throughout his brief ministry was to outline the pathway to eternal life for his followers. He had little concern with the temporal world, and the first generations of his adherents were equally unworldly. The church was able to maintain this outlook even after the empire's adoption of Christianity because the business of daily life remained entirely in the hands of a well-established imperial bureaucracy.

There was no separation of church and state in imperial Rome, but there was certainly a division of labor between the two powers. Once the Christian church was in place, it determined imperial cosmology, but the day-to-day interactions between humans and the productive world were left to the bureaucratic state. Unlike the followers of traditional Roman cults, Christians had no duty to the natural world. They did not celebrate its fertility at shrines to Priapus or honor the source of their nourishment by sacrifices to the penates.

For Christians, food and the fields were completely secularized, and although they had the potential to spark idolatrous worship, they had no positive religious meaning at all. In this sense, Christianity was a novel religion. The religions that the region had known before Christian conversion had regulated every aspect of life. Christianity concerned itself only with human ethical behavior and with the fate of human souls in this life and the next. The condition of the western Mediterranean environment today is largely a consequence of these two factors: the silence of Jesus (and, in time, Mohammad) on matters relating to ecology and the sharp divide between spiritual and pragmatic responsibility within the Roman Empire after its official conversion.[8]

In a groundbreaking article, the historian Lynn White neatly defined the antagonism between pagan and Christian responses to the natural world.[9] White overstated the case for Roman worship of nature spirits and the respect it guaranteed for landscape in general. Nevertheless, his central point remains true. Christianity reacted against geographically and temporally based Roman spirituality in much the same way the ancient Hebrews are generally understood to have responded to Canaanite nature worship. Both condemned the practice as a form of idolatry and a denial of the unique character and transcendent nature of God.[10] In pragmatic terms, the Christian response was more complicated. Some Roman deities were assimilated to the growing cult of saints, and Roman shrines sometimes retained their sanctity under new guises. These accommodations were for the most part occasional and local, and they had no effect on doctrine. For White, the bottom line was clear: Christian dogma replaced traditional ideals that were respectful of nature with ideals that authorized its exploitation: "By destroying pagan animism, Christianity made it possible to exploit nature in a mood of indifference to the feelings of natural objects. . . . Especially in its Western form, Christianity is the most anthropocentric religion the world has seen."[11]

Understandably distressed at this harsh critique, Christian theologians have in the last few decades begun to reexamine the tradition in hopes of finding a foundation within Christianity for the kind of ecological responsibility called for today. They have not found grounds for such attitudes in the words or actions of Jesus. Instead, they have resurrected a lost tradition of honoring the environment in the writings of a host of late classical and medieval thinkers. Primary among them is the North African bishop and church father, Saint Augustine. Augustine was one of the major voices establishing orthodoxy in the church that had only recently been officially sanctioned by the Roman Empire. He was also part of the first generation of Roman Christians who experienced the barbarian incursions into the heart of Rome.

Late Classical Theologies of Nature

In *Confessions*, Saint Augustine described the long process that led to his conversion to Christianity. In the immediate aftermath of that conversion, Augustine went with his mother to the Roman port of Ostia, where she was to set sail for Carthage. Together for the last time, the two of them sat in a tower overlooking a garden. As they looked out, all of the city and the natural world seemed to fall silent, and for a moment the two were conscious only of the presence of God. As Augustine reviewed this mystical experience, he described the relationship between God and nature that underlay their vision.

> What we said went something like this: "If to any man the tumult of the flesh were silenced; and the phantoms of earth and waters and air were silenced; and the poles were silent as well; indeed, if the very soul grew silent to herself . . . ; if fancies and imaginary revelations were silenced; if every tongue and every sign and every transient thing—for actually if any man could hear them, all these would say, 'We did not create ourselves, but were created by Him who abides forever'—and if, having uttered this, they too should be silent, having stirred our ears to hear him who created them; and if then he alone spoke, not through them but by himself, that we might hear his word, not in fleshly tongue or angelic voice, nor sound of thunder, nor the obscurity of a parable, but might hear him—him for whose sake we love these things— if we could hear him without these, as we two now strained ourselves to do, we then with rapid thought might touch on that Eternal Wisdom which abides over all.[12]

Contemporary Christian theologians have turned to this passage and others like it, to counter some of the charges that White leveled and to provide a foundation for Christian ecology. This rediscovered appreciation of nature is not based on the mandates contained within the Genesis account of creation but in an ongoing and largely nonbiblical relationship between God and his creation. Augustine defined that relationship in the imagined answer that all created things can offer to man's interrogation: "We are not God, but he made us." Because the created world bears the imprint of the God who made it, it can offer true and revealing information about him. Indeed, the beauty and order of the creation inspire and invite humans to search for that information.

In Augustine's theology, nature was a second revelation. God had expressed his personality and his intentions most directly in the sacred texts of the Old and New Testaments. Augustine and many others believed that God had also revealed himself through the world he created. From late antiquity through the High Middle Ages, it was common to refer to the "book of nature" and imagine nature as a second sacred text. The purpose of this text was clear. Its aim was to reveal God's character, not to sanctify his creation in and of itself or to establish limits on its exploitation. Understanding this relationship was largely an intellectual effort, and it inspired an encyclopedic lore about things. Isidore of Seville wrote a compendium called *The Etymologies*. His purpose was to provide a basis for understanding written texts, especially the Bible. On the symbolic level, Isidore's eytmologies explained why a particular creature was referred to in a particular biblical passage. The encyclopedic tradition that Isidore began fell into disuse for many centuries before it was revived in the High Middle Ages.

Alexander Neckham wrote his encyclopedic *De naturis rerum* (On the nature of things) around 1180. Sixty years later, Bartholomeus Anglicus, a Franciscan teaching in Paris, wrote *De proprietatibus rerum* (On the characteristics of things). These works and others like them included all kinds of information about their subjects gathered from multiple sources. The stated purpose of each was to offer practical information about the world. It was well understood, however, that all of these books were intended to show how the created world mirrored the character of its creator.

One of the clearest examples of this underlying purpose is found in the long tradition of entries on the word "pelican."

> Jacobus de Vitriaco in his book of the wonders of the East ... says that the serpents especially hate this bird. And so when the mother bird leaves the nest to get food, the serpent climbs the tree, and kills the young birds. And when the mother comes back, she mourns her offspring for three days, as it is said. Then she plunges her beak into her breast. The blood, pouring onto them, brings them back to life.
>
> The loss of blood weakens the mother, and the baby birds are compelled to leave the nest to get their own food. And some of them for love feed their mother, who is feeble, and some are unkind and neglect their mother. The mother pays attention, and when she returns to health, she nourishes and loves those birds that fed her in her need, and rejects her other children as unworthy and unkind, and will not allow them to live with her.[13]

Innumerable medieval sermons were preached on these characteristics of the pelican, none of which correspond to reality or observation. Depictions of the pelican in painting and sculpture into the Renaissance and beyond show the bird piercing her breast with her beak as blood drips out. No medieval cleric had any difficulty understanding that the pelican was a symbol of Christ, who pours out his blood for all humans and rewards those who reciprocate his love with eternal life. Despite such obvious allegory, the encyclopedists preferred to present their works as objective statements of fact.

Throughout late antiquity and the Middle Ages, the natural landscape of the Christian world included among its inhabitants clerics who professed a symbolic view of the created universe. Their way of life, for the most part, separated them from the day-to-day work of the fields and the pastures. They may have had a special fondness for created world and a special veneration for those parts of it that they thought most revealing of the mysteries of the faith, but they had little practical knowledge of plants, animals, or cultivation. The only exception to this divide between the clerical and the agricultural classes was to be found among the members of the Benedictine monastic order.

The order was founded by Saint Benedict in the sixth century CE. There had been Christian ascetics before Benedict, but they were men and a few women who lived solitary lives of prayer and self-denial in such harsh settings as the deserts of North Africa or the mountains of central Italy. Like many of his contemporaries, Benedict admired the piety of those who devoted themselves to prayer in such hostile places, but he also recognized the unusual level of spiritual maturity that such a life required. Many who went into the desert were simply not up to the challenge, and the conduct of ascetics was as likely to cause scandal as it was to advance the reputation of the church. Benedict thought that monks would be more successful in every way if they could be organized into communities under the leadership of authorities whose piety had been strengthened by age and experience.

To regulate this ideal community, Benedict set down a rule that determined the pattern of life for the multitudes of Benedictine abbeys that existed during the Middle Ages, and his rule continues to be the order's guide in the modern world. One of the forces that Benedict thought had played a generally mischievous role in solitary monasticism was idleness. The lone hermit did nothing but pray, and as the temptations of Saint Anthony, himself a desert ascetic, demonstrate all too well, the human mind is more than capable of filling hours meant for prayer with seductive fantasies. To avoid this temptation, Benedict decreed in his rule that monks in the order were to work.

This innovation was remarkable. Benedict's monks were not drawn from the peasant classes but from educated people of substance. Work was not something that any privileged group in the Roman world had ever admired. Intellectual labor was dignified and appropriate to literate men of standing, but physical labor, of the sort Benedict required, was absolutely destructive of social status. Status notwithstanding, the monks of the abbeys were to labor at something for some part of every day. Benedict considered work more than just a tool to combat idleness; for him it was a positive spiritual undertaking. Work was an expression of love for God and, like prayer and meditation, a way to strive for perfection.

Benedict clearly believed that the monks in his community would spend some part of their days in plowing and harvesting. This requirement of his rule, however, quickly migrated from weeding to reading. The majority of Benedictines did not work in the fields at any time during the Middle Ages. Instead they labored in the abbey copy rooms, or scriptoria, where books were duplicated, and in classrooms where novices were prepared. Still, the absolute separation that divided the rest of the clergy from the laboring classes broke down under Benedict's rule. The implications, even if the rule itself was honored more in the breach than in the observance, were still immense. As the pioneering environmentalist René Dubos pointed out, "By encouraging the combination of physical and intellectual work, they destroyed the old artificial barrier between the empirical and the speculative, the manual and the liberal arts. This created an atmosphere favorable for the development of knowledge based on experimentation."[14]

Experimentation included the opening of new fields and the application of methods and ideals that had been pioneered by the Greeks and Romans. Among the books that the Benedictines copied, there were several on Roman agriculture. Members of the Benedictine Order were virtually alone in preserving and studying these works, and without their efforts all would probably have been lost. On what became extensive agricultural holdings, the Benedictines were able to apply some of the principles of Roman agriculture that did not survive in the pragmatic culture of the peasants who worked the fields. In this way they preserved and practiced some of the constituent elements of the First Nature consensus, even though they would never have wished to describe their world in that language.

The population of Europe in late antiquity and the early Middle Ages was quite low. It was many times smaller than the population of the region had been during the Roman period, and, as we shall see in the next chapter, it was also much smaller than the population of the Muslim world, which began its rapid development in the seventh century CE. Reduced population meant reduced agricultural demand and a corresponding change in production. Because of abundant idle land, benefactors of the Benedictines and of the church in general were able to make donations of land that they had little use for. These donations guaranteed perpetual prayers for the souls of the donors in this life and the next and provided resources for the order. In general, the monasteries tried to make these gifts productive, and in the process, they transferred forms of land tenure, crops, and farming customs from one area to another.

Benedictines organized their scattered territories in the same way other large landholders did. They kept some of it for themselves and leased out the rest to tenants of various kinds. The lands they held for themselves, called demesne lands, were cultivated by the tenants of their farms, whose annual rents included not just a share of the harvest but a certain amount of labor on the order's fields as well. The monasteries were businesslike in the management of their holdings, and frequent inventories of properties, rents, and responsibilities were taken. A surprising number of these inventories from as early as the ninth century survive.

> Three [families] live in Neuillay. They hold a farm having
> 15 bunuaria of arable land and 4 arpents of meadow. They
> do service in Anjou and in the month of May at Paris. For
> the army tax they pay 2 sheep, 9 hens, 30 eggs, 100 planks
> and as many shingles, 12 staves, 6 hoops, and 12 torches; and
> they take 2 loads of wood to Sûtré. They enclose 4 perches
> with stakes in the lord's court, 4 perches with hedge in the
> meadow, and as much as necessary at harvest time. They
> plough 8 perches with winter wheat, 26 perches with spring
> wheat. As well as their labour and service, they spread ma-
> nure on the lord's fields. Each of them pays 4 denarii on his
> head.[15]

Bunuaria, arpents, and perches are all units of land and probably differed from place to place. Otherwise, the details of the rental obligations of these farming families are clear. This summary survey, in fact, is unusually detailed in laying out exactly what products and services the tenants of this farm are responsible for on a yearly basis. They owe service to the monks at their monastery in Paris and presumably at another in Anjou. They supply many kinds of small-dimension wood—presumably from coppiced forests—including fence stakes, firewood, barrel staves, and wood shingles. They plow a certain portion of the demesne lands for both winter and spring crops. They manure the fields. In addition, they pay a poll tax in coins (denarii) and an army tax that includes sheep, hens, and eggs.

By about the year 1200, population increases and the growth of urban centers brought changes to the Benedictine agricultural enterprise. Land was no longer as cheap as it once had been, and benefactors became harder to find. Though the money economy was far from the size of the Roman imperial one or the contemporary Muslim one, it was much expanded from its ninth-century low. With limited growth in their agricultural output because of decreasing donations and with rising costs for the commodities they needed, the Benedictines found themselves squeezed and forced to adapt. In general, they stopped farming their own demesne lands, which they had done for centuries, and rented them out. At this point they became more like the rest of the landholders in Europe: farm owners and overseers no longer actively involved in farm management.[16]

While the Benedictines over time became more and more like secular landowners, their preferences for cultivated crops always remained a little different. As a religious order that celebrated mass many times a day, the Benedictines needed ready supplies of wine. Since the ideal of each abbey was self-sufficiency, the monks introduced viticulture to any of their monasteries where grapes would flourish. In the Roman period, grape growing had been confined to the Mediterranean. In the unusually warm climate conditions that prevailed in the Middle Ages, suitable sites were as far north as England. Just as they required wine for liturgical use, and for daily consumption, they needed wax candles for ceremonies and copying work. A more typical Benedictine rental agreement than the one itemized above included rent to be paid in the form of a certain volume of wine and a number of pounds of beeswax.

Harshly critical as he was of the general Christian neglect of ecology, White made a special exception both for the Benedictines and for an order founded in the thirteenth century by Saint Francis of Assisi. Francis and his followers displayed a sensitivity to nature that White believed made them superior even to the older order. Dubos, on the other hand, felt that White's preference for the Franciscan love of nature in the abstract was a less valuable model of ecological responsibility than the Benedictine management of cultivation. The distinction between the two orders and the choice of one over the other is an important one with resonances in today's ecological debate. In preferring the Franciscans, White exalted a model of the natural world from which the human community stands apart. In essence, White depicted Francis as the counterpart of a modern-day environmentalist who identifies nature with wilderness uncontaminated by human presence. Dubos, on the other hand, recognized in the Benedictines an order that acknowledged the First Nature interdependency of the human community with its environment and made responsible ecological membership its goal.

> Francis of Assisi's loving and contemplative reverence in the face of nature survives today in the awareness of man's kinship to all other living things and in the conservation movement. But reverence is not enough, because man has never been a passive witness of nature. He changes the environment by his very presence and his only options in his dealings with the earth are to be destructive or constructive.[17]

Despite the Benedictine and Franciscan examples, the productive landscape played only a small part in the church's worldview. The productive landscape continued for the most part to be the concern of the secular community, which regulated it by tradition and pragmatic necessity. The fields, the pastures, and woodlands, once they were purified of pagan contamination, were managed in ways that bypassed Christian dogma almost entirely and maintained strong connections with Roman practices.

Peasant Agriculture in the High Middle Ages

Despite the many continuities in agriculture from the decline of the Roman Empire into the early Middle Ages, the overall impression is of discontinuity and dramatic change.[18] Slavery had been the Roman norm, but in the Middle Ages everyone involved in the agricultural enterprise from landowners to peasants to the communities in which peasants lived had clearly defined rights and responsibilities. No one party, including the wealthiest and most ruthless landlord, was free to overturn those patterns. This restraint was criticized during the eighteenth century, when it was repeatedly portrayed as a hindrance to agricultural reorganization. In the Middle Ages, however, when there was no sizable market for agricultural commodities, the system was well suited to the output that communities could consume and respectful of the needs of all the interested parties in the agricultural enterprise. This pattern of care extended to the land that was either farmed or pastured.

In many European countries along the Mediterranean, landowners held land granted to them by sovereigns in return for military service. A simple relationship between owning land and owing military service probably never existed in its pure form in many places, and the term that describes it, *feudalism*, is one that historians today dislike. The term does, however, capture something of the contingency of landholding by nobles. Sovereigns were hard pressed to replace nobles who were well established in their territories and well defended in their castles. Getting an earl to relinquish his holdings as punishment for failure to provide feudal service could be hard or easy depending on the power and political connections of the nobleman. But even a powerful noble who successfully resisted the demands of the sovereign to whom he owed his lands and titles would be impotent to challenge the customs of those underneath him. The feudal relationship, which has traditionally been portrayed as top down, was in reality one in which effective control from above was virtually nonexistent. Sovereigns had limited control over their barons, and barons, in turn, had little real control over their peasants.

Like the tenants of the Benedictines, the families who leased from secular lords paid rent to their landlord or his agent. Rent was usually paid with sheep, chickens, eggs, and grain. Cash payments were not unheard of, and some small farmers maintained animal stocks that could be sold for cash to meet these demands. Leaseholders also owed the landlord a certain number of days of service annually and seasonally. This labor could be devoted to infrastructure repair on the demesne lands—hedging, fencing, road building—or to plowing and helping with the desmesne harvest.

Farmers leased non-demesne lands from the landlord, but the leases were indirect, and village elders typically stepped in between the landlord and the individuals who farmed his land. The holdings of an individual farmer did not remain constant from decade to decade, and they were seldom consolidated. Village authorities assigned, surveyed, and periodically redistributed land. In a given year, a farmer might have a strip of rich plow-land near the river, a second on a hillside, and a third somewhere in between. The soils and exposures of the plots would be different, and the yield would differ accordingly. The aim of the village in distributing the agricultural land was undoubtedly a certain degree of equity, but all sorts of forces would have intervened to tilt the distribution in favor of one family or faction at the expense of another. The effect of forcing a farmer to cultivate different terrains amounted to a kind of insurance. If a field along the river was flooded out in a rainy year, another on the hillside might be especially productive. Multiple terrains and multiple crops created a diversity of products that more nearly duplicated the complexity of natural ecosystems and achieved some of the same safeguards that natural ecosystems have built in. Basically, scattered holdings supplied some of the diversity intrinsic in the Mediterranean agricultural enterprise from the start.

Not all the land that a village leased was distributed to individual farmers. A portion of it remained common land, where farm animals grazed. The animals were private property, but the grazing rights were shared by all the villagers. These rights were traditional, but that does not mean that they were implicit or subject only to the whims of debate and public memory. Grazing rights were spelled out in deeds and contracts. This protected the villagers not so much against encroachment by their neighbors as against encroachment by contractors who brought grazing animals onto village lands.

The study of these contracts is a lively if abstruse area of historical research. The existing contracts show that villages vigilantly guarded their property from animals brought through the villages by herdsmen during the seasonal migrations from the high summer pastures to the lowland winter pastures. According to the contracts, sheep could be turned out into fields only after the harvest. They could spend a contractually limited number of nights grazing before moving on. For an even more restricted period, sheep could graze between the rows of working vineyards. Goats were widely recognized to be the most destructive animals, and goat pasturing was regulated with extreme care. Goats moved through a village roped together and under the supervision of a goatherd. When they were allowed to graze, they were often tethered to a short lead fastened to a stake in the ground.

Given that grazing animals could do such harm to crops, it is a wonder that they were allowed passage at all. The fact is, however, that the passage was a source of cash for the village, and the animals were a source of the manure that fertilized the fields. Balancing the potential damage and the potential benefits of passing herds was an important part of the agricultural management that villages practiced. When traditional Mediterranean cultivation came under attack in the eighteenth century, the predominance of herding over grain production was a key issue.[19] Rome was remembered as a cereal-producing empire, and eighteenth-century agricultural economists thought that cereal cultivation was a sign of agricultural sophistication. Medieval villagers with their sheep and especially their goats were increasingly portrayed as backward and unproductive. What the agrarian philosophes apparently failed to grasp was the role that animals played in maintaining or enhancing field fertility. Medieval farmers used fallowing to maintain the fertility of their soils, but they also used the dung of herd animals.

The medieval system may seem restrictive—it was certainly portrayed that way by politicians who wanted to dismantle it—but it was one in which all parties in the productive enterprise, those who provided capital in the form of land, those who provided labor, and those who provided expertise all had some measure of power. Systems that replaced it, either in the Renaissance plantation or in the reformed eighteenth-century European economy, increased gross productivity, but at a high cost to the laboring community and to the land.

Despite the respect for tradition, medieval agriculture was not incapable of change and growth. As long as change was brought about without challenging the division of rights and responsibilities that defined the essential agricultural relationship, quite dynamic change was possible. The most dramatic changes in medieval agriculture took place in areas more or less remote from the Mediterranean littoral. Northern France, Germany, the Netherlands, and Great Britain experienced much greater change than did the Mediterranean basin, where agriculture was dominated by the mixed crops that had been traditional there from before the Roman period. When the Mediterranean technologies were taken north, however, new problems had to be solved.

The soils of the Mediterranean are shallow and dry, especially on the uplands cultivated in the Middle Ages. But if they were fragile, they were also easy to plow. The soils of northern Europe, on the other hand, were much denser and required much greater effort to turn over. New kinds of plows were required for these soils—plows that could cut deeper into the earth and turn the heavier earth from the cut furrow over on its side. The modified plows were equipped with wheels and pulled by teams of oxen. With the invention of the horse collar, horses could be substituted for oxen as effective draft animals, though the expense of maintaining horses limited their use.

New ways of maintaining or increasing soil fertility were also developed. Traditional farming had relied on alternating periods of productivity and rest for fields. In the Middle Ages a variant on this system came into widespread use. In the three-field system, spring crops alternated with both winter crops and periods of rest. Among the secondary crops introduced in this system were legumes, which increased human nutrition while adding vital nitrogen to the soil. This system of cropping was well adapted to northern farms where spring rains made a summer crop possible.

CHAPTER TEN

Muslim Ecological
Understanding

By the mid-eighth century, the Mediterranean world was divided into Christian and Islamic areas of influence. Though the two theological systems were hostile to each other, they shared many common beliefs. Both Christianity and Judaism influenced the dogma of Islam and remained a spiritual substrate within it. Christian and Muslim attitudes toward nature were similar, too: neither paid it much critical attention because both maintained a similar partnership with secular governments that ruled the material realm on principles unrelated to core theologies. Both were inheritors of substantial portions of the infrastructure and agricultural know-how of the Roman Empire. The Christian West experienced the empire's fragmentation and loss and had to struggle to regroup after the fall of Rome. The eastern Roman Empire included the richer and less damaged areas, the Nile Delta among them. Islam had the good fortune to assume the heritage of the Sasanian Empire, where agricultural experimentation had opened the door to crops native to climate zones beyond the Mediterranean.

The two major regional religions had significant differences besides territory and inheritance. In part because of its Sasanian legacy, the Islamic East was considerably richer in agricultural productivity and in crop-related infrastructure. Its management of agriculture was more hierarchical, and its markets were wider than those in the Christian West. Its population, especially its urban population, was many times that of the West. In population size, as in internal and external trade, agricultural productivity, and, indeed, almost any field imaginable, the Islamic East was more successful and more dynamic. Christian invaders were nonetheless able to seize and hold key Islamic territories for a time during the High Middle Ages. As was typically the case in the premodern world, superiority in resource management was no guarantee of protection from invasion. And although the Western crusaders were eventually forced out, they took with them in retreat a Levantine crop and a technology that were destined to transform the world in decisive and ultimately destructive ways.

Mecca, the holiest city of Islam, might look remote from the capital cities of the Roman, Byzantine, and Persian empires, but it was not marginal during the seventh century, when Muhammad was born there. Mecca lay within territory claimed by Byzantium. More importantly, it stood along one of the busiest international trade routes of the ancient world. Before the Portuguese circumnavigation of Africa in the sixteenth century, all trade between the Mediterranean and East Asia passed along one of only three international routes. The Silk Road brought a trickle of goods overland to cities in the Levant. A sea route from the Indian Ocean through the Red Sea and across Egypt to the Nile brought goods from East and South Asia to Alexandria. The third route traced the eastern coast of the Red Sea between the Gulf of Aden and the Sinai Peninsula. It passed through Mecca, which was well placed to benefit from the international trade in precious goods as well as the exchange of ideas.

Though polytheists themselves, the seventh-century residents of Mecca knew the dominant religions of their time, and the Qur'an in many of its verses reflects Jewish and Christian theology. The Muslim sacred book represents both Judaism and Christianity as revelations of the divine nature that led up to a third and final truth communicated only to Muhammad. According to Islam, each revelation was meant for a distinct community and for a distinct era in history: the Pentateuch for Jews, the New Testament for Greeks and Romans, the Qur'an for the Arabs. The successive revelations do not cancel each other out; rather, each revises its forerunners. For Islam the most important figures from the Jewish tradition are Abraham (Ibrahim) and Moses (Musa). Ibrahim is the patriarch of the religious community in Islamic theology as he is in Judaism and Christianity. Musa was the liberator of the Jews from captivity in Egypt, their leader during their wanderings through the desert, and a man of faith who battled idolatry. Through his unique relationship with God, he established the sacred law for his community. Like Musa, Muhammad was a political and spiritual leader and an enforcer of orthodoxy, but he was also a lawgiver and a leader of the people in both peace and war. The next great prophet after Musa was Isa— Jesus. Islam does not accept him as divine, nor does it acknowledge that he made any such claim. Muslims honor his mother, Mary, but they do not, as seventh-century Christians were beginning to do, venerate her as divine. Nor does Islam accept Jesus' partnership with God and the Holy Spirit in a Holy Trinity. Godhead in Islam remains one and undivided.

Christianity and Judaism contributed more than heroic exemplars to Islam. Both influenced Islamic cosmology. In the Arab tribal communities that gave birth to the new religion and supplied it with followers, the natural world appeared a harsh and unforgiving place. Communities struggling to maintain a pastoral way of life in this uncompromising environment never saw it as orderly or supportive of human endeavor. They imagined the desert as the battleground of gods and demons with ill-defined powers and conflicting aims.[1]

The book of Genesis gives pride of place to God's creation of the world, but the holy book of Islam, the Qur'an, pays little attention to the act of creation or its chronology. Rather than narrate once again the shaping of the world, the Qur'an emphasizes the world after creation and what it offers to human beings. What matters about the creation in Islamic thought is not how it was assembled but what its character is as a divine gift—specifically, creation exists first and foremost to nourish and sustain human beings. In one of its most suggestive characterizations of God, the Qur'an describes him as "He who has made the earth manageable for you, so you traverse through its tracts and enjoy of the Sustenance which He furnishes."[2]

[God] sends down rain from the skies, and with it brings out fruits wherewith to feed you . . . and the rivers (also) has He made subject to you.

And He has made subject to you the sun and the moon both diligently pursuing their courses: and the Night and the Day has He (also) made subject to you.

And He gives you of all that you ask for.

These verses grant humans authority and power over creation, but humans themselves are God's creation and depend on the world that God maintains. We are not self-sufficient beings set in a habitat that of its own nature meets our needs. Survival is an ongoing gift from God, and humans must pray to him for sustenance, which he grants not automatically but through his providence and mercy. Though we do not own or control the world, the Qur'an places few limits on our exploitation of it. What limits there are, are suggested by a small group of passages that describe the proper use of one of the region's most precious resources: water.[3] The importance of resource conservation is exemplified in a hadith, a traditional story, about the activities of the founder. Ritual cleansing is an important part of the Muslim preparation for prayer, but even in this case, Muhammad urged conservation.

God's Messenger appeared while Sa'ad was performing the ablutions. When he saw that Sa'ad was using a lot of water, he intervened saying:

"What is this? You are wasting water."

Sa'ad replied asking: "Can there be wastefulness while performing the ablutions?" To which God's Messenger replied:

"Yes, even if you perform them on the brink of a rushing river."[4]

In Islam humans are free to enjoy the bountiful resources that God has provided, but they are not free to use them irresponsibly, even to satisfy a ritual obligation. Excess, even in the highest cause, is not acceptable.

While the primary goal of the creation is to meet the needs of human beings, we are not the only beneficiaries.

... [T]he first purpose of all things is to proclaim, by means of their life and existence, the miracles of power and the traces of artistry of the Maker and display them to the gaze of the Glorious Monarch.

The second purpose of all existence . . . pertains to conscious creation. Everything is like a truth-displaying missive, an artistic poem, or a wise word of the Glorious Maker. . . .

The third purpose of all existence . . . consists of such minor consequences as the experience of pleasure and joy, and living with some degree of permanence.[5]

The full purpose of divine creation cannot be understood from a solely human perspective. God created the world "for all living beings."[6] He takes delight in all the parts of his creation; he contemplates every bit of it with satisfaction and admiration. Humans can share in this contemplation; every other creature, it would appear, also derives some sense of satisfaction from participating in the creation and from being assured of a rightful place within the natural order.

Nourishment is the tangible or material benefit of creation. A second and more significant gift is spiritual. The created world is made up of signs—*ayat*—that, if properly understood, reveal the nature, purpose, and beneficence of God. God has granted humankind a more explicit collection of signs as well. These are in the form of the holy books that culminate in the divinely created Qur'an. Together, these two collections of signs exist to enlighten people and to set the human community on the true and just path.

Saint Augustine believed that the created world was peppered with symbols that revealed the truth about God. In Islam, as in late antique Christianity, the essential fact to be discovered in any investigation of the natural world was not some biological mechanism but a reaffirmation of the power of God to create a massive and intricate system and to give it order and regularity. In Islam in particular, the topic of nature came down to a realization of human dependence on the bounty of God as that bounty is administered to humans through the created world. In this context, the appropriate human attitude is not an ecological one or even one that is centered on the identity of the gift itself. Humans owe gratitude to God the giver, and Muslims, like Christians, acknowledge few responsibilities to nature in and of itself.

Islamic ideals of creation no doubt inspired some regard for God's handiwork among pious men and women. But the principles outlined in the preceding paragraphs have only recently been articulated as a foundation for ecological thought and action in the Islamic community. They may represent little more than a search within the Qu'ran for verses that support or echo modern ecological principles. That they were articulated and applied in the Islamic world of the past is doubtful. Like the Christian world, historic Islam accommodated itself to existing governments and gave over control of productive life and the natural world to institutions that had been founded and governed for centuries on non-Islamic principles.

Though Muhammad was born in Mecca, resistance to his monotheism and to his claims to be a prophet, together with the long-standing rivalries that polarized Arab clans and tribes, made the city increasingly perilous for him and his followers. In 622 CE, leaders of the town of Yathrib invited his group to leave Mecca and take up local residence. Yathrib, now known as Medina an Nabi, City of the Prophet, or simply Medina, was an ancient oasis town with a history of intertribal warfare and a large, long-established and powerful Jewish community. Plagued by rivalries among all these factions, the town invited Muhammad to act as judge and arbiter of disputes. Despite Meccan opposition, the Muslim community managed to reach Yathrib in what would become year one in the Muslim chronology. The prophet created the first mosque there and built houses for his wives and family. He also fulfilled the demands of the leaders who had promoted and financed his relocation, in part by establishing the Constitution of Medina, a treaty among warring tribes and religions. Medina was the first Islamic community incorporated under an act of simultaneous political union and religious obligation.[7]

Once a concord had been reached in Medina, it was soon expanded to include surrounding tribes with links to groups inside the city. In a relatively short time, the Islamic community became a powerful local force, and tribes allied themselves with it for reasons of political expediency as well as spiritual commitment. Then, through a series of successful raids and negotiations, Muhammad won the allegiance of the tribes and factions in Mecca who had opposed him. Eight years after the escape to Medina, Muhammad and his followers returned to the city of his birth.

In 632, two years after his return, he died. The future of Islam and the confederation of tribes that he had brought into being and preserved in harmony were immediately threatened. Warfare broke out between tribes faithful to the Islamic confederacy and those attempting to break away. Though its dogma was still incomplete, the embryonic faith was able to motivate militant tribes to bring rebellious groups under control and to conquer new tribes and territories. For the Muslim community, victory in battle meant increased manpower and increased revenue as conquered tribes paid taxes to their conquerors. To recoup losses, defeated tribes more often than not made war on their unaligned neighbors. Tribes fell to Muslim conquest like dominos, and Muslim control quickly spread throughout the length and breadth of the Arabian Peninsula.

In 634 the Byzantine Empire sent a large force against Muslim raiders who were threatening villages in southern Palestine, then part of the imperial province of Syria. The second leader of the Muslim community, Caliph Abu Bakr, then near the end of his life, appointed Khalid ben al-Walid to take command of an Islamic army. The Muslim forces overcame the Byzantine forces in the battle of Ajnadayn and followed up their unexpected victory with a march through the Byzantine province. Driving north along the Mediterranean coast, they conquered Damascus by 636, then headed inland toward Baalbek, Homs, and Hama, which capitulated soon after. In 641, Muslim armies captured towns along the northern Euphrates River, which gave them control of the historic link between the Mediterranean and Mesopotamia.

A campaign against the Persian Sasanian Empire began in 637. Unlike the Byzantine Empire, which managed to establish a perimeter that Muslim invaders did not breach for centuries, the Sasanian Empire collapsed virtually on first contact. The emperor fled, and the area of modern Iraq came under Arab control. The mountainous terrain of modern Iran presented greater obstacles, and the conquest of this area took many decades. But at the fall of the Sasanian Empire in 641, a mere nine years after the death of Muhammad, Mus-

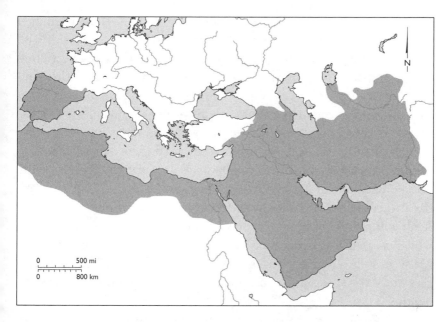

*Islamic conquests in the seventh to ninth centuries stretched from Spain across
North Africa to the Levant and beyond.*

lim forces were in control of the Arabian Peninsula, the Levantine
coast to the borders of Anatolia, and the whole of Mesopotamia.

Victory in the east was followed by a western campaign against
Egypt, which was the granary of the Byzantine Empire as it had
once been of Rome. By 643, Byzantine Alexandria, well fortified,
heavily garrisoned, and easily resupplied by sea though it was, fell
to the attackers. The Muslim army moved farther west along the
southern coast of the Mediterranean and took Tripoli the same year,
but from then on, difficult terrain and long supply lines, combined
with the determined resistance of tribes adept at desert fighting,
slowed their advance. The conquest of North Africa was not complete until the eighth century. By then, Spain had been overrun. The
drive to expand from Spain across the Pyrenees and into France met
decisive resistance from the Frankish general Charles Martel.[8]

The conquest of so much territory in such a short span of time
might logically have led to widespread conversions to the faith of the
Muslim victors, but this was not the case. Although Islam bound the
conquerors together, their goal was not the spread of their religion

but its protection. Muslims considered infidels on their borders a threat to Islam. The religious community campaigned to eliminate this threat, not to capture territory or to win converts. The victors sought to pacify or neutralize captured territories and to gather revenue from them. Under the rule of Muslim conquerors, therefore, subject peoples retained their religions, their language, their forms of agriculture, commerce, and manufacturing, and their customary laws. Islam and the Arab way of life remained the exclusive property of the victors. Being Muslim and being Arab were privileges that the first generations of Muslim conquerors saw no reason to share with the diverse peoples suddenly under their control. The model of the Arab conquerors appears to have been the Constitution of Medina, which created a confederation of believers and nonbelievers in which Muslims held a privileged and protected place in a pacified community and everyone shared responsibility for the general welfare and defense.

In keeping with the policy of religious exclusivity, early Muslim leaders made strenuous efforts to segregate Arab occupiers from civilian populations. In the military enclaves established in conquered lands Arab troops were garrisoned well out of reach of local populations. Before the invaders became soldiers, most of them had been Bedouin shepherds. Their traditional occupation and their ingrained sense of the appropriate use of land had favored pasture over cultivation. The ruling authorities of the first waves of Muslim advance, the successors of Muhammad called caliphs, along with the Arab elites of Medina and Mecca who were their closest advisors, insisted that captured lands under cultivation be preserved in their old forms and not transformed into pasture for horses, sheep, and camels. They also insisted that these lands become common property, not the spoils of war for individual bands of successful raiders. Top administrators in each new area were Arabs, but the functional administration of each conquered land remained in the hands of local powers.[9] These policies preserved indigenous systems of land tenure and land use.

The Constitution of Medina was more a treaty than a code of laws. The nations and cities that the invaders captured were already organized and governed in ways that were far more complex than the Arab tribes had ever needed to adopt for themselves. Unlike the

Byzantines or the Sasanians, the Arabs had no bureaucracies. They had no tradition of ruling cities or countries, and no system of governance to impose on conquered territories. They accommodated themselves to whatever form of organization that the conquered states had evolved. In the Levant, Egypt, and North Africa, they found themselves in charge of bureaucrats trained in Byzantine administration. In the Sasanian Empire, they commanded a different but equally efficient governing system.

After the death of Ali, the fourth caliph, his successor, Muawiyah, moved his court to Damascus. In Damascus, a Greek-speaking city with large Christian and Jewish populations and with all the trappings of Byzantine imperial culture, the governance of the Islamic territories changed. The caliphs became emperors. Their court culture became dominated by Greek protocol and Roman art and architecture. Having placed themselves at the pinnacle of a complex and highly ritualized imperial administration, the caliphs became increasingly shaped by its style and routines.[10] Though Arabic remained the official language of government, Arab manners were in decline, and the ruling elite was cosmopolitan. Some high officials in the caliph's court were neither Arab nor Muslim but prominent members of the indigenous communities.

When Caliph Hisham died in 743, the Syrian regime collapsed. A new dynasty, the Abbasid, seized the caliphate. To symbolize the new direction that their empire would take, they moved the capital from Damascus, with its Greek, Roman, and Byzantine heritage, to Mesopotamia. The move from Damascus ended an outside influence that had become discredited and introduced an equally powerful one that reshaped the court and its culture. In Mesopotamia, Persian language and literature were grafted onto the eclectic mix of influences that had already defined the caliphate. Planners laid out a round city named Baghdad on the banks of the Tigris River, and it grew rapidly. By the ninth century, development had pushed the city limits outward in every direction.

Within a hundred years of its founding, Baghdad had come to occupy nearly twenty-five square miles of land on both sides of the river. Its population, an estimated three hundred thousand to five hundred thousand, made it the biggest city in West Asia, Africa, or Europe. Baghdad was built where the Tigris is closest to the

Euphrates, and the agricultural land that nourished and sustained the city stretched from one river to the other. The ability to create and sustain a city of this size proves once again that environmental writers today are dead wrong when they characterize the Fertile Crescent of that era as infertile.

The Abbasids, secure in their new capital and backed by their coalition of supporters, transformed the caliphate once again, and with it the religion of Islam. This time the changes were more permanent and more fundamental. The Abbasid caliphs cut the cord that had for centuries bound Islam to Arab ethnicity. Full religious participation for all believers allowed the regime to draw its administrators and soldiers from ethnically diverse peoples united, as the Arabs had been originally, by their adherence to a common religion. Despite the Persian influences at court, however, Arabic remained the administrative and liturgical language, but it was a newly re-created classical Arabic grounded in the Qur'an, not the dialect of the conqueror tribes.

Because equal access was granted to all comers, and because membership in the community of Islam came to depend not on ethnicity but on the profession of faith, the rationale for preserving local laws and customs disappeared. If the religious and the political communities were to fully merge, then it was desirable that all barriers to full incorporation of the two be dissolved. The way of life of individual peoples had to be molded into one pan-Islamic system, and that system had to be sanctioned by and grounded in, not the laws and customs of multiple conquered peoples, but Islam.[11]

The Qur'an is by no means a book of laws. There are approximately six thousand verses in the whole book. Of these, some three hundred fifty, or about 5 percent, are clearly related to what is required, permitted, or ruled out for believers. Not surprisingly, the bulk of these prescriptions concern ritual behavior: the way to perform ablutions, the required daily prayers, the obligation to give assistance to those in need, and so on. Of the remaining verses that lay down laws, the overwhelming majority concern civil issues. A mere sixty verses, about 1 percent of the total, concern crime and punishment. Building a uniform code of law for a large and complex political system out of a fairly taciturn and frequently inconsistent text proved to be a daunting task.

The substitution of shari'a law—law based on the Qur'an—for the traditional laws and customs of individual peoples was neither immediate nor universal. Like Christianity, Islam concerned itself primarily with the human community and its ability to work together for the good of the faith. The nourishment of that community was essential, but Islamic law, like the Qur'an itself, had little to say on that subject. That silence was relatively inconsequential, however, because a governing bureaucracy was in place, and systems of land use and land tenure were stable and long-standing. A new codification of law would have little practical impact on old and well-established agricultural customs. Like Christianity, Islam essentially left the conduct of agriculture outside the day-to-day concern of religious authority. And like Christianity, Islam based its agricultural practices on an imperial heritage. For the Christian West, the inheritance was Roman. For the Muslim East, the inheritance was a combination of Roman-Byzantine in the Levant and North Africa and Sasanian in Mesopotamia and its surrounding area. God's creation might be idealized, and its revelations of God's nature reverently examined, but the landscape that nourished communities was purely secular and valued only in utilitarian terms.

Muslim Agriculture in Practice

The endowments that the conquered empires brought to the Islamic east were extraordinary. The western Roman Empire had provided a solid foundation for Christianity to build on, but that inheritance had been savaged. The Germanic invasions into Europe, Italy, and Roman North Africa decimated the population and destroyed much infrastructure. The toll grew heavier as widespread violence and uncertainty led to the decline of the regional markets that had sustained Roman agribusiness. The fragmented political systems of Europe that replaced the centralized government of Rome had no capacity and little incentive to reestablish the larger markets. The center of the western Roman Empire passed into the hands of popes, who often enough entertained imperial ambitions but lacked the training or the ability to manage an imperial state. In the west the old Roman Empire withered away; only vestiges, preserved at the level of village culture, remained viable.

In the east, the Byzantine Empire was far better off. Its roads, aqueducts, and trading networks were much less damaged by invasion, and its rulers remained engaged and interested in management. With the protection of a powerful navy, mercantile trade in the eastern Mediterranean survived long after the extinction of regionwide trade in the western Mediterranean. These distinctions made the pieces of the Byzantine Empire that Muslim conquerors made their own much more valuable properties than anything that was up for grabs in Europe during the seventh century. To their prime real estate in Egypt and the Levant, Arab conquerors added a second empire, that of the Sasanians, which included territories of modern Iraq and Iran. This conquest placed the entire Fertile Crescent in Arab hands, and though some contemporary writers have proclaimed the soil exhausted, deprived of its agricultural richness by generations of incompetent rulers, the opposite is true. Islam gained an incredible wealth of fertile land and agricultural know-how, especially irrigation technology, from the conquered Sasanian Empire.

As important as the territory of the Sasanian Empire was, the empire's greater contribution to Islam may have been the window that it opened on Indian agriculture. Long-standing trade through the Persian Gulf and the Indian Ocean had given the Sasanian Empire connections with the Indian subcontinent. Muslim armies captured northwest India in the eighth century, making it impossible for us to distinguish the crops that enriched the Islamic community after that conquest from others first cultivated and improved by Sasanian agronomists.[12] But whether directly or indirectly, the domesticates that entered the Mediterranean through the influence of India were extraordinarily important for Islam and ultimately for the entire world. Just as the Jordan Valley linked multiple climate zones and brought diverse products together, sparking the Neolithic Revolution, Islamic conquest of multiple climate zones created a single, if loosely integrated, community in a combination that yielded enormous benefits.

The area thus united was not only large but highly diversified. Its heartland lay in the semi-arid and arid lands of the southern and eastern Mediterranean, the Middle East and the Arabian peninsula; but it included tropical and semi-tropical regions in sub-Saharan Africa, monsoon-drenched lands in the Yemen and north-west India, near-temperate lands in the interior of Spain and regions with a severe continental climate in Central Asia. The variety of plant life was very great. So was the variety of human achievement: as the regions of this empire had developed in varying degrees of isolation from each other, they had produced a wealth of different traditions in every sphere of life from scholarship to agriculture. They thus had much to teach each other and much to learn. What is more the empire was strategically located with footholds on all three continents of the Old World. [13]

India was not the originator of most or even many of the new crops. Some had come there from China, others from East Africa. India was simply a way station on their global migration, but in India they were modified in ways that made a further step toward Mediterranean cultivation easier. India's climate, even in those areas bordering the Sasanian Empire, is subtropical or tropical. The Mediterranean region is generally colder and drier, and its seasons are different from the monsoon cycles that shape the agricultural year in South Asia. Taking crops from India and adapting them to the more rigorous climate of the Mediterranean required an additional adjustment, but an extension rather than a nullification of modifications that Indian farmers had already made.

Cotton was one of the most important crops that reached the Mediterranean via India. Ancient writers like Herodotus had known about cotton and, as more than one modern commentator has gleefully pointed out, believed that it grew on trees. The joke is on us, however; Indian cotton did indeed grow on trees. In the ancient world, cotton (*Glossypium arboreum*) was a woody-stemmed tree or large bush that grew year-round in subtropical climates. For it to survive the Mediterranean winter, an annual variety (*G. herbaceum*) had to be developed. No one knows exactly how this came about, but the end result was cotton that could be planted and harvested within a single growing season. Under the influence of Muslim farmers and horticulturalists, annual cotton became established in selected environments around the Mediterranean. Muslim farmers grew cotton in irrigated fields in the Jordan Valley, the Nile Delta, Sicily, and southern Spain.

Muslim farmers also acquired citrus fruits either from India or through Sasanian adaptations of Indian plants. Citrus crops, which we think of as characteristic of the Mediterranean, spread there slowly and irregularly. Bitter oranges, of the kind that English marmalade is made from, were probably the first variety to develop sufficient cold hardiness to move into the Mediterranean basin. Lemons and limes, which have different degrees of cold tolerance, followed. Sweet oranges made the leap next; grapefruit and tangerines, which have no wild cousins, were among the last to be introduced. Bananas took an equally long time to adapt and spread.

These originally tropical or subtropical plants were not the only foods to enter the Mediterranean through Muslim influence. Sorghum, a high-quality and highly productive grain, was one of the first and most important introductions. Other cereals included rice and durum wheat. Durum wheat is a high-gluten wheat used to make couscous, a dietary staple in North Africa, and pasta, the default food of Italy. Muslim farmers also brought sugarcane to the Mediterranean, a crop that was destined to transform international agriculture and commerce after the Renaissance. Other introductions were the coconut palm, the watermelon, the artichoke, the eggplant, and spinach.

Innovation in medieval Christian agriculture was generally cautious and slow. Innovation in Islamic agriculture, on the other hand, was swift, dramatic, and transformative. Combined with the dissemination of crops and increasing productivity, innovation helped generate and stimulate a robust economy.[14] Comparing the two agricultural traditions, practiced in territories that shared borders from the eighth century on, reveals sharp divergences from a common starting point. Though both had a base in the Roman imperial agricultural tradition, the Islamic polity moved well beyond that base when it incorporated the Sasanian Empire. Its openness to experimentation, and the agricultural markets that it developed on the basis of new crops as well as traditional ones like wheat, oats, and barley, stands in extremely strong contrast to the European approach.

Land tenure and capital investment were two other crucial factors that distinguished Muslim from European agriculture. As we saw in the previous chapter, landowners in Europe had limited control over the crops that their lands produced. Muslim proprietors, on the other hand, had rights nearly equivalent to those of the modern landowner. They could determine what crops were to be planted and direct the labor of those who worked the land. If they chose to plant wheat, they could direct their tenants and laborers to plant, cultivate, and harvest wheat. The wheat they produced would be sold to the residents of a city, not simply feed the workers who produced it. The population of the Islamic East, because of the large and growing nutritional base, was many times that of Europe. Muslim cities like Baghdad, Damascus, and Cairo housed hundreds of times more people than Rome, Paris, or London.

Wool was the only major agricultural commodity of the West, but the east had a market for every kind of agricultural product. While the Christian world subsisted on the produce of its farms, the Islamic polity had a developed agrarian economy. A wealthy Muslim landowner was well advised to invest in any of a variety of cash crops that would increase the economic productivity of his land. In the generally warmer and drier climate of the Muslim world, irrigation was the most common and most lucrative form of agricultural investment. Landlords could expect to harvest bigger crops in irrigated fields, and the increased profit from their sale would repay the investment in infrastructure.

The relative dynamism of the two agricultural systems also stands in sharp contrast. European farmers had repeated opportunities to take advantage of the same innovations and the same new crops as Islamic farmers. Evidence suggests, however, that they were extremely reluctant to do so. Crops like artichokes, spinach, and eggplants, to take a few random examples, were grown all the way to the frontiers of the Muslim sphere, but there their cultivation stopped. European farmers living just beyond the borders of Spain or southern Italy showed no interest in these crops. Even after the reconquest of both regions, European farmers who moved in neglected unfamiliar crops like sugarcane, rice, and citrus trees, which disappeared from the Christian world until their reintroduction in the Renaissance, a time when Christian and Muslim communities came to interact in radically new ways. The outcome of their interaction then was momentous not just for the region but for the entire world.

Islam: The First Thousand Years

Islam's initial period of rapid territorial expansion ended abruptly in the late thirteenth century, when Mongol invaders spread both west and east from their homelands in Central Asia. Under the powerful and brilliant war leader, Chinggis Khan, the Mongols created an empire that stretched from the Mediterranean coast east to the Pacific Ocean and from Moscow in the northwest to the Mekong River in Southeast Asia. Historians are of two minds when it comes to assessing the effects of their invasions.[15] Without question, the first wave of invaders took many lives and destroyed traditional cultures. Unlike the Arab invaders of many centuries before, who had also been nomadic pastoralists, the Mongols did not respect traditional land use in their conquered territories. Mongol conquerors routinely transformed fields into pastures. Though this transformation affected agriculture in the short term, it was not permanent. After the Mongol occupation, much pastureland was reclaimed for traditional irrigated agriculture.

The most lasting effect of the Mongol invasions was the devastation of Baghdad, the imperial seat of the caliph. The Islamic intellectual and cultural life centered on Baghdad had been dynamic and experimental. It was rooted in the heritage of three distinct cultural traditions: Arabic, Persian, and Greek. Its key institution, the Beit al-Hikma, or House of Wisdom, contained a great library with resources that rivaled those of the fabled Library of Alexandria. Along with thousands of Persian manuscripts left by the Sasanian emperors, the library contained many of the philosophical writings of the Greeks and much Greek literature. Arabic translations of books in the House of Wisdom were disseminated to Islamic communities throughout the Mediterranean. Translators in Sicily and Spain rendered the Arabic translations into Hebrew and Latin. During the Middle Ages these retranslations provided European theologians and scholars with access to Greek philosophy.[16]

Among the books in the Beit al-Hikma were many that reflected the strong interest of Islamic scholars in mathematics. Some texts detailed ancient Greek geometry and Mesopotamian astronomy; others chronicled mathematical developments in India. In that eclectic center, decimal numbers, the concept of zero, and the positional value of numbers were combined for the first time. Indian numbers, which came into use throughout the Islamic world, reached the West from the Levant. They are still called Arabic numerals in acknowledgment not of their source but of the culture from which the West obtained them. The intellectual culture of Baghdad also included a rich poetic tradition grounded in both Arabic and Persian sources. The vibrant and all-embracing culture of Baghdad was not wiped out by the Mongol invasions, but the intellectual openness and cosmopolitanism on which that culture had rested lost favor. A regime that had prided itself on its eclecticism became less daring and more fundamentalist in its thinking. Cultural syncretism became suspect, and the exploration of philosophy, mathematics, and the natural world declined.[17]

Turkic tribal members, originally from eastern Central Asia, were among the first groups to be driven westward by the advancing Mongol armies. Under pressure from the east, these tribes surged into northern Iraq. Caught between the Mongol hordes and the soldiers of the Byzantine Empire, these tribes, who would eventually become the chief Islamic power, remained for some centuries in a cultural crossfire.

At the death of the great Chinggis Khan, his son Ilkhan received the portion of the kingdom that included the whole of Mesopotamia with extensions eastward along the Persian Gulf and westward into Anatolia. The territory of Iran was not part of his inheritance. When the Ottoman Turks eventually took over Ilkhan's kingdom, Iran remained outside their empire. The exclusion of Iran from the Ottoman Empire had consequences that continue to be felt today. Iran fought frequent border wars with its neighbors. Always threatened on their eastern front, the Ottoman Turks were never free to commit their armies to an all-out attack on the West. The Ottomans endorsed Sunni Islam, one of the two main branches of the religion. The same accident of history that cut Iran off from membership in the empire cut it off from the Ottoman-dominated realm of Sunni Islam. In its isolation, it gradually turned to Shi'ite Islam and remains a majority Shi'ite country today. Hostility between the Ottomans and Iran also broke the cultural ties between Sunni Islam and the Persian language and literature that had been so powerful during the Baghdad caliphate. Arab thought and Arab tradition, not Turkic

or Persian traditions or Byzantine ritual, became the dominant cultural influences on the ethnic Turks of the Ottoman dynasties.[18] The
Ottoman conquest of the Byzantine Empire in 1453 removed the
long-standing barrier to a Muslim invasion of eastern Anatolia and
south-central Europe. Ottoman campaigns in the west reached their
high-water mark in the early sixteenth century. Late in the summer
of 1683, Muslim troops made a final and unsuccessful attempt to
capture the city of Vienna.

CHAPTER ELEVEN

Renaissance Landscape and Food

Anyone looking at the Mediterranean basin in the middle years of the fifteenth century would have seen a curious mix of the dynamic and the routine. Politically and militarily, the region was in turmoil. Ottoman troops were encircling Byzantium and preparing to move in for the kill. And just as they stood poised to end the final chapter in the millennial history of the Roman Empire, Ottoman religious leaders prepared to assume control of the community of Islamic nations. These sweeping political changes took place against a stable but sharply divided agricultural and ecological backdrop. On the European and Christian side of the sea, the traditions of peasant farming dominated. Landlords had minimal control over cultivation of the fields and forests that they held but in important senses did not own. Agricultural and ecological decisions remained primarily in the hands of informal community leaders who were strongly bound by tradition. Cultivation in this region was what eighteenth-century critics later labeled subsistence agriculture, meaning that it sufficed to feed the people who worked the fields and produced enough extra to feed the landed classes and the tiny urban populations. Ecologically the region was in balance. There were good years and bad years, but crops were usually large enough to meet the nutritional needs of the region's relatively small population. Cultivation was sustainable; cropping techniques kept the land from deteriorating and, in many cases, enhanced its fertility. It was certainly not the best of times from a cultural or political point of view, but by and large, the human community of the region lived in balance with its ecological resource base. The First Nature consensus was active on the land.

Agriculture on the Islamic side of the sea was decidedly different, but the ecological fit was about the same. Crops were more diverse, urban populations were larger, and a landlord's control over the harvest, which typically yielded cash, was much greater. The Islamic region's ability to recover from the devastations of the Mongol invasions gives important evidence of the continued ecological soundness of its agricultural regime. While the methods for ensuring harmony between the community and the resource base were very different from those practiced in the Christian regions of the littoral, the human impact on the region's ecology appears to have been about the same all around the sea.

Beginning in the fifteenth century, the resolute actions of a small country at the sea's western extreme turned the status quo on its head. Marginalized within a regional economy where power and wealth were concentrated at the far eastern end of the Mediterranean, Portugal took the lead in what became a decisive power shift when it launched a series of top-secret Atlantic voyages. Those voyages changed the character not just of the Mediterranean region but of the entire world. Although it is more usual to speak of the political, social, and economic implications of these voyages, world agriculture and ecology also experienced enormous changes as a consequence. New crops and radically new ways of exploiting land and labor increased the nutritional base—and the human population—while they eroded the First Nature balance between human communities and the landscapes on which they had long depended. The age of discovery, which was the starting point of the modern era, opened hostilities in the prolonged modern conflict between agriculture and ecology.

Portuguese Voyages

Under the sponsorship of Prince Henry the Navigator, Portuguese explorers pushed ever farther south on the west coast of the African continent. The hazardous journeys, which grew in length and scope with each successive sailing, tested and expanded naval technology. The passion that drove Prince Henry to expend his time, energy, and wealth on this series of Atlantic probes is in some ways as obscure as the record of the voyages themselves. His immediate and pragmatic motive was dominance in the African gold trade. Portugal had captured the North African town of Ceuta in 1415. The town was a haven for Moroccan pirates who harried Christian shipping in the fifteenth century. Depriving them of this important base of operations bought some security for Portuguese shipping. Ceuta was also an important market for the trans-African gold dust trade, which originated in Central Africa and flowed by various caravan routes across the Sahara to a handful of Mediterranean ports. Once the Portuguese captured Ceuta, Muslim traders took their precious commodity elsewhere. One of the clear goals of African exploration, then, was to make an end run around the trans-Saharan trade network and tap into the gold pipeline at or near its source, wherever that might prove to be.

The more abstract motive of the prince and his sailors reflected the crusading mentality that had served the Portuguese and the Spanish as they recaptured their home territories from the Muslim occupiers. As they saw it, sending Portuguese sailors and traders into Africa extended the boundaries of Christ's kingdom on earth. With luck they might create a hedge of Christian kingdoms around the borders of European Christendom. Instead, as everyone knows, the enterprise of conversion matured into a campaign of brutal conquest, exploitation, and mass enslavement. As the Portuguese ports of trade stretched south along the Atlantic coast, the riches of Africa, including men, women, and children, flowed northward to European ports. In 1532, when the first slave ships reached the Portuguese colony of Brazil, the slave trade in the Americas began; its horrors convulsed the world for the next three centuries; its aftershocks are still felt today.

The typical Mediterranean vessel was built for the sailing conditions of the inland sea, which were often challenging but less severe than those of the ocean. The Portuguese Atlantic voyages required ships capable of surviving swells that were considerably larger than those encountered on the Mediterranean, winds and currents that

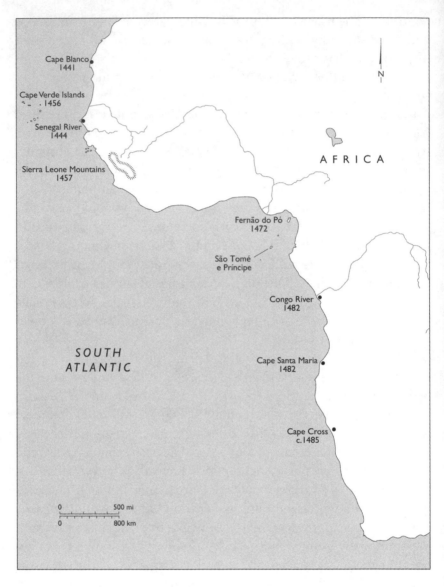

Cape Blanco
1441

Cape Verde Islands
. 1456

Senegal River
1444

Sierra Leone Mountains
1457

AFRICA

Fernão do Pó
1472

São Tomé
e Príncipe

Congo River
1482

SOUTH
ATLANTIC

Cape Santa Maria
1482

Cape Cross
c.1485

N

0   500 mi
0   800 km

The Portuguese established landfalls in West Africa as they pushed south in the age of exploration.

were stronger, weather that was less predictable and more violent. The first oceangoing vessels of the Portuguese were caravels. These were small ships, with keels and multiple masts fitted with triangular sails that favored maneuverability over speed. They had high, castle-like poop decks that both provided increased space on board and protected the ship from being washed over by wind-driven waves from behind. Unlike many Mediterranean vessels of the era, which were steered by oars, the caravels had a submerged rudder behind the keel that could be turned from the deck.[1]

As the sailing range of the ships and the experience of the sailors grew, the Portuguese developed even heavier craft called carracks. These larger vessels had two forward masts with square sails but retained the triangular sail on their rearmost mizzen mast. The new configuration increased speed in favorable winds. The multiple small sails could be worked one or two at a time by a relatively small crew. These new ships were bigger and so able to carry more goods to trade and greater supplies of food and water, which allowed for longer continuous voyages. They were also fitted with cannon, and their crews and officers were heavily armed.

Coastal sailing was the norm in the Mediterranean in the fifteenth century, as it had been in the Roman era. To avoid treacherous currents near shore and to take advantage of prevailing winds, the Portuguese Africa fleet often sailed well out of sight of land. With no landmarks to follow, navigators learned to depend on increasingly sophisticated instruments and the careful notations of voyagers who had come before them. With each successive trial, the Portuguese expanded the range of their charts. Since their maps included information known nowhere else in the world at that time, they were vigilantly guarded. Death was the penalty for betraying their secrets. Disinformation in the form of false charts and incorrect readings fill today's archives and make it almost impossible to tease out the voyages' true extent and chronology.

Some details are clear. In 1488, Bartolomeu Dias rounded the southern tip of the African continent and explored its eastern coast. Ten years later, Vasco da Gama embarked with a fleet of ships that traded along the East African coast before setting out on a northeast bearing to sail the six hundred nautical miles across the Indian Ocean. This voyage finally achieved the supreme goal, one the Portuguese could hardly have hoped for from the start: a chance to break into the East Asian luxury trade, which had long passed from Arab ships to Venetian galleys. Circumventing the eastern Mediterranean and reaching India directly, Dias cut out both Arab and Venetian middlemen. His voyage and those that came after it established safe ports for the Portuguese in the Indian Ocean.

In 1509 a mixed Muslim fleet that included ships of the Ottoman sultan and the Mamluk rulers of Egypt and forces from two Indian sultanates tried to drive the Portuguese away from India. Venetian captains advised them. Off the Indian city of Diu, a Portuguese fleet of eighteen heavily armed carracks took on a mixed fleet of generally smaller craft. Though more maneuverable, the smaller ships of the Muslim alliance were outgunned by the Portuguese. Adapted for near-shore sailing, these small ships rode low in the water, and the Portuguese ships towered over them. Arab boarding parties could not reach the decks of the taller ships. When their boats sailed in under the Portuguese cannon, the men aboard became targets for small arms fire from marines towering over them.

The decisive defeat by the Portuguese of a technologically inferior force at Diu ended Arab control of the Indian Ocean. After that, Muslim shipbuilding lagged behind European shipbuilding. European seafaring technology was more advanced. The Portuguese expanded their colonial outposts and gained control over the Strait of Malacca, between the Indian Ocean and the South China Sea (Pacific Ocean), a major choke point on the east-west ocean routes. After that, trade in the Indian Ocean passed to a succession of Atlantic-based sea powers. As early as the sixteenth century, it became all too clear to Asian rulers that no indigenous power could dislodge a European occupier; only another European fleet could do that. While Islam remained the dominant religion in the area, Christian Europeans controlled international trade. The Ottoman Empire, which in 1515 overwhelmed the Egyptian Mamluks and seized control of the whole of North Africa, was the biggest loser.

While the Portuguese were exploring the African coast, Spanish explorers, intent on an even wider end run around Arab-Venetian control of east-west trade, had stumbled on a new continent. Spanish adventurers grabbed the gold of the Incas, Mayas, and Aztecs. Although Portuguese diplomats negotiating in the papal court were able to secure a share of South American territory, they did not gain the immediate wealth that Spain enjoyed. Within a few decades, Spain's golden bonanza made the country rich beyond the dreams of avarice. In the long run, however, the wealth proved more a curse than a blessing. Spain did not invest in new technologies or new industries. To make matters worse, the increased gold and silver reserves from the New World drove up the cost of goods across Europe. Inflation put special pressures on agriculture, which faced higher costs but had limited means of increasing prices.[2]

In the short run, the wealth of the New World spurred ambitions in the Spanish monarchy that were played out in colonization in the Americas and in a series of territorial wars in Europe during the sixteenth and early seventeenth centuries. The Dutch were among the first to feel the might of a newly energized Spain. The Low Countries were possessions of Hapsburg rulers who came to power in Spain early in the sixteenth century. Rebellions against Spanish dominance brought eighty years of warfare during which the Dutch fleet grew both in imitation of and in opposition to the Spanish armada. The Dutch made small but important gains in the New World, but they had lasting success in East Asia, and they replaced the Portuguese at the Cape of Good Hope and in the Indian Ocean. Throughout much of the seventeenth century, centralized, monopolistic Dutch trading companies—especially the Dutch East India Company—dominated the world market in nutmeg, mace, cloves, and cinnamon. They came close to monopolizing the trade in pepper. This group of spices and a few others were the heart of a trade that had for a thousand years passed along corridors that Muslim rulers controlled. Revenues from this trade were exceptionally high.

Sometime allies of the Dutch against the Spanish, the English became major rivals of their cross-Channel neighbors in the seventeenth century. The English East India Company was founded a few years before the Dutch enterprise, but the latecomers were clear winners in the final competition. Officially the rivalry ended in 1688, when a Dutch prince, William of Orange and Nassau, became the new English king. In reality, the economic competition persisted and reached its resolution only in the eighteenth century, when income from the British trade with India exceeded the value of the Dutch spice trade.

Agricultural Exchange in the Age of Exploration

Opinion about the age of exploration, for centuries a source of pride in Europe, has within a single lifetime undergone a polar change. What was once labeled discovery has been downgraded to rediscovery. Indigenous peoples were there to greet Da Gama and Columbus, so in what sense can Europeans be called discoverers of what others already knew? For many regions of the world, European "discovery" opened the way to subjection, decimation, and despair. Exploration all too quickly led to epidemic diseases and the imposition of European control over native peoples. Still, for good or ill, the age of exploration remains a turning point in world and Mediterranean history, comparable in its effects to the greatest revolutions in human society, the Neolithic Revolution and industrialization.

The Levantine Neolithic Revolution, along with others in south China and northern South America, were rare, isolated moments when native plants were transformed in significant ways. First the plants were taken from their wild environment and transformed into crops. Then those crops were disseminated throughout the contiguous areas where climate allowed them to grow. When domestic plants and animals reached the edges of their tolerance for heat, cold, or dryness, or faced geographical barriers like deserts, mountains, and oceans, their dispersal stopped. The plants and animals of the Mediterranean Neolithic colonized all of Europe and the islands of the Atlantic, along with West and South Asia. The high steppe, desert, and mountain habitats of Central Asia did not support the cultivation of temperate climate crops, so the wave of advance of the Mediterranean Neolithic halted at their edges.

The domesticates of south China circulated through East Asia and the island archipelagos of the Pacific. A slow trickle of domesticates from the south Chinese Neolithic made their way westward for millennia, traveling overland on the long and twisting Silk Road or by sea through the equally tortuous routes from east to west. Whichever path a good happened to travel, it passed through the hands of many merchants and rested in the saddlebags or cargo holds of a number of carriers before it reached its final destination. The powers in every region through which these products passed enacted some kind of tax or tariff, adding greatly to the cost. Every

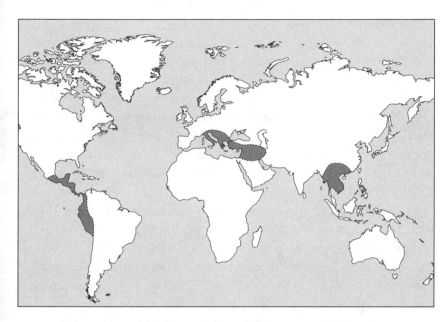

The sites of Neolithic Revolutions—where plants and animals were
domesticated—are few and scattered.

good traded over these transcontinental routes needed to be small,
light, and precious.

Under the restraints that limited east-west trade before the Renaissance, Asian domesticates could not play the same fundamental
role in the west that they did in the east. Still, there had always been
a trickle of commerce linking the Mediterranean and the south Chinese Neolithics; but before the Age of Discovery, European conquest, and colonization, products of the South American Neolithic
were completely isolated from the other two. Based principally on
the cultivation of corn (maize), squash of various kinds, beans, and
potatoes, the South American Neolithic spread in the pre-conquest
era from its base in northeastern South America to the ocean boundaries of the two American continents.[3]

During the sixteenth century, international shipping erased these
millennial boundaries, and domesticates spread through every region
where climate allowed their cultivation. The geography that had limited crop dispersal was replaced in the age of exploration by an ocean-
based world geography whose limiting factors were climate and soil

rather than the accidents of domestication history. The spread of domesticates transformed cultures and enriched the whole world's nutritional resources, and the result was an upsurge in world population.

In the classic book *The Columbian Exchange*, Alfred W. Crosby described both the benefits and the costs of commerce between the Old World and the New. Diseases like smallpox that ravaged New World communities were the most devastating of the unintended imports that Spanish explorers brought with them, and the suffering and death these diseases caused to unprotected communities worldwide has been well documented. Crosby also pointed out the number of domesticated plants and animals that reached the New World with the conquerors. These imports benefited not only European colonists but indigenous peoples. Horses, which reached the North American heartland well ahead of the Europeans who had imported them, transformed the lives of Plains Indians. It gave them a new and more effective way to hunt bison and a potent cultural symbol around which to build a distinctive way of life. In the Southwest, the Navaho lifestyle was completely reshaped around sheepherding. Sheep, like horses, were brought by the Spanish.

In the Old World, imported crops became cultural icons as well as dietary staples. The Irish potato famine was a tragic episode in the generally beneficial history of the New World root vegetable introduced into the European diet. Throughout northern Europe, the potato provided more nutrients per acre than the cold-climate grains—principally oats and barley—that had been the dietary staples before its importation.

In the Mediterranean region, the impact of new domesticates and imported commodities was also revolutionary. Consider the tomato. Given its prominence in southern Italian cooking and in the international versions of Italian food, it is impossible to imagine it as anything but native to Italy. In fact, the tomato is native to South America. From there, cultivation spread north to Mexico, where the Aztecs named it xitomatl. Spanish colonists brought the fruit and the last three syllables of its name to Europe in the mid-sixteenth century. At that time, the Spanish royal house of Aragon controlled Sicily and southern Italy with Naples as their capital. The nearby town of San Marzano, on the slopes of Mount Vesuvius, is still home to the most highly prized Italian tomatoes.

The "Columbian exchange"—Crosby's term, now widely adopted, for the exchanges of plants, animals, diseases, technology, and culture between the peoples on both sides of the Atlantic—provided many new crops to the Mediterranean region, but other domesticates reached the Mediterranean at about the same time through newly forged sea links to the east. Coffee, native to Ethiopia, was cultivated in Yemen as early as the fifteenth century. Its name in Arabic, *qahwah*, was originally a poetic epithet for the wine that Islam prohibited. Nonalcoholic coffee was an approved stimulant that came to be widely used by Sufi mystics. The beans were used medicinally in Venice by the end of the sixteenth century, and by 1640 coffee was being roasted, brewed, and served in specialty shops there that became the first cafés in Europe. The taste for coffee spread through the rest of the continent, and coffee plantations around the world soon augmented the supply that had made its way through the Ottoman and Venetian trading networks. Coffee was introduced to Europe through Mediterranean trade but was transformed into a widely used commodity by the network of colonial shipping and transplantation. Each culture that adopted coffee produced something like the coffee shop, but as any European traveler knows, the ambience and the favorite brew differ markedly from country to country.

Two of the best-loved foods of northern Italy are also imports. Polenta, a thick corn porridge to which multiple flavors can be added, is a favorite of northern Italian cooks. Corn entered the Italian diet from the New World. Rice came from the opposite side of the world. The Romans had imported small quantities from India, and Muslim farmers cultivated it in sites around the Mediterranean Sea. With the Christian reconquest of Muslim-held lands, however, rice cultivation disappeared in Europe until it was reintroduced in the fifteenth century.

Rice—the Harbinger

Although potatoes, tomatoes, and corn (maize) easily adapted to European gardens, rice was an altogether different crop. Rice is a grass, and it can be cultivated like oats or wheat in dry fields, but yields are much greater in a wet environment like the rice paddies of East Asia.

Creating this special environment where it had never existed before required many departures from tradition. As we saw in Chapter 9, Christian Mediterranean agriculture was bound by all sorts of rights, privileges, and customs. The peasants who worked the land had well-established ways of assigning and reassigning cropland, long-held views about how and what to plant, and controlled systems for guaranteeing the fertility of their soils. Innovations occurred, but they were slow to be adopted.

Cultivating rice on irrigated fields that were periodically drowned and periodically drained was not part of the tradition of the peasant cultivators of the Po Valley of northern Italy. To get them to do this unusual work required a new and more vigorous form of social control. This control was provided by despotic rulers—the Visconti of Milan—or capitalist managers from Venice. During the Renaissance, the despots of Milan were extending their reach into the Po Valley, and Venice was stepping up its conquests on the Italian mainland. As conquerors rather than traditional landowners, overlords from both cities were able to impose forms of social control and labor organization that overrode the rights and privileges of workers. By all accounts, this new form of management was not just demanding but abusive. Within twenty-five years of the first evidence of rice cultivation in the Po Valley, there are reports that rice workers, including many women and some children, were enduring long hours and miserable conditions in the fields.

Unlike traditional medieval agriculture, rice cultivation required a substantial capital investment. Land had to be acquired and fields combined so that a suitable cultivation environment could be created. Though the Po Valley was well watered, it was still necessary to acquire water rights to the natural flows and to the many canals that cut across the region. Bringing the water to the rice fields required ditches and channels to be cut, maintained, and skillfully managed. None of this work was cheap, none of it was self-sustaining, and none fell within the traditional obligations that peasants owed to their landlords. In addition to capital, the rice fields required labor on an unprecedented scale in a region that had been only marginally productive before.[4] As with the preparation of infrastructure, cultivation was also labor-intensive; throughout the growing season, large numbers of workers were employed. These characteristics of rice production meant that the grain had to be an economic commodity; it could not simply be another part of the subsistence agriculture of the Christian Middle Ages. The requirements of its production—capital investment, wage labor, and a cash market—were all novel and all pointless if the crop did not return a profit.

Rice cultivation transformed landscapes and overrode traditional labor rights. The owners of the fields did not respect the region's traditions or its ecology. In many ways, rice cultivation was a harbinger of things to come. It embodied a new sense of property, in which ownership implied absolute and unconstrained freedom of use—the right to unlimited exploitation. In most of Christian Europe an absolute sense of property with its attendant disregard for ecological limits and cultural traditions would not emerge until the eighteenth century.

Rice cultivation in the Po Valley also disenfranchised labor. Rice farmers were workers for hire, not peasants with inalienable rights of tenancy and a protected place in the manorial economy. This change of status led to immediate exploitation. The fact that ecological abuse and the exploitation of labor so often go hand in hand is evident from this first example. But rice remained a niche crop. It was not cultivated in many places, so the influence of the new agricultural regime that transformed the Po Valley was extremely limited. Only portions of Spain and southern France were involved in rice growing before the eighteenth century.

Sugar in Colonial Agriculture

Rice had the power to reshape agriculture and dismantle regional ecologies, to undo, in short, the traditional practices that sustained First Nature. But sugar was the crop that changed the world. Sugarcane is a domesticated version of a plant that probably originated in New Guinea but is now extinct in the wild. The crop was certainly cultivated in India and East Asia during the first millennium BCE and perhaps earlier. Herodotus mentions sugarcane. When the armies of Alexander the Great reached India, stalks of the plant and small quantities of sugar were sent back to the west.

In Alexander's era, sugar was brown and strongly flavored, but during the seventh century CE, Sasanian farmers and agronomists improved the refining process and produced sugar that was white and had a more intense sweetness. Their improbable process involved the use of ground limestone and bullock's blood. These two additives captured impurities, which could then be skimmed off the boiling syrup. A second boiling with egg white gave the sugar a snowy sparkle. The syrup was then poured into conical molds, which produced loafs that were hard enough to endure rough transport.

Sugar was a highly desirable product, but its labor-intensive refinement and the cost of transporting a heavy commodity over the great distances that separated the canefields from the final consumers made sugar a luxury good. Muslim farmers grew sugarcane in Sicily and Spain, but the crop was abandoned when Christians reconquered these areas. Muslim canefields in the Levant had a different and far more consequential fate. When crusader knights gained a foothold in Palestine during the twelfth century, they became military rulers over towns and villages where sugar was grown and refined. The crop was as capital- and labor-intensive as rice, and work in the canefields was both difficult and unpleasant. Slaves, who did not commonly do agricultural work in any part of the Mediterranean during the Middle Ages, worked in the Levantine sugar fields and processing mills. The crusaders recognized a good thing when they stumbled on it, and rather than suppress sugar cultivation or substitute crops from back home, they stepped into the role of the Muslim landowners they had ousted. In Spain and Sicily farmers refused to work newly captured Muslim canefields, so they fell into disuse. In the Levant, where workers were less autonomous, Christian landlords reaped the benefits.

As Muslim armies fought back, the crusaders' descendants lost their foothold in West Asia. Displaced sugar barons looked for new places where they could successfully grow the exceptionally lucrative crop. They took with them what they understood of sugar cultivation in the Levant. This included the most exploitative features of the cane culture, but it did not include those practices that had made the crop, along with other Muslim crops that were intensively cultivated, sustainable over the long term. Cyprus remained in Christian hands until 1570, and the Venetians made good use of the island as a producer of sugar. They established and exploited large plantations there and built sophisticated special-purpose refineries.[5]

Sugar production required capital and also political leverage; money by itself would not have been enough. In Cyprus, Venetian investment was supported by a monarchy that was sustained financially and diplomatically by the government. Building refineries, keeping them staffed with workers and stocked with the wood required for the repeated boiling of the sugar syrup was expensive. Paying workers and imposing onerous forms of labor on them was a necessity of the business, too, and here again the combination of finance and political muscle was crucial. Finally, bringing the finished product to consumers required merchant ships and naval security in the eastern Mediterranean, along with access to European markets. The Venetians had all of these in spades. When the Ottoman Turks finally deprived Venice of Cyprus, they struck an ultimately fatal blow to their empire and their financial viability.

When victorious Muslim forces drove Christian lords from the eastern Mediterranean, the sugar crop and its technologies moved further west. Although many sites were tried, sugar production eventually took hold most strongly not within the Mediterranean itself but on its fringes, in Atlantic islands that had been first discovered in the fourteenth century. For a while the Canary Islands were the center of Christian sugar production; they were eventually displaced by Madeira, where the crop was more successful. Columbus brought sugarcane to the New World in 1493, and its cultivation on Hispaniola initiated the long reign of sugar in the Caribbean.

Like rice, sugar was an agricultural crop that Mediterranean powers transplanted from one world region to another. Sugar became the first colonial crop, and the way it was financed, cultivated, and traded during the sixteenth century set the pattern for the other great colonial commodities that followed: rice, indigo, tobacco, cotton, coffee, cocoa, and tea. Sugar cultivation was the beta version of the international plantation economy. The plantation system, which relied on large field monoculture, slave labor, and international transport and finance was a form of land and labor exploitation that paved the way for the later adoption of these ecologically and ethically unsound practices worldwide.

The distinctive patterns of plantation agriculture that sugar pioneered have unmistakable Mediterranean roots, but sugar cultivation in the Christian Mediterranean itself was marginal primarily

because it violated norms of medieval agriculture there. When settlers migrate to new lands, they typically bring their crops and farming traditions with them. The farmers who settled New England
brought their wheat, rye, and barley, their horses, oxen, and milk
cows, their bees, and even their weeds with them. Once settled, they
did their best to re-create the English agricultural landscape they
had grown up in. Early Spanish settlers did much the same thing.
In Cuba, for example, they first cultivated olives, wheat, and grapes.
These crops were not successful. The soil, moisture, and temperatures in Cuba did not favor them, yet the few colonists persisted, just
as New England farmers did until the richer soils of the newly opened
Midwest drew them away.

Subsistence agriculture was viable in the colonial homelands,
where peasants could support themselves and grow a little extra to
feed others. In the colonies, however, subsistence was not enough.
Sixteenth-century Spanish and Portuguese colonies were not meant
to provide new homes for European migrants. There was no excess
population in Mediterranean Europe during the sixteenth century
as there would be later on, and both Spanish and Portuguese exploration was driven by economics. Voyages of exploration were unaf-
fordable unless a way could be found to make them self-supporting
and, if at all possible, profitable. The gold of the Incas temporarily
solved this problem for Spain. What made colonialism profitable in
regions without stores of precious metals was plantation agriculture.

The Portuguese were the most successful early explorers, establishing themselves in both the east and the west. Though their international dominance was short-lived, they briefly held all the key
pieces in their hands, pieces that they would assemble into a virulent
package that would serve as the model for every future colonial
plantation economy. By the sixteenth century, sugar producers had
evolved tried-and-true methods for every phase of crop management, from planting through milling, concentration, and distribution. They had shown, too, that sugar production could be moved
from one place to another.

During the course of the African explorations, the Portuguese
added the final fatal ingredient to the package. The island of São
Tomé off the West African coast served the Portuguese as a safe haven
from which they could trade with the Kingdom of the Kongo. As the

slave trade increased in volume and importance, and as its productive center shifted south along the African coast, this island became the headquarters of all facets of the Portuguese African venture. Sugar cultivation began there soon after Portugal colonized it in 1485, making the island the first site in the world where sugar production and African slavery were combined.

In the sixteenth century, Portugal reorganized its colonial government in Brazil and put control of territories there into the hands of entrepreneurial captains with unlimited rights to land and water and nearly absolute political authority. The captains in Bahia and Pernambuco in the Brazilian north soon put themselves in the sugar business. At first they worked the plantations with Indian slaves, but by the end of the sixteenth century, Africans brought directly across the South Atlantic became their major labor force. Once in Brazil, slaves were set to work in plantations where landlords controlled every aspect of their lives. Though their role was essentially economic— they were laborers, after all—the regime in which their labor was exploited was also a political one. Slaves had no recourse against an owner who held both an economic monopoly and absolute judicial authority. As in the rice economy of the Po Valley, the master had complete control over the conduct of a workforce without rights or traditions that in any way limited or mitigated his control.

This economic and labor-control system, developed and honed in Brazil, was exported either directly or as a model to every other region of the Americas where colonial crops were cultivated on a large scale. Sugar cultivation, which had always leapt from one locale to another as market and labor conditions dictated, predictably spread from Brazil to the Caribbean. On the islands of Jamaica, Barbados, Cuba, Haiti, and elsewhere, the plantation system of Brazil proved highly adaptable and highly profitable. Sugar was never a major colonial crop in the United States, but the plantation pattern was suited to other crops as well. Along the Carolina coast, plantation owners with huge slave forces cultivated rice and indigo. In the mid-Atlantic states, similar methods were used to cultivate tobacco. Cotton was the last of the colonial crops to be widely adopted; its colonial exploitation had to wait for the development of a mechanical means for separating the seeds from the lint of the cotton boll.

The Villa

On the cusp of the revolutionary change that discovery and colonization created, one country spearheaded an intellectual and cultural flowering. Beginning in the late thirteenth century, northern Italy, especially Tuscany, underwent a social revolution with a widespread impact. Though the term "Renaissance" is now in disrepute among scholars, the marked change in outlook that was once routinely signaled by that word cannot be dismissed so easily. The Tuscan city of Florence has long been seen as the origin of the multiple phenomena that make up the Renaissance. In 1100 it was one of many European centers of luxury cloth production. Florentine merchants sold their wares in seasonal markets throughout Europe. Since there were Florentine traders in many parts of the world, it became something of a matter of course for these merchants to extend credit to each other wherever they might be. The Florentine international banking industry grew from this relatively simple habit, based largely on transferable letters of credit. Other Italian cities were soon active in the credit business, and before the fourteenth century was old, Italian bankers were financing commerce throughout Europe and North Africa. When they extended credit to political leaders, their power and influence grew, along with the volatility of their investments.

Florence, Milan, Venice, and other northern Italian cities soon began to include merchants of enormous wealth among their citizens. What distinguished the wealthy of Florence and Venice from those in many other places was their ability to transform money into political power and their adoption of new and unprecedented ways to display and use their riches. Florence was an early leader in the creation of public architecture and city planning. Along with improvements in the urban fabric, Florentine commercial wealth financed a revolution in painting and sculpture. Both revolutions were attuned not only to the world of spirituality, as earlier Christian art had been, but also, for the first time since the Roman Empire, to the experiences and characteristics of the material world. Working with the newly invented or rediscovered (the evidence is unclear) art of perspective, Renaissance sculptors and painters created an increasingly refined representation of the landscapes of daily life.

The city of Florence had always been linked to the countryside around it: the food that nourished citizens came from fields and pastures nearby. But in the case of Florence, the relationship was individualized and intimate. Most city people had a country village somewhere in their past, and most maintained some ties with their home place. When people of even modest means migrated to the city, they held on to their village properties if they could. Country real estate was a popular form of investment for anyone who could afford it. The rents on farms, orchards, and vineyards often came in the form of produce, and at different seasons of the year, a city family might venture out into the countryside to collect their annual dues of olive oil, wine, or pork.[6]

The wealthiest Florentine merchant families followed that pattern; country real estate was one of their most common forms of investment. The interdependence of urban and agricultural life was celebrated in particular Florentine fashion by the creation of country estates that combined functional agriculture with refined leisure in a setting designed to encourage appreciation of the productive landscape. Like the estates of the Romans that once dotted the Mediterranean countryside, the Renaissance Italian villa was a glorified country house that linked agriculture and recreation. For the first time since the classical period, farming and the landscape that nourished the human community captured the attention of the wealthiest and most influential social class.[7] The First Nature conception appealed to the wealthy and powerful just as it was being expressed by artists of ability.

Early in the fifteenth century, Cosimo de' Medici bought a large farm near the little town of Careggi. After he consolidated political control over the city of Florence in 1434, he had the property remodeled. Throughout the fifteenth century, the Medicis and other prominent Florentine merchant families repeated the process. The same sort of sites were favored again and again, and each house "was set right in the midst of its podere, or farm, usually in an olive grove."[8] As the Medicis gained power in Rome in the fifteenth century, they commissioned villas in the papal city as well. The Villa Medici still overlooks Rome from the Pincian Hill a little north of the Spanish Steps. The Villa Madama, designed by the painter Raphael for Cardinal Giulio de' Medici, survives on its original site above the Vatican, but in a stripped-down form. The Este, Torlonia,

Aldobrandini, and other prominent families built elaborate villas on the city's outskirts and in sites farther afield.

The Villa Lante, one of the most celebrated Renaissance villas, was associated with two papal families, the Riario, relatives of Pope Sixtus IV, and the Montalto family of Sixtus V. Built far from Rome in the country outside Viterbo, the villa was under construction throughout much of the sixteenth century. It remained papal property until the nineteenth century. The Villa Lante begins on the outskirts of the little town of Bagnaia. Its upper end is buried in woods on the hillside above the town. The purpose of the villa, expressed in its layout, is to mediate between these two extremes, the forest and the town.[9]

Any comprehensive organization of landscape on this scale suggests a comparison with the greatest of all landscape-based works of art, Homer's shield of Achilles. The linking of wilderness, cultivation, and civilization in an orderly and harmonious totality that characterizes the Villa Lante and others of its kind recalls the similar linking on the shield, but there are important differences. The shield appears to be concentric and to group activities in relation to its twin urban centerpoints. The farther from the center, the farther from civilized organization. The Renaissance villa is organized not concentrically but along a single dominant axis. At the Villa Lante, that axis can be drawn from the woods downhill through increasingly formal settings. It transects the gardens and the country residence, placed at the meeting place of the wild and the cultivated and representing a balance between the two.

Seen from the monk's cell or the scholar's apartment, the world takes on a particular hue. Medieval clerics had recognized an ideal connection between plants, animals, and the hidden nature of God, a link that represented for them the sacredness of nature. These clerics, however, were almost completely divorced from both the peasants who worked the fields and the fruits of the peasants' labor. With the exception of special orders like the Benedictines, clerics preferred to leave agriculture to secular control. In the Renaissance, however, and for some centuries, the men and women who held power in Italy overcame this dichotomy and celebrated the real landscape, not an abstracted and spiritualized version of it. Moreover, they celebrated it in relation to their own earthly state rather than subsuming it under their devotion to a God veiled in mystery. To reason about their world and to contemplate their place within it, they situated themselves at the meeting place of the natural and the artificial in the middle of the landscape that sustained them.

The merchant princes of Florence and the noble families of Rome set themselves in a landscape over which they held real power. When they contemplated the hills and valleys, they were not looking with the delight of an indifferent spectator but with a ruler's eye. Ultimately, the Renaissance villa brought to life a philosophical ideal that would have been acceptable to the Stoics: the exercise of power must be grounded in the orderly processes of nature. Villa culture, then, was a remarkable counterpoise to the long history of Christian disregard for the active landscape.

The Renaissance has been portrayed with some accuracy as a time when the human image was widely depicted and the human scale was widely applied in the arts, in literature, and in philosophy. The famous drawing attributed to Leonardo in which a man with outstretched arms and legs appears to be the modulus—the underlying measuring unit—of primary geometric figures is one example. The associated phrase "man is the measure of all things" reflects the same point of view. Renewed attention to the human scale was reflected in study and imitation of the surviving monuments of classical art and classical writing. "Humanus sum et nihil humanum alieno a me no puto" (I am human and I consider nothing human to be alien to me), a phrase by the Roman playwright Plautus, signaled a common ground between the humanism of the Renaissance and that of the ancients. The human scale was the scale of the Tuscan villa. The villa brought the human community and the idealized landscape into a harmony that could be experienced as well as articulated.

The merchant dynasties of Florence were not the only elite group who embraced villa life and its ideals during the sixteenth century. The merchants of Venice had long shunned any form of involvement in mainland Italy, preferring overseas investments and colonial postings to life on terra firma. This attitude changed dramatically in the late fifteenth century, and by the middle of the next century, Venice was deeply involved in the great blood sport of the era, Italian politics. Venice did reasonably well in accumulating territories and very well in staving off powerful opponents like Spain and France, which came to dominate parts of Italy during the sixteenth century.

Along with political conquests, which were typically made through alliances and the creation of puppet governments, Venetian merchants also became property owners in the marshy flatlands of the north Italian coast. This watery landscape, cut through by channels and dotted with flooded fields where rice was cultivated, was more familiar and more comfortable to a Venetian than a drier environment might have been. They built villas in this area about the same time that Florentines were building theirs. The two landscapes had little in common—the flat watery plains of the Po and the Brenta watersheds were nothing like the hilly and agriculturally diverse landscape of Tuscany—but the great houses in both areas represented similar ideas.

Rich Venetians were fortunate to have one of the greatest domestic architects of any era to call upon. Andrea Palladio is still recognized as a supreme designer. His buildings were influential in his own era, and they captured the imagination of architects from the sixteenth century onward. Palladio created his most celebrated houses for the Venetian elite in the marshy landscapes around the town of Vicenza. The buildings now tend to be seen and described in isolation, but their original setting was agricultural. The main houses were set among secondary structures that served pragmatic purposes. Thomas Jefferson imitated this Palladian principle at Monticello, where he integrated the formal central house with a series of what he called dependencies, secondary structures connected to the main house where the businesses of farm and manufacturing went on out of sight. The model for both the Venetian villas and Monticello was a working farm, functionally integrated into the landscape and intimately linked to a formal suite of ceremonial rooms, a deliberate echo of the Roman villa's *pars urbana*. Some early Venetian estates in the region had been even more completely linked to agriculture. The attics of some early houses were designed as granaries to store rice. The windows of the main house, which stands higher than its surroundings, were positioned to give sweeping views over the rice fields. The Venetians, like the Florentines, appreciated the order created by a cultivated landscape. They saw themselves reflected in its contours.

CHAPTER TWELVE

Mechanistic Models and Romantic Wilderness

T he era of villa culture was little more than a moment in Western history.[1] The natural world and its intersection with food production and political power that the villa celebrated evolved in surprising directions as the Renaissance waned. The sixteenth and seventeenth centuries saw a dramatic change in the understanding of how the world and the universe were to be modeled. This change arguably grew out of the appreciation of the material world that grounded villa culture, but in the end it created a sensibility that was far from a down-to-earth point of view.

The First Nature concept had thrived historically within the same frame of reference. It was grounded in the visible material world that human beings experienced in their daily lives. That world was distinct from the conceptual world of the pre-Socratic philosophers, the cosmic imagery of the Platonists, and the heavenly perspective of Christian and other theologians. Renaissance culture had flowered within the First Nature framework, and it understood and celebrated the world on a human scale. The seventeenth and subsequent centuries introduced two scales beyond the limits of unaided human sight and so beyond the experience of daily life: the tiny and the vast scales of the microscope and the telescope. Of the two inventions, the telescope was the more immediately consequential. What it revealed to the observer established a new foundation for the cosmos. Its developers brought to prominence new techniques of analysis and established a new model for thinking about the world.

The sensibility of the post-Renaissance period was in many ways a reaction to that era's founding principles. Painting, architecture, and sculpture embraced a gigantism alien to Renaissance artists. The wars of religion that racked Europe beginning in the mid-sixteenth century put theocratic principles at the center of human concerns once again and destroyed any notion of a common human character or purpose shared across religious affiliation. Most decisively and most mysteriously, a fundamental turn occurred in what was still thought of as philosophy. With the exception of Aristotle and the first few generations of his followers, Greek philosophers had ruled out any constructive interaction between theory and observation. Indeed, the Greek insistence on the illusory nature of the world of becoming nullified any possibility that pragmatic observation could guide right thinking. Late Renaissance philosophers—men and women we would call scientists—were the first to see that observation, especially the controlled observation characteristic of experimentation, could provide valid insights into intellectual first principles. Pursuing this new approach to the investigation of the world and the cosmos, Galileo and others canceled out the humanistic grounding of the Renaissance and introduced a new measure, a new method, and a new model. The mechanistic world picture they postulated ended those Renaissance movements that might have reestablished First Nature as a principle for integrating human communities and the landscape on which they depended.

The invention of the telescope in the seventeenth century resolved old controversies about the cosmos and added new ones. Before the telescope revealed their true nature, the dark spots on the moon had been the subject of endless philosophical debate. Generally speaking, intellectuals had believed that the dark areas on the moon's face proved that the heavenly body closest to earth shared some of earth's fallen and corrupted nature. The dark spots, in other words, confirmed in the minds of generations the essentials of both Plato's and Aristotle's view of a distinction between natural law on earth and the physics that governed the upper planets. The telescope revealed that these dark areas were nothing more than landscape features with distinct reflective properties. Their presence had nothing to do with the substance of the moon and held no clue to its divine or mundane character.

The most controversial accomplishment of the celestial observers who watched the heavens through their telescopes was the deconstruction of the geocentric universe. This development was shocking and of great consequence. Just as modern creationists are fully invested in the dogma of the immediate divine manufacture of the world, religious authorities in the seventeenth century were committed to a geocentric universe. Theologians believed an earth-centered solar system to be the only planetary arrangement compatible with the relationship between God and humans that they understood. Without earth at the center of the universe, and hence at the center of divine attention and concern, how could God truly be the all-seeing, all-knowing deity they worshipped?[2]

Observations of the heavens accumulated after the idea of a heliocentric system was well advanced in the scientific community. The new data showed that the principle behind the old Ptolemaic system was wrong in another significant way. Aristotle had argued that bodies in motion above the earth naturally trace circles, while objects moving on earth trace straight lines. He saw these differences as proof of the incompatibility of celestial and earthly physical principles. But observations showed that the planets failed to exhibit the precise circular orbits Aristotle had predicted. Based on minute and detailed observations by Tycho Brahe, Johannes Kepler theorized that planetary orbits were elliptical.

Newton was the first to account theoretically for elliptical orbits and also the first to unite the mathematical description of planetary orbits with the linear physics that Aristotle believed existed only on earth.[3] Newton's law of gravitation, which rested on the work of many other researchers in the seventeenth century, stated that the attraction between two objects is proportional to their mass and inversely proportional to the square of the distance that separates them. The theory works for planets being pulled through their orbits by the sun as well as for apples falling to earth.

Newton articulated three laws of motion. The first law described the states of rest and motion and established that a moving object

will continue to follow its original trajectory unless some force in-
tervenes. The second addressed the way intervening forces change
motion. It related the intervening force to the mass of the moving
object and its acceleration, or change of velocity. (Aristotle had a
similar idea, but his theory related force, mass, and velocity, not acceleration.) Combining these two laws allowed Newton to describe
celestial and terrestrial motion in compatible ways. Motion in a
straight line is the norm in both. Since the planets do not move in
straight lines, a force must be acting on them to bend their paths.
This force is the gravitational attraction between each planet and
the sun.[4]

When these discoveries were added together, the universe suddenly became very different from the one that had been accepted as
firm fact for two millennia. The Newtonian universe was heliocentric, not geocentric, and that in itself was hard for the orthodox to
swallow. From the earth to the stars, the physics of the entire universe was uniform, an idea that shocked those who knew their Aristotle. The governing force in this homogeneous universe was gravity. In the universe of the ancient Greeks, planets moved because
deities pushed them around. Christian adaptations of the system
substituted angels. In Newton's universe, the power source may have
worked in a mysterious way, but the results were predictable and
definitely not divine, magical, or uncanny. Even if no one really
understood how objects attracted each other, the pull of attraction
was evident. Gravity was a fact of daily life on earth, and promoting
it to the role of planetary power source did not change its essentially
mundane character.

The intelligence exemplified in the order of the universe and
expressed in the formulas of the new scientists did not reside in
the material that made it up. Plato's *Timaeus*, which described the
universe as living, intelligent, and divine, ceased to be read.[5] God's
thought might have created the universe, but his thought could no
longer be expressed in the symbols and analogies dear to medieval
Christians.[6] It could, however, be captured in simple, concise mathematical formulas.

At this point in history, it might have been possible to preserve
a First Nature cosmology based on the landscape of daily life.[7] The
planets had lost their immaterial and divine attributes. The physical

principles that governed earth had been restored to primacy as universal forces, a status they had not enjoyed since the time of the pre-Socratics, when love and strife presided over the metamorphoses of earth, air, fire, and water. But times had changed. There was a new ideal in the minds of the intelligentsia, and it soon exerted its power.

The philosopher Alfred North Whitehead, a perceptive analyst of the governing ideas of the Newtonian revolution, recognized that the seventeenth-century understanding of the material of the universe and the mechanistic process of its activity strongly militated against any effort to restore the landscape to its ancient role as a cosmological symbol.[8] Mathematics and mechanics, not a productive agrarian landscape, underpinned the universe that seventeenth-century scientists codified.[9]

Newton's gravity, promoted to cosmological driving force, was a resource that humans harnessed to do mechanical work. When falling water turned the wheels of water mills, they were harvesting gravitational energy. Galileo demonstrated that the regular swing of a pendulum reflected the pull of gravity on its heavy bob. If the same gravity that turned the mill wheel or swung the clock's pendulum also powered the universe, then it was reasonable to see the universe as a mechanism of some sort. This analogy was brought to life in the early eighteenth century by two English clockmakers who designed an orrery, a mechanical device that replicated the movement of the planets around the sun. The mechanics of the orrery were based on the clock, which was one of the leading technologies of the seventeenth century.

The analogy of the clock or, more commonly, the watch played a part in many discussions of the Newtonian universe. The analogy was a keystone of the Deist argument about the relationship between God the creator and the solar system he brought into being: Like a watchmaker, God designed and built his cosmos, then wound it up and left it to run on its own. His design and his workmanship were both perfect, so the watch he made runs on forever without needing repair or resetting. For Deist theologians, this analogy represented a universe where order and reason are supreme and where God is aloof and takes no hand in the day-to-day conduct of his creation by causing miracles or answering prayers.

The watch analogy appealed even to thinkers who rejected the impersonal God of the Deists. In one of the first expressions of the theory that is now called intelligent design, the Christian apologist William Paley retooled the watch analogy to prove the "necessity of an intelligent Creator." He wrote: "The inference we think is inevitable, that the watch must have had a maker. Every observation . . . concerning the watch may be repeated with strict propriety concerning the eye, concerning animals, concerning plants, concerning, indeed, all the organized parts of the works of nature."[10]

In such a worldview, the mechanical was exalted because it reflected the inner workings of the greatest and most enduring machine, the universe itself. The biological, which resisted mechanical explanation, was another matter. The English philosopher John Locke fantasized about the mechanical processes that he believed would someday be discerned within what appeared superficially to be physiological processes.[11]

The search for the mechanisms of life put a premium on the structures of living forms and their grouping into coherent, rational systems. The microscope was an important tool in this investigation, and the greatest successes in eighteenth-century biology came in the anatomy of animals and the structures of plants. "The mechanical philosophy was certainly extended to living things. . . . But the 'animal machine' doctrine had limited applicability in an age when the best possible model was, literally, a piece of clockwork. Even with the help of the microscope, the mechanical philosophy could make little headway in the understanding of the more complex processes of life."[12]

With mechanistic cosmology in the ascendant, it was only natural that objects or processes with perceptible mechanical characteristics or at least analogues would be exalted at the expense of those that had none. Machinery seemed progressive, so industry gained an intellectual edge. Biological processes appeared mysterious and disorganized, so their manifestations, including agriculture, appeared retrograde. From the seventeenth century on, the mechanical and the industrial were cutting-edge cultural phenomena; farming was antiquated and ripe for capture by any mechanistic theory that convincingly described its dynamic.

The Social Machine

Because the study of plant and animal structure was gaining orderliness and explanatory power through a mechanical approach, the mysteries of human interaction were expected to yield to the same kind of investigation. One area that seemed especially apt for analysis of this kind was that of buying and selling. Money coursed through the body politic in mysterious but measurable ways as it influenced and responded to the interaction of farmers and merchants, buyers and sellers, commoners and princes. If the principles that governed the behavior of money could be understood with the clarity and the predictability of gravitational attraction, then societies could hope to rationalize production, stabilize prices, simplify taxation, and achieve other useful goals. The benefits promised to be enormous. At the end of the eighteenth century, Adam Smith took on this subject in his authoritative and still influential book *The Wealth of Nations*. He was not a pioneer. The book came at the end of a long debate that was both theoretical and pragmatic about the nature of the economic force that was increasingly competing with warfare as a measure of the power and influence of European states.[13]

Money was an ancient feature of well-organized societies, and eighteenth-century Europeans were sophisticated in their understanding of its nature, power, and limitations. What prevented many of them from seeing money as the universal engine of economic activity was not ideological blindness or unfamiliarity with the marketplace but, instead, the massive presence of an essential but largely nonmonetary economic engine in their midst. Money may not be everything, even today, but it is a great deal more like everything in the twenty-first century than it was in the eighteenth. Those things on which we cannot or will not put a monetary value are personal, for the most part. In the eighteenth century, there was no need to turn to the private sphere to find things that were priceless. Most of the essentials of life could be appropriately described as falling into that category.

Traditional farming was what eighteenth-century critics typically referred to as "subsistence agriculture." This term, which harked back to Aristotle's misconceptions about the development of the city from agricultural foundations, was intended to stigmatize this kind of farming as retrograde and ineffectual, but what the designation really meant in the eighteenth century was that agriculture existed mostly outside the realm of monetary exchange. The generally small crop surpluses that sustained Mediterranean cities gained an economic value through commercial exchange; farmers paid occasional taxes in cash rather than in kind, but most agriculture in the eighteenth century continued to be carried on as it had been for generations, with little or no money changing hands. People ate what they produced and bartered goods and services. What "subsistence agriculture" really meant was nonmonetized production.

Theorizing about economic activity on the basis of cash flow in the eighteenth century meant leaving agriculture, the largest employer and the largest institution, almost completely in the dark. A school of economic thinkers in France in the middle of the eighteenth century tried to deal with this difficulty by creating a theory of value that rested on the materials of subsistence rather than on the process of exchange. Called physiocrats, these theorists were led by a onetime court physician, François Quesnay, whose aim appears to have been to find an economic analogy for the circulation of the blood through the human body.[14] The physiocrats believed that primary value resided in the land and that agriculture realized an annual dividend on this national store of wealth.[15] That wealth was consumed when city dwellers bought food. It was also consumed, Quesnay argued, when people bought manufactured goods. The physiocrats thought of manufacturing as consumption rather than production.

This consumption view of manufacturing, the darling of the rival mercantilist school of economics, provoked fierce opposition. Nor did the physiocrats always help their own case. Much attention has been paid to a complex and confusing chart that Quesnay drew up to track the flow of economic activity through farm labor, food production, and consumption. From a modern economic point of view, the chart makes little sense, and it may be that even to the physiocrats themselves, it was not fully comprehensible. It was certainly pilloried by their enemies, but the physiocrats were not wrongheaded cranks; they were serious people who made an ultimately unsuccessful attempt to theorize about an important social institution that in their era had hardly been colonized by the cash economy.[16] It did not make sense to them to explain contemporary agriculture in terms of a medium of exchange that was hypothetically applicable to all buying and selling but which in pragmatic terms had made little inroads into farmers' lives.

Modern economics, the "dismal science," rests on the linked axioms that money is a means of exchange and that economic systems rely not on incalculable intrinsic values but on exchange values, established by markets.[17] We think of these statements as noncontroversial descriptions of reality, but historically the universal use of money and the acceptance of exchange value over intrinsic value required substantial intellectual adjustment and often wrenching social change. It is no accident that the seminal eighteenth-century theorist of money was not a Frenchman but a Scot. Adam Smith was much more comfortable taking exchange value as the foundation for his economic theories than Quesnay. Not only did Smith have greater insight into the economic process, but there was a much longer history of the penetration of money into agriculture in Britain than in France.[18]

In sixteenth-century Britain, land tenure and the rights of farmer-tenants had followed substantially the same lines as those still dominant in eighteenth-century France. For a variety of reasons, however, British landowners were both precocious and successful in annulling the traditional rights of their tenants. In a series of actions, British landlords slowly eliminated common lands that had for centuries served tenants on their estates. Once privatized and enclosed, these lands were turned into money-making ventures for the landlords. The farmers who had used them were in many cases dispossessed. Through these "enclosures," British landlords mobilized their estates to produce cash flow instead of continuing to accept rents in kind and traditional labor dues. Wool production was one of the capitalist ventures that British landlords moved into with increasing zeal.[19] By the eighteenth century, entire villages were being displaced to make room for herds of sheep. The enclosures and what came to be known as the clearances, which were particularly severe in the Scottish Highlands, created agricultural exiles who staffed the growing mines and mills of Britain, manned the imperial armies, or sold themselves into indentured servitude on New World plantations. In eighteenth-century Britain, then, where the monetization of agriculture was well advanced, it was much easier to conceive of money as a universal economic measure and unit of exchange. To catch up with what theorists regarded as the more advanced economy of Britain, France was urged to reorganize agriculture and the laws governing property. This did in fact occur, though it took the French Revolution with its overhaul of the traditional system of land tenure to bring it about.

When money activity emerged as the standard measure in economics, theorists began to question its nature. Yes, money was a medium of exchange, but it did not appear to be a neutral substance like a liquid, say, that would take the shape of whatever contained it. Nor did its action appear to be organic, like the circulation of the blood. Money appeared to be more like gravity, a force rather than a substance, and a force that shaped events. The operations of money appeared to follow some inner principles that were independent of law and social policy. Adam Smith summarized these mysteries as the work of an invisible guiding hand.[20]

His description suggested the workings of Providence. God moves in mysterious ways, yet everything he does serves a purpose, disguised from us perhaps, but known to him. Added to the moral force of this analogy was the purely mechanical similarity between the invisible hand of the economy and the invisible force of universal gravity. A concept with resonances both in the language of religion and in the progressive field of physics combined within itself the two strands of the Deistic model of cosmic order. The "invisible hand" symbolized both God's purpose for the creation and the mechanical means he had chosen to carry it out. This concept gave economics intellectual currency and cultural power. If economic activity depended on universal forces that were providentially guided, then societies needed to give them full scope to realize their purposes. In making this argument, French economists of the eighteenth century branded it with a lasting slogan, "Laissez faire, laissez aller." Leave the system alone, and it will steer economic affairs on their proper course.

The rise of economics as a discipline in the eighteenth century meant that social decisionmaking suddenly gained a new guiding principle. Alongside the developing conversations about political rights and political power, there were also animated and contentious

conversations about economic policy. The debate between the physiocrats and the mercantilists was only one of these; many others
focused on the role of manufacturing, the value of high versus low
wages, and the imposition of taxes and tariffs, to name just a few.
These conversations, like the political debates in France, also had
their role in thoughts and actions of the people. When Louis XVI
and his family were forced to leave Versailles and take up residence
in Paris, they were escorted into the city by a mob intent on two
things: expanding political rights and lowering the price of bread.[21]

During the seventeenth century, the conversation about famine
protection and the availability of bread at an affordable price migrated from agriculture to politics and economics. From that point
forward, the role of economic discussions in policy debates in governments expanded. Increasingly an economic rationale became the
last word in those conversations. More than any other emergent
force in the eighteenth century, economics with its calculus of means
and ends trumped reasoning about resource use. This was to prove
especially damaging to land and labor. The ascendancy of northern
Europe during the colonial era meant that materialistic science and
bottom-line economic thinking shaped world markets and social policy. First Nature, the Neolithic consensus, had been shared across all
classes in society. In the colonial era, in contrast, the reigning ideology was imposed by the intellectual, political, and agricultural elites,
who held power, however narrowly, over the disenfranchised.

Changes in Thinking about Nature

The mechanical view of the world that physics fostered and other
sciences strained to engage, imitate, or incorporate was indirectly
reflected in the way people viewed the landscape. As agriculture lost
its stature in the minds of theorists, it also began to lose its traditional place in the broader cultural imagination. This change was felt
in many ways and can be traced in forms of expression that range
from the musings of travelers to the writings of poets.

Writings about the landscape produced in the eighteenth century show a sharp divide. In the early part of the century, the human
world, the agricultural realm, and the province of uncultivated nature
were one continuous field with no internal boundaries. The poet's

or traveler's mind flowed from one to another without difficulty. By the end of the century, key writers had created a sharp divide within this continuum and separated the agricultural world from the world of nature. The middle ground between the human and the biological communities articulated by First Nature disappeared. The long-celebrated order and beauty of the rural landscape became a minor poetic theme; the sense of satisfaction and reassurance that poets had until recently felt in it was dismissed as unimportant; and the role of mediator that the farm landscape had long played was spurned as a new generation of poets declared themselves ready to confront nature face to face.

This abrupt and dramatic change of sensibility was as consequential for ecological understanding and action as eighteenth-century mechanistic or economic theory. In the field of ecological conceptualization, poets proved themselves to be the "unacknowledged legislators of the world," establishing within a remarkably few years an entirely new set of rules and expectations to govern the relationship between human and natural communities. The decisive changes after midcentury had roots in both France and Germany. Jean-Jacques Rousseau, a trendsetter in so many fields, was an important force in the changing response to landscape and to nature. The more decisive influence, however, came from German poets of the late eighteenth century, including Johann Wolfgang von Goethe. The English philosopher Edmund Burke and the German philosopher Immanuel Kant provided theoretical underpinnings for the new poetic ideal.

The radically new view of nature was first nurtured by scenery that had never before appealed to Europeans. It featured a well-known landscape that was visited only when necessary and more often endured than admired. The high Alps had been crisscrossed by paths since the Paleolithic period, but through travelers had always found the terrain forbidding and uncomfortable. Leopold Mozart and his son, Wolfgang, were among the many international travelers of the early eighteenth century whose itinerary took them across the Alps on their way to Italy. Mozart's biographer Hermann Abert, who was thoroughly familiar with the appreciation of that region that became universal among poets of following generations, expressed surprise that he was unable to find any trace of this later sensibility in the letters of the precocious Mozart and his father. The later writers, he noted, always included in their travelogues

> a series of more or less colorful images of the Alps. Of this we find not a single word in the accounts of either Mozart or his father. . . . Far more frequent are the references to the difficulties of crossing the Alps, to the snow and dirt and so on. Bozen struck Leopold as "dreary," while Mozart even described it as a "pigsty." There is not a single trace of the Romanticism usually associated with mountain scenery, and the Mozarts are still clearly in thrall to the essentially classical view of nature typical of the generation before Rousseau, in whom the wild beauty of the mountains inspired only terror and unease. . . . Only after the Mozarts had descended into the Valley of the Po, do we find more frequent accounts of their impressions of nature. Leopold had earlier written that his favorite scenery was the Swabian countryside, with its delightful mixture of woods and fields and parks, and in Italy, too, it is clear from his praise of Naples that what attracted most was the jocund charm of its park-like landscapes. As a true disciple of the Enlightenment, he never forgot the element of fruitful fecundity. Vesuvius, by contrast, left little impression on him.[22]

Goethe traveled through the Alps on his way to Italy in 1779. His impressions could not have been more different from theirs.

> Above the summits before us a light was revealing itself, the source of which we could not understand. It shone through the night like a glow-worm and we realized at last that it was none other than Mont Blanc. It had a strange, supreme beauty; it covered us with light and the stars were massing round it. It had not their twinkling glimmer, but it looked like a vast shining body, belonging to a higher sphere. It was difficult to believe that it had earthly roots.[23]

Out of tune as the Mozarts's reactions were with the new sensibility, their responses to the Alpine landscape were entirely in keeping with the sensibility of French poets of the early eighteenth century. To critics, these men and women appeared nostalgic, patronizing to those who did the hard work of agriculture, complacent and assured in their own superior social positions. Some poets may have been guilty of some of these failings, but by and large, the French poetry of the early eighteenth century reveals—as art had done since the Paleolithic—an appreciative attitude toward the landscapes that surrounded and sustained them. A poem written by a cardinal of southern French origin celebrates the fruitfulness of his native Provence.

> The worker's treasure and the shepherd's pride,
> the olive in my mind's eye is linked with the orange tree.
> How I love to contemplate the blue mountains
> which form long amphitheaters before my eyes
> where winter still reigns while blond Ceres
> has covered our fields below with the gold of her hair.
> It is sweet to remember the Rhône River as it opens its arms
> to separate our islands, then gathers in again her scattered
> treasures
>
> . . . .
>
> As the sun sets, I admire the celebrated vineyards
> where festoons of perfumed grapes hang from the vines,
> while towards the north the oaks ever green
> confront the thunder and brave the wintry blast.[24]

France itself inspired André Chenier to write a celebratory poem in much the same spirit. After contrasting France's moderate climate with the climates of less-blessed countries in the extreme north and south, he surveyed its natural resources.

> The oaks, the pines, and thick elm trees
> Shade our summits with useful branches;
> And the fortunate riverbanks at Beaune and Aix
> and the rich Aquitaine and the high Pyrenees,
> make rivers of delicious wines—
> matured on their shores—flow from bruising presses.
> Sweet-smelling Provence, beloved of the winds,

breathes her perfumed breath over the sea.
All along her coast, the orange and the lemon,
delicious treasures, gleam in their golden cloaks.
And further inland, on the slope of rocky hills
The fat olive forms its sweet liqueurs.[25]

These large themes do not overpower the poet, who takes the whole of Provence or the whole of France in stride. In another mood, a writer may realize that the world exceeds the reach of human consciousness. Faced with the same realization, a poet at the end of the century would dwell on the contrast between the spiritual human being and the overpowering might of brute nature, but in the early eighteenth century, poets accepted human limitations without losing their self-possession or their inherent optimism.

I love the depths of the ancient forests,
the robust old age and solemn height
of the oaks that Time and Nature, without us,
have raised high above our heads.
One breathes in these somber, majestic woods
a certain air of the venerable and the sacred;
it must have been the atmosphere of these mysterious places—
their profound silence and their solitary peace—
that made the Gallic people believe for so long
that the gods spoke only in the depths of the woods.
A man is unequal to their vast extent;
they halt his steps; they cloud his understanding;
a humble atom lost in so vast a space.
Even in the middle of the estate of which he is master,
he remains a lonely voyager on an immense surface.
A man can only truly possess a small place;
beyond the limits of his senses, he can find no pleasure;
if he owns too much land, his domains escape him.
So, proud by instinct, but conscious of his frailty,
he narrows the space he sets aside for himself;
he comes, on the slopes that he loves to walk,
To lay out a garden, to cultivate an orchard.[26]

Another extraordinary poem, by the Italian Giuseppe Parini, written in the middle of the eighteenth century illustrates the role that traditional agriculture still played then as a mediator between the poet and the natural world. Parini's poem describes the strength and invigoration that the poet feels when he is in the cultivated fields of his home region. A poet of Uruk might have felt erotically energized among the same fields, but Parini, whose poetic sensibility is like that of his French contemporaries, feels calm and reassured. When he is among familiar fields, all is right with the world.

Parini's poem contrasts the security and comfort the home fields inspire in him with his very different experience of the city. Despite the city-country opposition, the poem is about both cultural and personal responses to two agricultural regimes. The countryside where the poet feels at home is planted in wheat. What characterizes the city—Milan, in this instance—is not hustle and bustle but the cultivation of rice and hay in artificially flooded fields under the city's walls. What the poem offers, then, is more than just a view of the power of traditional agriculture to make humans feel at home in nature; it also contrasts this with the failure of exploitive, nontraditional agriculture to do the same.[27]

In the healthy air among my lovely hills,
I will pass tranquil days among the blessed folks
whom honest work has made robust and strong.
With an unburdened mind cleansed by pure waters,
I will celebrate in verse the healthy peasants
scattered through the fields at harvest time,
and their tireless bodies among the ripening grain

. . . .

saying "O fortunate folk who in perfect temper
breathe this air that is purged and purified!" . . .
Nature has given gifts of ample sky and pure air
to the city, but whom do these gifts serve
among all the luxury, the greed, and neglect?
It was not enough for you
that you had stagnant marshes all around.
You needed to bring the rivers
right under your city walls to flood your hayfields.

You sacrificed the common good
to feed a rich man's horses—
horses that trample honest men and women in the streets.[28]

In a later verse the poet returns to the healthy workers in traditional agriculture to contrast them with the pallid workers in the rice
industry, undernourished and afflicted with malaria.

Look at the faces painted with deathly pallor
of the exhausted workers among the accursed rice;
and tremble citizens that these people suffer among you.[29]

Written in the middle of the eighteenth century, such a poem
would seem impossibly old-fashioned by the century's end, when
farming landscapes had lost their hold on the imagination, to be replaced by geographies unmarked by human cultivation and beyond
the power of human beings to inhabit or influence.

Both Rousseau, the French innovator, and the German poets of
the later eighteenth century were thoroughly familiar with the French
poets who were their near contemporaries. They could hardly have
failed to be. Eighteenth-century France was the intellectual and artistic center of Europe. Cultivated men and women studied its literature, wore Parisian fashions, and may well have preferred the
French language to their native tongue. Apparently for personal
reasons, Rousseau rebelled against this overwhelming cultural force.
For essentially nationalistic reasons, German theorists and artists
resisted it as well.

Rousseau was the first French author of importance to portray
the landscape of the Alps in the manner that would become the hallmark of the new sensibility. While he did not fully share the enthusiasms of later romantic poets, he is clearly an important forerunner.
In this passage from his autobiographical *Confessions*, he describes his
reactions to different kinds of landscape: "It has never been the case
that flat landscapes, however beautiful they may be, appeared so to
my eyes. I need the torrents, the rocks, the pines and the deep woods,
the mountains, the rough paths to climb and descend, precipices on
both sides that make me truly afraid."[30]

In one of his most influential fictions, Rousseau has one of his central characters talk about the bracing effects of mountain scenery on his physical and mental states: "In essence, it is an impression shared generally by all people, though not all of them are aware of it, that in the high mountains, where the air is pure and clear, one feels greater ease in breathing, more lightness in the body, and greater serenity in the spirit. Pleasures are less powerful and the emotions are more moderate. Our thoughts take on a certain grandeur and sublimity proportionate to the affecting objects all around us."[31]

Fear, the emotion that Rousseau himself sought in his mountain forays, grounded the experiences that his character values: "This solitary place was for me a savage and desolate refuge, but one filled with those sorts of beauties that please receptive souls and appear horrible to others. A waterfall swollen with snow melt not twenty feet from us roared with the sounds of crashing rocks, sand, and debris as it poured out a stream of chalky water. Behind us a chain of inaccessible spires divided the rock shelf where we stood from that part of the Alps that is covered with glaciers."[32]

The steep slopes, the violent rush of the waterfall, the desolation and isolation of the region had for centuries appeared "horrible to others." Why, then, was this landscape so celebrated by the poets of the late eighteenth century that their responses became clichés in the nineteenth century? Harsh landforms satisfied a sensibility that had revolutionary characteristics. They combined intense emotion with a sense of transcendent purpose. A search for the transcendent necessarily rejected the calm, the orderly, and the everyday, the intellectual and emotional spaces that had long been occupied by the agricultural landscape. The high emotional pitch of these newly sought experiences ruled out mediation. So, not only did the agricultural landscape lose its ability to bridge the gap between humans and nonhuman nature, mediation of any sort in the encounter with nature was rejected as undesirable, even illegitimate.

Modern men and women are the inheritors of this radical tradition. Like many of the ideas of the nineteenth century, it remains a largely unexamined given in modern thinking about nature. Many in Europe and the United States continue to identify nature with the wild, with wilderness, and to think of it as transcendent, offering heightened experiences. There is a widely held belief that human intervention in nature destroys its defining characteristic of wildness. These attitudes eliminate any middle ground where humans and nature might interact constructively. In effect, this new characterization of nature meant and continues to mean that the First Nature agricultural landscape has lost its traditional role as the meeting ground of the human community with the natural world.

Two philosophers who speculated about the new eighteenth-century sensibility offered explanations of its psychological roots. One was the Englishman Edmund Burke and the other a Prussian, Immanuel Kant. Neither was much concerned with poetry, landscape in general, or the Alps in particular; instead, their subject was a concept in rhetorical theory known as "the sublime." Literary critics in the era of Rome's fall, deeply influenced by the revival that Plato's philosophy was then experiencing, focused attention on the sublime, and one of them, Longinus, wrote a treatise on the subject that resurfaced to influence men and women during the eighteenth century. Longinus thought of the sublime as a moment of exalted feeling combined with superior insight; it was something that a skilled orator might introduce at the climax of a speech. For Edmund Burke, the sublime was fundamental to human experience. It was not a mere technique in the toolbox of the speechmaker; it was a profound human emotion that could be evoked by art.

Burke distinguished the sublime from the beautiful in more or less the same way that Longinus had contrasted the overwhelming force of the sublime speaker with the less compelling power of the normal orator. In Burke's view, beauty appeals only to the civilized traits of an individual, or, we might say, to the conscious mind. Beauty rests on our capacity to appreciate order, regularity, and symmetry. The sublime, on the other hand, "pertains to the passions concerning, 'self preservation,'" so it appeals to the deepest instinctual strands in our nature. The primary emotional response in situations where self-preservation is at issue is terror, as a number of English theoreticians before Burke had acknowledged. While these theoreticians had assumed that the sublime was really the sigh of relief a person felt after escaping mortal threat, Burke's view was different. The "delight" that people felt in fearful situations was not what they experienced when they realized they were safe. Instead, as one author explains it, the delight "is the fear felt as they draw near to it, in other words, as they masochistically approach death. Not only terror but also pain itself (as long as it is not excessive) delights. As tension, moreover, terror and pain become exactly like lust, as Burke depicts it—'rapturous and violent.'"[33]

Immanuel Kant based his theorizing on Burke's distinction between the beautiful and the sublime.[34] Kant framed his argument in more complex terms than Burke had done. Burke was mainly interested in the individual's awareness of mortality. Rather than talk about death in the abstract, Kant framed death within a conversation about nature. For him the sublime—with its borderline approach to pain and extinction—was a feature of every human interaction with the natural world. In his view, the sensation of sublime terror was "evoked by objects or occurrences which reveal our powerlessness as natural beings to overcome the forces of Nature."[35]

For Kant the idealized flirtation with death does not end at this point. Kant's encounter with the terrifying in nature climaxes in a declaration of moral superiority. The individual recognizes the power of nature but at the same time realizes the confines of that power within the purely material sphere. Though as "natural beings," humans are weak, we also have an intellectual, emotional, and spiritual side. We have innate freedom and the capacity for both rational thought and ethical action.[36] Kant's individual encountering nature gains a new appreciation of all these distinctly human traits and a corresponding contempt for the brutal, materialistic realm of the natural. In Kant at least, though not in all romantics, Newton's soulless, mechanical, and material universe becomes a presence in the world of human experience.

Kant's identification of nature with the threat of mortality and the terror that threat evoked changed the entire valence of the natural world in both poetic and philosophical conversation. In the First Nature formulation, the cultivated world was a place where the civilized virtues of order and regularity prevailed. In Burke's philosophy, this realm was merely beautiful and evoked nothing more than the superficial delights associated with conventional pleasures. The wild landscape, however, promised the superior experiences of fear and pain and introduced the linked themes of death and moral ascendancy into what was coming to be conceived not as a partnership but as a face-off between humans and nature.

The early eighteenth-century taste for modest pleasures grounded in ordered fertility was displaced by a taste for intense sensation aroused by a forbidding landscape that threatened death. First Nature emphasized sociability, life, and vitality; the new sensibility of the late eighteenth century venerated the solitary, the extreme, and the deadly. A radical redefinition of the essentially human turned the confrontation between the human being and nature into a hierarchical one. Face to face with nature, humans proved their spiritual, rational, and ethical *superiority*. The same confrontation brutalized nature by emphasizing its material and mechanical character and its mindless capacity to do harm.

The consequences of this appreciation were, and remain, extremely significant, not just for the aesthete appreciating the power of the avalanche but for all of us as we engage the natural world. The First Nature landscape, "which stands ready to guide us step by step from . . . ordered beauty to the more somber and intricate aspects of life and nature, is absolutely cut asunder."[37] The new taste for the violent and terror-inspiring aspects of nature eroded the last intellectual underpinnings of First Nature. With this the great Neolithic cultural consensus collapsed.

PART III

Age of Crisis

CHAPTER THIRTEEN

Silence, Loss, and Catastrophe

The last decades of the eighteenth century were an unusually dynamic period in Mediterranean history. Within a few years, the region experienced unprecedented political, cultural, and economic change. Progressives characterized existing limits on the exploitation of land and labor as backward and pushed for reform. Inventors streamlined agriculture technologies, and industrialization drew down the farm labor force. When traditional constraints on the use of land and labor disappeared, nothing took their place. There was no new consensus to inspire respect for the land and its resources and no new rationale for environmental restraint. The Mediterranean world had entered an unprecedented era of self-created environmental illiteracy. The dismal environmental history of the nineteenth and twentieth centuries is a narrative of what happened after every voice advocating First Nature had been silenced.

The ethical vacuum that engulfed agriculture at the end of the eighteenth century still surrounds it today and leaves it enmired in environmentally unsound practices. For two centuries agriculture has existed in a state that sociologists call anomie, an absence of rules or norms. Except for the rights of ownership, little limits the use of land by those who have the right or power to possess it. Economic rationality has become the chief constraint on land use, and economics has gained increased authority and autonomy as the ground for social and environmental decisionmaking. During the eighteenth century, economics had earned cultural respect by allying itself with Deism. In the nineteenth century, economics gained an unexpected ally in Charles Darwin. Social Darwinism applied the presumed lessons of Darwinian evolution to the management of society. Not just political philosophy but economic theory as well, especially the old French ideal of laissez-faire, took advantage of the justifications for brutal competitiveness enshrined in the (often misinterpreted) concept of survival of the fittest. With a boost from Darwin's theories, economics could claim to be a fact of life, not just a social institution.

The fate of the Mediterranean environment became more and more closely linked to global movements. The importation into Europe of world crops had been going on since the Renaissance, and this generally beneficial movement accelerated in the nineteenth century. Colonialism, one of the region's deadliest exports, rebounded after centuries of exclusively extra-regional practice to invade the home sea. Colonies supplied raw materials. Ascendancy of the mother country over the colonies was enhanced as colonial masters industrialized.

France, whose once vast territories in the Americas had been reduced by war with Britain and by Napoléon's sale of the Louisiana Territory to the United States, looked around the Mediterranean for lands to replace a lost Atlantic Empire. The French found them in the short term in Egypt, which they occupied briefly under Napoléon, and in the longer term in Algeria, which they invaded in 1830. Though slavery played no part in these colonies or the protectorates that later supplemented them, the occupiers did introduce an entirely new and poisonous instrument of subjugation. Instead of placing real shackles on indigenous peoples, they burdened them with a new mythology that libeled their traditional ecological practices and justified foreign seizure of reputedly underutilized natural resources. This new environmental narrative played a major role in legitimizing colonial expropriations not just regionally but worldwide.

Nineteenth-century poetry and prose continued on the path that Rousseau and Goethe had pioneered. Literature engaged "nature" far more than before, and most of what we call nature writing has its roots in the century's romantic literature. The romantic concept of nature exalted wilderness while maintaining a strict divide between the human sphere and the natural world. Intrinsic to this divide was a sense of moral superiority discovered or disclosed through confrontation with nature. Face to face with a natural world that was typically characterized in Newtonian style as purely material, poets highlighted the spirituality of human beings. Nineteenth-century writers continued to polarize the human and the natural and consistently placed humans on a higher moral plane. Though largely unrecognized today, this sense of superiority still underlies many of our assumptions.

Spurred in many ways by the taste for landscape that romantic literature favored, travel to wild destinations increased. During the nineteenth century this trend became the foundation of a number of interrelated enterprises. Stimulated by industrial wealth and enabled by the rapid spread of rail transportation, the modern hotel industry developed with surprising speed. The goals of nineteenth-century travel, especially as train travel became more common, were new ones. The Grand Tour, the primary form of systematized travel in earlier times, was a privilege of the wealthy. Its purpose was educational, to expand the horizons and worldly experience of young gentlemen, and it focused on the cultural capitals of the Mediterranean world. But with romanticism, travel came to emphasize nature, and travelers visited the seaside or the mountains rather than cities. The south of France and the Italian coast were first affected by this new kind of travel. Like the Alps before their discovery by the romantic poets, the south of France had long been poor and agrarian. By the mid-nineteenth century, it was the scene of intense entrepreneurial development. By the third quarter of the century, it was the established retreat of European monarchs, nobility, and well-off bourgeoisie. The trend that began in that region has spread throughout the Mediterranean, and the impact of seasonal visitors is now a major strain on sensitive environments worldwide.

Colonialism Meets Industrialization

Cotton carried the colonial enterprise a decisive step beyond sugar, the crop that formed the plantation system.[1] Sugar went into the holds of merchant ships in Brazilian or Caribbean ports ready for market.[2] Cotton, on the other hand, required substantial work after harvest to turn the raw bolls into thread, thread into cloth, and cloth into clothing. By exporting and industrializing these final steps, Europeans were able to segregate the stages of production in ways that were economically beneficial to themselves and disadvantageous to their colonial suppliers. Ultimately, field production was the only work left to the colonial producers. Their enslaved labor force took the cotton from seeding to harvest, then the raw crop was shipped to the colonial homeland, where wage labor and increasingly autonomous machines did the spinning and weaving. Since most of the value added to the final product came from the postharvest stages of production, the colonial homeland—the metropole—gained an economic advantage over the primary producer, and this advantage grew bigger over time as mechanization increased.

Every stage of production favored the metropole over the colony. Purchasing additional slaves was expensive, and it increased output and profit by only a small percentage. The same funds invested in machinery increased not just production but productivity, and this increment came at a more profitable stage. Home governments made sure that the cotton their colonies harvested could only be sold in the metropolitan market, where a limited number of buyers sheltered from international competition were able to control prices. Metropolitan manufacturers of the finished product, on the other hand, had access to both wholesale and retail markets at home and abroad. Indeed, colonies became prime consumers of manufactured goods, including cloth made from the very cotton that they had cultivated.

This mature colonial cotton economy, like the sugar economy on which it was based, took a long time to develop. Cotton cultivation had begun in India during the Neolithic period. Early on, Indian textile workers learned the tricks of bleaching cotton to strip its fibers of the oils that resisted dying. The Romans knew about Indian cotton cloth, and Indian fabrics were much admired during the Middle Ages for their color and vibrant designs. Separating the useful fibers from the tenaciously held seeds is an especially tedious process, and in India this task occupied a large force of laborers.

At first the cotton trade, like every other trade with eastern Asia, was a drain on European precious metal reserves. Finding ways to turn a negative balance of trade into a positive one was essential if the relationship were to continue long term. The strategy that the European colonists adopted to shift that balance was transfer. Any eastern good that could be grown either in Europe or in a European colony would be removed from the international market and become part of a sheltered colonial exchange. The greatest cost saver and the innovation that dramatically transformed the colonial trade economy was the outright replacement of Indian labor by machines.

Techniques for spinning thread and weaving cloth were already familiar from the woolen industry that Britain had pioneered. Problems nonetheless went along with transforming a process devoted to one fiber to those appropriate to another. Once the problem of spinning strong thread was solved, the breakthrough technology that made cotton a viable industrial good was a simple device thought up by an American inventor, Eli Whitney, on the threshold of the nineteenth century. Whitney's gadget was more or less a reversed sieve. It combined a wire mesh that was too fine for cotton seeds to pass through with a revolving drum dotted with spines that plucked cotton fiber through the grid and left the seeds behind. Whitney's simple machine transformed the cleaning of a pound of cotton—a job once measured in days—into the labor of an hour. Mechanical ginning, rationalized production, machine milling, and international distribution in bulk carriers undercut the Indian cotton export industry and completely displaced it.

Both France and England were involved in the industrialization of cotton cloth production. Eventually machine-made cotton fabrics from these northern European industrial nations dominated the world market. English designs assumed a geometric look that bore little resemblance to the bright colors and rich block-printed patterns of the Indian originals. French manufacturers stayed much closer to their sources, producing fabrics still called *Indiennes*. The design palette that is now associated with Provence is largely defined by the colors and patterns of this cloth. *Indiennes* are imitations of an Indian export rather than an indigenous development, but they are now completely identified with the area that adopted it.

While northern Europe industrialized, the Mediterranean region remained mostly agrarian. North of some highly fluid boundary, manufacturing predominated. In that region, population moved from rural to urban areas as industry recruited masses of workers. South of this line, agriculture remained the major occupation, industry remained uncommon, and urbanization was slow-paced.[3] During the nineteenth century, the Mediterranean, once the center of the Western world, became a zone of primary production increasingly marginalized by a new world order that coalesced around industrial centers in northern Europe. In a world economy in which money dominated and industrial goods commanded high prices relative to the cost of food, the Mediterranean lost economic power and political clout simply by continuing as it had for centuries. The sea was further marginalized by innovations in oceangoing shipping that deprived it of its historic role as mediator between east and west. Sidelined by the new ocean routes of international trade, its ports lost commerce, which was increasingly concentrated on Europe's Atlantic seaboard. These factors hold true for the region as a whole; neither Christian nor Muslim nations were spared.

France Invades Egypt

At any time during the late fifteenth or sixteenth century, a European looking at the balance of power within the Mediterranean had good reason to be afraid. Ottoman influence was then rising to a crescendo in the eastern Mediterranean, and Ottoman influence was slowly but surely expanding into North Africa. A few decades after the Ottoman conquest of Egypt in 1515, Libya, Tunisia, and Algeria became integral parts of the empire.[4] At the time of the Ottoman conquest, Spain and Portugal were pursuing aggressive nationalist policies of conquest and Christianization. Invasions of North Africa by Christian armies were by no means to be ruled out, and Ottoman rulers worked to defend against piecemeal conquest.

When the long-anticipated European attack came, it was unlike anything that Ottoman rulers had prepared for. Neither Spain nor Portugal was the aggressor; the attack came centuries late; and it was directed at a part of Muslim North Africa that no one had considered vulnerable. In 1798, Napoléon launched a surprise invasion of Egypt. The rationale for the invasion was obscure at the time and has remained something of a mystery.[5] On July 21, 1798, elite Muslim cavalry attacked French infantry divisions that had been drawn up opposite them. Expecting the infantry formation to break under the terrifying impact of a mass charge, the horsemen drove straight into the invaders. The French held formation and delayed fire until the cavalry was almost on top of them. Then they launched coordinated musket volleys so powerful that the Muslim cavalry wheeled and retreated. The results of a second charge were identical, and the cavalry withdrew. This second failed charge ended the defense of Cairo, and the French occupied the city the same evening.

From Cairo, the French army drove southward, seconded by teams of experts who explored and chronicled the ruins of ancient Egypt. This scientific expedition, which resulted, among other things, in the uncovering of the Rosetta stone, is the face of the invasion that is best remembered in Europe. Muslim historians remember something quite different. The overwhelming French victory was a violent shock not just to the defenders of Egypt but to the entire Muslim world. Accustomed for more than a millennium to repeated victories against European armies, Muslims everywhere were stunned by the failure of their seasoned and disciplined troops to offer more than token resistance to a European invader.[6]

The most momentous change that the European powers brought about in Egypt was creation of the Suez Canal. This venture sponsored by the Egyptian government required substantial European investment. Eventually England, originally lukewarm about the project, was the major beneficiary of the canal, which provided more direct access to Asia, particularly India, than the route around Africa. The canal had the potential to restore the Mediterranean Sea to its pre-fifteenth-century position as the moderator of trade between east and west. The fact that it did no such thing illustrates dramatically the eclipse of the region in the trade and economic system then in force. The Mediterranean gave carriers from northern Europe shorter passage times between east and west. It did nothing to dislodge those powers from their dominant position in the world economic and geopolitical systems.[7]

France Invades Algeria

Napoléon's quixotic invasion of Egypt was a prelude to the far more devastating and far more consequential French invasion of Algeria. It began in 1830. If Napoléon's motives for invading Egypt are hazy, the motives of the French government for its attack on Algeria are all too clear.[8] To divert attention from mounting domestic failures, King Charles X sponsored the opportunistic venture.[9] His invasion soon matured into an occupation, and in 1841 the French appointed a new general to carry out more ambitious plans. No longer satisfied with a foothold, they determined on full territorial domination and a "pacified" countryside, where colonists from France could settle and prosper.[10] The military adopted a scorched-earth policy to wipe out the resources of the Arab opposition and to clear the ground for colonists. They drove Algerians from the most fertile soils and resettled them on marginal lands. Once cleared of native farmers, confiscated lands were redistributed among French nationals. Reduced to the rank of agricultural laborers on the domains of French farmers, Algerians were kept in check by economic pressures and by strict government control. For the first time, the full colonial package of economic and political subjugation was firmly in place in a Mediterranean country.

The Invention of Environmental Degradation

The decision to send French colonists into Algeria and the particularly vicious way that French forces cleared the ground were decisive not only for North Africans but for the entire Mediterranean basin, where generally less ambitious and less coercive colonial adventures continued through the end of the Second World War. The French invasion gave birth to an insidious pro-colonial propaganda weapon that had enormous, enduring consequences for the ecology of the region. As far as it is possible to determine today, Algeria before the French arrived was ecologically and agriculturally sound and healthy:

> Algeria was . . . fully self-sufficient in agricultural products and even exported surpluses, especially of grains. In the moun-

tains, fruit trees provided many of the primary crops, and
some grains were grown. The plains were largely given over
to cereal cultivation, mainly wheat and barley; vegetables
were also grown, in many areas with irrigation. In the deserts, livestock husbandry predominated, except in the oases,
where dates and vegetables provided the majority of agricultural products. In nearly all the rural areas livestock were
raised in numbers and combinations that varied with the region, the people, and the environment.[11]

Early French observers were equally positive. Though they argued that liberation from the Turks would improve agriculture, they
painted a glowing picture of the countryside, describing the "abundant agricultural and mineral products" and "thick" forests, "generally to be found in or near mountains with plentiful streams."[12]
    The highly positive assessment of the country and its resources
was about to change, but not because the facts had changed. As soon
as French administrators were required to make Algerian land available to colonists from France, they learned a different tune. In official documents, the country suddenly began to be described in terms
that were the opposite of those used in the precolonial era. This
crude and instant turnaround provided the ideological rationale for
the shift in policy. It created "an environmental narrative fundamentally different from the preconquest narrative. As early as 1834, and
possibly earlier, the Algerians began to be blamed for ruining the
land, and this accusation provided some in the military and the administration with a justification to expropriate it."[13]
    By midcentury this narrative was fully developed. Writing in an
official document in 1847, one French observer described the country and its people in the harshly critical terms that the new pro-
colonial, anti-Arab policies required. "This land, once the object
of intensive cultivation, was neither deforested nor depopulated as
today; . . . it was the abundant granary of Rome." The same report
paid special attention to the condition of the country's forests.
Woodlands that earlier, disinterested observers had described as
lush and abundant came to be portrayed as abused. The abuse was
blamed on Arab herders. The job of the French colonist in the landscape that French propaganda had labeled "degraded" was perfectly

clear. "It is our responsibility to raise Algeria from her fallen state, and to return her to her past [Roman] glory; for this privileged soil possesses all the elements of surprising fecundity, of a great prosperity."[14]

The damage caused by this self-serving pack of lies was enormous. In itself it represented official misconduct of breathtaking depravity. Worse, it masked the depredations of the French, who ravaged a verdant landscape and destroyed a highly successful indigenous way of life.[15] But the damage did not end there. Other European nations adopted the same environmental myth in service of their own interventions.

In the second half of the nineteenth century, a book on the plants and animals of the Bible offered an offhand critique of the environmental degradation of the eastern Mediterranean region. With evident unselfconsciousness, the book promoted the cause of European colonization and justified the growing British presence in Palestine.

> Though the manners and customs of the East are stationary, its *physical aspect* has greatly changed. Once the name was synonymous with fruitfulness and beauty, and there was scarcely a country in the Eastern world which was not rich by reason of its natural endowments; but time and the judgment-hand of God have wrought changes, and the fruitful places have become a waste. . . .
>
> Palestine has shared the same fate. The land of Israel— the "goodly land"—the land of promise—the Canaan which flowed with milk and honey, and was noted for its corn and wine—is no longer what it was. As compared with its former fruitfulness it is a wilderness.[16]

The damage this poisonous narrative created lives on today. Much contemporary environmental literature has taken European assessments of the Mediterranean environment from this era as true. Reliance on these fabricated accounts has skewed contemporary understanding of the state of the environment before colonization and belied the success of traditional practices of cultivation and land management. Innocently but fatally accepting crudely manipulated data as fact, environmental historians have painted a picture of preconquest deforestation and landscape degradation in the region that is as false and misleading as the twisted narratives on which it rests.[17]

Both within the Mediterranean and worldwide, colonial conquest was encouraged as a safety valve. Many believed that it could eliminate warfare in Europe. During the nineteenth century, this policy benefited the Ottoman Empire. Powerful nations agreed among themselves to preserve the empire, the so-called sick man of Europe, rather than risk coming to blows over its corpse.[18] At the end of World War I, this hands-off policy came to an abrupt end. As an ally of defeated Germany, the Ottoman Empire became fair game for the victors. Anatolia, its historic heartland, became modern Turkey. Other Ottoman territories were parceled out to European powers. France gained a protectorate in present-day Syria and Lebanon. Iraq fell into the British sphere of influence, along with Egypt, Saudi Arabia, Palestine, and Transjordan. Italy assumed responsibility for Libya and other countries in the Horn of Africa. France added Morocco and Tunisia to its North African portfolio.

Darwin and the Idea of the Natural

From the time of publication, *On the Origin of Species* sparked conflicts. Darwin's theory of evolution challenged the accepted interpretation of God's creation. In Genesis, God created generic light and darkness, but when it came to the creation of plants and animals, the biblical text descended to specifics. The common understanding was that the animals and plants that he created were unique and final. The notion that species were not distinct and immutable but in flux as the products of transformative change caused severe problems for theologians, as well as for many biologists.[19] To prove or refute this view, the emerging fossil record was scoured for transitional species that marked the passage from one species to another. The search was particularly intense and particularly polarized in the case of the "missing link" between apes and humans. This controversy affected acceptance of Darwin's theory.

Although this well-recognized clash between Darwinian theory and traditional cosmology was important, its effects on the conduct of daily life were considerably less than those brought about by the adoption of Darwinian concepts to underwrite social, political, and

economic institutions. Intellectually, Darwinism offered the opportunity for theorists in fields focusing on human organization to gain
the ostensible support of science. Darwin defined principles of the
natural world and declared certain immutable laws of nature in simple terms. Nature, the natural, and natural law were millennial pre-
occupations. To call a theory natural and frame it as an embodiment
of natural law was to give it enormous authority and persuasive power.

Shifts in descriptions of the natural order of the universe, like
Copernicus's and Darwin's, are rare, and they offer key opportunities for further change. Among other things, they make it possible
to promote or demote cultural principles of thought and action.
Newton's cosmology made geocentrism untenable, but that shift
was far less significant than its secondary effects. Newton's cosmos
favored the materialistic, the mechanical, and the mathematically
demonstrable. Every field of knowledge scrambled to reinvent or at
least redescribe itself in the language of these newly elevated principles. Some fields were well suited to materialistic and mathematical
structuring, but others were not. Even the least amenable sought
some kind of rapprochement with the principles that had shown such
spectacular results in Newton's work. Newton's laws were difficult,
though not impossible, to apply to social life. Darwin's theories, on
the other hand, were understood as embracing all life, including
human social life. They appealed to enough of the Newtonian universal principles to be considered good science, though they were
too speculative for many both inside and outside the scientific community.[20] Darwin stated his evolutionary principles with Newtonian
clarity, though without mathematical precision.[21] When Herbert
Spenser explained "natural selection" in a well-turned phrase, "survival of the fittest," Darwin did not hesitate to borrow it.[22]

Darwin's theories were ultimately more influential in European
social thinking than Newton's because he achieved a convincing connection between scientific explanation and historical concepts of the
natural. Darwin's simple formulas fit the political agendas of the day
and could be given immediate social application. The fact that his
principles seemed to lend aid and comfort to the strongest preju-
dices of his era—its racism and belief in European superiority, its
enthusiasm for unregulated competition in economics and politics,

its heedlessness of the benefits of cooperation, a self-congratulatory sense of progress—catapulted them to immediate popularity. Though his theories were resisted by theologians, scientists, and philanthropists, he was accepted as a national luminary and, upon his death, honored by burial in Westminster Abbey, not far from the grave of Sir Isaac Newton.

Making Economics Natural

Social Darwinism is the best known of the Darwinian pseudo-sciences, but economics, arguably, gained more than any other discipline from the appropriation of Darwin's ideas. The boost that Darwinism gave to the doctrine of laissez-faire was especially important.[23] Darwinism also offered a more up-to-date underpinning for economics than Adam Smith's conceptual linkup with Deist thought. Deism was no longer an influential idea in the nineteenth century, so the cosmological grounding for economic theory it once provided had become unpersuasive. Darwinism reestablished economics as a natural force. The economist John Maynard Keynes recognized the cultural power this connection provided:

> The parallelism between economic *laissez-faire* and Darwinianism ... is now seen, as Herbert Spencer was foremost to recognize, to be very close indeed. Darwin invoked sexual love, acting through sexual selection, as an adjutant to natural selection by competition, to direct evolution along lines which should be desirable as well as effective, so the individualist invokes the love of money, acting through the pursuit of profit, as an adjutant to natural selection, to bring about the production on the greatest possible scale of what is most strongly desired as measured by exchange value.[24]

Darwin's supporters in Britain are well known, but his influence spread rapidly to the Continent as well. As was the case in England, Darwin's strongest international influence was felt outside the scientific community. France and Germany were both particularly attuned to the social implications that could be drawn from Darwin's theories.

When Darwin published the *Origin*, France and Germany
were in the throes of socio-economic change and political
conflict. In France the legacy of the Revolution was one of
cleavage and political confrontation. . . . After the abortive
revolution of 1848, Germany also experienced political division against a background of brisk economic growth and
social change. After national unification under Bismarck, the
new Reich was fraught with continuing regional differences
and enmities, compounded by hostility between Protestants
and a sizeable Catholic minority. Abrasive class divisions were
reflected in the emergence of the largest socialist party in
Europe, in addition to a sharp differentiation between rural/
agrarian and urban/industrial subcultures.[25]

To these confused and battered nations, *Origin* promised to offer a
scientifically endorsed natural foundation for human social structure. The aim of social theorists studying his work was an ambitious
one; they hoped "to discover an authoritative body of beliefs capable
of uniting the nation around an ethical consensus."[26]

In France, when no biologist or botanist could be found to
translate Darwin's seminal work, Clémence-Auguste Royer was recruited. A largely self-educated expert in both economics and the
evolutionary theories of the French biologist Jean-Baptiste Lamarck,
she was known in the field of political theory as the author of a
well-respected study of taxation. Her concern with political ideals
prompted her to frame her translation of *Origin* in a social and economic context rather than a purely biological one. She even added
a preface of her own in which she not only pointed out the social
implications of his theories but scolded Darwin for his failure to
confront these issues directly, a defect she felt it her duty to correct.
In her work on taxation, she had described nature in progressive
terms as a "work of perpetual transition." She imagined human society as a biological organism and equated the economic laws of the
marketplace with the "immutable and universal . . . laws of biology
and physiology." She also drew a "parallel between the growth of
physical organs and the progressive elaboration of political institutions from primitive times to the present."[27]

Like many other interpreters of Darwin, Royer equated evolution with progress.[28] As she asserted in her preface, "Progress was a fact of the natural world affecting all species and from which it was vital to draw the relevant moral and political conclusions." Inequality was "natural and the foundation of the social division of labor." Among humans, as among animals, "the higher races seem destined to supplant the lower races and to make them disappear or slowly assimilate them." "Dedicated to all 'free men' the book extolled the virtues of individualism, economic freedom and competition."[29]

In Royer's formulation, as in the formulations of many of her contemporaries, economics was transformed. Like evolution, which encapsulated the competition among individuals and species that drove the progress engine, economics was a natural fact. To deny economic competition or to mute it through interference with its natural workings would be to risk thwarting the drive of nature toward human and social perfection. Neither money nor economics could remain what they had been with this kind of backing. From being market forces they became life forces. From being measures of the flow of goods and services, they became cosmological principles. These principles produced not a religion but certainly an ideology, one that is ascendant today and applies bottom-line thinking to every conceivable social decision, including those that impact the environment.

"Nature Red in Tooth and Claw": The Poets' View

Besides "survival of the fittest," Darwinians accepted another description of natural selection from an influential long poem by Alfred, Lord Tennyson. Tennyson's *In Memoriam A.H.H.* was published a decade before *Origin*.[30] Though its speculations on nature and evolution raise issues that Darwin also faced, Tennyson was actually responding to an anonymous work released in 1844 called *Vestiges of the Natural History of Creation*.[31] In the excerpted passages below the poet tries to reconcile the contradictions he finds between the processes of the natural world as biology was revealing them and fundamental principles of his faith. In canto 54 of the poem, he appeals to the belief in a providential God who permits evil in the short run but ensures that in time good will triumph.

I can but trust that good shall fall
At last—far off—at last, to all.

In the following canto, he takes the quest for divine justice to
the realm of existence that not only Christianity but Platonic philosophy appealed to. If justice in the world is elusive, then there must
be a life after death in which justice will be finally achieved. This
belief is championed by the divinity within all humans, in the soul.

The wish, that of the living whole
No life may fail beyond the grave,
Derives it not from what we have
The likest God within the soul?

Once these dogmatic positions have been established, the poet
turns to the challenges that nature, as it is exemplified in evolutionary thought, offers to faith.

Are God and Nature then at strife,
That Nature lends such evil dreams?
So careful of the type she seems,
So careless of the single life.

The "evil dreams" are sparked by the realization that Nature has
no interest in individual life. Rather, all natural mechanisms are
geared toward preservation of the species, "the type." If that was not
devastating enough, the poet then remembers the fossil evidence for
extinction of entire species:

"So careful of the type?" but no.
From scarped cliff and quarried stone
She cries, "A thousand types are gone:
I care for nothing, all shall go."

The poet is forced to conclude that Nature is indifferent to the
fate of all living creatures. It is simply a mechanism without purpose
or understanding. This conclusion is a tribute to the lingering power
of the Newtonian revolution that had reduced not just the stars but

all animate and inanimate being to mere material. From this viewpoint, plants and animals, like rocks and planets, have no spiritual character. Indeed, they confirm Nature's repudiation of spirituality altogether. For Tennyson, Nature is a literalist; from her point of view, "the spirit does but mean the breath."

Nature is even indifferent to the distinction—all-important to the poet and his contemporaries—between humans and the rest of the animate world. The poet expresses this realization in a rhetorical question:

> And he, shall he,
>
> Man, her last work, who seem'd so fair,
>
> . . . .
>
> Who trusted God was love indeed
>
> And love Creation's final law—
> Tho' Nature, red in tooth and claw
> With ravine, shriek'd against his creed
>
> . . . .
>
> Be blown about the desert dust,
> Or seal'd within the iron hills?

For Tennyson and for the majority of his audience, the interrogation of Nature led to the conclusion that the laws of nature are distinct from and far inferior to the laws of God. Natural law is cruel and thoughtless, ignorant of spirituality, and unaffected by love: "O life as futile, then, as frail!" Natural things are mortal; immortality is only for human beings, who are implanted with souls. Nature, in short, is outside the sphere of being that humans inhabit. We look at it across a divide that is stark and absolute. When we take stock of the differences between our humanity and the character of all other natural things, we are forced to acknowledge not just a difference in substance but a difference in value. And inevitably we must conclude that human culture is superior to natural processes and natural law. Tennyson returns us to the Kantian orbit, where the terrifying face of a purely material nature inspires the poet to extol human characteristics, which are, in Tennyson's case, underwritten by Christian dogma.

The Victorian view of nature represented here is markedly different from the view expressed in the poetic tradition of the early eighteenth century. It also takes a very peculiar slant on the biological itself. Take love, for example. Nature, as Tennyson sees it, presides over birth and death but not love. Tennyson must be imagining proper love as an utterly sexless sensation appropriate to Christian worship. This is not love as nature embodies it. Still, if reproduction is too prurient for Victorian conversation, maternal love might be worthy of mention. Many species of animals nurture and protect their young for prolonged periods. Protecting and training the young, which adults carry on, often at great sacrifice to themselves, is entirely natural, but this kind of love is missing from Tennyson's natural world.

Loveless nature is also characterized by uncontrolled appetites, which Tennyson calls "ravine." To serve those appetites, nature encourages unlimited predation, the drive that keeps it "red in tooth and claw." In fact, aggression in the biological community is restrained. It is human violence that knows no boundaries; we are far more likely to kill or wound intimates than any other species. The rules of animal behavior are different. Limits on aggression are widespread in the natural world. Predation involves death, but many forms of competition are limited, and there is widespread cooperation among packs, prides, flocks, and herds. Poets and others depicting nature in the nineteenth century paid little attention to the cooperative and symbiotic as opposed to the competitive. In developing the romantic myth of nature, Tennyson portrayed natural processes inaccurately and exaggerated those features that distinguished them from Christian idealism. He polarized the human community and its ecological surroundings and muddied the waters of responsible environmental thought. In both ways he was representative of his times.

Armed with this concept of nature as antagonist, nineteenth-century European men and women found it hard to acknowledge that they were biological beings dependent on air, water, food, and shelter for survival. They knew they were, of course, but they preferred to think of biological necessities as unworthy of consideration among enlightened and advanced people and nations. They regarded themselves as living on a higher plane defined by morally and spiritually guided thought and action. Savages and the poor were preoccupied with survival, but cultured Europeans devoted their lives to higher concerns. They sincerely believed themselves to be living in a world governed by law and custom rather than natural forces.

This extreme dichotomy was at the heart of the nineteenth-century conception of nature. A good example of the pervasiveness of this idea comes from a curious source. During the nineteenth century, classicists who studied ancient cultures came to the conclusion that the Greek idea of nature was similar to their own. The Greeks, they erroneously believed, had divided the world into two distinct spheres. One of them was governed by rules lumped under the concept *physis*, meaning "nature," a word from which we get "physics" and "physical." The other part of the world was subject to *nomos*, "law or custom." *Physis* ruled the natural world; human beings, on the other hand were subject only to laws and customs of their own devising.[32]

As we saw in Chapter 7, Greeks did not take this polarized view of the world at all; the classicists of the nineteenth century were projecting their image of the world into the past. So their scholarship tells us nothing about the Greeks, but it tells us everything about the nineteenth-century conception of nature. Once the romantic ideal took hold, it was so pervasive and so tenacious that it blotted out alternatives and seemed even to scholars to be a universal truth and not a recent cultural fabrication. Along with everybody else, scholars took for granted that nature and the world of human affairs stood on opposite sides of some unbridgeable divide. On one side of the divide stood the world that human beings made for themselves, and across from it stood the entirely different world of nature. Imagining a divide is probably the greatest difference between the romantic conception of nature and the First Nature view. It is also the greatest shortcoming of the romantic ideology. Because it polarized the world starkly and irreconcilably between what were seen as incompatible spheres of life, it denied even the possibility of a middle ground on which humans and nature could constructively interact.

The romantic sensibility was not limited to poets and their readers; it was the driving force behind the exploits of the explorers and adventurers of the nineteenth century. These men and women were driven by a need to seek out the harshest and most alien places for the sake of the emotional extremes they could experience and as a way of testing themselves. The romantic concept of nature as wild and brutal created a proving ground for Victorian strength and valor. Modern adventurers still court risk today. The men and women who climb Mount Everest or sail around the world alone or set off into the Alaskan wilderness with a penknife and a paperback are reenacting this romantic ideal. Though seldom indifferent to the places that they seek out, their focus is themselves. They do not climb Everest to find out what the mountain is like. They climb to discover if they will prove to be masters of their own fate. Wilderness is a realm where danger can be challenged and with luck overcome.

The romantic hero was a solitary individual. He—the hero was almost always a male—was imagined to have superior sensitivity and an uncompromising commitment to ideals. His goal in life was self-examination and self-actualization. He looked for challenges and faced them alone. He was not communal; the romantics had little interest in group action. Just as the world was divided between the civilized and the wild, the world of humans was atomized. Individuals lived and acted alone.

Before the romantic era, writing about nature had been essentially comic. Like much comic writing, it focused on the gratification of desire, festivity, feasting, and joy. In romanticism, nature lost its comic character. The wilderness ideal found two new forms of expression instead, both of which reflected the theme of progress. One was a bald celebration of the triumphant march of European civilization; the other was an appreciation of the cost of that progress. Europeans heartily congratulated themselves on their conquests of people they regarded as inferior and regions they regarded as ripe for exploitation. In another mood, they lamented the losses that seemed to them to be the inevitable collateral damage of progress. They felt sorry for themselves when they could not become like simple savages, innocently facing the challenges of nature. Wilderness played a part in both the triumphal and the elegiac commemoration. In modern nature writing, triumphalism is unthinkable. The wilderness theme remains firmly tied to the theme of loss and the acceptance of inevitable decline, degradation, and death.

Travel and Leisure

Men and women traveled to spas and country properties during the Roman era on the network of hard-surfaced, precisely engineered, and well-maintained roads. As the empire declined, the road network decayed along with it, and travel became increasingly difficult. During the Middle Ages, pilgrimage was the major motivator of elective travel. The Renaissance added classical study to the motives for restlessness. The Grand Tour, which systematized educational travel for the wealthy, remained the finishing school of gentlemen throughout Europe through the end of the eighteenth century. Crowded, slow, and uncomfortable carriages bounced along poorly maintained roads. They stopped nightly at inns where unwashed bedding, fleas, and stuffy rooms were the norm.

The railroads changed all that. They were fast and secure; they could be Spartan or luxurious. And they provided a way for the growing well-to-do classes to travel to all sorts of destinations. As rail networks expanded, they reached parts of the Mediterranean with little commercial life. The French coast east of Marseille and the contiguous coast of Italy—the Riviera—were one such region. With the arrival of the railroads and with energetic promotion by developers, the coastline was transformed. A loose chain of fishing ports and villages best visited by ship became an increasingly desirable series of resorts tightly strung along a coastal railroad. Within fifty years, an area long sustained by agriculture and fishing was transformed into the most fashionable resort in the world. Queen Victoria of England became an annual fixture at Cimiez, in the foothills above Nice. The tsar of Russia, the king of the Belgians, and Napoléon III of France all took holidays at the newly christened Côte d'Azur. Where royalty led, nobility and the merely rich followed. The once nearly inaccessible and modestly well-off region became a glittering international destination.

Substantial infrastructure was needed for the hordes of visitors arriving by rail. Developers built houses and villas. Entrepreneurs opened restaurants and shops, outfitted beaches, and created entertainments, like the Monte Carlo Casino. Towns everywhere along the Riviera were transformed. An old town with twisty streets leading down to the original harbor was soon engulfed by a modern grid on a much grander scale. The final product was similar to the multitude of colonial cities throughout the world with their "exotic" native quarters and their distinctly European esplanades and avenues.

The spread of towns and villas well beyond traditional city limits came at the expense of agricultural land. Fields, orchards, and vineyards disappeared, replaced by housing for visitors. As traditional infrastructure gave way to housing, locals found new sources of employment. Local knowledge that had kept the regional ecology in balance for generations was suddenly no longer called upon, and its influence declined, then vanished. Those now in charge of the region were more likely to be successful in the new economy of travel and tourism than in the old economy of agriculture and fishing. People with a very different stake in the region took command of its resources and its future.

CHAPTER FOURTEEN

The Modern Mediterranean

Around the year 1800, management of the city of Venice and its aquatic environs was wrenched from the hands of the local people who had maintained it for so long. Control passed to a succession of outsiders without local knowledge who over the years proved incapable of preserving either; subtle features of land and water that had been fine-tuned in the past slowly fell out of harmony. After the Second World War, Venice was invaded by unprecedented numbers of incomers, both transient and permanent; the local population shrank dramatically, and environmental deterioration accelerated its pace and vaulted to world attention. The past sixty years in Venice have been more destructive than any previous period in its history, and both the city and the lagoon are now in severe peril. There is no good reason to anticipate that either will survive even in the debased state that characterizes them today.

Two essential characteristics of the Venetian crisis are true of the Mediterranean region as a whole. The dramatic changes that the eighteenth century ushered in affected the region, as they affected Venice, at a relatively slow pace at first. After World War II, these forces accelerated dramatically. And as with Venice, the cause of the regionwide changes—changes that strongly impacted the environment—is, broadly speaking, a shift from local control to outside management. The regional transformation has a long history. The colonization of the southern and eastern Mediterranean that began with Napoléon's attack on Egypt is the plainest example of external takeover. The transformation of the Côte d'Azur from farmland and fishing villages to a tourist mecca is a more subtle version of the same process.

The most immediately devastating changes came with World War II. For five long years, the Mediterranean was an epicenter of intense, prolonged, and exhausting conflict. Victors and defeated alike emerged from this brutal experience in a state of near exhaustion. Millions were without adequate food, clean water, or shelter. Social services were minimal. The massive work of rebuilding was repeatedly hamstrung by shortages of all kinds. Decimated by death and disease and trying to cope with dislocation, the laboring population was too weak for the task at hand. Infrastructure had been destroyed, especially in nations occupied by Axis troops, among them France, what is now Ukraine, the Balkan states, Italy, and Greece. Nature, evidently offended by the monstrous conduct of war, took revenge in the immediate postwar years. Weather between 1945 and 1947 was capricious and severe. Hot, rainless summers alternated with winters of record-setting cold. Farms were already suffering from war damage, and farmers were overwhelmed. Famine threatened regionwide.

Colonial regimes in their various manifestations rapidly disappeared after the Second World War only to be replaced by a more centralized global political system revolving awkwardly around the twin poles of US and Soviet influence. An exhausted Europe became, like the majority of nations everywhere, contested terrain on which the two foes of the Cold War scrambled for political advantage. US foreign policy in the Mediterranean and in Europe at first had humanitarian aims, but it refocused around the grand strategy of containing Russian expansion. Both the United States and the Soviet Union took a hand in restoring regional agriculture as part of their foreign-policy initiatives. The United States was first and most successful with the Marshall Plan. Even after the famine eased, both nations used food aid and agricultural expertise to garner influence. But interest in the Mediterranean was never primarily agricultural for either country. In the immediate aftermath of the war, the Soviet Union made determined forays beyond its borders to secure at least a foothold in Turkey, Greece, and Libya. Determined to counter these thrusts, the United States increased its military presence in the region. For both world powers, the main draw of the Mediterranean came from its oil reserves.

Casualties during the war had been staggering. After the war the population rebounded slowly, then exploded. As the world recovered from the war and prosperity spread, population pressure in the most vulnerable parts of the region was intensified by a vastly expanded leisure market. When second homes in Mediterranean countries, especially in Spain, Italy, and southern France, became affordable for people with modest incomes, expatriate populations soared. The replacement of old towns and farms by sprawling resorts was accelerated.

The Mediterranean was transformed piecemeal from a landscape shaped by agriculture to one reshaped for a variety of purposes that were all too frequently alien and ill-conceived. Regional autonomy and regional concerns have been submerged within the incompatible agendas of a mixture of powers and international players. Environmental degradation is now endemic. The region is drowning under a tide of incomers with little or no ability to correctly assess and address the disaster around them. Let us look more closely at the acceleration of change after the war.

Ravaged by War

The complex and devastating chain of events began in the aftermath of the Second World War. In late February 1946, less than six months after the final victory over Germany, the United Nations General Assembly took the measure of the devastation.

The damage caused by war and the dislocation of agricultural production resulting from the shortage and dislocation of labour, the removal of draught animals, the shortage of fertilizers and other circumstances connected with the war have caused a serious fall in world production of wheat. In addition, a large number of countries, including some of those which are normally the largest producers of grain, have suffered serious droughts and have therefore reaped abnormally small crops. The supply of rice is also so short as to threaten a famine in certain areas.[1]

The threat that survivors faced in the early months of 1946 hinged on the ravages of war and the meager output of a poor growing season in 1945. Food shortages, already severe, grew markedly worse during the following winter, which was one of the harshest that the European continent had ever experienced.[2] In France intense cold destroyed the winter wheat crop. Wartime grain rationing, which had been suspended during the armistice, was reimposed in 1946; the daily bread ration dropped still further in the spring of 1947. Controlled sales of bread and sugar continued in France until 1949.[3] During the winter of 1946–47, heavy snows blocked roads and ports in Italy, preventing the distribution of food to cities and towns, and severe storms caused coastal damage.[4]

This unusually bitter winter was followed by a summer so hot and dry that one meteorologist wondered whether Europe was experiencing a climate change.[5] French wheat production in 1947 fell to less than half its prewar level. This shortfall required the nation, a net exporter of grain before the war, to import wheat and other cereals to feed its people, expending a "significant part" of its scanty cash reserves.[6]

On June 5, 1947, US Secretary of State George Marshall delivered a momentous speech in which he summed up the disasters threatening Europe.

The town and city industries are not producing adequate goods to exchange with the food-producing farmer. Raw materials and fuel are in short supply. Machinery is lacking or worn out. The farmer or the peasant cannot find the goods for sale which he desires to purchase. So the sale of his farm produce for money which he cannot use seems to him an unprofitable transaction. He, therefore, has withdrawn many fields from crop cultivation and is using them for grazing. He feeds more grain to stock and finds for himself and his family an ample supply of food, however short he may be on clothing and the other ordinary gadgets of civilization. Meanwhile people in the cities are short of food and fuel. So the governments are forced to use their foreign money and credits to procure these necessities abroad. This process exhausts funds which are urgently needed for reconstruction. Thus a very serious situation is rapidly developing which bodes no good for the world. The modern system of the division of labor upon which the exchange of products is based is in danger of breaking down.[7]

The foreseeable consequence of failing to address Europe's crises was disaster. Without American aid, Marshall predicted, Europe would face "economic, social and political deterioration of a very grave character."[8] The Marshall Plan, which grew out of this speech, has typically been portrayed as a program for economic recovery, but that phrase captures only one part of the multipronged US initiative. The plan addressed all the interconnected problems Marshall had identified: food production, intrastate commerce, industrial recovery, commercial and government finance.

A New World Order

Like all the European combatants, Britain was severely beaten down by war's end, and one of the most immediate effects of its weakened condition was rebellion throughout its colonial empire. Exhausted and losing its hold on its colonies, Britain simultaneously lost the rationale for Mediterranean involvement and the means to pursue it. In an unusually abrupt political volte-face, the British government abandoned Mediterranean involvement altogether and passed the torch to the United States.[9] Both the massive initiatives of the Marshall Plan and the British withdrawal from a centuries-long role as arbiter of Mediterranean affairs meant that the conduct of geopolitics in the postwar era would weigh heavily on the United States.

Many had seen in the wartime alliance between the Soviet Union and the democratic West the promise of a new era of international cooperation. At war's end, a world governed by the two most powerful nations acting in consort was a dream that appeared to be within reach. The Soviet dictator, Joseph Stalin, put an abrupt stop to the dream in a grim speech in early 1946 predicting inevitable hostility and war.[10] Reaction, especially in the US government, was strong

and immediate. George F. Kennan, then chargé d'affaires in the
Moscow embassy, sent back what has come to be known as the "long
telegram," in which he critiqued Stalin's speech and explained its
implications: that the Soviet Union was "more dangerous and insidious than ever before."[11] Kennan later outlined a US foreign policy
designed to meet and counter Soviet initiatives worldwide. His doctrine of containment served as the recipe for US foreign policy
through most of the latter half of the twentieth century. It transformed the Marshall Plan from a humanitarian campaign to one
arm of a political strategy that aimed to counter the appeal of communism in poor and hungry countries.

The doctrine that Kennan spelled out influenced every Mediterranean state during the forty years that the Soviet Union continued
in existence. Individual rulers callously and self-consciously took
advantage of the international rivalry to extort military aid and financial support from one or the other superpower. Egypt and Syria
were especially adept in courting the Soviets. Israel and Saudi Arabia were the most consistent regional friends of the United States.
Along with the need to contain the USSR, oil made the eastern
Mediterranean "an economic and strategic area of vital importance"
to the United States.[12] For decades after the war, the Mediterranean
was invisible from a geopolitical perspective unless thrown into the
spotlight by either of two dominant issues, oil or communism.

Oil

Colonial powers had always wanted more or less the same thing
from countries in their sphere of influence. They imported raw materials, preponderantly agricultural products, and they coerced their
less industrialized colonies to buy goods manufactured in the metropole. They developed infrastructure and increased education in
their areas of influence primarily to further these two commercial
goals. At first, the discovery of oil fit within this paradigm. Its role in
the economic relationship between metropole and colony was more
or less the same as that of an agricultural commodity. What first
promoted oil from the rank of just another colonial raw material to a
prime regional resource was sea power, which, before World War II,
was the principle of European international control.

Superior ocean-sailing technology had built European world domination since the Renaissance, and control of the oceans remained the key to colonial empires worldwide. Around the turn of the twentieth century, it became clear to some forward-looking British admirals that oil might offer a way to increase naval power and further secure naval dominance. British warships had already made the switch from sail to steam in the nineteenth century. Coal was one of the few natural resources found in the British Isles in sufficient quantity to power both national industries and the vast fleet of commercial and military vessels that kept the global empire in constant and effective communication.[13]

Despite a domestic supply of coal and a well-secured infrastructure of refueling stations, there were disadvantages to the use of coal to power military vessels. Coal is immensely heavy. The work of filling a battleship with coal was prolonged, physically demanding, and hazardous. Stokers on board moved the coal from bins to the fireboxes of multiple boilers. Though the job seemingly required nothing more than strength and endurance, skill came into play. It was the stokers rather than the officers or the engineers who controlled the speed of ships and the distance traveled between refuelings. Proficient teams made ships sail farther and created the least volume of visible smoke and the fastest speed. In battle, accelerating, maintaining speed, conserving fuel, and being minimally visible all created strategic advantages.[14]

Oil was the answer to many of coal's shortcomings. It was easy to fill the storage tanks of a docked ship with oil by piping it from an onshore reserve. It was just as easy to transfer the oil from onboard tanks to burners. Most importantly, regulating the heat in each firebox was a matter of turning a valve. Pound for pound, oil produced twice as much heat energy as coal, so ships refitted to burn oil had nearly twice their former range. Firing up the boilers and preparing to go to sea was faster on an oil-powered vessel; top speeds were higher, and the telltale plume of black smoke from coal-powered engines working at peak load was replaced by a thin wisp of exhaust. In 1914, at the urging of Winston Churchill, then First Lord of the Admiralty, the British navy adopted oil in its biggest and most powerful battleships. The conversion of the rest of the fleet to oil power came quickly after that.

Growing appreciation of the strategic value of oil spurred European interest in the countries of West Asia. In 1901 the Iranian government granted the first concession for oil exploration to a European entrepreneur. In 1908 the first well began producing. By 1912 crude oil was being pumped and piped to a refinery at the head of the Persian Gulf. Access to the region, which, with the exception of Iran, was then part of the Ottoman Empire, assumed increasing importance in European geopolitical thinking.

At the end of World War I, the treaty of San Remo, negotiated in 1920, dismembered the Ottoman Empire.[15] During the days of negotiation that led up to ratification, England and France worked out a plan for sharing the region's oil reserves. Oil discoveries in Iraq came a decade after the end of the war. By 1939, Iraqi oil had reached Mediterranean ports. Small-scale production had begun by then in Bahrain and Saudi Arabia. Despite the value of oil, returns were modest for the producing nations. Few locals worked in the oil fields, where most employees were foreigners. Royalties from oil production were scarcely sufficient to even out the balance of payment deficits that plagued most nonindustrialized countries. Before World War II, the oil industry duplicated the economic inequalities of colonialism, though the name "colony" was assiduously avoided.

More than any other single resource, oil was the key to success or failure in World War II. No European combatant had a sufficient domestic supply of oil. Securing fuel for their armies and air forces became a major preoccupation. Both sides wanted to capitalize on eastern Mediterranean suppliers. The Allies alone consumed seven billion barrels of oil during the war. Some historians believe that the Allied defeat of Nazi Germany was a consequence of the differing qualities and quantities of petroleum-based fuels available to either side. Differences in resource bases and resource management may well have determined the outcome of the war.[16]

Foreign Aid and Agricultural Policy

Agricultural development played a part in US and Soviet foreign policy after World War II, but it was one factor among many that caused geopolitical head butting. The domestic agricultural policy of the Soviet Union combined collectivization of farm resources, nationalization of land, and state management of production with state-controlled distribution. The US model resisted government management of the economy and relied on market forces to set production priorities. Despite these differences in ideology, both world powers urged similar programs of agricultural development in the Mediterranean and elsewhere. Both had vast internal grasslands under cultivation, and this geographical commonality played an enormous, and largely unacknowledged, role in the agricultural methods that each nation touted for foreign adoption.[17] The Great Plains of the United States and the rich soils of Ukraine could be most successfully exploited using mechanization, large-field cultivation, single crops, chemical pesticides and fertilizers, and large-scale irrigation.[18]

When Mediterranean farmers were introduced to methods labeled progressive by either superpower, the result was the destruction or abandonment of traditional local methods of cultivation. Mechanization replaced handwork. Monocultures edged out traditional mixed crops. Land consolidation eliminated the advantages of farming multiple terrains. The use of chemical fertilizers and pesticides, obtained at great cost, replaced traditional practices of manuring cropland and allowing fields to lie fallow. Irrigation brought immediate benefits to dry regions, as it had done in the Roman era, but there were important differences. Roman farmers crafted intricate systems to trap and channel rainwater, which was renewed annually. Modern farmers dig deep wells to tap buried aquifers. In a decade or two, they use up water accumulated over generations. The result is increased productivity in the short run with depleted aquifers and subsiding land as the long-term consequence. While short-term upticks in production occur, local infrastructure, created in some cases over millennia, and local knowledge, on which traditional agriculture in the Mediterranean had depended, are destroyed or lost.[19]

Areas that could not be modified to fit the ideal model of postwar agriculture were abandoned more often than not. Traditional farming could have continued, but it had become either unprofitable or culturally unacceptable. In Greece, farms and farming villages have been emptying out over the past fifty years. Today nearly half the Greek population lives in or near Athens or Thessaloníki. Traditional agricultural lands are untenanted and uncultivated. Terraces fall down; olive trees collapse under their own unpruned weight.

Houses and barns rot away as the land around them returns to Mediterranean scrub. As farms and villages disappear, those with knowledge of the soil, the crops, and traditional techniques of cultivation scatter. Few masters of traditional cultivation and the infrastructure that sustained it are left. They have little or no opportunity to use their hard-won skills, and there are almost no young farmers to succeed them.

The Mediterranean Landscape Today

According to an article in the French magazine *France-Soir*, one quarter of a billion people were expected to vacation somewhere on the Mediterranean coast in 2010. This transient population would exceed the year-round population by about one hundred million.[20] That makes the entire Mediterranean more or less the equivalent of Venice in terms of the ratio between locals with a long-term investment in the health and welfare of the region and casual incomers with little or nothing at stake. Indeed, some visitors seem to have no interest whatsoever in where they happen to be. British tour companies offer young men and women "clubbing" packages to beach resorts where other young men and women are the main attraction. The Spanish island of Ibiza is a longtime destination for this kind of travel. Cyprus, Kos, Zante, Corfu, and Crete are popular; Turkey and Bulgaria have both recently entered the list. Tourism of this kind involves no appreciation of place, no cultural awareness, and certainly no sense of responsibility. Clubbers want a place where egregious behavior will be overlooked. Those who provide for them are looking for a ready source of cash.

Most visitors come to the Mediterranean to savor the beaches, the vineyards and olive groves, the local food, "quaint" villages, and peaceful solitude. They come to experience turquoise water, to lie on manicured sand or rocky beaches. In the evening they expect to dine on fresh fish, to sample local wines, and to eat just-harvested fruit and vegetables.

To meet their needs, the Mediterranean fishing fleet is going out ever farther in search of economically viable catches. In every fish market from Venice to Fez, shoppers note the disappearance of fish once locally caught or cultivated and their replacement by ocean species. As technologically advanced fleets move beyond traditional fishing grounds, they impinge on the grounds of still-local fishers. Traditional fisheries along the west coast of Africa, once exploited by local people using small boats and hand lines or nets, are now fished by mechanized European trawlers. Unable to compete, African fishers load their boats with human cargoes and make for the Azores or the Canaries or the volcanic islands of Italy.[21]

When a vacationing family gets tired of the seaside, they take a walk in the hills to sit under olive trees or beside vineyards and admire the view. Some find the attractions of the region irresistible: they buy a second home. A Tuscan farmhouse with its own vines and olive trees, with cypresses lining the drive and a view over the fields into the valley below may be far out of their price range. But there are plenty of less picturesque villages and hillsides without sea views that are affordable today and will not be tomorrow, so the second-home culture spreads ever wider, and agricultural land shrinks. Traditional care for the land vanishes along with it.

This scenario was once played out in confined areas of the Mediterranean coast; it is now a regionwide phenomenon. From east to west the landscape is being reshaped to attract vacationers. The United States faces almost exactly the identical dilemma in the management of its public wilderness: what attracts visitors is diminished, then destroyed, as more and more people flock to enjoy it. In the Mediterranean, vestiges of the traditional character of the region are what draw incomers, but satisfying their appetite for land, housing, and infrastructure can only come at the expense of what they have come to see. Like the picturesque villages of Les Baux and Èze in southern France, like the splendid city of Venice, the region as a whole is filling with shops selling imitations of vanishing local specialties to busloads of tourists who are none the wiser.

Conclusion
What Is to Be Done?

A long look into the deep past has revealed a very different history from the one that most environmentalists have imagined. As the roots of our current environmental crisis come to light, it becomes increasingly clear that the damage was done when Mediterranean culture abandoned an ancient system of understanding. First Nature, the early consensus view of our place in the world, linked the human and biological communities through agriculture. Abandonment of First Nature occurred in fits and starts over millennia, but by the end of the eighteenth century, every intellectual and emotional piece of this consensus view had been wrecked or abandoned. From that point on, First Nature ceased to govern ecological thought and action. The crisis that haunts us came to birth when environmental exploitation was no longer restrained by time-tested ideals or traditional methods.

The most unexpected and significant truth uncovered here is this: our era of crisis is an aberration. In the Mediterranean, humans have had a long and constructive relationship with the land. The current environmental crisis, though prolonged and severe, does not dominate the Mediterranean story. Living in the middle of the crisis, as all of us do, makes its historical abnormality hard to grasp.

The Roman rhetorician Cicero recognized the difficulty of critiquing one's own experience and coined a phrase, "the tyranny of the present," to sum it up. Born into an era of crisis, it is natural for us to assume that the past was similar and that the future will be substantially the same. Cicero believed that we study the past to free ourselves from the tyranny of the present and to learn the trick of framing our own time and place in a broader context. In the long-term context of Mediterranean history, the crisis that threatens us is no less real or urgent; it remains cataclysmic, but it is also exposed as an abnormality. If the current environmental crisis were an economic event, we could call it a "bubble." Though it has lasted much longer than the dot-com bubble or the housing-market bubble, it occupies a sliver of time. From an expanded perspective, the current environmental crisis is just like the notorious economic bubbles, a short-term eruption in a long-term situation of stability.

Finding a way out of either an economic or an environmental bubble requires putting events in the wider context that Cicero recommended. It does no good to keep applying the same logic that created and inflates the bubble. "Business as usual" and the lock-step thinking that accompanies that approach only make bubbles grow bigger. Solutions come from thinking outside the bubble, and throughout this book, the past environmental history of the Mediterranean region has shown itself to be a good place to look for a way to recalibrate and reinvigorate our understanding. Acknowledging the environmental soundness of the Mediterranean before the bubble erupted in the nineteenth century and recognizing the forces that maintained ecological health for millennia before that time enable us to rethink the crisis of our era. By recognizing what ecological health depended on, we can imagine how to produce it today in a creative way. With luck we will be able to make repairs and bring down the bubble before it bursts. It will burst. They always do.

Recovery depends on regaining the practical knowledge that sustained Mediterranean cultivated landscapes and accepting once again the First Nature concept that perceived the unity of the human community and the natural world in terms of those landscapes. First Nature lies in plain sight in writings from the past, in archaeological studies, and in those vestiges of the historic Mediterranean agricultural landscape that remain intact. Above all, First Nature is omnipresent in the food that sustains human life on earth today.

As we look back over history, however, we need to make another unaccustomed intellectual effort. The inventor of psychotherapy, Sigmund Freud, urged members of his new profession to adopt a particular style when listening to their patients. Don't listen for particulars that you can assemble into your own theory of the case, Freud advised. Listen instead "with evenly-suspended attention" to everything that the patient offers.[1] What that advice means in the present context is illustrated by two of the more widely publicized ways the Mediterranean heritage has been attended to in recent years. The Mediterranean diet has been a subject of repeated interest among nutritionists and public health specialists. The surprising longevity of island dwellers in remote areas of Sardinia and on the Greek Island of Ikaria have attracted attention. In both cases, researchers have focused on isolating the factors that produce the results that they desire—a decrease in heart disease and a general uptick in longevity. They pinpoint one or two potentially adoptable foods or actions that others could take advantage of to be healthier and live longer.

What this book urges, what it offers, is listening in the way Freud recommended. If we attend to the full narrative of the human engagement with the Mediterranean landscape through agriculture, we hear a complex story. Rather than taking a reductive approach to that story—listening for those details that seem salient to us from a single perspective—it is beneficial to capture the multiple threads that run through the narrative. By capturing the richest version of the Mediterranean interaction with the biological world, we can discover important matters that our questioning, limited by the tyranny of our present, could not anticipate. Mature historical systems, like mature ecosystems, interact internally in complex ways. A responsible account of environmental history needs to be complex itself.

No obstacle is posed by a lack of material to study or by the richness of the tradition we contemplate. But a seemingly insurmountable barrier remains. We may be ready to appreciate the cultivated landscape as an image from our shared past, but the tyranny of our present pushes us in another direction altogether. This is especially true for Americans, whose conception of nature has been dominated for the past two hundred years by the ecological ideal that denigrated the cultivated landscape. For us and for multiple generations before us, the keyword for thinking about nature has been "wilderness." Two hundred years of art and literature underwrite our sense that "nature" means "wild nature," the biotic world untouched by humans. Henry David Thoreau's slogan still stirs us: "In wildness is the preservation of life." Though an American expression, it is grounded in the eighteenth-century literary traditions of France and Germany.

Heretical or not, there are good reasons to reject wilderness as the poster child for biological life. This is not to reject wilderness itself but only to reject its role as stand-in for the whole of nature. If we ask ourselves whether the wilderness concept, during its two-century reign, has done a good job of standing up for the natural world, the answer has to be a resounding "No!" During that short time, more damage has been done to the landscape than ever before in human history. This is a terrible irony. We have honored wilderness in our hearts and minds while we have ravaged every bit of it we could get our hands on. Either we have been consistently perverse and hypocritical, or the wilderness concept has not offered sound guidance as we have engaged with the world in which we live and upon which we depend.

There are clear reasons why the wilderness ideal has failed to point to or sustain environmentally sound action. First among them are the historical and conceptual foundations of the ideal, discussed in Chapter 12. The idea of wilderness has been adopted by environmentalists and ecologists, but it was pioneered by poets and philosophers whose concerns were far removed from biology. The wilderness ideal has come to embrace and embody nature as a whole, though it originally focused on dramas of human emotion and spirituality that could only be staged in the grand arena of disinterested natural forces.

What fascinated eighteenth-century writers like Rousseau, Goethe, Burke, and Kant was the way humans reacted to nature in what they thought of as its purest and most exemplary form. For these thinkers, the human *experience* of landscape was primary, and their theories led them to favor encounters in savage landscapes where the stakes were high. So they focused on men and women who risked death in frightening places. What began as a philosopher's intellectual exercise or a poet's means to push creative boundaries soon developed into a taste for fear. Romantic writers were addicted to emotional extremes; they hungered for storm-wreathed Alps and blasted heaths. They taught that such powerful landscapes created in receptive individuals a quasi-religious feeling of awe or exultation, inspired by a sense of imminent danger and hedged with mortal terror.[2]

The high drama of romantic poetry entered popular culture, and thrill seeking in the natural environment is still a big part of how we engage with nature. We measure ourselves against it. We invite it to do its worst, and when it does, we publish best sellers about death on Mount Everest, the perfect storm, a mauling by a grizzly, or survival with an arm pinned under a fallen boulder. We have not rejected the romantic poets' confrontational stance in the face of "brute nature"; we have instead taken what was for them an elite pastime and source of literary inspiration and marketed it for mass entertainment.

Nature as proving ground and antagonist is not the most destructive side of the wilderness ideal. What makes the ideal such a critical problem is the internal contradiction that surfaces whenever the concept is called upon to clarify or guide the relationship between humans and their environment. Since "wilderness" is defined as the world without human intervention, the wilderness concept insists that there is nothing constructive that humans can do for the environment. Wilderness, and by extension nature itself, is a finite resource that is beyond our aid or repair. It can diminish, but it cannot grow; we can do nothing but hurt it more. On the subjects that interest us most—how to act responsibly in the natural world and how to roll back the damage we have already done—the wilderness concept says the only thing it is capable of saying about nature: "Leave it alone."

That never was a sufficient answer, and the two centuries of unremitting environmental degradation show all too plainly just how misguided a watchword it is. We have not left wilderness alone in the past, and there is no reason to believe we will do so in the future. It will not help to be told once again, "Hands off nature." We need to understand how to put our hands *on* nature in a beneficial way. Constructive and sustainable cooperation with nature was the theme

of First Nature, and it is primarily for that reason that we must recapture its truths.

A remarkable example of the contradictions and policy miscues
that the wilderness ideal leads to is provided by the creation of a new
national park in the interior of Sardinia. The Gennargentu National
Park, established by the Italian legislature in 1991 at the urging of
international organizations, encloses nearly 150,000 acres of mountainous territory in the island's interior. Those who proposed a park
saw central Sardinia as "one of the last, untouched areas of pristine
natural wilderness remaining in Italy and Europe."[3]

Sardinians from the many mountain communities that border
on the vast Gennargentu massif held a different view.

> The farthest reaches of these Gennargentu municipal terri-
> tories, including the slopes of Gennargentu mountain itself,
> have been used by their ancestors for millennia for collecting
> natural plants and hunting wild animals, for raising sheep
> and goats, and for cultivation. This so-called uninhabited
> wilderness was anything but that; every peak, every valley,
> every spot was known, named and used by its highland in-
> habitants. . . . The inhabitants scoffed at the idea that the land
> and forests and animals had to be protected from them.[4]

In the twenty years of the park's existence, devastating forest
fires, which had been controlled by the herds systematically grazing
on the underbrush, have burned out of control. The change of management from farmers and herders with rich First Nature traditions
of local knowledge to experts from outside with a different conceptual outlook has so far not served the region well.

The noted environmental writer Bill McKibben proclaimed the
end of nature in a groundbreaking book. What he meant by that
shocking announcement was that wilderness—nature beyond human
influence—no longer existed. The death was quite recent, he said,
and it was caused by human-generated atmospheric pollution. Since
the air respired by every terrestrial organism now contains some
chemical emitted by a manufacturing process, there is no longer
any place on earth beyond human influence, so there is no longer any
"nature."[5]

McKibben's aim, like the aim of so many environmental writers, was to alarm readers into a greater awareness of environmental problems. He was focusing on pollution, its causes, and ways to ameliorate it. He was not calling into question the conceptual foundation of the wilderness-nature link. All the same, his conclusions have important implications for that connection. If McKibben was right and there really is no wilderness anymore, then we are relieved of the burden of trying to protect it from ourselves. We are free to choose whether to continue to intervene in a negative way, as we have for so long, or to begin to act positively. We are free to think about the best ways to cultivate the world. Replacing the wilderness concept with the model of the landscape transformed for cultivation is the most constructive step we can take as we rethink nature, our place in the natural world, and programs for responsible engagement in and with the biological community.

The writing and teaching of environmental literature helps keep the wilderness ideal ever present in the consciousness of each new generation. Even though the literature that engages nature is millennial in scope and worldwide in breadth, modern writers and teachers focus almost entirely on the products of the past two hundred years— the centuries of crisis. It is rare to find an acknowledgement even from these well-informed people that writing about nature preceded English romanticism; that there is a Mediterranean tradition of writing about nature; that there is a preromantic tradition of writing about nature; that there is a tradition of writing about nature that is not rooted in wilderness. These facts would almost certainly be news to the average student enrolled in Literature and the Environment 101.

The craft of environmental writing as it is currently practiced could also benefit from a wider perspective. Passionate as the writers are, and committed to the greater good, nearly all nature writers remain trapped in the contradictions of wilderness. In the tyranny of their present, they are left with the task of chronicling and lamenting the tragedy of the disappearing wild. Broadening the scope of nature writing would allow another theme: the possibility of fruitful and joyful collaboration with the land that sustains us all. Rethinking the fundamentals of environmental engagement without the albatross of wilderness around the necks would make the nature writer's task more hopeful.

Along with abandoning the wilderness ideal, we need to make another cultural recalibration. Since the eighteenth century, economics has been the enemy of environmentalism. Bottom-line thinking helps companies make money and workers earn a living, but over the past two centuries, the economist has become a virtual dictator with veto power over any social project that cannot pass the comparative cost test. Should solar and wind power replace coal-generated or nuclear-generated electricity? The environmentalist says yes to both; the economist says no. The economist's trump card is always the same: cost parity. Unless proponents of clean energy can demonstrate costs per kilowatt hour that equal those for coal or nuclear power, the economist declares the project dead in the water.

There is a new generation of economists and accountants, however, whose work is known and increasingly respected by fellow professionals but is virtually invisible so far. Neither the general public nor government officials know of their proposals, nor do all but a few in the environmental community. What these economists offer is different from the kind of bottom-line argumentation that traditional economics relies on.[6] Instead of looking at markets only, the domain of the conventional economist, the emerging economists are attentive to all the costs of an activity, including those that are not reflected in market price. The case of coal-generated electric power offers a good example of the difference between their calculations. The market price of coal-generated electricity in the United States hovers around eleven cents per kilowatt hour; the French pay double and the Italians nearly three times that rate. Yet none of these numbers represents the true cost of electricity per kilowatt hour, because these market prices silently factor in subsidies and the utilities' own successful strategies for transferring or laying off costs. The conventional economist's bottom line, then, is a sum that glides over additions and subtractions that environmental economists take into account.[7]

Governments underwrite electric power production in various ways, among them tax breaks and the creation and maintenance of infrastructure that supports the power grid. Since these costs are not paid by the utilities themselves, they are not reflected in market price. But they are real costs, and someone pays them. The same is true of costs that can be passed on to others. In the case of coal-fired plants, the greatest cost that is passed on represents liabilities associated with impacts on the environment and public health. Pollutants increase the incidence of human respiratory diseases and aggravate the acidity of rains that damage ecosystems. Utilities have not been forced to pay for much of the disease and ecological damage their emissions cause, but their liability is a real and calculable cost. These costs are undetected by the standard economist and by the decision makers he or she advises. New methods of accounting look at the full spectrum of costs associated with the generation of electricity from coal, both those paid by the industry itself and reflected in its market price and those paid for in ways that the market overlooks.

When the new kind of accounting is applied to the production of energy, the bottom line is markedly different. Because environmental and health costs, which are left out of market accounting, are real and important in this form of analysis, the overall costs of alternatives can be compared, not just the costs that make it into a market price calculus. When real costs are toted up, both solar and wind power are fully competitive with coal- and nuclear-generated power.[8] As more economists embrace full-spectrum accounting, environmentalists can stop butting heads with economists. And if policy makers embrace it as they make environmental decisions, there is every reason to believe that environmental conservation and repair will accelerate.

If nature can be reimagined without wilderness as its representative and if a new economics that is no longer the enemy of environment can prevail, what remains to be done? The biggest intellectual and cultural hurdle that still must be negotiated is the state of modern agriculture itself. Agriculture was more brutally savaged after the abandonment of First Nature than any other sphere of human activity. Deprived of all the traditional protections, agriculture became just one more form of environmental exploitation. With a few exceptions, in its present state agriculture offers no guidance for responsible ecological action.

Fortunately, there are signs that some areas of contemporary agriculture are changing. Still, the overall picture is disturbing. Few things are more repellent than a factory pig farm surrounded by lagoons of decaying manure. Or a muddy feedlot where calves live in their own filth while their brief life spans are accelerated by fodder spiked with hormones. Both are contemptible abuses of both domestic animals and the ecosystem. Where crops require hand labor, human beings are often the victims. Recent exposés of farm labor in southern Italy have shown the exploitation of undocumented workers and the control of the harvest by organized crime, and this is by no means an isolated example.

Market forces and the inexorable pressures of international competition are held up as the demons that drive farmers to work in ways that at least some find unwelcome. But what holds for the economics of energy production is true of farming as well. When the true costs are totaled up, the economic picture becomes strikingly different. Massive government subsidies, indirect benefits in the form of infrastructure, and protective isolation from liability and health-related costs make contemporary agriculture economically viable. The cost of addressing the obesity that modern crops create would itself be sufficient to tip the balance in favor of ecologically sound practices.[9] Without subsidies and insulation from liability, agribusiness would have to be reconfigured in ways that are more responsible to land, labor, and consumers.

It is all too easy to forget, however, that while idealism continues to feed our concept of nature, farms feed our bodies and minds. Until and unless we can all be entirely nourished by machine-made synthetic foods—a development that most of us would view with revulsion—farming will continue to be the mainstay of the human community. Agriculture nourishes all of us, and agriculture remains culture's pragmatic connection to the biological world. We should not try to overcome our repugnance at the abuses of modern farming. We should continue to raise holy hell about the devastation of public health that modern food processing and marketing have created. At the same time, we need to recognize that farming keeps an unprecedentedly large world population alive. That is not an insignificant or unworthy achievement.

Food literacy is becoming a watchword among food writers and their growing audience. It is an important theme and one that can help to overcome the ignorance that shrouds contemporary farming.

This book suggests a second dimension to food literacy. Our look at food history takes the conversation about where nourishment comes from an important step further. Food literacy discussions typically address the link between the farm and the table. The expanded notion of food literacy advocated here focuses on the question How did the world accumulate its stock of edible plants and animals? The answer, amply certified by genetic research, cites one or another of the world Neolithic Revolutions.

Critics like Jared Diamond, who recently characterized the Neolithic as the "greatest disaster in human history," seem especially prone to forget where food comes from.[10] Farms feed us, but what farms feed us *with* has for millennia been, and will continue for the foreseeable future to be, the descendants of wild plants and animals brought into the human community by Neolithic farmers and herders around the world. If we stigmatize the Neolithic as the origin of the diseases of civilization, we are remembering much less than half the story. The Neolithic lives on in the crops that make up the world's food supply. Without the Neolithic agricultural revolutions, there would be nothing for our farms to raise and nothing to eat on our tables. Far fewer of us would exist to sit at those barren tables.

Domesticates are not casual bits of human capital that might within a generation or two become outmoded and worthless; the entire human community depends on them. The domesticate products of the Mediterranean—wheat, olives, milk, grapes—are among the most precious human resources. Along with the domesticates of the south Chinese Neolithic and the New World Neolithic, they represent monumental human achievements that bring daily delight, sustenance, and comfort. Understanding just how rare and precious domesticates are and honoring the generations whose care and labor created and maintained them is a vital and insufficiently acknowledged part of food literacy.

Understanding, too, that modern versions of domesticates are not the same as earlier varieties is important. "Wheat flour" may appear to refer to the same product today as it did a hundred or a thousand years ago, but that is not the case. Contemporary commercial wheat represents a small part of the spectrum of wheats cultivated historically. It is chosen for extensive cultivation because it has characteristics that suit contemporary planting, harvesting, shipping, and storage conditions. It is milled and processed, packaged and shipped in ways that ancient grains were not. All of these actions influence its nutritional value, but they also reflect choices based on considerations other than nutrition. Studying the history of domesticates uncovers the choices that agribusiness has made and challenges the notion that the most modern or the most commercially viable crop is necessarily the most healthful.

Dramatic evidence of how narrowly commercially produced foods represent the spectrum of cultivars comes from many sources. Of the hundreds or thousands of distinctive apples once grown in the United States, the supermarket offers at most 1 percent. The percentages may be slightly higher for pears, tomatoes, lettuce, onions, or potatoes. In every instance, the loss of species is deep enough to make the preservation of varietals a serious preoccupation with seed banks throughout the world. Even foodstuffs that we may think of as commodities—rice and cornmeal, for example—have been heavily affected by the tendency of factory farming to cultivate a minimum of varieties. In coastal South Carolina and Georgia, archivists and agricultural researchers have joined with farmers and chefs to resurrect varieties of corn and rice with unique growth patterns, complex flavors, and increased nutritional value.[11]

Farming is not the same everywhere, and it does not always present the same face to the world. The American feedlot is obscene, but many agricultural landscapes are places of great beauty. Though many of us appreciate the majestic in nature enshrined in the Swiss Alps or the barren cliffs towering above the Dead Sea, we are also drawn to beautiful cultivated landscapes. Despite the ravages in the Mediterranean during the past two hundred years, a traditional agricultural landscape still survives there in many places. And despite transformation, abandonment, and neglect, this landscape remains lovely and productive.

It may no longer be possible to look out from the terrace of the Villa Lante and see a sixteenth-century garden, but the view is still compelling. What one sees from this vantage point and from hundreds of other hillsides in Tuscany, Spain, Tunisia, and many other places around the Mediterranean is a landscape that is both beautiful and bountiful. Because a wide range of nourishing and delicious foods are produced, the landscape that produces them is pleasing

not just to look at but to depend on. We can understand intellectually and feel emotionally what Homer represented on the shield of
Achilles. A functioning landscape lets us feel the warmth and sense
of security that ancient men and women knew.

On a recent trip, climbing the steep trail from Èze Bord de Mer
to Èze Village on the outskirts of Nice, I saw little evidence of an
agricultural past. Housing dominated the lower levels of the hillside;
it sprawled along a pricey coastline. Walled villas, tied only to the
vista and to road access, are surrounded by wasteland, where plants
that can manage on their own are free to grow. The villas perch on
the hillside but do not enter into any kind of relationship with it. The
vacationers who come and go are isolates, too, and show little love
or understanding for the land. Trash and litter blow from their small
yards into the scrub, where it remains until it rots away. Above the
villas, in a zone without real estate potential, there is nothing but
maquis, the tough, drought-resistant mix of shrubs and weeds that
is climax vegetation in this arid region. Here and there among the
shrubs, on a bit of south-facing hillside, it was possible to see the
remains of terraced farm plots and the rotted or burned trunks of
long-dead olive trees.

Further inland, near the mountain town of Sospel, the landscape
is different. The traces of the farming past are abundant. In every
direction, terraces cut across the landscape; often they are visible
only as bare traces, but sometimes they are planted with young olive
trees to supplement or replace aged orchards. As the rural population declined after World War II, forests replaced farms; some
woods were planted, and some were random second growth. While
the coastal region grew out in scrub, this better-watered, higher-
altitude inland region became covered with big trees. Ironically, the
ability of the soil to sustain oaks and pines was almost certainly a
consequence of its previous life. Trees thrived in the deep soil of the
terraced landscape, so the woods here are filled with tumbledown
walls.

I found myself thinking of the drystone walls that edged the
fields of New England and now run through the woods wherever
farms were abandoned. Anyone who has ever come upon them realizes the tremendous energy it must have taken to clear the land. The
farmers of southern France were known, like those of New England,

for their perseverance, thrift, and industry. But here they went the New World farmers one better. Not only were the stones gathered and piled along the edges of their fields, they were organized into retaining walls—some more than head high—and backed with earth to create deep soil. Thousands of miles of these walls endure—testimony to the extraordinary investment in infrastructure that traditional farmers of the region once made.

Not all their work has been consumed by opportunistic trees. There is evidence here and there of new rural pioneers, men and women who have chosen to clean and repair the walls and to use them in the traditional way to guard and sustain crops of various kinds. Rather than seeing the work of their ancestors as outmoded, they are reusing it for the purposes originally intended. This is certainly one of the most hopeful signs anywhere of a dawning recognition that the traditions of the region made sense in the past and have promise for the future. The *New York Times* reports that the economic crisis in Greece is sending many young men and women back to the land and to a life of farming.[12] Planners believe that forests, even second-growth, post-agricultural forests, encourage tourism, but the land of the Mediterranean region can offer more than a way to cater to the tastes and needs of outsiders. Rural pioneers are discovering that potential.

Most of the human community abandoned First Nature long ago, but in many parts of the Mediterranean, the landscape transformed for agriculture remained faithful to it. These vestigial landscapes commemorate First Nature, even though men and women have forgotten. To uncover the secrets of the consensus and the harmony that First Nature created between the human community and the biological community, we need to reactivate the landscape as these pioneering farmers are doing. Terraced and other landscapes need to be renewed and used as they were meant to be used so that they do not just nourish and delight but also instruct.

There is much that can be done to help individuals reclaim the land as well as to use the agriculturally transformed landscape for broader purposes. Governments at every level must learn to treat the remnants of the traditional Mediterranean farm landscape as a resource to be protected and preserved. Along with the land and the crops, the traditional skills used to create, cultivate, and maintain the

Rural pioneers are recapturing the agricultural potential of a reforested landscape in southern France. (Photograph by author.)

landscape need to be recovered. I do not mean to endorse the misguided efforts that some Balkan countries are now making to preserve or re-create their agricultural past to entertain tourists. Nostalgia and remastered authenticity are not the issues. What is needed is far more consequential: preservation of ways of working that have long been successful in sustaining the health of the Mediterranean region.

The history of wilderness preservation offers a useful lesson in revitalization. Among the influential essays of the ecological writer Aldo Leopold are two on the value of wilderness.[13] The details Leopold outlines in those essays are closely tied to the uniquely American experience of wilderness, but the themes that he emphasizes are broad and can serve as guidelines for agrarian landscape preservation as well. Wilderness for Leopold was primarily a place for pleasurable experience. With proper encouragement, the experience could lead not just to recreation but to increased knowledge and understanding. The forms of understanding encompassed history, ethics, and ecology. Though embedded in a different biological region and a different cultural and historical context, Mediterranean cultivated landscapes promise benefits in each of the areas Leopold outlined.

Leopold began with an unexpected link between recreation in wild places and American history. The American wilderness was a place where travel by canoe and pack train could be experienced for fun. These forms of recreation recapitulated experiences during the national expansion westward by way of river networks and overland trails. Participating in river and trail travel was a way to act out a history lesson. Leopold argued, too, for an ethical dimension to the wilderness experience. Thoughtful hunting, fishing, and camping, the activities most commonly carried out in wild or semi-wild places, teach a rudimentary kind of environmental ethics. The lessons of care and conservation learned from field and stream could become foundations for a broad sense of ecological responsibility. Finally, as a scientific ecologist, Leopold knew that wild places as mature biological communities were a precious source of data for scientific study. Leopold recognized their value as models of ecological health.

Writing in the 1940s, when the majority of Americans still had some farm connection, Leopold focused on the pioneer era in national development, which few, if any, of his readers had experienced firsthand. Today only a fraction of the population has any direct experience of farms and farming. Opening the wilderness happened during a brief moment in American history, but farms have been the major cultural engine through most of history, and there would be enormous value in having more people experience traditional farming. Preserving Mediterranean cultivated landscapes and encouraging visitors, much in the vein of contemporary agri-tourism, would communicate that history firsthand.

Leopold understood the need to preserve examples of every kind of wild ecosystem. Tall-grass prairies are not interchangeable with short-grass prairies, nor are forests of giant sequoias interchangeable with forests of long-needle pines. The composition and formative principles of each are markedly different. He recognized that a parcel of every wild ecosystem needed to be preserved. The same is true of Mediterranean agricultural landscapes and the techniques that maintained them.

Farms in Tuscany are not the same as those in the Levant or North Africa. Preservation needs to be regionwide, but it does not have to be coordinated. One of the advantages that agricultural landscape preservation holds over wilderness preservation is a differing

dependency on geographical scale. Leopold, in common with ecologists in general, recognized the importance of size and contiguity
in wilderness preservation. A wild ecosystem that is too small or that
is islanded by development typically loses its ability to thrive. Species that are wide ranging, like the grizzly bear, bison, and elk, cannot be contained even in the largest preserves. Their native ranges
extend well beyond park boundaries into habitats that have lost their
ability to sustain them or that have become zones where humans
will not accept them. In wild ecosystems size matters.

In Mediterranean agricultural landscapes, however, even a small
isolated farm can preserve valuable information. This is partly due
to the nature of the Mediterranean landscape itself with its multiple,
repeated small geographical units that each recapitulate regional variation within themselves. This geography makes possible preservation on a number of scales, and in a region as politically fragmented
as the Mediterranean basin, that is an advantage. Intra-regional cooperation has been the precondition for much United Nations– and
European Union–sponsored environmental action. The barriers to
cooperation remain substantial in a region marked by antagonism on
both the economic and the religious fronts. The divisions between
rich and poor, which seem to be growing rather than diminishing,
have reduced the effectiveness of international efforts. Preserving
the traditional agricultural landscape, however, can be undertaken at
virtually any scale. A town or village can do useful work, and so can
a regional authority or a transregional one. Individual projects might
all look different, but each could be viable and valuable.

From a more general ecological perspective, it is important to
recognize how closely traditional agriculture in the Mediterranean
mimicked the fundamental traits of naturally occurring ecosystems.
It was diverse, complex, self-regulating, and resilient. Traditional
farmers made adaptive use of local material to build enduring infra-
structures that captured surface water and enhanced soil fertility.
They combined crops and pasturing to increase the benefits of both.
They protected against crop failure through cultivation of a variety
of different terrains and crops. The diversity and complexity of traditional agriculture made it reliable and sustainable. These essential
characteristics make it an important object of ecological study. What

separates this landscape from wild ecosystems is equally significant. This vibrant, sustainable landscape was built and managed by its human members. Unlike wilderness, which excludes humans except as visitors, the Mediterranean landscape as it was transformed for agriculture serves as a paradigm of a long-term constructive human engagement with the surrounding biological community.

The men and women who still remember the techniques that managed this landscape are themselves a valuable and rapidly disappearing resource. For the past two hundred years experts have assumed that they know better than the old farmers, that the traditionalists are fools with nothing to teach. It is almost too late to correct that mistake. Much has been lost, the landscape has been degraded, and local knowledge has died away. But there is still much that can be recovered and studied and reimagined.

Farm labor is a touchy subject in the modern Mediterranean, where the trend in most countries has been to demean manual work and to shorten both the workweek and the entire working career. Farmwork is hard work. In some seasons it requires long hours of physical labor. Generally speaking, however, when compared with a repetitive industrial task or work at a desk or computer terminal, the work is varied and challenging, and it calls on a range of manual and intellectual skills. Farming is, overall, a highly skilled occupation. A small farmer has to be an expert at any number of things that vary from crop to crop and from season to season. Restoring respect for labor and for the skills, diligence, and responsibility of a farmer is a necessary part of First Nature agriculture and also an unexpected benefit.

The emphasis here is not on the quaint and picturesque. The farm workers involved in a revitalization of farming cannot be reenactors or costumed staff. The purpose of recovery and preservation is to create a living cultural and ecological laboratory: a working farm. The purpose of bringing back what worked in the past is to study traditional methods and to learn to use them creatively and to enhance them with modern techniques. If new tools and sophisticated technology can make old jobs easier without compromising their success, then they should by all means be used. Change has always been part of the culture of farming, but the test of viability must be success in the long term. Too many of today's technological advances have sacrificed long-term ecological health for short-term gains. Millennial thinking is needed.

Understanding traditional farming would anchor a shift in values. This shift needs to begin with an appreciation of the history of food and its culture, of the land that produces the food, of the men and women who care for the land and for what it yields. The shift may already be happening, as indicated by, among other things, the growth and spread of slow food restaurants, edible landscaping, community gardens and backyard gardening, community-supported agriculture, farmers' markets, and local-food consumerism. Appreciation of food and farming is one route to appreciation of the cultivated landscape, and appreciation entails an ethical commitment to its preservation.

Research is important. Preservation is important. Long-term thinking is important. But as the history of farming in the Mediterranean shows, the key to the well-being of the land is a shift in our attitude toward the cultivated landscape. Human beings had it right during the Neolithic period and for many, many centuries after that. The Mediterranean landscape, transformed for agriculture, and the First Nature concept that sustained that landscape are the keys to well-being not just for the Mediterranean region but for the whole earth.

Notes

Introduction

1. Lauritzen, *Venice Preserved*, 23–31.
2. Lauritzen, *Venice Preserved*, 33–35.
3. Fletcher and Da Mosto, *La scienza per Venezia*, 32–43.
4. McGregor, *Venice from the Ground Up*; Lauritzen, *Venice Preserved*, 35–73.
5. Salvadori, *Per e contro Venezia*, 81–109.
6. Diamond's critique is based on theories about the origins of agriculture that are no longer accepted by prehistorians. See Chapter 4.
7. White, "Historical Roots of Our Ecological Crisis."
8. Leopold, "The Land Ethic," in *Sand County Almanac*, 201–26.

Chapter One. The Paleolithic Landscape

1. The title of King's article, "The Reputed Fossil Man of the Neanderthal," refers to the site and not yet to the hominid, and "Neanderthal man" occurs with the same geographical sense throughout the article. King describes the find, the haphazard preservation of the bones, and their preliminary study. He notes earlier finds and also counters the arguments that these were animal bones or those of a diseased or "primitive" modern human.
2. In 1871, after *Origin*'s positive scientific reception, Darwin published *The Descent of Man*. There he pointed to the links between humans, chimpanzees, and apes and speculated that the origins of human life were to be found in Africa.
3. The debate was live and unscripted. No single authoritative account of it survives. Those who attended remembered it in very different ways, and over time an account of a supercilious, mocking fundamentalist countered by a serious and eloquent spokesman for pure science emerged as the

accepted version. Wilberforce's published review of *Origin* shows the cleric's appreciation both for Darwin's work and for the scientific method in general. By the time King discovered conclusive evidence in the fossil remains of a Neanderthal man, the lines in the debate had already been drawn. Creationists today are still forced to reckon with the quarrymen's discoveries, which have been augmented by hundreds of others that represent dozens of extinct hominid species. Some among them still draw rather forlornly on Virchow's alternative explanation.

Bones of premodern humans had been discovered before the Neanderthal finds. A premodern human skull was recovered in Belgium in 1829; a second was excavated in Gibraltar in 1848. Before *Origin* these finds were anomalies, objects without a context. After Darwin, as King quickly showed, they became key bits of evidence. Albert Einstein once declared to fellow physicist Werner Heisenberg that "theory determines the boundaries of what we can observe." The science of prehistory, which was born and rapidly came to full flower in the second half of the nineteenth century, exemplified this absolutely. Without Darwin's theory and the intense debate about human origins that it sparked, there would have been no way to classify hominid remains and no motive to seek them out. For a discussion of the influence of Darwin on nineteenth-century cosmological and social thought, see Chapter 13.

4. The original mitochondrial DNA examination was carried out by Svante Pääbo of the University of Munich and others on a small sample from the arm bone of the Neanderthal described by King. This is the so-called type skeleton of Neanderthal man. Subsequent research on a "38,000 year old Neanderthal fossil" was reported in Green et al., "Analysis of Neanderthal DNA." The final word on Neanderthal and anatomically modern human genetic history will probably not be written for some time.

5. New research shows that hominids, presumably Neanderthals, reached the island of Crete 130,000 years ago. This precocious seafaring raises the possibility of unanticipated points of entry into the European continent. Strasser et al., "Stone Age Seafaring in the Mediterranean."

6. The periodic expansion and contraction of polar ice in Europe and its effect on species distribution is discussed in Hewitt, "Genetic Legacy of the Quaternary Ice Ages." The periodic massing of the populations in small and long-isolated refuges reduced genetic variation and accelerated the development of distinctive Neanderthal features—like the shelving brow—that have no obvious value as adaptations.

7. Wreschner et al., "Red Ochre and Human Evolution." The evidence for Neanderthal use of ochre consists of the "sprinkling of a human body at Le Moustier, the deposition of bones, jasper and ochre around the head of a male at La Chapelle aux Saints, two skeletons in whose vicinity red ochre abounds at Qafza." Solecki, "Shanidar iv."

8. As one report sums up: "The prehistory of human fire has undergone

major rethinking in recent years. It now seems that none of the 'classic' examples of early fire-use, . . . hold up under modern scrutiny, either because the source of burning is equivocal . . . or because the general site integrity can be questioned. . . . However, more recent discoveries, excavated with modern methods, do indicate that fire was used by hominids during the Middle Palaeolithic . . . and perhaps earlier." Rigaud et al., "Mousterian Fires from Grotte XVI."

9.   Foreman, *Confessions of an Eco-Warrior,* 56.

10. The Cro-Magnon, a looming shelter rock in the Dordogne region of southwest France, was the scene of their first discovery in 1868, five years after the publication of King's Neanderthal identification. The pair discovered the skeletons of five hominids of great antiquity but of nearly modern physiognomy. The current scholarly preference is "anatomically modern human" (AMH) rather than "Cro-Magnon" for these peoples. Though "Cro-Magnon" is now out of favor with prehistorians, it remains in common use.

11. The details were first published by Edouard Lartet and Henri Christy in *Reliquiae Acquitanicae.*

12. The overlapping of the cultures of anatomically modern humans and Neanderthals is exhaustively described in Bar-Yosef and Pilbeam, *Geography of Neanderthals and Modern Humans.*

13. Altamira Cave in Spain, the scene of this discovery, had first been explored some five years earlier. Explorers uncovered ancient artifacts, but the paintings went unnoticed. A visit to the Paris Exhibition of 1878, where objects used by premodern humans were prominently displayed, led Marcelino Sanz de Sautuola to revisit the cave. As he searched for remains like those he had seen on display in Paris, his nine-year-old daughter wandered deeper into the cave. She returned to tell her father that further inside she had seen pictures of oxen painted on the walls. Her father recognized that the animals were in fact bison, which had been extinct in Europe for thousands of years. In 1880 he published his discoveries in a book entitled *Breves apuntes sobre algunos objetos prehistóricos de la Provincia de Santander.* Sautuola's assertions that these paintings were the work of people who had shared the region with the long-vanished bison were fiercely contested, especially by French scholars. Twenty years after the first publication of the paintings, though, the leading French antagonist admitted his error and acknowledged the antiquity and importance of the Spanish finds. Cartailhac, "Les cavernes ornées de dessins." Long a favorite of visitors, the cave suffered damage that led to its closure in 1977. Modern visitors must content themselves with a full-size replica of one portion of the cave.

14. He lists Altamira and five French caves, Lascaux, Niaux, Les Trois-Frères, Font-de-Gaume, and Les Combarelles. Breuil, *Four Hundred Years of Cave Art.*

15. Two authoritative books on the cave and its extraordinary riches have already appeared: Chauvet et al., *Dawn of Art;* and Clottes et al., *Chauvet Cave.*

16. The German director Werner Herzog was granted unprecedented access to the cave. Paintings can be seen in his quasi-documentary film *Cave of Forgotten Dreams*, released in 2011.

17. Lewis-Williams and Clottes, "Mind in the Cave." In this book one of the principal investigators at the Chauvet Cave, Jean Clottes, drawing on the work with contemporary hunter-gatherers by anthropologist David Lewis-Williams, suggests a reading of the paintings that draws on the psychic transformation of shamans: "During the Upper Paleolithic, we argue, the limestone caves of Western Europe were regarded as topographical equivalents to the psychic experience of the vortex and a nether world. The caves were the entrails of the underworld, and their surfaces—walls, ceilings and floors—were but a thin membrane between those who ventured in and the beings and spirit-animals of the underworld. This is the context of west European cave art, a context created by interaction between universal neuropsychological experiences and topographically situated caves. When people of the Upper Paleolithic embellished these caves with paintings and engravings of animals, signs and, less commonly, apparently human figures, they were at times exploiting certain defined altered states to construct, in each cave, a particular socially and historically situated underworld."

18. Dissanayake, "What Art Is and What Art Does."

19. Dissanayake, "Aesthetic Incunabula," 343, 335.

20. Dissanayake, "Aesthetic Incunabula," 343.

21. Dissanayake, "Aesthetic Experience and Human Evolution," 148.

22. Nelson, *Make Prayers to the Raven*, 15.

Chapter Two. Neolithic Revolutions

1. The old view is well represented in Childe, *Man Makes Himself.*

2. Jared Diamond is one of the ecologically based critics who relies on the traditional critique in his linking of domestication history, social elites, and state-sponsored violence. See Chapter 5. The same historical misconception underlies the critique of contemporary political economists like Guillermo Algaze (*The Uruk World System*) who portray Mesopotamia as a founding example of imperialism.

3. The valley was unusual in several ways: "Distinctive climate and environmental diversity at a plate boundary explains the unusual spatial context within which farming began. A similarly unusual context in time is provided by the events accompanying the termination of the last glaciation: increasing warmth and moisture in an interval before postglacial conditions had stabilized." That is, it was "an unusual time in an unusual place,

when the elements were shaken up and reconfigured in the presence of behaviourally modern human populations." Sherratt, "Diverse Origins," 3.

4. Sherratt, "Diverse Origins," 8.

5. "It was the unique characteristics of that intimate intermixture of the desert, the steppe and the sown which made the area between the Mediterranean and the Persian Gulf into such a powerhouse of innovations." Sherratt, *Economy and Society*, 157.

6. Moore, "Abu Hureyra Project," 69.

7. "Some thirty-five different foreign minerals have been identified, including rock for axes, grinding stones, pigments and beads as well as several varieties of flint and very large quantities of obsidian." The obsidian came from two kilometers (one and a fifth miles) away. Sherratt, *Economy and Society*, 254.

8. Cities like Çatalhöyük that were at key points on trade routes into the mountains of Turkey and Iran, "where traffic-flows of resources such as obsidian were concentrated, had nodal positions and an enhanced incentive to sedentism." Sherratt, "Diverse Origins," 14.

9. The finds of the first expedition to the site are presented in Mellaart, *Catal Huyuk*. The site was reopened thirty years after the initial dig. Annual reports during the fifteen years of ongoing excavations directed by Ian Hodder can be read online at www.catalhoyuk.com. Mellaart called the city Catal Huyuk; Çatalhöyük is the spelling preferred by the current excavators.

10. See also Hodder, *Domestication of Europe*, 8–10.

11. In the original publication about the site, Mellaart expressed surprise that no such quarter was found. Social differentiation was so fundamental a part of theory at the time of the excavation that he assumed that the dig had failed to uncover it, not that it did not exist. Although only a fraction of the site has been excavated, the buildings are remarkably uniform; there is no differentiation of large elite or public buildings. Sherratt, *Economy and Society*, 254.

12. Mellaart, *Catal Huyuk*, 106.

13. See Hodder, *Domestication of Europe*, 7–8.

14. The walls of another shrine in level VII (VII.1) are painted in patterns very like those found on contemporary Turkish kilims: diamond patterns with multiple parallel edges and grids with diamonds inside them. In level VI.B.44, two jaguars butt heads between buttresses decorated with kilimlike diamond patterns. In level VII.8 there is a painting of a bull on one wall with what appears to be a horned altar on a platform in front of it. In shrine VII.45 there is an image of a human with outspread arms and legs pressed against the buttresses in the center of the wall. The figure has been interpreted as a woman giving birth. In shrine VII.31 the images of bulls' heads and birthing mothers are combined.

15. Recent excavations of such sites reveal, among other things, an art that

"depicts in three dimensions . . . the kinds of subjects otherwise encountered in rock art." Hodder, *Domestication of Europe*, 7–8. The animal art of Çatalhöyük lends support to Sherratt's notion that the rise of the city had close connections with those scattered locations where trade and other advantages allowed foragers to become sedentary.

16. Since the eighteenth century, scholars and agronomists have put a great deal of theoretical and ideological emphasis on grain production. They see it as more significant and more advanced than herding in terms of the development of human society. V. Gordon Childe and many other more traditional scholars associated large-scale grain production with the rise of elites, the creation of social differentiation and social hierarchy, widespread trade, and the rise of the state form of political organization. Sherratt's research has reversed chronologies and disabled many of these connections, showing, for example, that trade was an early feature of domestication.

17. Sherratt sums up the remarkable achievements at the north end of the valley. "All this is literally fantastic, but gave rise not only to rectangular houses of increasing constructional skill and perhaps to experiments in animal-keeping which provide the background to the first domestication of ovicaprids." The flowering of extraordinary social forms at the northern end of the rift "was only one part of the Neolithic revolution . . . ; it was its dialectical conjunction with developments taking place in other parts of the network—with which it was increasingly combined, from 8000 BC onwards—which gave rise to the classic combination of cereal cultivation, domestic livestock and village life that was to spread with such speed in subsequent millennia and to provide the basis for subsequent developments within the Fertile Crescent." As Sherratt argues later in the same article, "It is the diversity of lifeways that came together, not the size of their calorific base, which explains their complexity." Sherratt, "Diverse Origins," 5–6, 14.

18. Mazoyer and Roudart, *History of World Agriculture*, 93–94.

19. Roughly speaking, there were three primary Neolithic events: in the Mediterranean, in south China, and in northern South America. Each of these Neolithic events combined and redistributed the domesticates of multiple smaller centers; and some scholars rate the independence of these smaller centers more highly than others, leading to the notion that there were as many as six Neolithic event centers.

20. Davidson, *Oxford Companion to Food*, 845.

21. See Steven Diamant, review of *The Emergence of Civilization: The Cyclades and the Aegean in the Third Millennium BC* by Colin Renfrew, *American Journal of Archaeology* 77 (1973): 346–49.

22. Arroyo-Garcia et al., "Multiple Origins of Cultivated Grapevine."

23. The literature on Franchthi Cave is extensive. Among the most notable works are van Andel and Sutton, *Landscape and People of the Franchthi Re-*

gion; Perlès, "Long-Term Perspectives"; Jacobsen, "Franchthi Cave"; Hansen, *Palaeoethnobotany of Franchthi Cave;* and Farrand, *Depositional History of Franchthi Cave.*

24. The rapid transition from Paleolithic to Neolithic at Franchthi contrasts with the much slower pace of transition at Jericho and Abu Hereyra. This suggests that a Neolithic package already developed elsewhere was imported to Franchthi.

25. The classic description of transhumance is in Braudel, *The Mediterranean,* vol. 1.

26. West and Zhou, "Did Chickens Go North?"

27. Larson et al., "Worldwide Phylogeography of Wild Boar."

28. Hobbes, *Leviathan,* chap. 13.

29. The pioneering work expressing this view is Paul Shepard's *The Tender Carnivore and the Sacred Game.* A curious manifestation of the sentimental rediscovery of the Paleolithic is the wildlife park in Holland devoted to reconstructed pre-Neolithic fauna. There are others scattered around Europe where scientists are attempting to reintroduce genetically engineered Pleistocene megafauna. The Rewilding Movement, which underlies these projects, is based on both scientific and romantic ideals. See Kolbert, "Recall of the Wild."

30. Cordain et al., "Origins and Evolution of the Western Diet."

31. Papathanasiou, "Health Status." A substantial percentage of that research, however, concerns New World sites and the transition from foraging to agriculture in a region that is culturally analogous but where particular changes of diet do not match up. The agricultural transition in the New World was based on foods that were not cultivated in the Old World.

32. Papathanasiou, "Health Status," 381.

33. Papathanasiou, "Health Status," 384.

34. Papathanasiou, "Health Status," 388.

35. Caldwell and Caldwell, "Was There a Neolithic Mortality Crisis?" 159.

Chapter Three. The Spread of Farming Culture

1. The movement of farming technology through the Mediterranean region is illustrated in the endpaper map in Anthony, *Lost World of Old Europe.*

2. Engels, *Origin of the Family* (1884); Graves, *White Goddess* (1948).

3. Gimbutas's words are quoted in Stanton and Stewart, *Feminisms in the Academy,* 206. Then comes a discussion of the whole Goddess movement: "The 'facts' about past societies that the Goddess movement cites are based on the existence of artifacts (such as female statuettes) and interpretations of certain decorative motifs (e.g. spirals) as female. Certain architectural features are then viewed as sacred or religious, as are their associated female characteristics or attributes. . . . In many versions all the diverse goddesses from various circum-Mediterranean locales and

varying time periods . . . are brought together and coalesced into one. . . . All too often the values or attributes of the coalesced goddesses are subsumed under some form of 'fertility' or other biological function, perpetuating an equation of women with nature." Though admitting variations, the Goddess proponents' account of life in Old Europe, with its direct continuities from the Paleolithic, suggests overall a society that is "matrifocal, sedentary, peaceful, art-loving, earth-and-sea bound." Stanton and Stewart, *Feminisms in the Academy*, 207, 210.

4. Milne, "Ecocriticism." The ecofeminist Ynestra King "teases out some of the inherent feminist critiques and contradictions of ecofeminism by locating it along a feminist continuum between rational feminism, which would reject any link between woman and nature as a dangerous acknowledgment of biological determinism, and radical feminism, which would argue that women are more natural than men." Milne, "Ecocriticism."

5. Douglass W. Bailey, "The Figurines of Old Europe," in Anthony, *Lost World of Old Europe*, 113. My account of Old Europe rests on material in David Anthony's anthology.

6. Douglass Bailey, a contemporary commentator on the figurines, imagines the objects being handled in a variety of different contexts. Rather than tangible expressions of a goddess cult, the female figurines are, in Bailey's view, representations of a communal ideal. What that ideal might be he leaves to the imagination. Bailey argues that the power of the figurines "rested not in any specific reference to the divine, but rather in their condition as miniature objects, and the ways that miniature objects open up the minds of the people who hold and see them, facilitating deepseated understandings of what is appropriate in terms of body appearance membership within a group." Psychological studies, he says, "have shown that something very odd happens to the human mind when one handles or plays with miniature objects. Most simply put, when we focus our attention on miniature objects, we enter another world, one in which our perception of time is altered and in which our abilities of concentration are affected." Bailey, "Figurines of Old Europe," 125, 122.

7. For example, at Golyamo Delchevo in Bulgaria, "there were not identifiably male figurines in the houses of the excavated town; all of the figurines that could be assigned a gender were female. Yet all of the high-prestige graves in the nearby cemetery, marked by exotic trade goods and metal, belonged to men." Anthony, *Old Europe*, 45.

8. Anthony, *Old Europe*, 45.

9. Anthony, *Old Europe*, 45, 48.

10. From the fifteenth century onward, Indo-European languages spread far beyond their earlier geographical limits and are now spoken over much of the globe.

11. In language as in many other things, the Levant is an extension of Africa into Asia. Its primary languages, Arabic and Hebrew, are linked to the in-

digenous languages of Ethiopia, Egypt, and North Africa. Turkish, which originated in the steppes of East Asia, is not an Indo-European language. Within the broadly contiguous swath of ethnicities that join Europe to East and South Asia, there are patches where remnant languages hold out. The Basques of Spain, the Finns and the Hungarians, and the Georgians of the Black Sea coast all speak languages that do not belong to the Indo-European family.

12. "V. Gordon Childe assumed that large-scale migrations would have been associated with the prehistoric diffusion of Indo-European languages and . . . therefore searched the archaeological record for a material culture horizon that was distributed widely enough to qualify as the archaeological manifestation of that diffusion. Linguistic evidence suggested that any such horizon should be located in the temperate zone, should represent a culture familiar with copper/bronze and wheels, and should predate the 2d millennium BCE. . . . He saw [such a] complex as originating in the Ukrainian North Pontic steppes, a region favored by some linguists as a probable homeland for Proto-Indo-European languages." Anthony, "Kurgan Culture," 291.

13. Anthony, "Kurgan Culture," 291.

14. Cavalli-Sforza's work is thoroughly described in Sykes, *Seven Daughters of Eve.*

15. Renfrew, *Archaeology and Language.*

16. However plausible the model may be, its ability to convince rests on shifting ground. The current picture of mitochondrial DNA distribution in Europe and the current thinking about the pace of genetic mutation are fundamental to it. New research will probably modify these factors in unpredictable ways. The long and involved history of post-Neolithic population movements in Europe is a complicating factor of the greatest importance. So far genetic research has been comfortably allied with an ideal of deep history. In time we may find that the genetic echo of events that unfolded thousands of years ago is fainter and more ambiguous than we now are prone to think.

17. "Though these societies were late to join the movement, they preceded the Mesopotamian flowering of agriculture by centuries. In the case of monumental construction and the elaboration of fixed material culture, it helps us to understand why the most spectacular monuments of Neolithic culture, in the form of megalithic tombs and ceremonial monuments, lay in the west and north of Europe, not in the Balkans—in areas where the 'Mesolithic' inheritance was the strongest, not in the areas where cereal production was most effective." Sherratt, "Diverse Origins," 14. Some prehistorians put these late converts in the Mesolithic period, a transitional phase between the Paleolithic and the Neolithic.

18. He goes on to say that the image of the house is not casual but associated with "male-female relationships, which are themselves linked to compe-

tition between lineages for control of labour." Such structures are "ways of coping with and involving material culture in similar social strategies." Hodder, "Burials, Houses, Women and Men," 53.

19. "Aggregated communities were not possible," says Sherratt. "This interpretation of the social basis of the megalith-building groups . . . does not imply that such groups were essentially egalitarian—in the sense that there was no conflict of interests between different status- and kinship-groups—for it is basic to the idea of such ritual-centered organizations that that competition took place between (probably exogamous) local units, and that certain sections of the population (notably senior men) exercised authority within them. But authority was localized, and there was no hierarchy in the sense of successive tiers of authority: rather, dominant groups promoted a common ideology which supported their own interests within the unit." Sherratt, *Economy and Society*, 145. Though Sherratt's description applies specifically to northern European groups, it can reasonably be extended throughout the megalithic zone.

20. Until recently no early villages had been discovered among the islands, and no early cemeteries. In the 1990s, foundations of modest rough-built houses of loose stone and mud brick were uncovered. These small scattered settlements are dwarfed by the several megalithic complexes that survive.

21. J. D. Evans's *The Prehistoric Antiquities of the Maltese Islands* is the most complete survey of all the archaeological sites described here.

22. Hodder argues that the "elaboration of the entrance area, the facades and forecourts, the closing of the [monuments] and the difference in ritual and artifacts inside and outside . . . all indicate the same concerns with an inner/outer dichotomy, with control and seclusion. No more eloquent testimony of the latter principles could be provided than the false portals." Hodder, "Burial, Houses, Women, and Men," 63.

23. "In Atlantic Europe in both early and later phases the position of women is emphasized in the context of communal ritual, outside the domestic sphere. Here women are depicted and the domestic 'house' context is elaborated. Women as reproducers, as the source and focus of the lineage, are here celebrated. . . . Women as reproducers and their position in the domestic context are, in the context of ritual, appropriated for the lineage, as a whole. Their services are for the lineage alone and this control is legitimated by the ancestors and by higher authorities." Hodder, "Burial, Houses, Women, and Men," 64.

Chapter Four. Uruk and Egypt, the Great Powers

1. Shortly after 3500 BCE, traders, explorers, and warriors from Uruk began to impinge on their neighbors. This aggression has typically been seen as resource-driven, but see note 4 below.

2. Lawler, "Archaeology: North Versus South." On Uruk in general, see especially the essays in Rothmann, *Uruk Mesopotamia and Its Neighbors*; Collins, *Uruk Phenomenon*.

3. Many of the most valuable of these tablets passed into the hands of private collectors and did not become available for scholarly study until the late 1980s. Representatives are now in the British Museum, the Louvre, and the Metropolitan Museum of Art in New York. The bulk of the collection is held by the University of Berlin. In 1990 the tablets were exhibited and a catalogue prepared. Portions of that catalogue have been published in English, and the text, by Hans J. Nissen and others, remains the most authoritative work on early cuneiform. The title of the publication, *Archaic Bookkeeping, Early Writing, and Techniques of Economic Administration in the Ancient Near East*, is revealing.

4. I am summarizing the argument in Rothman, *Uruk Mesopotamia and Its Neighbors*, 27–84. Uruk's trade has been characterized as imperialistic. According to Guillermo Algaze, in *Uruk World System*, Uruk functioned as a high-volume agricultural producer and manufacturing center while villages and lesser states in its periphery produced raw materials. This notion is based on a number of assumptions. The first is that Uruk was resource poor and that its foreign policy was driven by the need to obtain the wood and stone that it lacked. The second unstated assumption of this critique is that both trade and manufacturing are late stages in economic and social development and that they are dependent on the production of an agricultural surplus. Grain was not a commodity that peripheral centers lacked, and there is little reason to believe that they would have needed to trade for it with Uruk rather than grow it themselves. Detailed records of trade do not indicate asymmetry of the kind that Algaze assumes. Finished goods and raw materials flowed in both directions to and from Uruk. See also Stein and Wattenmaker, "On the Uruk Expansion," 66–69.

5. My discussion draws on Shaw, *Oxford History of Ancient Egypt*.

6. On Badarian culture in Egypt, see Stan Hendrickx and Pierre Vermeersch, "Prehistory," in Shaw, *Oxford History of Ancient Egypt*, 40–43.

7. After the Aswan High Dam was completed in 1970, as Scott Nixon points out, "Egypt switched from the system of irrigation used since the time of the Pharaohs to agriculture based on essentially constant irrigation. . . . Two important consequences of this change were the need to expand and improve an already extensive system of drainage canals in order to halt or reduce salinization of the soils and the need to increase the application of synthetic fertilizer to replace the nutrient-rich sediment formerly delivered with the flood." Nixon, "Replacing the Nile."

8. This important theme is explored fully in Chapter 13.

9. Ehrlich and Ehrlich, *One with Nineveh*, 4.

10. Ehrlich and Ehrlich, *One with Nineveh*, 4, 5. This book is clearly meant as an indictment of the administration of U.S. President George W. Bush.

Nineveh is just a convenient stalking horse. Hubris was the charge leveled by Greek historians and dramatists against the Asian kings who attacked them. Failure in resource management is the key concept that Jared Diamond has also pointed to in a series of op-ed pieces and in his book *Collapse*.

11. Roberts, *The Holocene*, 130–31.
12. Diamond, *Collapse*, 174; Diamond, "Infertile Crescent."
13. Diamond summarizes the focus of his book *Guns, Germs, and Steel* as "how some people came to dominate other people" (7).

Chapter Five. The Primacy of Landscape in West Asia

1. Black et al., *Electronic Text Corpus of Sumerian Literature* [*ETCSL*], t4.08.30 33.
2. Black et al., *ETCSL* t.4.08.30 47–60.
3. Black et al., *ETCSL* t.4.08.16 seg. C, 12–27.
4. On wilderness in modern culture and ecology, see Chapter 13.
5. Black et al., *ETCSL* t.4.07.3 18–28 passim.
6. Black et al., *ETCSL* t.4.07.3 29–38.
7. "Baal advanced, [his penis] tumescent; Divine Hadd [his] pha[llus] erect. Moist was the nethermouth of Virgin Anat." Wyatt, *Religious Texts from Ugarit*, 158–59: Baal Cycle, 1.10 iii 5–10 passim.
8. KTU 1.101: "A Hymn to Baal Enthroned," in Wyatt, *Religious Texts from Ugarit*, 388–90 passim.
9. Wyatt, *Religious Texts from Ugarit*, 89: Baal Cycle, 1.3 iv 10–20 passim.
10. Wyatt, *Religious Texts from Ugarit*, 120–21: Baal Cycle, 1.5 ii 1–8 passim.
11. Wyatt, *Religious Texts from Ugarit*, 135: Baal Cycle, 1.6 11 30–35 passim.
12. Wyatt, *Religious Texts from Ugarit*, 160: Baal Cycle, 1.10 iii 35.
13. M. Smith, *Ugaritic Baal Cycle*, xxv.
14. Hoffner, *Hittite Myths*, 15.
15. M. Smith, *Ugaritic Baal Cycle*, 122–23.
16. As logical as this beginning point might seem, it is not the one that was typically chosen by other West Asian cosmologies. These cosmologies reflected a world that had come under the control of a supreme god through a struggle that often endured through multiple generations. See Hall, "Does Creation Equal Nature?"
17. The week in Genesis is also the beginning of historical time, which in the Torah stands as the record of God's interaction with his chosen people.
18. White, "Historical Roots of Our Ecological Crisis," 1205.
19. "The religion of the Yahwist's epic was thus a religion of the earth, more precisely a religion of the agrarian highlands of Biblical Israel. . . . By consequence, the earth, which defined the character and contours of human life, assumed ultimate value in Yahwistic thought. No philosophical or theological dualism is present by which the world can be conceived in

terms of two distinct ontological orders—human and world, history and nature, spirit and body, mind and matter—which may then be weighed against one another to determine their relative value.... Only with the rise of apocalyptic thought, late in Israelite history, is this unified conception of reality and its absolute valuation of earthly existence modified." Hiebert, *Yahwist's Landscape*, 153.

20. In one verse (Exod. 20:18) that describes the reaction of the people to the manifestations on Mount Sinai, the text stops referring to fire and smoke and describes what the "people saw" and heard as "the thunderings, and the lightnings."

Chapter Six. Mediterranean Trade and Regional Cooperation

1. Materials from the Uluburun shipwreck were displayed at the Metropolitan Museum of Art in an exhibition entitled *Beyond Babylon*, November 18, 2008–March 15, 2009. The catalog of the exhibit, with the same title, edited by Joan Aruz and others, offers a wealth of information not only on the wreck but on Mediterranean trade in the era.

2. Paul Krugman, in *Geography and Trade*, emphasizes this dynamic in modern markets, where economic activity gradually overcomes the effects of geography.

3. "Many elements in the course of history have colonized the [Mediterranean] Basin thanks to the number of geographic and climate events that periodically occurred in this part of the world.... The region's physical environment and climate have changed radically since the Mesozoic, with the result that biological composition of the different regions of the Basin and migration routes of invading species have changed repeatedly. Opportunities for invasion and secondary speciation have been continually renewed. As a result, one can find species originating from such different biogeographical realms as Siberia, South Africa, and even some relics of the Antarctic continent.... The Mediterranean thus must be considered as a huge 'tension zone' ... lying amid the temperate, arid and tropical biogeographical regions which surround it, a zone where intricate interpenetration and speciation has been particularly favored and fostered as compared to the more homogeneous regions to the north and south." Blondel and Aronson, *Biology and Wildlife in the Mediterranean Region*, 31.

4. Jared Diamond once postulated that the success of the Levantine Neolithic as compared with that of Africa and the New World depended in part on the shape of the Eurasian continent. The Eurasian continent runs roughly east to west, the Americas stretch from north to south, and Africa stretches south from the equator. From his point of view, the west Eurasian advantage lay in climate homogeneity. Eurasia was more of a piece than either of the other two land masses, so innovations could more easily

spread. Innovations in either of the other continental masses needed to spread along a north-south axis, where differences in heat and cold meant very different climates, each of which might be inhospitable to the domesticates of the neighboring climate zone. This view assumes that the spread of cultivation rested on climate homogeneity, but the Mediterranean challenges that notion. Diversity and the ability to successfully absorb new species are its major characteristics as a biological region. Its ability to accept, adapt, and spread the Neolithic discoveries of West Asia rested on its openness rather than on insularity.

5. The standard text on Mediterranean ship history is Casson, *Ships and Seamanship*. On Bronze Age shipping, see Wachsmann, *Seagoing Ships and Seamanship*, 69.

6. Clutton-Brock, *Horse Power*.

7. The best known and most important site with evidence of extensive use of horses is assocated with a people called the Sredni Stog. Their principal site, Dereivka, is located on the Dnieper River north of the Black Sea and just beyond the limits of Old Europe. The remains of more than fifty horses have been excavated at the site. What use the culture made of these horses is clear only to a degree. One key point of disagreement among archaeologists who study the history of horse domestication is the date at which horses were first ridden. The generally accepted date is the first millennium BCE, but individual researchers point to evidence that suggests that riding occurred much earlier. At Dereivka, for example, excavators have found worked bits of deer antler pierced with holes that could be bridle parts. Abnormal wear on the teeth of some horses excavated at the site lends support to the notion that they had worn bridles with bits.

8. "By the beginning of the Iron Age, wild horse populations had declined, and today, only one putative wild population, the Przewalski's horse, remains. Therefore, a scenario consistent with the archaeological record and genetic results posits that, initially, wild horses were captured over a large geographic area and used for nutrition and transport. As wild populations dwindled because of exploitation or environmental changes, increased emphasis was placed on captive breeding." Vilà, "Widespread Origins of Domestic Horse Lineages," 474.

9. Vilà, "Widespread Origins of Domestic Horse Lineages," 474.

10. Clutton-Brock, *Horse Power*, 68–69.

11. Kalenka, *Horse in Human History*, 65.

12. Hyland, *Horse in the Ancient World*, 26.

Chapter Seven. The Greek Link between Landscape and Cosmology

1. The ancient Greeks' debt to the great civilizations of West Asia has only recently been recognized and acknowledged. Because of their antago-

nism to the Persian Empire, the fifth-century Greeks downplayed that connection and repeatedly asserted that their culture was self-made and free of Asian influence. Groundbreaking studies—Walter Burkert's *The Orientalizing Revolution* and M. L. West's *The East Face of Helicon*—have shown that Hellenic claims of cultural independence were more wishful thinking than fact. Like the West Asian people with whom they shared technologies and ideas, the Greeks understood the order of the world in terms of landscape.

2. Homer, *Iliad* 18, 535–40, trans. A. S. Kline, *Poetry in Translation*, http://poetryintranslation.com/.

3. Homer, *Iliad* 18, 540–60.

4. Homer, *Iliad* 18, 575–90; the quotation is continued in a following paragraph. The lion attacking a bull is one of the most common images in the art of West Asia. It appears in monumental sculpture, on pottery, and in hundreds of copies on cylinder seals.

5. The "means of life" was fire:

> But Zeus in the anger of his heart hid
> it, because cunning Prometheus deceived him.
>
> . . . .
>
> But afterwards Zeus who gathers the
> clouds said to him in anger:
> "Son of Iapetus, surpassing all in cunning, you are
> glad that you have outwitted me and stolen fire.
>
> . . . .
>
> But I will give men as
> the price for fire an evil thing which will gladden
> their heart as they embrace their own destruction."
> So said the father of men and gods, and laughed.

Hesiod, *Works and Days*, 44–60 passim.

6. In Hesiod's words:

> And he told famous Hephaestus to make haste and mix earth
> with water and to put in it the voice and strength of a human,
> and mold a sweet, lovely maiden-shape, with a face like the immortal
> goddesses; . . . golden Aphrodite would give her
> beauty that inspires cruel longing. . . .
> And he charged Hermes the guide, the Slayer of Argus, to put into
> her a shameless mind and a deceitful nature.

Hesiod, *Works and Days*, 60–70.

7. "A twofold tale I shall tell: at one time they [i.e. the roots] grew to be one alone out of many, at another again they grew apart to be many out of

one. Double is the birth of mortal things and double their failing; for the one is brought to birth and destroyed by the coming together of all things, the other is nurtured and flies apart as they grow apart again. And these things never cease their continual interchange, now through Love all coming together into one, now again each carried apart by the hatred of Strife. So insofar as they have learned to grow one from many, and again as the one grown apart grows many, thus far do they come into being and have no stable life; but insofar as they never cease their continual interchange, thus far they exist always changeless in the cycle." Kirk, Raven, and Schofield, *Presocratic Philosophers*, 287.

8. Since the concept of the four elements was fundamentally wrong, every effort to break down substances into these constituent parts failed. For Empedocles, however, the issue was not the chemical composition of materials but the theory's ability to mediate between seemingly irreconcilable states. Like the cosmological poets of West Asia, Empedocles was trying to account for the difference between the ideal and the real. Kirk, Raven, and Schofield, *Presocratic Philosophers*, 238.

9. On Parmenides, see Kirk, Raven, and Schofield, *Presocratic Philosophers*, 239–63. See also Osborne, *Presocratic Philosophy*, 1–79.

10. "There are just these [elements], but running through one another, they become different things at different times and yet ever and always the same." Kirk, Raven, and Schofield, *Presocratic Philosophers*, 290, frag. 349.

11. Kirk, Raven, and Schofield, *Presocratic Philosophers*, 289–90, frag. 349.

12. "Friends who live in the great city of the yellow Acragas, up on the heights of the citadel, caring for good deeds, I give you greetings. An immortal god, mortal no more, I go about honored by all, as is fitting, crowned with ribbons and fresh garlands; and by all whom I come upon as I enter their prospering towns, by men and women, I am revered. They follow me in their thousands, asking where lies the road to profit, some desiring prophecies, while others, long transfixed by harsh pains, ask to hear the word of healing for every kind of illness." Kirk, Raven, and Schofield, *Presocratic Philosophers*, 313, frag. 399. I rearranged the last line.

13. Herodotus described the teaching of one such philosophical school founded by a follower of Pythagoras: "He built a hall in which he received and entertained the leading citizens, and taught them that neither he nor his guests nor any of their descendants would die, but that they would go to a place where they would survive for ever and possess every good thing." Herodotus, 4:95, in Kirk, Raven, and Schofield, *Presocratic Philosophers*, 218.

14. "There is an oracle of Necessity, ancient decree of the gods, eternal, sealed with broad oaths: when anyone sins and pollutes his own limbs with bloodshed, who by his error makes false the oath he swore—spirits whose portion is long life—for thrice ten thousand years he wanders apart from the blessed, being born throughout that time in all manner of

forms of mortal things, exchanging one hard path of life for another. . . . Of these, I too am one, an exile from the gods and a wanderer, having put my trust in raving Strife." Kirk, Raven, and Schofield, *Presocratic Philosophers*, 315, frag. 401.

15. Kirk, Raven, and Schofield, *Presocratic Philosophers*, 315, frag. 401.

16. This is not a popular dialogue today, though historically it has been among the philosopher's most influential. During the Middle Ages, when the rest of Plato's dialogues were unknown in Europe, the *Timaeus* was widely read. Its concepts were extremely influential in the Renaissance. Since that time, however, it has been considerably less studied and less valued.

17. Like all Plato's works, the *Timaeus* is a dialogue with multiple speakers and multiple points of view. The point of view in the *Timaeus* is supplemented and to a degree contradicted in other dialogues. Given its unique status as a cosmological argument from one of the most authoritative of Greek philosophers, however, the *Timaeus* cosmology as it is outlined here was widely accepted as Plato's own view on these issues.

18. Though the language and logic of this passage is specifically Platonic, the narrative pattern is familiar. Essentially, *Timaeus* offers an explanation of how the work of the wholly good, rational, and divine craftsman could encompass imperfection, irrationality, and ethical failure. In the biblical creation story, Adam's disobedience to God's command caused the Fall, which blighted human life. In *Timaeus*, it was the recalcitrance of the original material from which the earth and everything on it was formed that accounted for imperfection.

19. Plato, *Critias* 111 a–d, trans. W. R. M. Lamb, in *Plato*, vol. 9, Loeb Classical Library (Cambridge: Harvard University Press, 1929).

20. "Everything that Nature makes is means to an end. For just as human creations are the products of [craft], so living objects are manifestly the products of an analogous cause or principle, not external but internal." Aristotle, *On the Parts of Animals*, I.i (641b).

21. "And that the heaven, if it had an origin, was evolved and is maintained by such a cause, there is therefore even more reason to believe than that mortal animals so originated. For order and definiteness are much more plainly manifest in the celestial bodies than in our own frame; while change and chance are characteristic of the perishable things of earth." Aristotle, *On the Parts of Animals*, I.ii (641b).

22. Aristotle, *Politics*, 1.2.

23. Aristotle, *Politics*, 1.1.

24. Pomeroy, *Oeconomicus*, 45–46.

25. Pomeroy, *Oeconomicus*, 52.

26. Pomeroy, *Oeconomicus*, 52.

27. Household production has effectively masked the degree to which women contributed to the wealth of the family and of the polis. By the same

token, economists have underestimated the cumulative economic impact of small-scale agriculture. Things too dispersed for easy theoretical summing up tend to be lost in the mix not just in the eyes of Greek philosophers but in the eyes of modern analysts as well.

28. Carter, *Discovering the Greek Countryside*, esp. chaps. 1 and 5.
29. All quotations are from Torrance, *Encompassing Nature*, 421–22.
30. See "Epicureanism," in Sedley, *Cambridge Companion to Greek and Roman Philosophy*.
31. Torrance, *Encompassing Nature*, 403.
32. Lucretius, *De rerum natura* 1, 250–63. Translation mine.
33. It is highly unlikely that Lucretius had any direct knowledge of the hymns to Dumuzi and Inana. The resemblances between the two result from their choice of a common subject and their approach to that subject.

Chapter Eight. Roman Agriculture

1. Pliny, *Natural History* XVIII.285; Varro, *On Agriculture* I.1.6; and Varro, *On the Latin Language* VI.16.
2. Livy, *Ab urbe condita* 3, 26–29.
3. Dyson, *Roman Countryside*, 13–35.
4. This description is based on Barker et al., *Mediterranean Valley*.
5. My summary of agriculture in Roman Libya is based on Barker, *Farming the Desert*.
6. Barker, *Farming the Desert*, 346.
7. Barker, *Farming the Desert*, 347.
8. Hughes and Thirgood, "Deforestation, Erosion, and Forest Management," 60.
9. Erdkamp, *Grain Market in the Roman Empire*, 225–305.
10. On the Delta and agriculture, see Qadri, "Delta after the Pharoahs"; David Peacock, "The Roman Period," in Shaw, *Oxford History of Ancient Egypt*, 422–45.
11. Casson, *Ships and Seamanship*, 297–300.

Chapter Nine. Medieval Christian Ecological Understanding

1. "Several writers cite this breakdown of law and order as a cause of the decline of agricultural investments in the Mediterranean basin, particularly in the Middle East. Thirgood ascribes the contraction of settled agriculture in the Eastern Mediterranean largely to political instability and economic decline in the disintegrating Roman Empire and to the invasion of nomadic tribes. He notes that the landscape was transformed from agriculture to pastoralism, and that failure to maintain terracing on the hills hastened soil erosion." Deacon, "Deforestation and Ownership," 347.

2. Carter, *Discovering the Greek Countryside*, 39, 43.
3. Deacon, "Deforestation and Ownership," 343. Donald Hughes and J. V. Thirgood, in "Deforestation, Erosion, and Forest Management," argue that the forests were devastated by mining, cooking, and warfare. They also note the conservation efforts of both individuals and the state and the apparent awareness among ancient writers of the link between forest cover and erosion.
4. Reale and Dirmeyer, "Modeling the Effects of Vegetation," 165.
5. Meiggs, *Trees and Timber*, 377.
6. "In a . . . recent book, concerned with the history of forests, it is claimed that by the end of the Empire the destruction of readily accessible forests in Italy caused the import of wood from North Africa, Spain, and other Mediterranean areas. This is a popular view, but it is not firmly based on evidence." Meiggs, *Trees and Timber*, 382.
7. Whether private or public, invocations of the gods satisfied the Romans in a number of ways. As one author notes, "Piety meant honoring the gods as they deserved. Religious festivals yielded a twofold pleasure: besides enjoying oneself, one did one's duty. The pagans never asked the faithful how they 'really' felt; hence we have no way of knowing. Paying homage to the gods was a solemn way of enjoying yourself. Fortunate were those who, more than others, felt the presence of divinity and whose souls were moved." Veyne, "Roman Empire," 194.
8. Christianity engaged the Roman Empire in two different ways. In the West religious and secular authority were divided. In the East they were united. In both regions, however, a division of responsibility arose between secular and religious authority.
9. "In antiquity every tree, every spring, every stream, every hill had its own *genius loci*, its guardian spirit. These spirits were accessible to men, but were very unlike men; centaurs, fauns, and mermaids show their ambivalence. Before one cut a tree, mined a mountain, or dammed a brook, it was important to placate the spirit in charge of that particular situation, and to keep it placated." White, "Historical Roots of Our Ecological Crisis," 1205.
10. But see Hiebert, *Yahwist's Landscape*; and the discussion of Genesis in Chapter 5.
11. White, "Historical Roots of Our Ecological Crisis," 1205. "Christianity inherited from Judaism not only a concept of time as nonrepetitive and linear but also a striking story of creation. By gradual stages a loving and all-powerful God had created light and darkness, the heavenly bodies, the earth and all its plants, animals, birds, and fishes. Finally, God had created Adam and, as an afterthought, Eve to keep man from being lonely. Man named all the animals, thus establishing his dominance over them. God planned all of this explicitly for man's benefit and rule: no item in the physical creation had any purpose save to serve man's purposes. And,

although man's body is made of clay, he is not simply part of nature: he is made in God's image." White, "Historical Roots of Our Ecological Crisis," 1205.

12. Augustine, *Confessions*, book 9, chap. 10, par. 25.

13. Bartholomaeus Anglicus, *De proprietatibus rerum* (Johannes Koelhoff, 1453), book 12, chap. 30: "De volatilibus." Translation mine. Another example is Isidore's description of the pelican in *Etymologies*, book XII, chap 7, secs. 27 and 32.

14. Dubos, "Franciscan Conservation versus Benedictine Stewardship," 57.

15. University of Leicester, *Carolingian Polyptyques: St-Germain-des-Prés: Neuillay*, trans. P. Dutton, http://www.le.ac.uk/hi/polyptyques/index.html.

16. About this time, the Cistercians, an offshoot of the Benedictines, began recruiting lay brothers who worked directly in agriculture and carried out the Rule of Saint Benedict to the letter, which the monks themselves were no longer willing or able to do.

17. Dubos, "Franciscan Conservation versus Benedictine Stewardship," 59.

18. "Lynn White's book *The Transformation of the Roman World* generated a change in our overall view of history. Its title signaled the final overthrow of the 'catastrophe theories' as promoted, for example, in Edward Gibbon's classic *Decline and Fall of the Roman Empire*. Since then, two important theses have been advanced. The first is that the initial stage of the transition from antiquity to the Middle Ages is to be sought in various changes that took place within the Roman world. The second thesis is that the so-called 'barbarians' made use of classical institutions in the course of their invasions and their subsequent ethnogenesis, the process in which a group of people becomes a tribe." Karl Brunner, "Continuity and Discontinuity of Roman Agricultural Knowledge in the Early Middle Ages," in Sweeney, *Agriculture in the Middle Ages*, 21.

19. Analogous arguments were made by French colonial administrators in the nineteenth century to challenge the legitimacy of Arab cultivators in North Africa. See Chapter 13.

Chapter Ten. Muslim Ecological Understanding

1. The Qur'an challenged the polytheism of the pagan Arabs by referring to nature as an assembly of orderly, meaningful, and purposive phenomena and inviting them to study its order so that they could deduce from it the existence of God, who reveals and manifests his power and mercy through the universe. According to the Qur'an, nature, "having a firm and well-knit structure with no gaps, no ruptures, and no dislocations, is one of the grand handiworks of the Almighty." Like a mirror, it reflects the power, beauty, wisdom, and mercy of its creator. Ozdemir, "Toward an Understanding of Environmental Ethics," 8.

2. This and the following passages are quoted in Ozdemir, "Toward an Understanding of Environmental Ethics," 25–26.

3. "The Qur'an and the *sunna*, stipulating that water is the basic need of life, place a number of obligations and responsibilities upon Muslims: the conservation of existing water supplies in the best possible way; the prevention of any activity that might lead to the pollution of water resources or spoil the purity and characteristics of the water; and never adopting an extravagant or irresponsible attitude in the consumption of water." Ozdemir, "Toward an Understanding of Environmental Ethics," 15.

4. Ozdemir, "Toward an Understanding of Environmental Ethics," 14, 33 n. 33.

5. Ozdemir, "Toward an Understanding of Environmental Ethics," 26.

6. Ozdemir, "Toward an Understanding of Environmental Ethics," 23.

7. Significantly the contract recognized the rights of the substantial Jewish community in Yathrib in both secular and religious terms. Jewish monotheism and the history of God's revelations to the Jewish community were accepted not as equivalent to but as compatible with the undertakings and obligations of Islam. As members of the community so defined, the Jews shared the obligation for its active defense.

8. When Persia and Armenia fell at about the same time as Spain, the Muslim empire reached its medieval limits. Despite repeated and costly attempts to conquer Anatolia, the heartland of the Byzantine Empire, Muslim armies were unsuccessful. From that time on, the Islamic realm and its neighbors remained in essential stalemate without major permanent gains of territory on either side until the fifteenth century, when the monarchs of Aragon and Castile drove the last Muslims from Spain, and Ottoman Turks conquered Greece, the Balkans, and Hungary. In 1453, they finally conquered Byzantium.

9. Lapidus, *History of Islamic Societies*, 36.

10. Lapidus, *History of Islamic Societies*, 51.

11. Vikor, *Between God and the Sultan*, 21–30.

12. "Probably some of the crops moved into the Sasanian Empire in the fifth, sixth and seventh centuries. They may include sugar cane, sorghum, eggplants, spinach, bananas, plantains and rice, the last of which (along with cotton, which was not grown in the Sasanian empire) was also grown by the sixth century in the Jordan valley, where the extremely warm climate and the availability of irrigation favoured its introduction. Since the sources which throw light on late Sasanian agriculture are few, uninformative and difficult of interpretation, we cannot be sure that even this limited diffusion from India into the Sasanian empire occurred in pre-Islamic times … but as much else was transmitted from India into the syncretic civilization of the Sasanians, it does not seem improbable that at least a few of our crops were also diffused." Watson, *Agricultural Innovation*, 78.

13. Watson, *Agricultural Innovation*, 91–92.
14. Barbier, *Scarcity and Frontiers*, 182–83.
15. For an unusually positive view of the Mongol invasions, see Jack Weatherford, *Genghis Khan and the Modern World*.
16. See Gutas, *Greek Thought, Arabic Culture*; and Lyons, *House of Wisdom*.
17. Hourani, *History of the Arab Peoples*, 85.
18. Lapidus, *History of Islamic Societies*, 226–47.

Chapter Eleven. Renaissance Landscape and Food

1. Lavery, *Ship*, 70.
2. "At this time the very unimaginative system of management did not allow the treasure to be employed usefully in Spain or the colonies, and this vast capital benefice, a windfall equivalent to five or ten years' national income, was largely lost through ignorance and the rigid habits of a monarchy in theory absolute, in fact limited in ability. This affected the whole of Europe, not least Portugal, which was a dependency of Spain from 1580 onward. By 1640, when Spain relinquished her dominion over the country, Portugal had lost forever her premier position as an Atlantic trader, settler, and merchant. Portugal was overtaken by the Dutch, and the Dutch by the English and French, in the sugar trade, in the colonies, and in the slave trade itself." Hobhouse, *Seeds of Change*, 55.
3. "Though it was rich in grains and vegetables, the New World Neolithic included only turkeys as a domestic animal. This characteristic not only ruled out an independent discovery of the traction complex, but it also left the continental diet deficient in protein. Lifestyles in the New World evolved to link cultivation with hunting." Sherratt, *Economy and Society*, 189.
4. The heavy clay-rich soils of the Po Valley required the deep heavy plows commonly confined to the soils of northern Europe. The marshy environment meant that malaria was rampant. Before rice and corn were cultivated in the valley, the most common use was for winter pasture.
5. Maria-Louise Von Wartburg, "Design and Technology of the Medieval Refineries of the Sugar Cane in Cyprus" in Malpica Cuello, *Paisajes del Azúcar*, 81–116.
6. "Wherever records are complete enough, or where representative last wills have been studied, we find the rich and middling families of urban society characteristically possessed of farms or scattered pieces of productive land. Their town houses were stocked with corn, cheeses, wine, oil, meats, fruits in season, or whatever other produce came from their own lands. According to the best advice, these stocks were meant ideally to suffice for periods of up to two years. . . . The farms of citizens usually lay within a twenty-mile radius of the city." Martines, *Power and Imagination*, 164.

7. Appreciation of the productive landscape, however, did not include appreciation of the primary producers. Like the Romans before them, the men and women of the Italian Renaissance saw no connection between their urbanity and sophistication and the character of country people. In fact, "The urban record public and private, prosaic and literary, is rich in the virulent prejudice of a landowning patriciate which exhibited derision and distrust for the neighboring peasantry and for those who worked the farms." Martines, *Power and Imagination*, 164.

8. Newton, *Design on the Land*, 59.

9. "Thus from a symbolically wild site the water progresses down the slope through several transitional stages to reach its most sophisticated form in the Lower Garden. So too with the vegetation of the villa. The high southern end is virtually embedded in the woods of the hillside; the Fountain of the Dolphins is an area relatively shaded by a mixed stand of native trees. From there on down the slope the cover thins until on the terrace of the Fountain of Light as at the main-floor level of the casini, the sunlight filters down through the translucent leaves of the old plane trees to cast a pattern of dappled sun and shadow on the ground, the last hint of shade before the sunny expanse of the colorful Lower Garden.

"For most observers what makes the Villa Lante such a compelling experience is probably the handling of spaces in a wonderfully comfortable rhythmic sequence from level to level." Newton, *Design on the Land*, 105–6.

Chapter Twelve. Mechanistic Models and Romantic Wilderness

1. On villa culture, see Chapter 11.

2. Reconceiving the universe as heliocentric did not change the fact that all observations of planetary motion were still made from earth and so continued to reflect the motion of celestial bodies relative to an observer who was himself in motion.

3. For an authoritative and readable account of this development, see Einstein and Infeld, *Evolution of Physics*, 3–55.

4. Gravity also attracts planets to each other, which causes slight changes in their orbits.

5. On Plato's *Timaeus*, see Chapter 7.

6. On Christian nature symbolism, see Chapter 9.

7. On landscape-based cosmology, see Chapter 5.

8. "There persists . . . throughout the whole period the fixed scientific cosmology which presupposes the ultimate fact of an irreducible brute matter, or material spread through space in a flux of configurations. In itself such matter is senseless, valueless, purposeless. It just does what it does do, following a fixed routine imposed by external relations which do not

spring from the nature of its being. It is this assumption that I call 'scientific materialism.' Also it is an assumption which I shall challenge as being entirely unsuited to the scientific situation at which we have now arrived." Whitehead, *Science and the Modern World*, 25–26.

9. "The dominance of the idea of functionality in the abstract sphere of mathematics found itself reflected in the order of nature under the guise of mathematically expressed laws of nature. Apart from this progress of mathematics, the seventeenth-century developments of science would have been impossible. Mathematics supplied the background of imaginative thought with which the men of science approached the observation of nature. Galileo produced formulae, Descartes produced formulae, Huyghens produced formulae, Newton produced formulae." Whitehead, *Science and the Modern World*, 46.

10. Paley, *Natural Theology* (1802), quoted in Ratzsch, "Teleological Arguments for God's Existence."

11. In the eighteenth century, chemistry began to supply those answers, and it, too, was a mathematical science depending on abstract relationships among material substances.

12. Bowler, *Norton History of the Environmental Sciences*, 93.

13. See Meek, *Precursors of Adam Smith*.

14. On Quesnay and the economic debate in eighteenth-century France, the classic treatment is Weulersse, *Le mouvement physiocratique en France*. See also Larrère, *L'invention de l'économie*.

15. The physiocrat's analogy implies that land is like a trust fund, and agriculture is like a variable annuity paid out by the land through the application of labor. The physiocrats summarized their doctrines in a celebrated diagram, well described in McNally, *Political Economy and the Rise of Capitalism*, 110–21.

16. Given that agriculture dwarfed every other enterprise of the era, including manufacturing, theirs was not a foolish attempt, though it was ultimately a failure both politically and theoretically. The attention to land among the physiocrats is also significant. They appreciated land as a primary value. They understood its value not only in productive terms but in social terms as well. What had long secured the wealth and prominence of families even in post-feudal Europe was land ownership. Lands and titles were the foundations of wealth and prestige. Such lands were seldom if ever sold, so their monetary value was anyone's guess, yet their productivity and social power were indisputable.

17. This issue was clouded in the eighteenth century by the widespread attribution of intrinsic value to precious metals.

18. See especially Hutchison, *Before Adam Smith*, 27–87, 185–227.

19. "'But I do not think that this necessity of stealing arises only from hence; there is another cause of it, more peculiar to England.' 'What is that?' said the Cardinal: 'The increase of pasture,' said I, 'by which your sheep,

which are naturally mild, and easily kept in order, may be said now to devour men and unpeople, not only villages, but towns; for wherever it is found that the sheep of any soil yield a softer and richer wool than ordinary, there the nobility and gentry, and even those holy men, the abbots, not contented with the old rents which their farms yielded, nor thinking it enough that they, living at their ease, do no good to the public, resolve to do it hurt instead of good. They stop the course of agriculture, destroying houses and towns, reserving only the churches, and enclose grounds that they may lodge their sheep in them." Saint Thomas More, *Utopia*, trans. Ralph Robinson (Rockville, MD: Tark, 2007), 20. On Quesnay and the British example underlying the reform of French agriculture and economy, see McNally, *Political Economy and the Rise of Capitalism*, 85–121.

20. "Every individual is continually exerting himself to find out the most advantageous employment for whatever capital he can command. It is his own advantage, indeed, and not that of the society which he has in view. But the study of his own advantage naturally, or rather necessarily, leads him to prefer that employment which is most advantageous to society. . . . He intends only his own gain, and he is in this, as in many other cases, led by an invisible hand to promote an end which was not part of his intention." A. Smith, *Wealth of Nations*, vol. 1, 477.

21. Public provision of bread had a long and venerable history. The Romans provided bread to a portion of the citizens of Rome. After the collapse of the empire, the early church carried on with the distribution, often from the very same buildings the Roman administrators had used. In the city of Venice, to take only one subsequent example, the availability of bread flour was an important public concern. The city built large and prominent granaries at key points along the Grand Canal to highlight their care for public nourishment. Their prudence is represented allegorically in the porch of the Basilica of Saint Mark's, where mosaics describe in great detail the provisions that Joseph made to protect the Egyptians against famine.

22. Abert, *W. A. Mozart*, 152.

23. Goethe, *Italian Journey*, quoted in Shoumatoff and Shoumatoff, *The Alps*, 213.

24. Cardinal de Bernis, "Sur l'amour de la patrie." The source of all poems in French is *Poésie française*, "Les grands classiques": poesie.webnet.fr/lesgrandsclassiques/index.html. All translations mine.

25. André Chenier, "A la France."

26. Antoine-Marin Lemierre, "Les jardins."

27. On early Italian rice cultivation and its dismal effects on land and labor, see Chapter 11.

28. Giuseppe Parini, "La salubrità dell'aria," in Petronio, *Civiltà nelle lettere*, 862–67. Translation mine.

29. Parini, "La salubrità dell'aria."

30. Quoted in Reymond, *L'Alpe romantique*, 9.
31. Reymond, *L'Alpe romantique*, 10.
32. Reymond, *L'Alpe romantique*, 10.
33. Sertoli, "Burke, Edmund."
34. "It is undoubtedly upon this foundation that Kant erects his theory, in which fear, corresponding to Burke's 'passions relating to self-preservation, which turn mostly on pain or danger,' suggests a principal case of sublimity." Bosanquet, *History of Aesthetic*, 275.
35. Bosanquet, *History of Aesthetic*, 277.
36. "In opposition to Burke, Kant would come back to the 'noble passions,' thus humanistically reproposing the idea of Art as the expression of full and sovereign Subjectivity (humans as rational and moral beings), not the expression of a dissipated subjectivity that only longs to lose itself into Otherness." Sertoli, "Burke, Edmond."
37. Bosanquet, *History of Aesthetic*, 278.

Chapter Thirteen. Silence, Loss, and Catastrophe

1. Cotton was one of the first agricultural products to fill the holds of larger ships. By 1625, the English alone were importing more than two hundred thousand bolts of Indian cotton. Total imports in Dutch and French ships may have been as great. Anquetil, *Les routes du coton*, 48.
2. Sugar refining took place in multiple small-scale operations near where the crop was harvested, and did not become a metropolitan industry.
3. For a novel and revealing comparison of the North-South dynamic in the United States and Italy, see Doyle, *Nations Divided*.
4. Morocco, the westernmost North African state, never came under Ottoman control and remained an independent Muslim principality.
5. By defeating the combined forces of Cleopatra and Marc Antony, Octavian secured control over the Roman Empire and made himself Caesar Augustus. The most venerated of French kings, the sainted Louis IX, led an army of Crusaders to Egypt in 1248. Napoléon may have planned to associate himself with the first Roman emperor and the most venerated French monarch by adding the conquest of Egypt to his résumé. The national purpose in supporting the invasion is more complicated. The project had a long history among European and French intellectuals. In a 1670 paper, the German philosopher and political theorist Gottfried Wilhelm Leibniz discussed the advantages of turning intra-European aggression outward and directing it toward non-Christian peoples. Two years later, he wrote directly to Louis XIV and pointed out the advantages of French control of Egypt. The main benefit, he suggested, was control of the shortest route between the east and the west. *Leibniz: Political Writings*, 34. This idea lurked in the minds of generations of French royal counselors, but once the British captured French New World colo-

nies in the mid-eighteenth century, the project gained new vitality. Why not replace lost American colonies with others nearer to hand? Egypt offered productive land, and its ruling class could provide a market for luxury goods in a land that was an easy sail across the Mediterranean rather than an ocean away. Napoléon's expedition was also anchored in the geopolitics of Europe in the immediate aftermath of the French Revolution. During the course of the French Revolution, the English navy had shown repeatedly that it could advance well into the Mediterranean.

6. While French troops and experts roamed the countryside with no fear of local resistance, English forces were landing. They marched against the French army—abandoned now by Napoléon, who had returned to France, where he was appointed First Consul—and defeated it. As Bernard Lewis notes, the Muslim world was forced to learn another sobering lesson. Not only was a European power free to invade a Muslim country at will, but only a second European power could dislodge that invader. In a hundred years the Ottoman military had slipped so far that it was forced to stand on the sidelines while European powers settled the issue of who would rule its territories. The experience in Egypt confirmed what the Ottoman navy had learned in the Indian Ocean in the sixteenth century. European technology, firepower, and coordinated military operations could overwhelm the bravest and most determined opposition from traditional troops.

The French occupation of Egypt provoked a strong Islamic reaction. Muhammad Ibn Abd-al-Wahhab founded a Muslim sect that is often called Wahhabism. Ibn Abd-al-Wahhab urged a return to the original and authentic form of Islam and a rejection of innovations that had transformed the religion during is millennial history. As successive governments of Egypt became increasingly dependent on European powers— primarily England, which maintained significant influence over the country well into the twentieth century—and increasingly influenced by European ideals, the Wahhabi advocated a return to the pure hadith and sharia of the Prophet and of the first four caliphs. For these reformers, the fall of Egypt to Christian invaders was not a sign that Europe had grown in power and influence but an indication that Islam had lost its way. Lewis, *What Went Wrong?*, 31.

The worldwide influence that the teachings of Ibn Abd-al-Wahhab now enjoy is a result of a pact between the religious reformer and a minor Arab leader of the eighteenth century named Muhammad Ibn Saud. In the nineteenth century, through a series of alliances and local wars, not unlike those that Muhammad himself had organized in the same terrain during the seventh century, Ibn Saud's descendants established their control over much of the Arabian Peninsula. Though their success was mixed, in the aftermath of the First World War, the Saudi dynasty displaced the traditional rulers of Mecca, members of the Hashemite family, who claimed multiple genealogical connections with the family of Muhammad. With the blessing of the British protectors of the region, the Saudis assumed control of the sacred cities. The Hashemite dynasty was removed to what is now Jordan, where they continue to rule.

The Saudi dynasty continues to promulgate doctrines of the eighteenth-century reformer that are often criticized as xenophobic, misogynistic, and intolerant of religious diversity. The ideology of the movement has been widely disseminated throughout the Muslim community in religious schools sponsored and paid for by the oil wealth of Saudi Arabia. Hostile and aggressively repressive movements like the Taliban, the Egyptian Brotherhood, and Al Qaeda have been linked to Wahhabi fundamentalism, though many dispute the connection. The Wahhabi movement, whatever its current role in the world, gained strength in an era when the power of Islam was under European attack in its core territory.

7. Lapidus, *History of Islamic Societies*, 572.
8. Post-Napoléonic France was a web of contradictory political impulses. The republican ideals of the revolution lived on in the minds of many. The European powers that had decided the nation's fate at the Congress of Vienna, however, made it clear that restoring the monarchy was their choice for conquered France, and many French citizens agreed. Though Louis XVIII assumed power as a constitutional monarch, he conspired to control elections and undermine the power of the representative assemblies. At his death in 1824, his younger brother, an embittered ultra-royalist, ascended the throne as Charles X. Within a few years, his government was in crisis. In the same year an insult to the French ambassador offered a pretext for a naval blockade of the North African city of Algiers.
9. Hourani, *History of the Arab Peoples*, 269–71. The rationale for invasion was even more tenuous than the diplomatic pretext for the blockade. The French could point to a time-honored motive for war in the western Mediterranean: pirates. Pirates were active on the Barbary Coast in the nineteenth century as they had been for centuries. The port city of Algiers was one of their most important bases, and though European fleets had been sent against them again and again, the menace continued.
10. Originally geared to the Ottoman model of ruling through local leaders, the French changed their approach after 1843. A combined military and civil administration centered on regional Bureaux Arabes assumed direct control of the country.
11. Davis, *Resurrecting the Granary of Rome*, 27.
12. Davis, *Resurrecting the Granary of Rome*, 23.
13. Davis, *Resurrecting the Granary of Rome*, 23.
14. Davis, *Resurrecting the Granary of Rome*, 38. The brackets are in the original.
15. The lies that the French and other European colonial administrators told about the countries they wished to claim for themselves came true for the

most part under their administration. Within a few decades of French conquest and colonization, the Algerian environment became every bit as abused and degraded as French apologists claimed it had been before colonization. The people who portrayed themselves as the revivers of Roman abundance themselves caused the greatest harm to the land they had seized: "In western Algeria (Oranie), the nineteenth and twentieth centuries witnessed large-scale forest clearance and massive soil erosion. French colonial settlement after 1850 drove Arabs and Berbers into the higher reaches of the Tell, where their cultivation quickly led to ecological disasters. Shortly after clearing fields they found yields in decline and abandoned their land to try again elsewhere. Here, as in southern Italy and all of Spain, political forces promoted sudden shifts in land use patterns, with devastating consequences. Algeria, far more than Morocco or Tunisia, felt the environmental consequences of colonial power." Davis, *Resurrecting the Granary of Rome*, 38.

16. Knight, *Bible Plants and Animals*, 1.
17. For a summary of the Algerian situation, see McNeill, *Mountains of the Mediterranean World*, 355.
18. The Berlin Conference of 1885 established formal guidelines for occupying coastal countries in sub-Saharan Africa. The principles became a blueprint for European dominance of the African continent, a process that occurred with a minimum of conflict among the colonial powers, though with extraordinary loss of life and liberty among Africans.
19. They also created problems for some anatomists who believed, like Cuvier, that past species had become extinct but that evolution did not account for the distinct character of any species.
20. In France, for example, their acceptance was hampered by a prevailing positivism, which demanded far more physical evidence and much less speculation than Darwin offered.
21. "Darwin abandoned the Newtonian model of dynamical explanations in important respects and came to a novel conceptualization of dynamics for biological systems. . . . Living systems were infinitely more complicated than Newton's planetary system. Biological 'elements' had characteristics that were changing in time: they had a history. All the interactions of organisms whether with one another or with the environment were non-additive, non-instantaneous, and exhibited memory. It was the ahistorical nature of the objects with which physics dealt that gave the Newtonian scheme the possibility of a simple, mathematical description. It was precisely the *historical* character of living objects which gave biological phenomena their unique and complex features." Schweber, "Wider British context," 48–49.
22. Spenser's phrase first appeared in the fifth edition of *Origin of Species*, published in 1869. It far outpaced the use of "natural selection," and especially, "the preservation of favoured races in the struggle for life," which

was Darwin's own subtitle for *Origin*. If Darwin did not have mathematical simplicity on his side, he had at least a slogan-like statement of his essential principle. In broader terms, Darwin outlined grounds for a rapprochement between materialistic science and biological description. This was a resolution that botanists and biologists had been working to achieve since the late eighteenth century.

23. That there were two sides to the picture that Darwin painted—not just competition but cooperation as well—was neglected by theorists whose version of social Darwinism was aggressive. In France, where the political spectrum was broader, there was more of a debate about the implications of Darwin's theory for social policy and economics than in England, where "survival of the fittest" was the watchword. On Darwinism in France, see Glick, *Comparative Reception of Darwinism*, 117–67.

24. Keynes, "End of Laissez-Faire."

25. Hawkins, *Social Darwinism*, 123. On Germany, see also Glick, *Comparative Reception of Darwinism*, 81–116.

26. Hawkins, *Social Darwinism*, 123.

27. Quoted in Hawkins, *Social Darwinism*, 124–25.

28. Darwin wrote about the "descent of man," but most nineteenth-century enthusiasts of his theories were believers in human "ascent" from primitive beginnings. For progress-minded thinkers, evolution could easily be equated with the continual improvement of the human race that idealist philosophers had theorized and popular thinkers took as gospel. Influential writers soon identified "survival of the fittest" as the key principle on which human progress had depended. For them, to deny it pride of place in social planning was unimaginable.

29. Quoted in Hawkins, *Social Darwinism*, 125.

30. Tennyson, *In Memoriam A.H.H.*, cantos 54–56 passim.

31. In the twelfth edition, printed in Edinburgh in 1884, long after Darwin's *Origin* and *Descent of Man*, Robert Chambers, the author, finally acknowledged his work.

32. Bill McKibben efficiently summarizes this view of Greek thinking in *The End of Nature*, 64–66.

Chapter Fourteen. The Modern Mediterranean

1. United Nations, *Yearbook, 1946–1947*, 75. Among the Recommendations to the General Assembly was "the furnishing of maximum assistance, including technical assistance, to promote the expeditious re-establishment of agricultural production." See also the report of the Economic and Social Council on pp. 478–96.

2. In France "the winter of 1946–47 was very cold and very dry. . . . In February there were twenty-seven days of below freezing temperatures. Sparse snow covered the ground for only two days in December, eleven in Janu-

ary, and nineteen days in February. The soil remained frozen from January 6 to January 11 to a depth of 20 centimeters, from January 23 to January 30 to a depth of between 20 and 30 centimeters, [throughout] February to a depth exceeding 30 centimeters, and in March to a depth approaching 30 centimeters." "Observations phenologique à UCCLE (I.R.M.) pour l'anée 1947," Smithsonian/NASA Astrophysics Data System. Translation mine.

3. Broder, *Histoire économique de la France*, 114, 125

4. "Il gelido inverno, 1946–1947," meteolive.leonardo.it.

5. Visser, "Le climat change-t-il?" 1–3.

6. Broder, *Histoire économique de la France*, 125. Translation mine.

7. Marshall, "Marshall Plan Speech."

8. Marshall, "Marshall Plan Speech."

9. The situation came to a crisis on Friday, February 21, 1947, not because of any new Soviet moves but through an epochal action by the British government. On that date the British ambassador delivered a simple diplomatic note to the Americans. The note contained a dire assessment of the economic and security needs of both Greece and Turkey. After acknowledging the severity of the situation, the British government candidly but officially declared that it "could no longer be of substantial help in either. His Majesty's Government devoutly hoped that we [the United States] could assume the burden in both Greece and Turkey." Acheson, *Present at the Creation*, 217.

10. Looking back over the war, Stalin characterized it in two ways. It was a war for survival, a war to the death between fascist and democratic nations. This characterization was one that his British and American allies could happily accept. More menacingly, Stalin characterized the war as "the inevitable result of the development of world economic and political forces on the basis of present-day monopolistic capitalism. Marxists have more than once stated that the capitalist system of world economy contains the elements of a general crisis and military conflicts, that, in view of that, the development of world capitalism in our times does not proceed smoothly and evenly, but through crises and catastrophic wars. The point is that the uneven development of capitalist countries usually leads, in the course of time, to a sharp disturbance of the equilibrium within the world system of capitalism, and that group of capitalist countries that regards itself as being less securely provided with raw materials and markets usually attempts to change the situation and to redistribute 'spheres of influence' in its own favor—by employing armed force. As a result of this, the capitalist world is split into two hostile camps, and war breaks out between them." Stalin, "Speech Delivered by J. V. Stalin."

11. "Basically this is only the steady advance of uneasy Russian nationalism, a centuries old movement in which conceptions of offense and defense are inextricably confused. But in [the] new guise of international Marxism,

with its honeyed promises to a desperate and war torn outside world, it is more dangerous and insidious than ever before." Kennan to Byrnes, ["Long Telegram"].

12. Oren, *Power, Faith and Fantasy*, 481.

13. To maintain the range of British shipping, the government created depots throughout the world where supplies of coal were stored. Not all the coal came from Britain; Bermuda, a major Atlantic station, got most of its coal from the United States, and coal from Australia supplied the Pacific stations. At the peak of the operation, around 1910, there were British coaling stations in the Mediterranean, at Gibraltar and Malta. Stations in Hong Kong, north Borneo, Fiji, and New Guinea supplemented the more secure depots in New Zealand and Australia.

14. On coal and the British navy, see Thomas Brassey, *The British Navy* (London: Longmans, Green, 1883), vol. 4, 318.

15. By the terms of the treaty, the Saudis gained control over the bulk of the Arabian Peninsula. The Hashemites, descendants of the Prophet and traditional rulers of Mecca, were moved to Jordan. Palestine was created, and the Jews were promised a homeland.

16. This is Diamond's argument, and it is appropriate in this context, but his insistence on promoting this modern example into a pattern in history and applying it to eras when conflict was carried out in entirely different ways is mistaken.

17. Both societies advocated crop improvement through experimentation and the development of hybrids, though their approaches in this area were guided by markedly different principles. For decades Soviet agronomists officially embraced the genetic theories of Jean-Baptiste Lamarck. Under the leadership of biologist Trofim Lysenko, and with Stalin's blessing, they repudiated Darwin and embraced Larmarck's signature thesis: that characteristics an organism acquired in one generation could be passed on through genetic means to future generations. With this theory as their guide, Russian agronomists tried to improve grain stocks. Many believe that adherence to this pseudo-science caused the repeated Soviet crop failures before and after World War II.

18. The agricultural programs that the United States and the USSR favored were also fostered by the United Nations. The UN organization responsible for disseminating these practices was and remains the Food and Agricultural Organization (FAO). Its charge is to improve agricultural production worldwide. In the first decades of its existence, FAO programs reflected the ideals of industrialized agriculture; the fit with traditional farming was poor. The FAO emphasized the cultivation of high-yield grain crops to produce a marketable surplus. Unlike the United States and Soviet Union, whose agricultural policies were seldom called into question, the FAO faced severe criticism from many different directions. The organization, which is headquartered in Rome, has been repeatedly portrayed

as an inefficient, self-serving bureaucracy with a bloated staff of function-
aries and relatively few agricultural specialists. In response to these charges,
the FAO dispersed its staff into the field and redirected research toward
traditional agricultural practices that are better suited to particular soils
and cultures. Making small improvements in traditional practices rather
than advocating sweeping change is the organization's current goal.

19. The US Department of Agriculture urged increased meat consumption
in developing nations. Meat eating was celebrated as a sign of development, but in reality it was intended to expand the market for American
grain. Increased meat consumption drove up the local cost of grain and
introduced health problems seldom seen before in the region.

20. Gonzale, "Méditerannée."

21. The most viable fishery at the moment is off the Egyptian coast. For many
years after the completion of the Aswan High Dam, which ended annual
flooding on the Nile, the number of fish shrank. Nutrients in the flood-
waters had supported the fish population, and when the floods ended, the
river stopped making its annual deposits in the sea. Fishing has recently
become profitable, thanks to the nitrogen-rich pollutants entering the
Nile from Cairo sewage and from Delta agricultural runoff.

Conclusion

1. Freud, in "Recommendations to Physicians Practising Psycho-Analysis,"
amplified: "It consists simply in not directing one's notice to anything in
particular and in maintaining the same 'evenly-suspended attention' (as I
have called it) in the face of all that one hears."

2. The taste for terror in landscape was closely tied to a budding interest
in horror, which the romantic poets discovered and mined for similar
effects. The modern horror movie, the amusement park thrill ride, and
the taste for a wilderness experience all have common roots in the literature of the early nineteenth century.

3. Salzman, *Anthropology of Real Life*, 53. This controversy is the focus of
Heatherington, *Wild Sardinia*.

4. Salzman, *Anthropology of Real Life*, 53.

5. McKibben, *End of Nature*, 47–94.

6. Krugman, "Building a Green Economy."

7. Muller, Mendelsohn, and Nordhaus, "Environmental Accounting."

8. "Environmental accounting is a system for indexing, organising, managing and delivering data and information on the environment via physical
or monetary indicators. It constitutes an indispensable tool for applying
the sustainable development concept and now commands acceptance as a
means of ensuring the preservation of the environment in Europe. Conventional instruments of economic analysis do not in fact enable political
decision makers to measure reliably the effectiveness of the environmen-

tal policies implemented or the impact of economic policies on the environment. It is therefore necessary to adopt suitable environmental monitoring and information systems which can serve as a basis for political decisions. By taking this step, political decision-makers would be able to report the environmental outcomes of their actions to the communities under their authority, relying on dependable data and constantly updated information on the state of the environment, to incorporate the variable 'environment' into the official decision-making process at every tier of government and to make the environmental effects of policies more transparent." Parliamentary Assembly of the Council of Europe, *Environmental Accounting*, summary.

9. Some of the cost of combating obesity is already being met by governments. Ironically, those governments both subsidize the agribusiness that creates obesity and spend funds to combat it.

10. As early as 1987, Diamond was blaming the ills of the modern world on the Neolithic invention of farming. "Besides malnutrition, starvation, and epidemic diseases, farming helped bring another curse upon humanity: deep class divisions." Diamond, "Worst Mistake."

11. Anson Mills in Columbia, South Carolina, has for almost two decades had as its goals "to grow, harvest and mill near-extinct varieties of heirloom corn, rice, and wheat organically, and re-create ingredients that were in the Southern larder before the Civil War. Grits, cornmeal, Carolina Gold rice, graham and biscuit flour, milled fresh for the table daily, had helped create a celebrated regional cuisine—America's first cuisine, the Carolina Rice Kitchen." http://www.ansonmills.com/about-us-page .htm. Rice cultivation and research is the focus of the Carolina Gold Rice Foundation, carolinagoldricefoundation.org.

12. Rachel Donadio, "With Work Scarce in Athens, Greeks Go Back to the Land," *New York Times*, January 9, 2012.

13. Leopold, "Wildlife in American Culture" and "Wilderness," both reprinted in his *Sand County Almanac*.

Bibliography

Abert, Hermann. *W. A. Mozart*. Trans. Stewart Spencer. New Haven: Yale University Press, 2007.

Acheson, Dean. *Present at the Creation: My Years in the State Department*. New York: Norton, 1987.

Acsadi, Gy., and J. Nemeskeri. *History of Human Life Span and Mortality*. Trans. K. Balas. Budapest: Akademiai Kiado, 1970.

Algaze, Guillermo. *The Uruk World System*. Chicago: University of Chicago Press, 1993.

Allain, Jean. *International Law in the Middle East: Closer to Power than Justice*. Burlington, VT: Ashgate, 2004.

Ambrose, Stanley H. "Paleolithic Technology and Human Evolution." *Science* 291 (2001): 1748–52. Online.

Ammerman, Albert J., and Paolo Biagi, eds. *The Widening Harvest: The Neolithic Transition in Europe—Looking Back, Looking Forward*. Boston, MA: Archaeological Institute of America, 2003.

Anquetil, Jacques. *Les routes du coton*. La Fleche, France: JC Lattès, 1999.

Anthony, David W., et al. "The 'Kurgan Culture,' Indo-European Origins, and the Domestication of the Horse: A Reconsideration (and Comments and Replies)." *Current Anthropology* 27, no. 4 (August–October 1986): 291–31.

Anthony, David W., ed. *The Lost World of Old Europe: The Danube Valley, 5000–3500 BC*. The Institute for the Study of the Ancient World. Princeton, NJ: Princeton University Press, 2010.

Aristotle. *Metaphysics*. Cambridge, MA: Harvard University Press, 1969–75.

Aristotle. *On the Heavens*. Cambridge, MA: Harvard University Press, 1939.

Aristotle. *On the Parts of Animals*. Trans. William Ogle. Perseus Digital Library, http://www.perseus.tufts.edu/hopper/.

Aristotle. *Physics*. Trans. R. P. Hardie and R. K. Gaye. Internet Classics Archive, classics.mit.edu.

Aristotle. *Politics.* Trans. Benjamin Jowett. Ancient Greek Online Library, greek texts.com.

Arroyo-Garcia, R., et al. "Multiple Origins of Cultivated Grapevine (*Vitis vinifera* L. spp. Sativa) Based on Chloroplast DNA Polymorphisms." *Molecular Ecology* 15, no. 12 (2006): 3707–14.

Aruz, Joan, et al., eds. *Beyond Babylon: Art, Trade and Diplomacy in the Second Millennium BC.* New Haven: Yale University Press, 2008.

Arvidsson, Stefan. "Aryan Mythology as Science and Ideology." *Journal of the American Academy of Religion* 67 (1999): 327–54.

Atkins, Peter, et al. *People, Land and Time: An Historical Introduction to the Relations between Landscape, Culture and Environment.* London: Arnold, 1998.

Augustine, Saint. *Confessions and Enchiridion.* Trans. and ed. Albert C. Outler. Christian Classics Ethereal Library, ccel.org.

Augustine, Saint. *On Christian Doctrine.* Ed. and trans. D. W. Robertson Jr. Indianapolis: Bobbs-Merrill, 1981.

Aveni, Anthony. *People and the Sky: Our Ancestors and the Cosmos.* New York: Thames and Hudson, 2008.

Bahn, Paul G. "Sex and Violence in Rock Art: Are Cave Paintings Really Little More than the Testosterone-Fuelled Scribblings of Young Men?" Book review. *Nature* 441 (June 2006): 575–76.

Barbier, Edward B. *Scarcity and Frontiers: How Economies Have Developed through Natural Resource Exploitation.* Cambridge: Cambridge University Press, 2011.

Barker, Graeme, ed. *The Biferno Valley Survey.* London: Leicester University Press, 1995.

Barker, Graeme, ed. *Farming the Desert: The UNESCO Libyan Valleys Archaeological Survey.* 2 vols. Tripoli: UNESCO Publishing Department of Antiquities Society for Libyan Studies, 1996.

Barker, Graeme, et al. *A Mediterranean Valley: Landscape Archaeology and Annales History in the Biferno Valley.* London: Leicester University Press, 1995.

Barton, George A. *Royal Inscriptions of Sumer and Akkad.* New Haven: Published for the American Oriental Society by Yale University Press; London: H. Milford, Oxford University Press, 1929.

Bar-Yosef, Ofer, and David Pilbeam. *The Geography of Neanderthals and Modern Humans in Europe and the Greater Mediterranean.* Cambridge, MA: Peabody Museum of Archaeology and Ethnology, Harvard University, 2000.

Batten, A. H. "Aristarchus of Samos." *Royal Astronomical Society of Canada Journal* 75 (1981): 29–35. Online.

Bauman, Richard A. *Political Trials in Ancient Greece.* London: Routledge, 1990.

Bellwood, Peter, and Colin Renfrew, eds. *Examining the Farming/Language Dispersal Hypothesis.* Cambridge: McDonald Institute for Archaeological Research, University of Cambridge, 2002.

Black, J. A., G. Cunningham, J. Ebeling, E. Flückiger-Hawker, E. Robson, J. Taylor, and G. Zólyomi. *The Electronic Text Corpus of Sumerian Litera-*

ture [*ETCSL*]. Faculty of Oriental Studies, Oxford University, 1998–2006, http://etcsl.orinst.ox.ac.uk/.

Blake, Emma, and A. Bernard Knapp, eds. *The Archaeology of Mediterranean Prehistory.* Oxford: Blackwell, 2005.

Blondel, Jacques, and James Aronson. *Biology and Wildlife in the Mediterranean Region.* New York: Oxford University Press, 1999.

Bosanquet, Bernard. *A History of Aesthetic.* London: Allen and Unwin, 1922.

Bowler, Peter J. *The Norton History of the Environmental Sciences.* New York: Norton, 1993.

Braudel, Ferdinand. *The Mediterranean and the Mediterranean World in the Age of Philip II.* 2 vols. Berkeley: University of California Press, 1996.

Breuil, Henri. *Four Hundred Years of Cave Art.* Trans. Mary E. Boyle. Montignac, France: Centre d'études et de documentation préhistorique, 1952.

Bright, William, ed. *International Encyclopedia of Linguistics.* 4 vols. New York: Oxford University Press, 1992.

Broder, Albert. *Histoire économique de la France au XXième siècle: 1914–1997.* Paris: Editions Ophrys, 1998.

Brush, Stephen B. *Farmer's Bounty: Locating Crop Diversity in the Contemporary World.* New Haven: Yale University Press, 2004.

Bryce, Trevor. *The Kingdom of the Hittites.* Oxford: Oxford University Press, 2005.

Bryce, Trevor. *Life and Society in the Hittite World.* Oxford: Oxford University Press, 2002.

Burkert, Walter. *The Orientalizing Revolution: Near Eastern Influence on Greek Culture in the Early Archaic Age.* Cambridge, MA: Harvard University Press, 1992.

Caldwell, Bruce K., and John C. Caldwell. "Was There a Neolithic Mortality Crisis?" *Journal of Population Research* 20, no. 2 (April 2012): 153–68.

Carman, John, and Anthony Harding, eds. *Ancient Warfare: Archaeological Perspectives.* Phoenix Mill, England: Sutton, 1999.

Cartailhac, Emile. "Les cavernes ornées de dessins: La Grotte d'Altamira (Espagne), mea culpa d'un sceptique." *Antropologie* 13 (1902): 348–54.

Carter, Joseph Coleman. *Discovering the Greek Countryside at Metaponto.* Jerome Lectures, 23rd series. Ann Arbor: University of Michigan Press, 2006.

Casson, Lionel. *Ships and Seamanship in the Ancient World.* 2nd ed. Baltimore, MD: Johns Hopkins University Press, 1995.

Cavalli Sforza, Luca. "Returning to the Neolithic Transition in Europe." In Ammerman and Biagi, *Widening Harvest,* 297–314.

Cavalli Sforza, Luca, and M. W. Feldman. *Cultural Transmission and Evolution: A Quantitative Approach.* Princeton, NJ: Princeton University Press, 1981.

Chambers, Robert. *Vestiges of the Natural History of Creation.* London: Chambers, 1884.

Chauvet, Jean Marie, et al. *Dawn of Art: The Chauvet Cave: The Oldest Known Paintings in the World.* Trans. Paul G. Bahn. New York: Abrams, 1996.

Childe, V. Gordon. *The Aryans.* New York: Knopf, 1926.

Childe, V. Gordon. *Man Makes Himself.* New York: New American Library, 1951.

Clottes, Jean, et al. *Chauvet Cave: The Art of the Earliest Times.* Trans. Paul G. Bahn. Salt Lake City: University of Utah Press, 2003.

Clottes, Jean, and Jean Courtin. *La Grotte Cosquer.* Paris: Seuil, 1994.

Clutton-Brock, Juliet. *Horse Power: A History of the Horse and the Donkey in Human Societies.* Cambridge, MA: Harvard University Press, 1992.

Colledge, Sue, and James Conolly, eds. *The Origins and Spread of Domestic Plants in Southwest Asia and Europe.* Walnut Creek, CA: University College London Institute of Archaeology Publications, 2007.

Collins, Paul. *The Uruk Phenomenon.* British Archaeological Reports International Series 900 (2000). Oxford: Hadrian Books, 2000.

Cooper, P. J. M., et al. "Improving Water Use Efficiency of Annual Crops in the Rainfed Farming Systems of West Asia and North Africa." *Experimental Agriculture* 23 (1987): 113–58.

Cordain, Lorin, et al. "Origins and Evolution of the Western Diet: Health Implications for the 21st Century." *American Journal of Clinical Nutrition* 81 (2005): 341–54.

Crosby, Alfred W. *The Columbian Exchange: Biological and Cultural Consequences of 1492.* Westport, CT: Greenwood Press, 1972.

Crouch, Dora P. *Water Management in Ancient Greek Cities.* New York: Oxford University Press, 1993.

Curtin, Philip D. *The Rise and Fall of the Plantation Complex.* Cambridge: Cambridge University Press, 1990.

Dahl, Erik. J. "Naval Innovation from Coal to Oil." *E & P.* July 1, 2006. Online.

Darwin, Charles. *The Descent of Man and Selection in Relation to Sex.* 2 vols. London: Murray, 1871.

Darwin, Charles. *The Origin of Species by Means of Natural Selection; or, The Preservation of Favoured Races in the Struggle for Life.* London: Murray, 1859.

Davidson, Alan. *The Oxford Companion to Food.* Oxford: Oxford University Press, 1999.

Davis, Diana K. *Resurrecting the Granary of Rome: Environmental History and French Colonial Expansion in North Africa.* Ohio University Press Series in Ecology and History. Athens: Ohio University Press, 2007.

Deacon, Robert T. "Deforestation and Ownership: Evidence from Historical Accounts and Contemporary Data." *Land Economics* 75 (1999): 341–59.

Delson, Eric, and Katerina Harvati. "Return of the Last Neanderthal." *Nature* 443 (October 19, 2006): 762.

Diamond, Jared. *Collapse: How Societies Choose to Fail or Succeed.* New York: Viking, 2005.

Diamond, Jared. *Guns, Germs, and Steel: The Fates of Human Societies.* New York: Norton, 1999.

Diamond, Jared. "Infertile Crescent: The Decline of Iraq." Op-ed. *Seattle Times Newspaper,* July 20, 2003. Online.

Diamond, Jared. "The Worst Mistake in the History of the Human Race." *Discover Magazine,* May 1987, pp. 64–66.

Dissanayake, Ellen. "Aesthetic Experience and Human Evolution." *Journal of Aesthetics and Art Criticism* 41, no. 2 (1983): 145–55.

Dissanayake, Ellen. "Aesthetic Incunabula." *Philosophy and Literature* 25, no. 2 (2001): 335–46.

Dissanayake, Ellen. *Homo Aestheticus: Where Art Comes From and Why.* New York: Free Press, 1992.

Dissanayake, Ellen. "Komar and Melamid Discover Pleistocene Taste." *Philosophy and Literature* 22, no. 2 (1998): 486–96.

Dissanayake, Ellen. "What Art Is and What Art Does: An Overview of Contemporary Evolutionary Hypotheses." In Colin Martindale et al., eds., *Evolutionary and Neurocognitive Approaches to Aesthetics, Creativity and the Arts,* 1–14. Amityville, NY: Baywood, 2007.

Doyle, Don H. *Nations Divided: America, Italy, and the Southern Question.* Athens: University of Georgia Press, 2002.

Dubos, René. "Franciscan Conservation versus Benedictine Stewardship," in J. R. Berry, ed. *Environmental Stewardship,* 57–63. London: T & T International, 2006.

Dyson, Stephen L. *The Roman Countryside.* Duckworth Debates in Archaeology. London: Duckworth, 2003.

Ehrlich, Paul R., and Anne Ehrlich. *One with Nineveh: Politics, Consumption, and the Human Future.* Washington, DC: Island Press, 2004.

Ehrlich, Paul R., and Peter H. Raven. "Butterflies and Plants: A Study in Coevolution." *Evolution* 18 (1964): 586–608.

Einstein, Albert, and Leopold Infeld. *The Evolution of Physics from Early Concepts to Relativity and Quanta.* New York: Touchstone, 2008.

Empedocles. *The Poem of Empedocles.* Ed. and trans. Brad Inwood. Toronto: University of Toronto Press, 2001.

Erdkamp, Paul. *The Grain Market in the Roman Empire: A Social, Political and Economic Study.* Cambridge: Cambridge University Press, 2005.

Evans, J. D. *The Prehistoric Antiquities of the Maltese Islands: A Survey.* London: Athlone Press, 1971.

Fall, Patricia L., et al. "Seeds of Civilization: Bronze Age Rural Economy and Ecology in the Southern Levant." *Annals of the Association of American Geographers* 88, no. 1 (1998): 107–25.

Farrand, W. R. *Depositional History of Franchthi Cave: Stratigraphy, Sedimentology, and Chronology.* Bloomington: Indiana University Press, 2000.

Fletcher, Caroline, and Jane Da Mosto. *La Scienza per Venezia: Recupero e salvaguardia della città e della laguna.* The Venice in Peril Fund. Turin: Allemandi, 2004.

Foley, Jonathan. "Boundaries for a Healthy Planet." *Scientific American* 302, no. 4 (April 2010): 54–57.

Foreman, Dave. *Confessions of an Eco-Warrior.* New York: Harmony Books, 1991.

Foss, John E. Review of *Soils and Societies: Perspectives from Environmental History. Geoarchaeology* by J. R. McNeill et al. 24, no. 1 (2009): 111–12.

Freud, Sigmund. "Recommendations to Physicians Practising Psycho-Analysis." In James Strachey, ed., *The Standard Edition of the Complete Psychological Works of Sigmund Freud,* vol. 12: *The Case of Schreber, Papers on Technique, and Other Works,* 109–20. London: Hogarth Press and Psychoanalytic Institute, 1911–13.

Furley, David. *The Greek Cosmologists.* Vol. 1. Cambridge: Cambridge University Press, 1987.

Galloway, J. H. *The Sugar Cane Industry: An Historical Geography from Its Origins to 1914.* Cambridge: Cambridge University Press, 1989.

Gantz, Timothy. *Early Greek Myth: A Guide to Literary and Artistic Sources.* Baltimore, MD: Johns Hopkins University Press, 1993.

Gardiner, Robert, ed. *The Earliest Ships.* Conway's History of the Ship. London: Conway Maritime Press, 1996.

Glick, Thomas F. *The Comparative Reception of Darwinism.* Chicago: University of Chicago Press, 1988.

Gloudemna, Nikki. "The Not-So-Fertile Crescent." *Mother Jones,* July 2009. Online.

Gonzale, Alexandra. "Méditerannée—La plus belle mer du monde est à nos pieds." *France-Soir,* June 4, 2010. Online.

Goren-Inbar, Naama, and John D. Speth, eds. *Human Paleoecology in the Levantine Corridor.* Oxford: Oxbow Books, 2004.

Green, Richard E., et al. "Analysis of One Million Base Pairs of Neanderthal DNA." *Nature* 444 (November 2006): 330–36.

Grenville, J. A. S. *A History of the World in the Twentieth Century.* Cambridge, MA: Harvard University Press, 1994.

Grove, A. T., and Oliver Rackham. *The Nature of Mediterranean Europe: An Ecological History.* New Haven: Yale University Press, 2001.

Gunderson, Lance H., et al., eds. *Foundations of Ecological Resilience.* Washington, DC: Island Press, 2010.

Gutas, Dmitri. *Greek Thought, Arabic Culture.* London: Routledge, 1998.

Hall, W. David. "Does Creation Equal Nature? Confronting the Christian Confusion about Ecology and Cosmology." *Journal of the American Academy of Religion* 2005 (73): 781–812.

Hansen, J. M. *The Palaeoethnobotany of Franchthi Cave.* Bloomington: Indiana University Press, 1991.

Hawkins, Mike. *Social Darwinism in European and American Thought, 1860–1945.* Cambridge: Cambridge University Press, 1997.

Heatherington, Tracey. *Wild Sardinia: Indigeneity and the Global Dreamtimes of Environmentalism.* Seattle: University of Washington Press, 2010.

Herodotus. *The Landmark Herodotus: The Histories.* Ed. Robert B. Strassler. New York: Pantheon Books, 2007.

Hesiod. *Works and Days.* In Homer and Hesiod, *Hesiod, the Homeric Hymns, and Homerica, with an English Translation by Hugh G. Evelyn-White.* New and rev. ed. Cambridge, MA: Harvard University Press, 1936. Online.

Hewitt, Godfrey. "The Genetic Legacy of the Quaternary Ice Ages." *Nature* 405 (June 22, 2000): 907–13.

Hiebert, Theodore. *The Yahwist's Landscape: Nature and Religion in Early Israel.* New York: Oxford University Press, 1996.

Hobhouse, Henry. *Seeds of Change: Five Plants That Transformed Mankind.* New York: Harper and Row, 1987.

Hodder, Ian. "Burials, Houses, Women and Men in the European Neolithic." In Daniel Miller and Christopher Tilley, eds., *Ideology, Power and Prehistory.* London: Cambridge University Press, 1984.

Hodder, Ian. *Domestication of Europe.* London: Wiley-Blackwell, 1998.

Hoffner, Harry A. *Hittite Myths.* 2nd ed. Atlanta: Scholars Press, 1998.

Horden, Peregrine, and Nicholas Purcell. *The Corrupting Sea: A Study of Mediterranean History.* Oxford: Wiley-Blackwell, 2000.

Hourani, Albert. *A History of the Arab Peoples.* New York: MJF Books, 1991.

Hughes, Donald, and J. V. Thirgood. "Deforestation, Erosion and Forest Management in Ancient Greece and Rome." *Journal of Forest History* 26, no. 2 (1982): 60–75.

Hutchison, Terence. *Before Adam Smith: The Emergence of Political Economy, 1662–1776.* Oxford: Blackwell, 1988.

Hyland, Ann. *The Horse in the Ancient World.* Westport, CT: Praeger, 2003.

Inglis, Fred. *The Delicious History of the Holiday.* London: Routledge, 2000.

Irwin, Robert, ed. *Night and Horses and the Desert: An Anthology of Classical Arab Literature.* Woodstock, NY: Overlook Press, 1999.

Isidore of Seville. *The Etymologies (or Origins).* Ed. W. M. Lindsay (Oxford: Oxford University Press, 1911). LacusCurtius, http://penelope.uchicago.edu/Thayer/E/Roman/home.html.

Jacobsen, T. W. "Franchthi Cave and the Beginning of Settled Village Life in Greece." *Hesperia* 50 (1981): 303–19.

Jastrow, Morris, ed. *An Old Babylonian Version of the Gilgamesh Epic.* Ed. Morris Jastrow; trans. Albert T. Clay. The Project Gutenberg eBook.

Johnson, Allen W. *The Evolution of Human Societies: From Foraging Group to Agrarian State.* 2nd ed. Stanford, CA: Stanford University Press, 2000.

Kalenka, Pita. *The Horse in Human History.* Cambridge: Cambridge University Press, 2009.

Kaltsas, Nicolaos, and Alan Shapiro. *Worshiping Women: Ritual and Reality in Classical Athens.* New York: Alexander S. Onassis Public Benefit Foundation, 2008.

Kennan, George, to James Byrnes. ["Long Telegram"], February 22, 1946. Harry S. Truman Library and Museum, http://www.trumanlibrary.org/

whistlestop/study_collections/coldwar/documents/index.php?document
date=1946-02-22&documentid=6-6&pagenumber=1.

Keynes, John Meynard. "The End of Laissez-Faire." 1926. *Panarchy: A Gateway to Selected Documents and Websites,* panarchy.org/keynes/laissezfaire.1926
.html.

King, William. "The Reputed Fossil of the Neanderthal." *Quarterly Journal of Science* 1 (1864): 88–97.

Kirk, G. S., J. E. Raven, and M. Schofield. *The Presocratic Philosophers: A Critical History with a Selection of Texts.* 2nd ed. Cambridge: Cambridge University Press, 1983.

Knight, Alfred Ernst. *Bible Plants and Animals.* London: James Nisbet, 1889.

Kolbert, Elizabeth. "Recall of the Wild." *New Yorker,* December 24, 2012.

Krugman, Paul. "Building a Green Economy." *New York Times,* April 7, 2010. Online.

Krugman, Paul. *Geography and Trade.* Gaston Eyskens Lecture Series. Lueven, Belgium: Leuven University Press; Cambridge, MA: MIT Press, 1993.

Krugman, Paul. "The Role of Geography in Development." Paper prepared for the Annual World Bank Conference on Development Economics, Washington, DC, April 20–21, 1998. Online.

Krugman, Paul. "Who Cooked the Planet?" Op-ed. *New York Times,* July 25, 2010. Online.

Landstrom, Bjorn. *Ships of the Pharoahs.* Garden City, NY: Doubleday, 1970.

Lapidus, Ira M. *A History of Islamic Societies.* 2nd ed. Cambridge: Cambridge University Press, 2002.

Larrère, Catherine. *L'invention de l'économie au xviiie siècle.* Paris: Presses Universitaires de France, 1992.

Larson, Greger, et al. "Worldwide Phylogeography of Wild Boar Reveals Multiple Centers of Pig Domestication." *Science* 307 (March 11, 2005): 1618–21.

Lartet, Eduoard, and Henri Christy. *Reliquiae Acquitanicae: Being Contributions to the Archaeology and Paleontology of Périgord and Adjoining Provinces of Southern France.* Ed. T. R. Jones. London: Williams and Norgate, 1865–75.

Lauritzen, Peter. *Venice Preserved.* Bethesda, MD: Adler and Adler, 1986.

Lavery, Brian. *Ship: The Epic Story of Maritime Adventure.* Smithsonian National Maritime Museum. New York: DK Publishing, 2008.

Lawler, Andrew. "Archaeology: North Versus South, Mesopotamian Style." *Science* 312 (2006): 1458–63.

Leibniz, Gottfried Wilhem, Freiherr von. *Leibniz: Political Writings.* 2nd ed. Ed. Patrick Riley. Cambridge Texts in the History of Political Thought. Cambridge: Cambridge University Press, 2001.

Leopold, Aldo. *A Sand County Almanac and Sketches Here and There by Aldo Leopold.* New York: Oxford University Press, 1949.

Levy, Thomas, et al. "New Light on King Narmer and the Protodynastic Egyptian Presence in Canaan." *Biblical Archaeologist* 58 (1995): 26–35. JSTOR Online.

Lewis, Bernard. *The Crisis of Islam: Holy War and Unholy Terror.* New York: Modern Library, 2003.

Lewis, Bernard. *What Went Wrong? Western Impact and Middle Eastern Response.* Oxford: Oxford University Press, 2002.

Lewis-Williams, David J., and Jean Clottes. "The Mind in the Cave—the Cave in the Mind: Altered Consciousness in the Upper Paleolithic." *Anthropology of Consciousness* 9 (2008). Online.

Liverani, Mario. *Uruk: The First City.* Ed. and trans. Zainab Bahrani and Marc Van de Mieroop. London: Equinox, 2006.

Locke, John. *An Essay Concerning Human Understanding.* Ed. Alexander Campbell Fraser. Oxford: Henry Frowde; New York: MacMillan, 1894.

Lyons, Jonathan. *House of Wisdom.* New York: Bloomsbury, 2009.

Malpica Cuello, Antonio. *Paisajes lel Azúcar: Actas del Quinto Seminario Internacional sobre la Caña de Azúcar, Motril, 20–24 de Septiembre de 1993.* [Granada]: Diputación Provincial de Granada, 1995.

Marshall, George C. "The Marshall Plan Speech," June 5, 1947. George C. Marshall Foundation, http://www.marshallfoundation.org/library/Marshall PlanSpeechfromRecordedAddress_000.html.

Martines, Lauro. *Power and Imagination: City-States in Renaissance Italy.* New York: Knopf, 1979.

Mathseon, Susan B. "The Mission of Triptolemus and the Politics of Athens." *Greek, Roman, and Byzantine Studies* 35, no. 4 (Winter 1994): 345–77.

Mazoyer, Marcel, and Laurence Roudart. *A History of World Agriculture.* Trans. James H. Membrez. New York: Atlantic Monthly Press, 2006.

Mazzoleni, S., et al., eds. *Recent Dynamics of the Mediterranean Vegetation and Landscape.* Chichester, England: Wiley, 2004.

McAuliffe, Jane Dammen, ed. *The Cambridge Companion to the Qur'an.* Cambridge: Cambridge University Press, 2006.

McGregor, James H. S. *Venice from the Ground Up.* Cambridge: Harvard University Press, 2008.

McKibben, Bill. *The End of Nature.* New York: Doubleday Anchor, 1990.

McNally, David. *Political Economy and the Rise of Capitalism: A Reinterpretation.* Berkeley: University of California Press, 1990.

McNeill, J. R. *The Mountains of the Mediterranean World: An Environmental History.* Cambridge: Cambridge University Press, 1992.

Meek, Ronald L. *Precursors of Adam Smith.* London: Dent, 1973.

Meiggs, Russell. *Trees and Timber in the Ancient Mediterranean World.* Oxford: Clarendon Press, 1982.

Mellaart, James. *Catal Huyuk: A Neolithic Town in Anatolia.* New York: McGraw-Hill, 1967.

Mellars, Paul. *The Neanderthal Legacy.* Princeton, NJ: Princeton University Press, 1996.

Metz, Helen Chapin, ed. *Egypt: A Country Study.* Research completed 1990. Federal Research Division, Library of Congress, Country-Data.com.

Milne, Anne. "Ecocriticism." 2nd ed. *The Johns Hopkins Guide to Literary Theory and Criticism.* 2005. http://litguide.press.jhu.edu/.

Moore, Andrew M. T. "The Abu Hureyra Project: Investigating the Beginning of Farming in Western Asia." In Ammerman and Biagi, *Widening Harvest,* 59–74.

Muller, Nicholas Z., Robert Mendelsohn, and William Nordhaus. "Environmental Accounting for Pollution in the United States Economy." *American Economic Review* 101 (August 2011): 1649–75.

Nelson, Richard K. *Make Prayers to the Raven: A Koyukon View of the Northern Forest.* Chicago: University of Chicago Press, 1983.

Newton, Norman T. *Design on the Land: The Development of Landscape Architecture.* Cambridge, MA: Belknap Press of Harvard University Press, 1971.

Nissen, Hans J. "The Archaic Texts from Uruk." *World Archaeology* 17 (1986): 317–34.

Nissen, Hans J., et al., eds. *Archaic Bookkeeping, Early Writing, and Techniques of Economic Administration in the Ancient Near East.* Chicago: University of Chicago Press, 1993.

Nixon, Scott W. "Replacing the Nile: Are Anthropogenic Nutrients Providing the Fertility Once Brought to the Mediterranean by a Great River?" *Ambio* 32 (2003): 30–39.

Oren, Michael B. *Power, Faith, and Fantasy: America in the Middle East, 1776 to the Present.* New York: Norton, 2007.

Osborne, Catherine. *Presocratic Philosophy: A Very Short Introduction.* Oxford: Oxford University Press, 2004.

Ozdemir, Ibrahim. "Toward an Understanding of Environmental Ethics from a Qur'anic Perspective." In Richard C. Foltz et al., eds., *Islam and Ecology: A Bestowed Trust.* Publications of the Center for the Study of World Religions. Harvard Divinity School. Cambridge, MA: Harvard University Press, 2003. 3–38.

Papathanasiou, Anastasia. "Health Status of the Neolithic Population of Alepotrypa Cave, Greece." *American Journal of Physical Anthropology* 126 (2005): 377–90.

Parliamentary Assembly of the Council of Europe. Committee on the Environment, Agriculture, and Local and Regional Affairs. *Environmental Accounting as a Sustainable Development Tool.* Doc. 10071. February 11, 2004. Online.

Pearce, Fred. "Fertile Crescent 'Will Disappear This Century.'" *New Scientist* 13, no. 19 (July 27, 2009). Online.

Peregrine, Peter N., and Melvin Ember, eds. *Encylopedia of Prehistory.* 9 vols. New York: Kluwer Academic/Plenum, 2001–3.

Perlès, C. "Long-Term Perspectives on the Occupation of the Franchthi Cave: Continuity and Discontinuity." In G. N. Bailey, E. Adam, E. Panagopoulou, C. Perlès, and K. Zachos, eds., *The Palaeolithic Archaeology of Greece and Adjacent Areas* (BSA Studies 3), 311–18.

Petronio, Giuseppe. *Civiltà nelle lettere*. Vol. 2. 4th ed. Florence: Palumbo, 1968.

Plato. *Timaeus*. In *Plato in Twelve Volumes*, vol. 9. Trans. W. R. M. Lamb. Cambridge, MA: Harvard University Press; London: William Heinemann, 1925. Online.

Pomeroy, Sarah. *Oeconomicus: A Social and Historical Commentary*. Oxford: Clarendon Press, 1998.

Qadri, Kanwal. "The Delta after the Pharoahs: The Archaeological Evidence." C-paper in archaeology, Department of Archaeology and Ancient History, Uppsala University, Uppsala, Sweden, 2004. Online.

Rahman, Fazlur. *Major Themes of the Qur'an*. 2nd ed. Minneapolis: Bibliotheca Islamica, 1989.

Ratzsch, Del. "Teleological Arguments for God's Existence." *Stanford Encyclopedia of Philosophy*. http://plato.stanford.edu/.

Reale, Oreste, and Paul Dirmeyer. "Modeling the Effects of Vegetation on Mediterranean Climate during the Roman Classical Period. Part I: Climate History and Model Sensitivity." *Global and Planetary Change* 25 (2000): 163–84. Online.

Reale, Oreste, and Jagadish Shukla. "Modeling the Effects of Vegetation on Mediterranean Climate during the Roman Classical Period. Part II: Model Simulation." *Global and Planetary Change* 25 (2000): 185–214. Online.

Renfrew, Colin. *Archaeology and Language: The Puzzle of Indo-European Origins*. New York: Cambridge University Press, 1987.

Renfrew, Colin, ed. *The Megalithic Monuments of Western Europe*. London: Thames and Hudson, 1983.

Renfrew, Colin. "The Neolithic Transition in Europe: Linguistic Aspects." In Ammerman and Biagi, *Widening Harvest*, 327–36.

Reymond, Evelyne. *L'Alpe romantique*. Grenoble: Presses Universitaires, 1988.

Rigaud, Jean-Phillipe, et al. "Mousterian Fires from Grotte XVI." *Antiquity* 1995. Online at bnet.

Rippin, Andrew, ed. *The Blackwell Companion to the Qur'an*. Oxford: Blackwell, 2006.

Roberts, Neil. *The Holocene: An Environmental History*. Oxford: Blackwell, 1989.

Rothmann, Mitchell S., ed. *Uruk Mesopotamia and Its Neighbors*. Santa Fe, NM: School of American Research Press, 2001.

Ruddiman, William F. "The Anthropogenic Greenhouse Era Began Thousands of Years Ago." *Climatic Change* 61, no. 3 (2003): 261–93.

Runciman, Steven. *The First Crusade and the Foundation of the Kingdom of Jerusalem*. Vol. 1 of *A History of the Crusades*. Cambridge: Cambridge University Press, 1987.

Saggs, H. W. F. *Civilization before Greece and Rome*. New Haven: Yale University Press, 1989.

Salvadori, Renzo. *Per e contro Venezia: Storia e cronaca (1945–2001) di una città in pericolo di estinzione*. Venice: Supernova, 2002.

Salzman, Philip Carl. *The Anthropology of Real Life: Events in Human Experience.*
  Prospect Heights, IL: Waveland Press, 1999.
Schweber, Silvan S. "The Wider British Context in Darwin's Theorizing." In
  David Kohn, ed., *The Darwinian Heritage*, 35–69. Princeton, NJ: Prince-
  ton University Press, 1988.
Sedley, David, ed. *Cambridge Companion to Greek and Roman Philosophy.* Cam-
  bridge: Cambridge University Press, 2003.
Sertoli, Giuseppe. "Burke, Edmund." In Michael Groden, Martin Kreiswirth,
  and Imre Szema, eds., *The Johns Hopkins Guide to Literary Theory and Crit-
  icism.* 2nd ed. Baltimore, MD: Johns Hopkins University Press, 2005–12.
  http://litguide.press.jhu.edu/.
Shaw, Ian, ed. *The Oxford History of Ancient Egypt.* Oxford: Oxford University
  Press, 2000.
Shepard, Paul. *The Tender Carnivore and the Sacred Game.* Athens: University of
  Georgia Press, 1998.
Sherratt, Andrew. "Diverse Origins: Regional Contributions to the Genesis of
  Farming." In Colledge and Conolly, *Origins and Spread of Domestic Plants*,
  1–19.
Sherratt, Andrew. *Economy and Society in Prehistoric Europe.* Edinburgh: Edin-
  burgh University Press, 1997.
Sherratt, Andrew. "Reviving the Grand Narrative: Archaeology and Long-Term
  Change." *Journal of European Archaeology* 3 (1995): 1–32.
Sherratt, Andrew. "What Would a Bronze-Age World System Look Like? Re-
  lations between Temperate Europe and the Mediterranean in Later Pre-
  history." *Journal of European Archaeology* 1 (1993): 1–57.
Shoumatoff, Nicholas, and Nina Shoumatoff. *The Alps: Europe's Mountain
  Heart.* Ann Arbor: University of Michigan Press, 2001.
Smith, Adam. *An Inquiry into the Nature and Causes of the Wealth of Nations.*
  2 vols. Ed. Edwin Cannan. Chicago: University of Chicago Press, 1977.
Smith, Mark S. *The Ugaritic Baal Cycle.* Vol. 1: *Introduction with Text, Transla-
  tion and Commentary of KTU 1.1–1.2.* Supplements to Vetus Testamentum,
  vol. LV. Leiden: E. J. Brill, 1994.
Smith, Mark S., et al., trans. *Ugaritic Narrative Poetry.* Atlanta: Scholars Press,
  1997.
Solecki, Ralph. "Shanidar iv: A Neanderthal Flower Burial in Northern Iraq."
  Science 190 (1975): 880–81.
Stalin, Joseph V. "Speech Delivered by J. V. Stalin at a Meeting of Voters of the
  Stalin Electoral District, Moscow, Feb. 9, 1946." Marxists Internet Archive,
  http://www.marxists.org/reference/archive/stalin/works/1937/12/11.htm.
Stanton, Domna, and Abigail J. Stewart, eds. *Feminisms in the Academy.* Ann
  Arbor: University of Michigan Press, 1995.
Steele, Robert. *Medieval Lore from Bartholomaeus Anglicus.* The Medieval Besti-
  ary, bestiary.ca.

Stein, Gil, and Patricia Wattenmaker. "On the Uruk Expansion." *Current Anthropology* 31 (1990): 66–69.

Stewart, J. R. "The Ecology and Adaptation of Neanderthals during the Nonanalogue Environment of Oxygen Isotope Stage 3." *Quarternary International* 137 (2005): 35–46.

Strasser, Thomas F., et al. "Stone Age Seafaring in the Mediterranean: Evidence from the Plakias Region for Lower Paleolithic and Mesolithic Habitation of Crete." *Hesperia* 79 (2010): 145–90.

Sullivan, Meg. "UCLA-Dutch Team Uncovers Egypt's Earliest Agricultural Settlement." UCLA International Institute, http://web.international.ucla.edu/institute/.

Sweeney, Del, ed. *Agriculture in the Middle Ages: Technology, Practice, and Representation.* Philadelphia: University of Pennsylvania Press, 1995.

Sykes, Brian. "European Ancestry: The Mitochondrial Landscape." In Ammerman and Biagi, *Widening Harvest,* 315–26.

Sykes, Brian. *The Seven Daughters of Eve.* New York: Norton, 2001.

Tabak, Faruk. *The Waning of the Mediterranean, 1550–1870.* Baltimore: Johns Hopkins University Press, 2008.

Tennyson, Alfred, Lord. *In Memoriam A.H.H.* 2nd ed. New York: Norton, 2003.

Tilley, Alec. *Seafaring on the Ancient Mediterranean.* British Archaeological Reports, International Series, 1268. Oxford: Archaeopress, 2004.

Torrance, Robert M., ed. *Encompassing Nature: A Sourcebook—Nature and Culture from Ancient Times to the Modern World.* Washington, DC: Counterpoint, 1999.

United Nations. Department of Public Information. *Yearbook of the United Nations, 1946–1947.* Lake Success, NY: Department of Public Information, 1947.

United Nations. Division for Sustainable Development. *Environmental Management Accounting Procedures and Principles.* New York: United Nations, 2001.

United Nations. World Health Organization. Interim Commission. *Chronicle of the World Health Organization.* Vol. 1. New York: World Health Organization, 1947.

van Andel, T. H., and S. B. Sutton. *Landscape and People of the Franchthi Region.* Bloomington: Indiana University Press, 1987.

Vasey, Daniel E. *An Ecological History of Agriculture.* Ames: Iowa State University Press, 1992.

Veyne, Paul. "The Roman Empire." In Paul Veyne, ed., *A History of Private Life: From Pagan Rome to Byzantium.* Cambridge, MA: Harvard University Press, 1987.

Vikor, Knut. *Between God and the Sultan: A History of Islamic Law.* Oxford: Oxford University Press, 2005.

Vilà, Charles, et al. "Widespread Origins of Domestic Horse Lineages." *Science* 291 (2001): 474.

Vileisis, Ann. *Kitchen Literacy: How We Lost Knowledge of Where Food Comes From and Why We Need to Get It Back.* Washington, DC: Island Press, 2010.

Visser, S. W. "Le climat change-t-il?" *Pure and Applied Geophysics* 12 (1948): 1–3.

Wachsmann, Shelley. *Seagoing Ships and Seamanship in the Bronze Age Levant.* London: Chatham, 1998.

Ward, Cheryl A. *Sacred and Secular: Ancient Egyptian Ships and Boats.* AIA Monographs. New Series, 5. Dubuque, IA: Kendall Hunt, 2000.

Watkins, Calvin. "Culture History and Historical Linguistics." In William Bright, ed., *International Encyclopedia of Linguistics*, vol. 1, 319. New York: Oxford University Press, 1992.

Watson, Andrew M. *Agricultural Innovation in the Early Islamic World: The Diffusion of Crops and Farming Techniques, 700–1100.* Cambridge: Cambridge University Press, 1983.

Weatherford, Jack. *Genghis Khan and the Modern World.* New York: Three Rivers Press, 2005.

Wells, Spencer. *The Journey of Man.* New York: Random House, 2002.

Wengrow, David. "Rethinking 'Cattle Cults' in Early Egypt: Towards a Prehistoric Perspective on the Narmer Palette." *Cambridge Archaeological Journal* 11 (2001): 91–104.

West, Barbara, and Ben-Xiong Zhou. "Did Chickens Go North? New Evidence for Domestication." *Journal of Archaeological Science* 14 (1988): 515–33.

West, M. L. *The East Face of Helicon: West Asiatic Elements in Greek Poetry and Myth.* Oxford: Clarendon Press, 1997.

Westley, Kieran, and Justin Dix. "Coastal Environments and Their Role in Prehistoric Migrations." *Journal of Marine Archaeology* 1 (2006): 9–28.

Weulersse, Georges. *Le mouvement physiocratique en France.* Paris: Alcan, 1910.

White, Lynn. "The Historical Roots of Our Ecological Crisis." *Science* 155 (March 10, 1967): 1203–7.

Whitehead, Alfred North. *Science and the Modern World.* Lowell Lectures, 1925. New York: Macmillan, 1944.

Whittle, Alasdair. *Neolithic Europe: A Survey.* Cambridge: Cambridge University Press, 1985.

Whitty, Julia. "Making Iraq Fertile." *Mother Jones.* December 2008. Online.

Wilkinson, Toby A. H. "What a King Is This: Narmer and the Concept of the Ruler." *Journal of Egyptian Archaeology* 86 (2000): 23–32. JSTOR Online.

Wreschner, Ernst E., et al. "Red Ochre and Human Evolution." *Current Anthropology* 21 (1980): 632.

Wright, Clifford A. *A Mediterranean Feast.* New York: Morrow, 1999.

Wright, M. R. *Cosmology in Antiquity.* London: Routledge, 1995.

Wright, Mary. "Contacts between Egypt and Syro-Palestine during the Protodynastic Period." *Biblical Archaeologist* 48 (1985): 240–53.

Wroe, Stephen, et al. "Megafaunal Extinction in the Late Quaternary and the Global Overkill Hypothesis." *Alcheringa: An Australasian Journal of Palaeontology* 29 (2005): 291–331.

Wyatt, Nicholas. *Religious Texts from Ugarit.* London: Sheffield Academic Press, 2002.

Yon, Marguerite. *The City of Ugarit at Tell Ras Shamra.* Winona Lake, IN: Eisenbrauns, 2006.

Index